THE FAMILY BOOK OF HOME ENTERTAINING

THE FAMILY BOOK OF

Home Entertaining

by Florence Brobeck

Illustrated by Helen Disbrow

DOUBLEDAY & COMPANY, INC.
Garden City, N.Y.

For Mary Ann and Will Jones
and their children

PREFACE

The first "best" party I remember happened in a house in a tiny village, which has long since vanished from the map. My mother and I were the only guests. We had walked through the hot June sunshine from a small, nearby town. I was only five years old, but a long walk, especially in June when the wild flowers were in their gayest, most spendthrift blooming in the Ohio meadows, was nothing unusual for us. This day's walk had a purpose other than gathering armfuls of field flowers. My mother wanted me to see the little community where she had lived as a child. It was Canalport, a cluster of houses on the banks of a once busy waterway. Her childhood there had been adventuresome and thrilling, with daily rides on the backs of the big black mules that plodded along the towpath pulling the barges in the now nonexistent canal.

At Canalport, after I had looked at the towpath and canal bed and tried to imagine my mother as a little girl on the back of a mule, she took me to call on some cousins who lived in the village. The house was shaded by tall, old elms and looked friendly and cool. It was full of surprises, too, for me. As we crossed a side porch to knock at the screen door, I saw a pan of taffy cooling in an open window. The next moment we were swept up in welcoming hugs by two tall, laughing, young lady cousins, who were as pleased to see us as if we had come with news of an inheritance.

They made a big pitcher of lemonade while we sat in wicker rocking chairs on the shady porch. They brought out with it from the kitchen a plate of large, soft sugar cookies so fresh that they were still slightly warm. Then, best of all, the small visitor was asked if she cared to help pull the taffy. It was a glorious finish to a fine afternoon. I can't remember anything about the end of the party—how we got home, or how much taffy I ate—but it was a day that is still surrounded with a rosy glow. It was my first "best" party.

Visits to an aunt's farm, to my grandmother's home in another small Ohio town, and the Sunday dinners and Sunday-night suppers that my mother prepared for visiting relatives and friends (the house was always full of them) belong in the same class of parties where a warm welcome, good humor, good food, and relaxed talk combined to send everybody home at the end of the day in a happy mood. The wit, tall tales, and high good humor of one of my uncles and my father's answering wit and sense of fun sparked these parties, and so did the charm of one aunt in particular and my mother's good cookery.

The essence of these good times was absorbed and cherished by me. It educated and sharpened my appreciation of all kinds of hospitality that came in later years. In my first days in New York there were many small dinners in a little apartment near Columbia University. The hostess planned them for me, bringing together in her tiny living room interesting men and women she thought I would enjoy knowing. I remember her with special appreciation because she always invited a man for every woman guest. They were politicians, musicians, newspapermen, actors, a retired Supreme Court Justice who was a fabulous raconteur. Men and girls and older women, too, entertaining and good company, came to her dinners, which she cooked and served. Her husband carried in the great roasts to the table, and, at the end of dinner, made the coffee himself.

In those first years in New York my newspaper columns made many friends for me. One was a French antique dealer whose house on East Fifty-fifth Street was as famous for its Sunday-night suppers as for the collections of ancient valuables that crowded its five floors.

The cellar contained an old kitchen, and the owner had cleared space among the old and authentic Chinese costumes and furnishings he had lent the *Chu Chin Chow* production years before, and some of the rare Arabian robes borrowed by Valentino, for a great, long monastery table. He covered the table with anything handy. For one dinner it was a beautiful Spanish bedspread, another an ecclesiastical lace cloth from an auction of a cardinal's estate. He set his table with fine Canton dinner plates and the handsomest silver and crystal goblets, for the twelve to twenty or more guests who came on Sunday nights.

We were always invited for seven o'clock. But we stood about in the main-floor shop half an hour or so, while the host belowstairs, arrayed in a museum-piece Japanese or Persian robe, cooked the dinner. Summoned down to the table, we often found the evening's feast to be a giant-size, delicious crab-meat omelet, high and wide, on a great Chinese platter. Our host served us, then returned to the kitchen. While we, the strangely assorted guests oh'ed and ah'ed over the food, he busied himself making our salad and Turkish coffee, and finally sat down at the head of the table to take coffee with us. I never saw him eat anything at these dinners. Perhaps he was too full of amazement and satisfaction or amusement at the array of men and women he had gathered around his table. Most of them were colorful individuals from the Metropolitan Opera, the movies, and the theatre all over the world. In addition, on one occasion or another, there was a traveling French schoolmarm, the widow of his favorite druggist, the plumber who had been working in the house that week, a writer or two, and a couple of members of the New York Society for Psychical Research.

Everybody talked across the table, down its length, and to side partners, stopping only to enjoy second helpings from the huge omelet platter and large slices of crusty French bread spread with sweet butter. The secret of the success of these dinners? Good food, warm affection on the part of the host for every one of the young, old, and middle-aged around his big table, and the curiosity, interest, or fascination everyone there had in everyone else, in talking and in hearing what was said.

Other "best" dinners include summer-night parties in a quiet country house in New Hampshire, a gem of architectural beauty with Regency and Georgian furniture, exquisite color everywhere, fresh flowers, and a museum collection of antiques. The meals were planned with care by a hostess who liked to see happy people around her table. They were prepared to perfection by a family cook who could draw upon dairy, poultry yards, farms, berry patches, great refrigerators, and her own skill to give us matchless dinners.

Among my "best" parties a certain annual Philadelphia terrapin luncheon must be included. Superb dinners, evening parties, and these luncheons were part of the hospitality in an old Pennsylvania stone house. The cook was Irish, a Botticelli beauty whose fame in the kitchen was known around Europe as well as in Philadelphia and New York, and to every chef on the French Line because she and her mistress crossed to France every year, sometimes twice or more often, and she used the journey to wheedle, bribe, and charm new cookery secrets from the ship's chef.

The parties her mistress gave for Philadelphia musical and publishing people were not only famous for the gourmet quality of the dishes served but for the beauty of the occasion. The house was filled with Chippendale furniture and silver brought from an ancient Irish castle by the owner when she married her Philadelphian. Her garden was full of roses. Her taste so cultivated, restrained, and sensitive that she could combine flowers and the old furnishings of the house to create an atmosphere of such charm that guests relaxed, looked their best, and acted like good children at a birthday party. Even a stormy-browed orchestra conductor famous for his bad manners purred and spoke civilly at her parties.

Other "bests"—a fish fry with an um-pah village band for dancing; one tuba too many in the brassy ensemble made the sambas sensational. A barn dance on a Missouri sugar farm. Wonderful Sunday-night suppers and music around the fireplace of a Fayette, Missouri, home. A breakfast in a country house in Surrey, England. Luncheon in a garden in Sweden. Luncheon on a sunny terrace on the river Elbe, in Dresden.

Especially, there was a breakfast on the sunny stone steps of a little studio in Manchester, Vermont. Before my hostess could lift her kitchen coffeepot onto the tiny studio gas burner, her neighbor presented us with breakfast. She had made coffee, and arranged hot rolls, butter, honey, marmalade, and a handful of ripe cherries in a suit box she had lined with green paper. She carried box and coffeepot across the garden path to the studio door, managing on the way to lay a few fresh zinnias on the cover of the box. No breakfast has ever looked so appetizing, tasted so good, or was eaten in better company.

More "best" parties are described in detail, with guidance on how to give them, in various sections throughout this book. I don't like to mention the worst parties, one of them being a fiasco of my own in which the baked ham did not bake; a series of disasters followed one after the other out of the kitchen from the dinner's beginning to its end. And another evening's buffet supper for which a number of agreeable people had assembled: two of my guests (new friends) disapproved of everyone present, kept silent, looked stern, sent out waves of black magic toward everybody, and almost, but not quite, managed to turn the evening into a shambles.

Between the best and the worst are the mildly boring parties—the frustrating and annoying ones with show-off hosts and name-dropping guests. The ones where the conversation is about business or politics, or personal and local and family topics, of interest to only one or two guests at best. There are the countless occasions on which unconscious rudeness or carelessness, or a messy, uncleaned house, or poor food badly cooked and served long after the hour specified in the invitation greet the guests. Or a tired, harassed hostess tries to function with her mind on something besides her guests. Or a host insists on games, games, games when his adult guests prefer to dance, or sit quietly after dinner and talk, or listen to records, or look at television. Just as bad are parties for teen-agers planned by someone outside their age group—and children's parties that have not been planned down to the tiniest detail of what to do and what to serve, and that do not include either professionals or mothers of some of the children as helpers.

All of your parties can be "bests." Even the beginning party-giver need not have a failure or a near failure, a not-so-good party. Rules and guidance for all kinds of entertaining have been worked out by experienced hosts and hostesses all over America and elsewhere in the world to help themselves when they entertain. For this book a great many successful party-givers sent me their best menus, game ideas, decoration and color schemes, and suggestions for new easy ways to plan and give dinners and to insure success for parties for all ages.

I wrote more than three hundred letters to women, and men, who are famous for their entertaining at home or who are professional party specialists, and to widely-traveled friends who are as likely to go to an Eskimo party or one in South Africa as well as to entertainments at less exotic addresses. I called on and consulted games importers and manufacturers, specialists on sports and tournaments, talked with psychologists who know children and adolescents, with P.T.A. members, folk dance authorities, record collectors. I called on officials of government and university departments from which movie films can be borrowed or rented, and on officials at the United Nations for community and school-party material developed by the U. S. Committee for U.N.I.C.E.F. I wrote to home economics departments in state colleges and universities all over the country for information on how girls and boys, young hostesses, and older homemakers in their communities entertain.

America is a party-giving country! Everything from a quiet birthday dinner for Mother prepared by the young teen-agers of the family to a gala Mardi gras supper dance in a family playroom—all are in the pages which follow.

INTRODUCTION

One of the warmest, most knowledgeable, and successful hostesses I know is Florence Brobeck. There's very little about the art of entertaining—and it is an art—that her homemaker's heart, nurtured in the Midwest from which she comes, doesn't know.

When she writes in this book about socials and lawn festivals, she does so with the authority of one who has taken part many times in just such activities to which she has lent a willing helping hand.

Florence well knows the importance of teen-agers' first parties, and she goes to great pains to tell *everything* about the running of a variety of them, from Box Socials and Square Dances to Pajama Parties, complete with menus and recipes and helpful hints for the parents of the hostesses.

A vital and enthusiastic world traveler, she also writes with great authority and flair on the subject of entertaining in a variety of foreign styles. She shows you exactly how to put on a foreign dinner, complete with menus, recipes, table decorations, and entertainment, in such a way that your friends and yourself will feel that on this occasion you have journeyed together happily to a foreign land.

This is a helpful, practical book on home entertaining by a woman with a most distinguished background as an editor and writer—and the recipes she gives *cook*. The decorations she suggests make the kind of beautiful party setting for which she herself is well known.

The ideas in this book are workable, feasible, and easy to reproduce.

Happy entertaining!

AMY VANDERBILT

A WORD TO THE SUCCESSFUL HOSTESS

Successful entertaining is pleasurable entertaining for the guest and for *you*. A successful hostess is a relaxed hostess, one who conveys the warm spirit of hospitality, one who is confident of her cuisine, her knowledge of etiquette, and is blessed with a measure of imagination and enthusiasm. Following are a few suggestions and ideas to start you off as a happy and confident hostess in your own home.

Sources and Aids for the Party-giver Menu planning for any home entertaining is not the chore it used to be. To help young homemakers and beginning hostesses, the women's magazines glow with beautiful color photographs of new dishes, new products, new ways to economize and yet set a fine table. New products and appliances are appearing in the shops every month to make hospitality easier. Both are shown and their uses described in these monthly publications. No party-giver can afford to ignore these magazines since they bring her a steady stream of fresh ideas and inspiration. So do the handsome home furnishing and decorating magazines in which menus, color schemes, and new slants on home entertaining are shown every month.

No party-giver can afford to be without a large general cookbook and one or more smaller speciality and foreign cookbooks. There is menu help and decoration ideas in foreign food shops, markets, and restaurants. A sound volume on etiquette is a source of strength and guidance for many kinds of hospitality. Good manners, knowing what to do, being courteous are priceless qualities. They keep a host from asking a musician guest to play or sing (for his supper), a lawyer or interior-decorator guest to give free advice, or a physician guest to diagnose. They guide a hostess in what to say when her guests ask, "Shall we dress up?" She must be specific. It is either a dress-up party or one to which your guests wear their daytime clothes. To say, "Wear what you like," is confusing and someone is sure to be embarrassed at dressing up too much or not enough.

Imagination and enthusiasm are other essential possessions of the party-giver. So is derring-do or being inventive. I asked the most famous party-goer I know—he is the most widely traveled, too—to tell me about the best parties on his long list. He surprised me by saying they are the dinners, suppers, dances, barbecues, and movie evenings, which his favorite hosts in his home town give in a special party room they built themselves.

They call this room The Shed. Their home stands on a city lot, the backyard separated by a whitewashed brick wall from their driveway to the garage. Across the back of the yard they built a brick terrace and surrounded it with flower borders. Beyond and adjoining the terrace is The Shed. Originally a one-story garage, the man of the family knocked the front and one side out of the structure and opened it onto terrace and yard, extending the roof to overhang part of the terrace. He painted the cement floor bright orange, but changes the color from time to time if a party color scheme calls for it. He built, in the center, an in-the-round fireplace with a huge iron fire basket on legs. On cool autumn nights guests sit around it to enjoy a buffet supper. He installed a barbecue along one wall of the garage-shed, placed long tables against another wall, and piped music in from the house. As many as forty guests can be given supper in this party shed in fine weather when they can spill over onto the terrace and yard.

For these big parties, the host and his wife hang Swedish and Japanese lanterns in the trees and around the yard and terrace and place small, brightly-colored tables and chairs everywhere. Shed and terrace make an ideal dance floor. On rainy or cool nights The Shed is cozy for a smaller crowd to dance and have supper.

These hosts also give winter dinner parties in their house dining room, which they have decorated and furnished with a long marble-top table and Italian chairs. One wall of the room is mirrored. The only illumination is from many candles on the table and in wall sconces. Some of their favorite frequent guests are local university teachers and foreign visiting instructors. Sometimes the guests have planned the dinner and cooked it. One night a Chinese couple from the university cooked and served a very unusual Peking dinner for a large party in this home. Another night two Russian scientists from the local research institute were hosts at this family's table, preparing and serving a superb Russian meal. When these enthusiastic party hosts plan costume parties, the menus are designed around the theme of the evening. They are imaginative and inventive hosts who enjoy party-giving and they open their home to their friends many times during the summer as well as throughout the winter.

The same kind of imagination and inventiveness can be scaled down to minimum budgets and produce unique settings, delicious dishes, good times. Dozens of color schemes and decoration ideas are given throughout this book to help beginning hostesses use the accessories already on hand in their homes, or those they can buy from local shops to make their dining room, living room, and party table effective and the occasion a success.

The Subtle Art of Entertaining More important than a new centerpiece or unusual decor is to know and abide by the taste of your guests. If they are ardent games fans, plan the evening that way whether it is bridge, canasta, poker, guessing games, treasure hunts, bowling in a basement playroom, or playing darts on the back porch.

If the friends you have invited like conversation, or listening to records, or have come in to see a certain TV program with you, or to hear election returns, or simply to meet a new neighbor, keep the after-dinner period to doing whatever you have told them you will do after dinner. Some guests resent being asked to play games, including charades and similar party stimulators. Various amusingly bitter articles have been published about the behavior of the hostess who, according to one man, forces guests to play games because she is empty-headed and fears her company is likewise or she would leave them alone to make conversation with each other. The problem of what to do at parties is dealt with in detail in the various party plans given throughout this book.

Formal, Semiformal, Informal That troublesome word *formal,* which pops up in magazine articles and conversation about parties, is not found in this book (except right here and in a side reference to debuts). Some party-givers wrongly describe any event at which the guests wear evening clothes as "formal." The word has a special meaning in the world of hospitality. A formal luncheon or dinner is given only in homes where there is a chef and kitchen helpers, a butler and menservants to prepare a traditional menu and serve it according to long-established custom to guests seated by time-honored rules of protocol, at a table elegantly arrayed with the superlative in silver, crystal, porcelain, and other accessories.

Or a host or hostess gives a formal luncheon or dinner for an important personage, public figure, or visiting dignitary in a private suite of a fine hotel or restaurant where a competent, European-trained staff is responsible for the exacting procedure and perfection of such an occasion.

The nearest thing to a formal luncheon or dinner which the average hostess can offer, or wants to offer, is *semiformal* luncheons and dinners, that is, those prepared by a home cook and served by one or two waitresses. But *informal* luncheons, dinners, and buffet suppers, cooked and served by the hostess with the help of her husband and family or with the aid of a part-time maid, are the rule in most homes today.

None of these is correctly referred to as formal even when host, hostess, and guests wear evening clothes. Nor is any home dance or any other kind of party called formal simply because evening clothes are worn by all present. Such dressing up adds a special festive atmosphere and is preferred by many people especially at holiday parties, dances, and many other occasions described in this book. But what you wear depends on what you and your crowd like to do, the part of the country in which you live, and what your hostess asks you to wear.

Invitations, for example, to a formal affair are especially engraved for the event, or hand written in Spencerian script, the phraseology restricted to the stilted style dictated by good taste and the conventions of Society in the late nineteenth century. Many kinds of modern invitations, invitation cards, and forms are discussed throughout this book.
The Versatile Kitchen A vitally important room in your home at party-giving time is the kitchen. It must be ready with equipment and utensils to function perfectly on large and small jobs, to do what your menu demands of it.

This does not mean that, to give a party, you must have a big, handsomely equipped kitchen. But the supply of pots and pans, cutlery, and kitchen towels used to prepare family meals from day to day is seldom sufficient when a party is in preparation. Let the menu, decided on well ahead of the party date, guide you in buying any new necessities. Use any new utensils bought for the party meal at least once in a trial preparation of the dishes before the day of the party.

Among the rewarding additions to a home for party use are electric table cookery devices, such as a small oven, skillet, broiler, toaster, and warming tray. A serving cart is almost an essential not only to save steps but because it can be decorative as well as useful and carry a large punch bowl, or big wedding cake, or the heavy soup marmite around the room to guests. Or a cart can be used at a child's party to wheel a record player and its gay tunes around the room, or to bring in the birthday cake on its musical stand. Or when the dining room is small, a service cart can hold the coffee maker, cups and saucers, or other accessories. Various uses for this handy, wheeled assistant are mentioned in party plans throughout this book.

Table-service dishes, such as a large soup marmite, individual soup casseroles, and casseroles of many other sizes, shapes, and kinds make buffet supper and home dinner serving easy, as shown in the recipes given with parties. A crêpes Suzette pan, a Swedish plättar pan for those delicious little pancakes, a regular pancake griddle, a waffle iron can add good eating to suppers and brunches, kitchen parties, and playroom meals.

One of the most satisfying additions to a kitchen utensil supply is a collection of ring molds and fancy molds of various shapes and sizes for aspics, gelatin salads and desserts, cakes, puddings, and frozen desserts.

You cannot do without a sturdy, easy-to-use can opener and a foolproof corkscrew. You will find a meat grinder almost an essential. Food grinders for crumbs, cheese, nuts, crackers, and a mincer for parsley and other greens add to the pleasure of preparing a party menu. Add a blender or mixer or both for juice and milk drinks if there are teen-agers around, also because these devices are time savers and do many jobs for a busy cook.

Party cakes are more effective if baked in special pans, such as four-, six-, or nine-inch square and round pans—keep sets for tier cakes. You can find star, bell, wreath, lamb, rabbit, Santa Claus, and other cake pan shapes to help make children's cakes "different." Cupcake pans and spring-form and tube pans for angel cake are also good additions to the party kitchen. Cookie cutters, molds, and varied forms come in handy when preparing a children's party as well as when giving a kitchen work party for all ages.

Some hostesses say that large sugar and spice shakers, a pepper mill, extra-fine slicers and knives, two or more spatulas, wooden spoons, and a pancake turner are helpers they do not want to be without. Poultry shears, a butter curler, brochette skewers of various lengths, and decorative skewers for roasts are good additions. And for barbecue cooks, there are heat-proof gloves, special long-handled forks, turners, and skewers—all practical and necessary as well as decorative.

A steak plank may be one of your favorite accessories. You may want a Turkish coffeepot, perhaps an espresso coffeemaker, and certainly one extra-large coffeepot and a large-quantity urn for serving coffee to a crowd. For teen-agers soda fountain sundae dishes, real ice cream soda glasses and their metal holders, long-handled soda spoons, and an endless supply of colored sipping straws are good things to have on hand. So is a large glass pitcher in which punch or an iced soup is mixed to place in refrigerator to chill. An ice tub in which to chill bottles of soft drinks is a good addition to the teen-age party supply.

An insulated, ice-cube bucket, an easy juicer, a cutting board for fruits, and the right knife for the slicing make fruit-drink mixing and serving easy. You may need a few large-quantity, restaurant-size kettles for occasional big parties; some hostesses borrow or rent these from club, school, church, or caterer. You may want a deep-fat fryer for butterfly shrimp, doughnuts, croquettes, and other fried delicacies. You will need one or two heavy, cast aluminum or iron skillets for sukiyaki, the Japanese favorite that is cooked at the table.

Other necessities in some kitchens are a heavy wooden chopping and slicing block, asparagus steamer, which also is used for many other foods, large colander or wire salad washing basket, iron popover and corn-stick pans, an extra tea kettle, extra roasting pans, an inexpensive light plastic tray for use in the refrigerator and a light, decorative one for use in the dining room.

Several young homemakers insist that one of the most important helpers in the kitchen is space for a menu board in front of or near their worktable or countertop. Besides the menu thumbtacked up before their eyes, there is a detailed schedule beside it. This lists the time to start the dish and what to do next step by step, for complete preparation of the menu—everything written out as reminders so that nothing is left undone, nothing started too soon, or left to be done too late, hastily and badly, and all dishes are ready to serve at the same time.

CONTENTS

Suburban Dwellers • Invitations • Planning and Decoration • Menus • Entertainment.

Wedding Anniversaries Invitations, Color Schemes, Table Decorations, Gifts, Favors, Entertainment, Menus and Recipes for: 1st Wedding Anniversary through the 9th Wedding Anniversary • Suggestions for the 10th Wedding Anniversary through the 14th Wedding Anniversary • Complete Plans for the 15th, 25th, and 50th Wedding Anniversaries.

Engagement Luncheon What It Is • Who Gives It for the Engaged Girl • Whom to Invite • Menu • Decoration • All Procedures • Invitations.

Engagement Dinner Family Party • Procedure • Invitations • Decorations • Menu and Recipes.

Bachelor and Ushers' Dinner Giving It at Home • Menu.

Gift Showers for Engaged Girls and Married Couples Invitations, Decorations, Gifts, Menus, Recipes for Menus and All Details for: Bath Shop Shower • Book-and-Record Shower • Clean-Up Shower • Clothes Closet Shower • Fix-It Shower • Games Shower • Home Decorating Showers • Kitchen Cutlery Shower • Kitchen Utensil Shower • *Other Popular Showers:* Lingerie Shower • Pantry Gifts Shower • Table Setting Shower • Stork Shower.

Wedding Breakfast and Reception Where to Find Helpful Information and Professional Catering Services • How to Plan All Details for the Home Breakfast and Reception • Arrangement of Room for Bride's Table and Guests • Seating • Decorations • Traditional Menu • Bride's Cake • Wedding Cake • Small Weddings • Afternoon and Evening Weddings: Menus, Decorations, and Procedure.

Spring *St. Patrick's Day:* Shamrock Chowder Supper—Invitations • Decorations • Menu • Recipes • Entertainment • Other St. Patrick's Day Parties • A Green Menu. *Arbor Day:* Family and Community Parties • What to Serve. *Easter:* Brunch—Invitations • Decorations • Menus • Recipes • Easter Dinner—Decorations • Menus. Passover and The Seder—Menus. *May Day and Child Health Day:* Pick-up Luncheon for May Day Basket Makers—Menu and Suggestions • Tray Luncheon Menus. *Memorial Day or Decoration*

CHAPTER   4   **CHILDREN'S PARTIES**   **164**

TRADITIONAL FAMILY PARTIES

Birthdays

Family birthday parties begin with those gently hilarious occasions when a small cake bearing one gleaming pink or blue candle is brought in from the kitchen to the one-year-old's high chair while admiring relatives, young and old, sing "Happy Birthday dear Baby, to you!" Next year two candles, then three, and soon several more shine from the annual cake.

When we are past the age of the circus party, bright balloons, and grab-bag gifts, a birthday so personal, so especially one's own day is still the best possible excuse for inviting friends in for festivity. We can plan a simple birthday cake-and-coffee evening, a luncheon or dinner. Or we can turn any of the costume, dancing, regional, picnic, and other kinds of entertainments described in the following pages into a special birthday festival by simply saying so, and adding a candle-topped cake to the refreshments.

For all name-day and birthday events, decorations, color schemes, and traditional themes can be stimulated and influenced by the lists of Birthstones, Flowers of the Month, and Flowers of Astrological Signs given at the end of the chapter. The budget, time of year, space available, age, number of guests, special interests of the guest of honor are other considerations. With these inspirations and limitations the general rule is: plan all details carefully as in all other kinds of entertaining (see A Word to the Successful Hostess). Then be as imaginative and interesting as possible.

There are typical birthday parties for a high school or prep school girl on vacation, and easy celebrations which older children can carry out for their parents, and grandparents' birthdays. Teen-age parties, as well as other teen-age social activities, are given in detail in Chapter 5, "Teen-age Parties."

Girl's Birthday Luncheon For a birthday luncheon during spring vacation for a high school or prep school daughter, in late March or early April.

Invitations may be telephoned. Or with this special color scheme in mind, they may be written on red-edged note paper:

> Tuesday
>
> Dear Helen,
>> Mother thinks my birthday is a good excuse for a luncheon party. So do I! We both hope you can come, Thursday, April 8th, at 12:30 noon.
>> At my home, 221 Acacia Boulevard.
>>> (signed) Margaret
>
> R.S.V.P.
> Waverly 4–2211

Color Scheme Since this birthday is an Aries date on the astrologers' calendar, the Aries red (see end of this chapter) might be followed with satisfying and dramatic effect. For this, use a red linen tablecloth and a small red carnation corsage on each folded red napkin. Make the table centerpiece of red and white carnations and red roses in a low crystal, silver, or pottery bowl. Select all-white china, or solid-color pink ware, clear crystal glassware or red glassware, and your prettiest silver.

Menu For diet-conscious girls, the menu could be a cup of herb-seasoned bouillon with heated cheese crackers, ripe olives, lemon gelatin salad ring filled with icy-cold crab-meat salad, finger sandwiches of whole-wheat bread and butter, white-frosted birthday cake with tiny red candles on it. With the cake, serve pineapple sherbet or ice cream, and hot coffee or tea.

Opening birthday presents afterwards, and talk, bridge, or listening to new gift records turn this into a party to be remembered.

Mother's Birthday When a family of young teen-age children give a birthday party for their mother, one of them should be appointed leader or organizer of the planning and cooking. And they should confer on menu and guests with their father, who usually is pressed into service of assorted kinds for the event.

For success, which means good things to eat nicely served, every step must be planned ahead (see the section on How to Give a Dinner in Chapter 15 for general guidance). This planning starts with the guest list, then invitations telephoned or written. A shopping list must be made and all supplies bought. The house must be cleaned, all table accessories freshly washed and made ready.

Someone is assigned the job of decorating the dining room, porch, living room, or wherever the party table will be placed. Someone must set the table, arrange a centerpiece, place dessert plates, coffee cups and saucers, and other dishes exactly where they will be needed.

Decorations For either an ice cream supper or a larger menu, decoration of the table might be a low arrangement of garden flowers in a glass bowl, and a special little bouquet for the guest of honor to wear in her hair or on her dress. Or, decoration which adds a more festive air can be made with wide crepe-paper streamers in Mother's favorite colors. These can be hung from a central point in the ceiling and fastened to side walls with gummed tape to look like a striped tent top. Streamers should be about 10 inches wide. For length of each, measure from ceiling center to side wall; amount of crepe paper needed can be estimated if one package is bought, measured, and cut ahead of time.

Two strips of different colors of the same paper laid down the length of the center of the table make a colorful area for the flower centerpiece. Paper napkins to match crepe paper add still more color.

Invitations The invitations, if not telephoned or given in person, are written by the children on their best note paper:

Monday

Dear Aunt Bee,
    We are having a birthday party for Mother on Saturday night, May 31st. We hope it will surprise her, so don't tell her if you see her. Dad says, and so do we, *please* come. 6 o'clock.

(signed with children's names)

Menu For success with this kind of family party, especially if the children are preparing it as a surprise party, the simplest menu is best, such as, birthday cake, Mother's favorite ice cream, coffee made by Dad, which might follow the family supper. This need not be a surprise party, although a surprise is the most fun. But it is difficult to surprise Mother unless she has a full schedule of club, church, or other work that keeps her outside the house for most of the party day. The idea of any birthday party for her is to save her work, give her pleasure, and remind her that her birthday is important to the family.

The light menu is ideal for a Saturday evening, perhaps after a hearty late luncheon earlier in the day. If family appetites demand something more filling at the party, first serve a platter of cold cuts easily assembled from delicatessen or grocery store and a tray of hot buttered, brown-and-serve rolls and buns, mustard and relishes, so that everybody can make his own sandwich. With a bowl of crisp mixed salad greens with chive-seasoned cottage cheese, iced tea or coffee, and milk shakes for the younger members, this is a meal not too difficult to prepare. If there are experienced teen-age cooks in the family, a good casserole of chicken or tuna fish may be prepared instead of the cold cuts.

After guests have finished sandwiches and salad or a hot main dish, all plates, serving plates, and silver are carried to the kitchen. Then the cake with its lighted candles is brought in while everybody sings the birthday song. Dad, who makes the coffee, does his share by bringing in the freshly-made brew and serving the grownups' cups or refilling iced coffee glasses.

After-supper Entertainment What to do after supper? The guest of honor will open her presents, most of them wrapped by the children in more of the bright crepe paper. These can be simple gifts that they know their mother wanted. For this very special, once-a-year party Dad may have rented a movie projector for the evening and an old silent movie full of fun, or a projector and colored slides showing a tour of some wonderful faraway country. Both movies and projectors can be rented in most cities—consult the classified telephone directory, or a librarian, school teacher, or the moving picture theatre operator (see Index). Sometimes a school or museum owns projectors and films as well as slide sets and will lend or rent them.

Shop your town's possibilities thoroughly for something which your mother and the guests will enjoy. A new Perry Como record, or maybe she likes opera and seldom gets to hear one? A new LP record album of opera favorites would provide a whole evening of music, which grownups could listen to over their second cups of coffee, and the children could appreciate as background music to their own table and floor games of dominoes, Scrabble and others.

Or a darts tournament with prizes is fun for old and young. So is an impromptu art class. School crayons, large sheets of drawing paper, drawing boards made of stiff cardboard cut from old suit boxes and grocery store cartons are passed out to all guests. Prizes are given for the best sketch of Mother, or of one of the children, or of the parakeet in his cage, or the family dog. The sketching should be timed by a scorekeeper with a watch. After two or three models have posed, the sketches should be hung up for judging. The guest of honor, one child, and one guest might be judges. Prize ribbons, blue for First, red for Second, white for Third, can be pinned on the winners, and possibly prizes distributed as well.

Prize ribbons are easily made, using plastic-back ribbon and gold paint, a job that should be done *before* the day of the party. Prizes might be a small bud vase with a garden flower in it, a small toy that is wound by its key and walks across the floor to make everybody laugh, or, for a man, a miniature chess set now available everywhere in toy stores for less than fifty cents.

Father's Birthday A surprise party for a man of the house is more easily planned and carried out because he is away most of the day at his work. Mother or one of the older children telephones the invitations, or sends notes like those sent for the Mother's birthday party. Invite his best friends. Be sure to tell each that the party is a surprise and ask everyone to come at exactly the time you want to assemble the crowd.

Decorations Decorate the table with a bowl of fresh fruit, or flowers from the garden, or leaves and pine from the woods. If he likes golf or some other sport, miniature golf bags and clubs or other sports items from toy shops and ten-cent store might be used around the centerpiece. Or surround it with gaily wrapped presents from family and friends, which he will open after the birthday song and blowing the candles.

To add party atmosphere, fill big jars with fresh rhododendron or other large greens or flowers and place around the room. Or make big "bouquets" of those plastic toy whirligig windmills on long sticks. Some of the party budget money would be well spent on two or three dozen of these in assorted colors. (Maybe your local toy shop or ten-cent store will sell a box of them to you wholesale.) They should be bunched loosely in wide glass jars. Their bright, lively colors are just right to start the fun at the surprise party. At the end of the evening, they can be given as favors to departing guests.

Menu Plan a menu of the dishes Father likes best. For instance, fried oysters with coleslaw or that standby meat loaf he always asks for, with a big casserole of scalloped potatoes, fried apples, warm corn bread, the birthday cake, his favorite ice cream, and coffee.

After-dinner Entertainment If his card-playing cronies are guests at this party, the rest of the evening can be spent as usual with them around a card table. The other guests and family can play card or table games, or enjoy records in the living room. If Dad likes Gilbert and Sullivan operas, an LP recording of his favorite gives him a musical birthday.

There are LP records of railroad songs, amusing with guitar, banjo, accordian accompaniments, very singable too, and the whole party will like them. Or if he likes to hear poetry or a play read aloud, there are wonderful selections listed in special sections of record catalogues at music shops. Or ask some friend who plays a guitar to bring it to the party, and after supper have a family sing of old-time favorites.

At the end of the evening, provide a pitcher of iced tea or fruit punch and any leftover birthday cake, or the newest batch of cookies made by the children, before guests start home.

Grandmother and Grandfather Birthdays

Invitations may be telephoned or written to friends of the same age as the birthday celebrant as well as to any younger people he or she especially likes. The time of day for the party, the food to be served, the kind of entertainment depend on the age and health of the grandparent. Most frail, elderly people do not care for, or are wearied by, planned entertainment and a big dinner. But they will enjoy seeing friends at an afternoon party or an early evening get-together to chat awhile and will blow candles on a cake, cut it, and be happy to serve it with ice cream and coffee. Even the very old can enjoy dispensing this simple hospitality.

There are, of course, those amazing exceptions, strong-minded ancients who "love a party!" For them, plan or let them plan the kind of entertainment they like. Invite their gang, cronies of the same spirit, or let this lively grandparent do his own telephoning of invitations. This may be the kind of party where paper hats and horns, gay costumes, records for dancing, or tables for bridge are in demand. These lively elders do not belong in the category of Old Dears who live alone or with an indulgent and loving family, and whose birthday is a little sad (another milepost) and almost the only social event of their year.

The young grandparent For an active man or woman who leads a busy life, an amusing party can be planned around his or her younger days.

Decoration—College class colors and old college photographs, pennants, banners, can be used, the more the better. Some may be borrowed from friends and relatives or from the college itself (write to the Publicity Department at the college) if the party is planned far enough ahead. Wide, inexpensive plastic ribbons or streamers of crepe paper in the college colors are pinned or tacked over windows as draperies, or pinned to the draperies already hung at windows. A centerpiece of flowers of the month or the school flower, place cards of the turn of the century, or 1910, made from old Valentines, dance programs, and similar bits from your attic, or cutouts from old magazines and books—all set the tone for "do you remember" conversation.

Invitations Old dance programs might be used as invitations. Write across each, "You are invited to a Birthday Party for Mrs. Joel Evans, by her grandchildren." Add day, time, address, telephone number, and R.S.V.P.

Another Variation If the college theme does not apply for this grandparent, another decoration scheme might be an old-time country grocery store set up in the kitchen or dining room. Old-fashioned candy jars (now available in glassware departments, kitchenwares shops) filled with goodies, a cracker barrel with a large assortment of crisp crackers in their original boxes, opened and grouped in the top of the barrel, a superb Cheddar cheese, open jars of pickles, relishes, a hand-crank ice cream freezer, coffee grinder.

Menus These decorations are used to create old-time atmosphere but they and their contents supply part of the menu. An old-fashioned glass cake stand holds the birthday cake. To add atmosphere, hang up cutouts from old newspapers and magazines, old State Fair posters, framed photographs borrowed from the local library, merchants, museum, and college.

If a help-yourself buffet luncheon or supper menu of greater possibilities than this atmospheric, crackers-and-cheese menu is preferred, serve a casserole dish such as scalloped oysters, or stuffed deviled crabs, or oven-baked chicken as a main dish, with small baked potatoes split and seasoned, then the cake and coffee. Or in warm weather, serve a porch meal of such old favorites as cold baked ham, chicken salad or cold fried chicken, potato salad, relishes, hot biscuits, chocolate ice cream, and the birthday cake with iced tea or coffee.

Entertainment Music or old films might be the entertainment feature after the refreshments. For the music, records of old songs from various parts of the country are available through Folkways Records & Service Corporation, 117 West Forty-sixth Street, New York 36, New York.

Such records include cowboy songs, various regional ballads by local singers (Bay State, Virginia, North Carolina, Texas, Kansas, Kentucky are a few of the areas listed, also sailors' songs, soldiers' songs, work songs, songs of other countries. The catalogue includes so much music on nostalgic themes that almost any early sport, hobby, career, or enthusiasm of a grandparent can be had in records to make the birthday party one to be remembered.

Gifts Family and friends can find in local shops many gifts that older people enjoy, such as an enlarging glass for the reading table, earphones for radio so he or she can rest in bed and hear a program without disturbing the rest of the family, new solitaire decks, refreshing cologne, a knitting bag, a soft warm shawl knitted by a member of the family, hand-knit neckties, slippers, footstool, gifts of golf clubs, gardening gloves, books, magazine subscriptions. The family album brought up to date with new photographs from distant relatives makes a thoughtful gift.

Opening the presents can be the high point of any grandparent's party. Handsomely wrapped, perhaps piled high on a coffee table, or in the center of the dining table, they emphasize the love and generosity of family and friends.

Especially appreciated is a round-robin letter from all members of the family who could not come to the party. This letter must be planned and started on its way two or three weeks in advance of the party—even longer if it must go to Europe or other faraway places. It is sent first to the most distant relative whose name heads the list, with a request that he or she add his news to it and send the letter on its way to the next name. The last relative must mail it to the original sender well ahead of the party date. The reading of this letter can be the finale of the party, with second cups of coffee, second helpings of cake all around.

Reception or Open House Still another kind of grandparent birthday celebration is the reception or open house planned for a man or woman who in younger days played some outstanding role in the community. An old musician may be "serenaded" by former pupils or friends who played with him in a band, orchestra, or string ensemble. An art teacher or painter may have pupils come to his home on his birthday to unveil his portrait done by a former student. Men and women who have been school teachers, librarians, have taught Sunday School class, or have connections with the public through some other profession in one sense belong to the public. A birthday reception is easily managed on a porch, or in a living room.

Invitation might be inserted in a local or school paper:

Birthday Reception

The family and friends of Mrs. Emily Jameson, who taught
history for many years at Centerville High School, will hold
Open House in Honor of her 75th Birthday

Saturday Afternoon	At The Family Home
3 to 5 PM	34 Main Street
September 21st.	

Friends and Former Students Invited

Menu If the number of guests is small, a menu of birthday cake and coffee or punch can be served. For a larger crowd cookies or sandwiches, or both, with coffee, tea, or punch. For a very large crowd, neighbors and friends may want to share with the family to provide the refreshments and to help receive and serve all guests.

Decorations The house can be festive with flowers and greens in bouquets and arrangements on tables and mantelpiece. The dining-room table, lighted with candles and decorated with flowers or autumn leaves and fruit, is the center from which refreshments are served, with a member of the family or a friend helping in the kitchen and two or more taking turns at the serving table. (See section on *How to Give a Tea* in Chapter 15.)

A special place should be provided for the guest of honor, such as a sofa around which chairs are grouped, so that guests have a chance to visit with her or him. Then they move along to the refreshment table to be served, making room for others around the guest of honor. No planned entertainment is necessary.

Home Birthday Treasure Hunt When a family celebrates a birthday alone with no outside guests, the gift-giving can take the form of a household treasure hunt. Amusing, mysterious wrappings are used, packages hidden behind books, in golf bags, in the waste basket, the cat's basket, Mother's sewing basket, in the kitchen breadbox, under a bed, and as many unlikely hiding places as possible. Old newspapers, butcher-shop brown paper, wallpaper, bandana handkerchiefs, fancy paper are used as wrappings; all kinds of ribbon, strings, cords. Each hidden gift must bear the name of some member of the family.

The hunt is better fun if a time limit is set, with someone holding a watch and calling out some such warning as, "Five minutes to go or forfeit the prize." Besides the birthday celebrant, all members of the family take part in the hunt, finding surprise gifts for themselves, which have been hidden during the day.

The hunt can precede a supper or come after refreshments, depending on ages and other factors.

General Birthday Information

Birthstones

January	Garnet
February	Amethyst
March	Bloodstone and Aquamarine
April	Sapphire and Diamond
May	Agate and Emerald
June	Emerald, Pearl, Moonstone
July	Ruby and Onyx
August	Carnelian, Sardonyx, and Peridot
September	Sapphire and Chrysolite
October	Aquamarine, Opal, and Tourmaline
November	Topaz
December	Turquoise and Zircon

Flowers of the Months

January	Carnation and Snowdrop
February	Violet and Primrose
March	Jonquil and Daffodil
April	Sweet Pea and Daisy
May	Lily of the Valley and Hawthorn
June	Rose and Honeysuckle
July	Larkspur and Water Lily
August	Poppy and Gladiolus
September	Aster and Morning Glory
October	Calendula and Cosmos
November	Chrysanthemum
December	Narcissus and Holly

Flowers of Astrological Signs

March 21 to April 20	Aries	All small red flowers; red carnation, red roses
April 21 to May 20	Taurus	All flowers
May 21 to June 20	Gemini	All double flowers; lilac

June 21 to July 22	Cancer	Lotus and immortelles, lily and jasmine
July 23 to August 22	Leo	All golden and deep yellow flowers
August 23 to September 22	Virgo	All flowers of the lily family; white rose, heliotrope
September 23 to October 22	Libra	All balms, pansy, violet, primrose
October 23 to November 22	Scorpio	Chrysanthemum; all large red flowers
November 23 to December 21	Sagittarius	All climbing vines and flowering trees
December 22 to January 19	Capricorn	All black and dark-hued flowers; dark poppies, tulips
January 20 to February 18	Aquarius	Blue and white flowers; acacia
February 19 to March 20	Pisces	White and orchid flowers; all sea plants; ferns, mosses, white narcissus

Recipes for Birthday Parties

BIRTHDAY CAKE

2½ cups sifted cake flour	½ cup soft shortening
3 teaspoons baking powder	1 cup plus 2 tablespoons
1 teaspoon salt	milk
4 egg whites	1 teaspoon vanilla
1½ cups granulated sugar	

Start oven at Moderate (375°F.). Grease two 9-inch layer pans, then line bottoms with waxed paper and grease paper.

Sift flour, baking powder, and salt together three times. Whip egg whites stiff, gradually beating in ½ cup sugar. When mixture stands in peaks set bowl aside. Cream shortening with remaining 1 cup sugar until light and fluffy, beat in flour mixture, a little at a time, alternating with milk and vanilla. Then beat egg white mixture thoroughly into cake batter. Pour into greased pans. Bake 25 minutes, or until cake tester inserted in center of layers comes out clean. Let cool in pans on cake rack 15 minutes. Then loosen cake with spatula, invert on rack, lift pan off cake. Peel off paper. Repeat with second pan. When layers are cool put together with this frosting between them, and frost top and sides generously:

BIRTHDAY CAKE FROSTING

2 egg whites	½ teaspoon salt
1½ cups granulated sugar	1 teaspoon vanilla or other
⅓ cup water	flavoring
1 tablespoon light corn	
syrup	

Combine all ingredients except flavoring in upper part of double boiler. Beat with mixer at high speed, 1 minute, or beat quickly and smoothly with hand beater. Place over rapidly boiling water and continue to beat 7 to 9 minutes, or until mixture stands in peaks when beater is raised. Remove pan from hot water. Add vanilla, continue beating until smooth enough to spread. This recipe makes filling and frosting for two 9-inch layers, which will serve eight.

You can, of course, use any other favorite filling and frosting. When topping is firm, use a plain tube of your cake decorating set and write

Happy Birthday, the name of the celebrant, or other greetings; or add frosting flowers or swirls of delicately tinted butter cream frosting. But leave room for the candles.

Small candles of one color are usually set in a border around the cake, and one larger candle is placed in the center. Or the entire top of the cake is dotted with candles. An all-white cake with white candles is popular but many hostesses prefer to use candles in one of the colors of the party decorating scheme or a rainbow of two, three or more colors arranged helter-skelter over the cake's top.

Other Kinds of Cake An angel food, chiffon, or sponge cake may be preferred to a layer cake. These as well as layers are easily made using the excellent cake mixes now available, some with frosting included in the package. Colored frostings, delicately tinted with pure food coloring are favorites for some cakes, and for lettering also; the easily made butter cream frostings adapt nicely to scrolls, flowers, and other decorations, but are less satisfactory for lettering a name and date.

A local baker may be famous for his birthday cakes, or a caterer may be available whose cakes have made his reputation. One in New York makes birthday cakes for boys' parties in the shapes of baseball bats, footballs, and other masculine sports equipment. Pans for fancy shapes are available, or a cake may be baked in a large, shallow, square or oblong pan and amusing forms cut from it using a homemade paper pattern. These cutouts may be put together as a layer cake—and it is fun to use different colored filling between layers in the same cake, such as currant jelly between two layers and mint jelly between next two—or frost the cutouts as single-layer cakes, and decorate with small candles, or with a cluster of flowers or fruit and one large candle in the cluster (see "Children's Parties," Chapter 4).

Recipes for Girl's Birthday Luncheon

BOUILLON WITH CURRY-FLAVORED WHIPPED CREAM

½ pint heavy cream
1 teaspoon curry powder
4 (10½ oz.) cans beef bouillon
1½ cans water

1 tablespoon each chopped chives and parsley
1 teaspoon orégano
1 teaspoon dried sweet basil

Whip cream stiff, gradually adding curry powder. Taste, and judge amount of this seasoning; curry powders vary in their intensity. The whipped cream topping should have a delicate curry flavor. Set seasoned whipped cream aside. Combine bouillon and water in saucepan; heat to boiling. Add parsley, chives, and herbs. Lower heat; cover and let simmer 5 minutes. Serve in warmed bouillon cups with spoonful of whipped cream on top. This recipe makes 6 servings.

If bouillon must be prepared ahead of time, combine bouillon and water and heat to boiling. Do not add seasonings. Cover and place in refrigerator. At serving time, skim any fat from top and reheat bouillon with the seasonings indicated.

LEMON GELATIN SALAD RING
WITH CRAB-MEAT SALAD

2 tablespoons plain gelatin	1 tablespoon sugar
¼ cup cold water	½ teaspoon salt
½ cup boiling water	Water cress or lettuce
1½ cups lemon juice	
2 tablespoons grapefruit juice	

Soak gelatin in cold water for 5 minutes. Add boiling water and stir about 2 minutes, or until gelatin completely dissolves. Stir juices, sugar, and salt in. Let cool. Rub 1-quart ring mold with olive oil or cooking oil. Pour gelatin into mold. Set in refrigerator for at least 2 hours, or until firm. Unmold on chilled salad platter. Fill center with crab-meat salad. Garnish with small clusters of water cress or very small hearts of lettuce. Recipe makes 6 servings.

To unmold gelatin ring: Set mold in shallow pan of hot water 30 seconds. Lift out, loosen jelly around edges with thin sharp knife. Invert serving platter over mold, turn both right side up; tap mold all around. If jelly does not fall out easily, cover outside of mold with towel wrung out of very hot water. Let stand 2 minutes. Tap mold again and ease jelly out.

CRAB-MEAT SALAD

2 cups flaked cooked, canned, or quick-frozen crab meat	1 tablespoon lemon juice
	1 teaspoon salt
	½ teaspoon pepper
1 cup finely diced celery	¾ cup mayonnaise
1 tablespoon minced onion	

Clean crab meat carefully, removing all large and small cartilage. Combine with other ingredients. Toss lightly with fork and spoon. Chill in covered bowl in refrigerator until serving time. Heap in center of gelatin ring on platter. Recipe makes 6 servings.

Recipes for Mother's Birthday Party

GREEN SALAD

Your best cookbook, the one that you use regularly, contains many salad recipes. But a recipe for tossed green salad is given here because some cooks think a good salad is simply a big bowl filled with greens and salad dressing over all. A green salad to be appetizing and delicious should look washed and be crisp, and consist of pieces of greens and vegetables just the right size to eat with a fork.

For this salad have all vegetables and greens washed thoroughly, drained, rolled in a towel, and placed in refrigerator to chill. Do not mix salad until ready to serve it or it will wilt and be soggy.

3 red tomatoes	2 teaspoons salt
½ clove garlic	Freshly ground pepper or
6 red radishes	½ teaspoon pepper
1 head romaine	French dressing
1 head iceberg lettuce	½ cup crumbled Roquefort
1 bunch water cress	or Blue cheese
3 or 4 pieces parsley	

Scald tomatoes by pouring boiling water over them. Let stand 2 minutes. Drain, skin them, let cool in refrigerator. Cut tomatoes in quarters. Rub salad bowl with garlic, then discard the garlic. Slice radishes thin. Break romaine and lettuce in bite-size pieces into the bowl; cut water cress and parsley very fine with kitchen scissors over the other greens in bowl. Add tomatoes and radishes. Sprinkle all lightly with salt and add a quick grind of pepper or the ½ teaspoon of pepper. Pour 1 or 2 tablespoons French dressing and the cheese over all. Lift the mixture lightly with salad fork and spoon so the dressing coats all. Serve at once onto chilled salad plates. Recipe makes 6 servings.

If you have a very large salad bowl, and want to double this recipe, it will still be appetizing because the greens are crisp and well seasoned, and the right size, and the combination of flavors is so good.

EASY CHICKEN OR TUNA CASSEROLE

5 tablespoons butter or margarine
4 tablespoons flour
¾ teaspoon salt
⅛ teaspoon pepper
⅛ teaspoon nutmeg
¼ teaspoon celery salt
2 cups milk
½ cup light cream
2 cups cut up, cooked chicken or canned tuna fish

1 canned pimiento cut in small dice
2 tablespoons minced parsley
3 tablespoons grated cheese
2 tablespoons bread crumbs
Paprika

Start oven at Moderately Hot (400°F.). Melt butter or margarine in saucepan, stir flour in and mix until smooth. Add salt, pepper, nutmeg, and celery salt. Add milk slowly, stirring all the time until smooth. Add cream, stir continually, cooking over low heat until mixture thickens and boils. Add chicken or tuna fish, pimiento, and parsley. Pour into buttered 2-quart casserole. Sprinkle top with cheese and crumbs, and with paprika lightly. Bake in Moderately Hot oven (400°F.) about 20 minutes, or until top is lightly browned and bubbly. Recipe makes 6 servings.

For larger party make the recipe twice, using 2 identical casseroles.

Recipes for Father's Birthday Party

FRIED OYSTERS

1½ pints bulk oysters (36 oysters)	1 egg, slightly beaten
1½ cups fine dry crumbs or corn meal	2 tablespoons water
	4 tablespoons butter or margarine
½ teaspoon salt	Tartare sauce or chili sauce
¼ teaspoon pepper	

Drain oysters, examine, and remove any bits of shell. Pat oysters dry on paper towel. Dip each in crumbs or corn meal seasoned with salt and pepper, then into egg mixed with water, then into seasoned crumbs again. Let stand 10 minutes to dry. Fry in butter or margarine in heavy skillet, or in deep hot fat. When browned on both sides, drain a few minutes on thick paper towels. Serve on warm platter. Recipe makes 6 servings.

For 8 to 12 guests, double this recipe. Keep fried oysters hot in pan in hot oven (leave the oven door open) until all are cooked.

Do not overcook; oysters should be taken from pan as soon as coating is lightly browned.

STANDBY MEAT LOAF

2 pounds ground beef	¼ teaspoon pepper
¼ pound finely chopped salt pork or bacon	1 tablespoon salt
2 eggs, slightly beaten	1 onion, peeled and chopped
1 cup milk	1 cup soft bread crumbs
3 tablespoons butter, melted	3 strips lean bacon
3 tablespoons ketchup	Tomato sauce

Start oven at Moderate (375°F.). Combine meat with eggs, milk, butter, ketchup, seasonings, onion, and crumbs. Shape in loaf in greased 8-by-4-inch baking dish. Lay strips of bacon on top. Bake in Moderate oven (375°F.) for 45 minutes, or until well browned. Serve with Tomato sauce or reheated leftover gravy. This recipe makes 6 servings.

For 8 to 12 guests, mix loaf twice, use 2 baking pans. Do not try to make an extra-large loaf by doubling recipe.

Recipes for Grandparents' Birthday Parties

SCALLOPED OYSTERS

½ cup butter or margarine
4 cups soft bread crumbs
1¼ teaspoons salt
⅛ teaspoon pepper

1 tablespoon lemon juice
3 tablespoons finely minced
parsley
24 drained oysters (1 pint)

Start oven at Hot (450°F.). Melt butter or margarine, stir crumbs, seasonings, lemon juice and parsley in; mix well. Arrange a layer of drained oysters in buttered 2-quart baking dish, cover with crumb mixture. Repeat layers, making top layer crumbs. Bake in Hot oven (450°F.) for 20 minutes. This recipe makes 6 servings.

For larger number of guests fill another pan or two; do not try to bake all in one extra-large pan.

OVEN-COOKED CHICKEN

Allow ½ broiler for each
serving
Butter
Salt
Pepper

Orégano
Curry powder
Celery salt

Select plump broilers of about 2 pounds' weight. Have poultry dealer split them and break joints.

Start oven at Hot (500°F.). Clean, rinse, pat chicken dry with paper towel. Rub generously with butter, sprinkle inside and out with salt and pepper. Place skin side up in baking pan. Bake in Hot oven (500°F.) for 15 to 20 minutes. Reduce heat to Moderate (325°F.). Baste with melted butter mixed with a little orégano, curry powder, and celery salt. Continue baking for 20 to 30 minutes, or until chicken is browned and done. Baste 2 or 3 times with the seasoned butter.

This is an easy recipe for a very large party. Large shallow baking pans holding six or more pieces can be put on both shelves of oven at once.

Christenings

In many families a christening is an occasion for a luncheon, tea, or reception following a church or home ceremony. Guests, besides the parents and godparents, include the clergyman, grandparents, possibly other members of the family, and intimate friends. If the clergyman has a wife, as in Protestant denominations, she also is invited to the christening as well as to any social affair that follows it.

The question of church or home christening depends on the religious denomination of the parents who, in either case, follow the suggestions of their clergyman as to place and time of the ceremony, the necessary accessories for his use (in a home ceremony), the duties of godparents, and similar details.

A church christening might be followed by luncheon at the baby's home or the home of one of his godparents or grandparents, a home christening by a tea or reception.

Invitations to the christening party may be telephoned, given in person, or written on small white fold-over cards or note paper:

Tuesday

Dear Marie and John,

Our new daughter, Barbara, is to be christened at home, Friday afternoon, October 12th, at three o'clock. It will mean so much to both Will and me if you can be here for the ceremony and stay afterwards for the small reception. Dr. Brown and his wife and a few other friends will be here.

Devotedly,

R.S.V.P.   (signed)

Tuesday

Dear Marie and John,

Our new daughter, Barbara, is being christened at church Sunday, October 14th, after the service. Both Will and I hope you can be there for her christening, and then come home with us afterwards for luncheon. Father Connoly will come to lunch, so will Joe and Celia (the godparents, no less!) and a few others. Buffet and very informal, but with-

out you the party will not be the completely happy occasion
we want it to be.

Devotedly,

R.S.V.P. (signed)

Menu for such a luncheon served either at the dining table, small
tables, or buffet is much the same as a wedding reception menu but
with a fruit punch or other beverage included for toasting the baby's
health and future.

Here is one menu: Hot clam bouillon with celery-seasoned whipped
cream, chicken or ham mousse or creamed chicken in puff pastry shells,
green peas, asparagus vinaigrette, hot biscuits, christening cake, lemon
sherbet or ice cream in fancy molds, demitasse, and the fruit punch to
toast the baby. Omit the bouillon if the luncheon is served buffet.

Or, if the weather is warm, the menu might be: honeydew melon
with fresh lime sections and mint leaves, chicken salad in lemon aspic
ring, stuffed celery, small hot rolls, iced tea or coffee, apricot sherbet
parfait, christening cake, and the punch for the toasts.

For either luncheon the usual careful planning, as for any entertaining, is necessary, and in this case at least one helper in the kitchen is
essential. Without kitchen help and someone to take charge of the
baby, a luncheon following a church christening cannot be managed
smoothly and satisfactorily. To come in at lunchtime with guests and
the baby, who may be restless after the morning episode, means that
the house must be in readiness and the table set before going to church.
Cookery and other jobs have to be done on Saturday, and on Sunday
morning before you leave for the church, so that only a final few minutes of kitchen work are necessary after church.

The bouillon can be made on Saturday and kept in a jar in the
refrigerator, ready to skim and reheat. Cream must be whipped and
seasoned at the last minute for topping the bouillon. Chicken or ham
mousse can be made on Saturday and placed in the refrigerator. Or
creamed chicken made Saturday can be kept in a covered glass jar in
the refrigerator ready to reheat at lunchtime. Pastry shells are made,
too, or bought at a bakery on Saturday and only need to be put in the
oven for crisping when the bake-and-serve biscuits go in. Asparagus is
cooked Saturday, the vinaigrette dressing made, and both kept in the

refrigerator, the sauce to be poured on drained asparagus just before serving.

Christening cake is made or bought Saturday. Sherbet or ice cream molds are made or bought and stored in freezer or packed in ice. Fruit punch is mixed and chilling in a glass jar in the refrigerator. With one kitchen helper, and someone to look after the baby, you can easily serve this luncheon in a few minutes after coming in from church.

Or a tea reception for that afternoon, or one to follow an afternoon home christening, may be more easily managed. But this too calls for detailed planning. As for the luncheon, the tea table should be made ready before the time of the afternoon ceremony, with cups and saucers, silver, napkins, small plates, trays for the tea and coffee service in place, sugar bowls filled, cream, sliced lemon, and other accessories ready.

In the kitchen, sandwiches have been made, wrapped in waxed paper, covered with a damp towel, and placed in the refrigerator. Punch has been mixed and placed in the refrigerator to chill. Petits fours or cake, ice cream, and all other dishes on the tea menu (see below) are ready to be served.

After the ceremony in the living room, while family and guests congratulate the baby, someone must go to the kitchen and put on water to boil for tea and coffee. Sandwiches are transferred to serving platters and placed on the table, the punch is poured over ice in a bowl or pitcher and placed on a tray on a side table or buffet where glasses or cups are ready.

The party begins with toasts to the baby. Then coffee and tea are brought in. Guests go to the table to be served. (See section on "How to Give a Tea" in Chapter 15.) For success, someone must look after the baby in his room—he will be tired, possibly complaining and unsocial, by this time. Someone must also be helper in the kitchen, to keep coffee- and teapots freshly full, sandwich platters refilled, and to bring cakes and sherbet or ice cream to the table a little later.

Menu for such a tea or reception might be: small, thin delicious sandwiches of various shapes and assorted breads with fillings such as lobster and mayonnaise, ham salad, sliced cucumber, chopped water cress and mayonnaise. Petits fours frosted with pale icings such as pink, blue, yellow, and white, or christening cake, small ice cream molds in flower forms, coffee, tea, and the punch complete it. Small, pretty dishes of mints and other candies, salted almonds, and pecans add to the festivity of this tea table.

A Christening Cake is traditional in some families. It may be any delicious family favorite or a white fruit cake. Some of it, like a wedding cake, is served at the party, the rest being cut and packaged in gift boxes for the guests. In some families boxes of candy are given to godparents and guests (a French custom) at a christening party. Or a personal gift of value, such as a piece of jewelry with the name of the baby and date of christening engraved on it, is given each godparent.

Gifts to the baby may be a silver spoon, silver mug, knitted sacques, or even one share in a blue-chip stock!

Decoration for luncheon, tea, or reception of this kind is usually arrangements of the more delicate "baby" flowers, such as lily of the valley, or violets, babies'-breath, delicate ferns, or even sprays of very tiny orchids, sweet William, pinks and sweet peas in pale colors, forget-me-nots, the smallest wild flowers such as spring beauties, or all-white petunias, or small white or pink roses in a table centerpiece or as small bouquets at each place. In some communities a home garden and nearby woodland can supply enough flowers and greens for the occasion.

A suitable choice of table linen for this party is a delicate white organdy cloth and napkins, or white linen mats and napkins, or perhaps a fine old family cloth, the gift of a grandparent for the occasion.

Those important christening day photographs are made after a luncheon or during a tea reception. Family camera fans can make photographs of parents with the new baby, group pictures of grandparents, parents, and baby, snaps of godparents and baby, also of the clergyman, parents and baby, and as many others as time and the mood of the baby allow.

In addition to gift boxes of the christening cake, the flowers from the table and other bouquets about the house are sometimes divided among guests when the party is over, making lovely reminders of a happy occasion.

Recipes for Christening Parties

CHRISTENING CAKE
WHITE FRUITCAKE

2 cups sifted all-purpose flour	1 cup dried currants
1 teaspoon baking powder	½ cup diced candied orange peel
¼ teaspoon salt	1½ teaspoons grated lemon peel
1 cup soft shortening	
1 cup sugar	1½ cups chopped candied cherries
5 eggs	
1 tablespoon lemon juice	½ cup sifted flour
1 cup slivered almonds	

Start oven at Moderately Slow (300°F.). Grease loaf pan 10-by-5-by-3 inches; line bottom with waxed paper and grease paper.

Sift flour, baking powder, and salt together. Cream shortening with sugar, then with eggs until light and fluffy, or about 4 minutes with mixer set at *cream*. Beat in (at low speed on mixer) flour mixture and lemon juice; add almonds, currants, peel, and cherries until just mixed. Pour into prepared pan. Bake 1¾ hours, or until cake tester inserted in center comes out clean. Let pan cool on rack 15 minutes. Then loosen cake gently with thin sharp knife and invert on rack. Remove paper. Turn cake. Let cool completely. This recipe makes 10 or more large servings, or 20 or more gift-box pieces.

See also Birthday Cake

CHICKEN OR HAM MOUSSE

1 tablespoon gelatin	2 teaspoons prepared mustard
2 tablespoons cold water	
½ cup boiling water	Cayenne
2 cups ground cooked chicken or boiled ham	½ cup heavy cream, whipped stiff

Soak gelatin in cold water 5 minutes. Dissolve by adding boiling water and stirring. Combine with chicken or ham, mustard, a few grains of cayenne, and the whipped cream. Pour into fancy 1-quart mold, which has been lightly rubbed with olive oil or cooking oil. Chill until firm.

To serve, turn mousse out onto chilled platter. Garnish with parsley, water cress, or small lettuce cups of tartare sauce or pickle relish. This recipe makes 6 servings.

For larger party, make recipe twice, using matching molds.

Bar Mitzvah and Bat Mitzvah

Many Jewish families celebrate their children's religious coming-of-age with a home reception—Bar Mitzvah for sons, Bat Mitzvah for daughters.

The Bar Mitzvah means literally "son of the commandment" in Hebrew, and is applied to a boy who has reached his thirteenth birthday and is then expected to assume his religious duty and his responsibilities as a Jew.

Jewish families in America, of every shade of religious belief, Orthodox, Conservative, and Reform, solemnize this occasion with traditional services in their local synagogues and temples. On any Saturday following closely on his thirteenth birthday, the Bar Mitzvah is called to read from the Torah scroll, the Bible in the original Hebrew. He reads two portions, one from the Pentateuch, and a portion from the Prophets.

In the Orthodox ceremony, the services are conducted in Hebrew, while in the Conservative and Reform, portions are rendered in English. The Bar Mitzvah sometimes delivers a discourse on a portion of the Bible, or in some congregations he offers an original prayer. The lad in most cases today delivers his discourse in English. Then the rabbi evokes God's blessings on him, and from then on he is regarded as having reached his religious maturity.

Since Jews regard their synagogue or temple as "a House of Prayer for all peoples," and inasmuch as the Bar Mitzvah service is held during the regular Sabbath services, anyone and everyone is permitted to attend. In the Orthodox synagogues and in some of the Conservative temples, the men sit in one section while women are usually seated in a specially assigned part of the sanctuary or the balcony. This regulation is not observed in Reform temples.

In Orthodox or Conservative synagogues both men and women are required to wear head coverings. Yarmulkes (skull caps) are available in most synagogues, though frequently parents at the Bar Mitzvah of their son supply these caps traditionally worn by men, upon their entrance to the house of worship. However, it is permissable for a man to wear his own hat if he prefers. In Reform temples the wearing of a head covering for a man is optional, but women traditionally wear hats.

Guests who attend the religious service should arrive early and remain to its conclusion. It is not advisable to bring infants or young children who may create disturbances during the religious service. No greetings or congratulations should be extended until after the conclusion of the service.

The Bar Mitzvah service, which is a solemn religious occasion, is also a joyous one and is always celebrated with a reception or party in honor of the event, arranged by the parents. Guests come by invitation only. The party generally takes place immediately after the religious service. Depending upon the circumstances of the parents, the celebration may take the form of a simple wine and cake Kiddush (a ceremony to proclaim the holiness of the Sabbath, or of a festival) held in the community hall of the synagogue, where the family of the Bar Mitzvah act as hosts to the worshippers, or an elaborate catered reception may be given in a hotel or at home. Young children and infants may be brought to this reception after the religious services are over.

Since Saturday is the Jewish Sabbath, Orthodox and Conservative families postpone the reception until the evening or the following day. Reform Jews are permitted to hold such receptions outside their homes on the Sabbath.

At Orthodox and Conservative social functions, even when held outside the synagogue, it is a mark of respect for men to wear their hats or skull caps, but headcovering is not required of women. Since these celebrations are generally held on Saturday, Orthodox and Conservative Jews do not permit smoking. This is true of some Reform congregations as well. If the party is traditional, the dietary laws will be observed; that is whenever meat is served, no butter or milk will be available.

Non-Jews invited to the reception should present gifts to the boy because it is customary to mark his emergence into religious maturity with significant presents. His parents or his grandparents present him with a tallith, the fringed prayer shawl which he wears during the religious service at his Bar Mitzvah. Among traditional families the boy is also presented with "tephillin"—the phylacteries which the Bible symbolizes as a "sign upon thy hand and frontlets between thine eyes," which he is expected to wear during daily week-day prayers. The congregation or his rabbi presents him with a Bible or prayer book.

Gifts that will enable him to continue his education (secular or religious) are in keeping, such as savings bonds or cash, which can be applied towards his college education. Equally acceptable are personal items, such as a watch, cuff links, ring, or wearing apparel.

Relatives and friends try to strike a balance between an average teen-ager's interests and the solemnity of the occasion by giving him books, both those which deal with the history of the Jews and Jewish cultural and religious contributions, as well as current books of Jewish interest and knowledge; records or albums of Jewish religious services for various holidays and festivals, many of them recorded by Metropolitan Opera stars who are also outstanding cantors; recordings of contemporary Israeli folk songs; various craft items such as wood carvings, book ends, and book marks, pottery items and religious articles.

Bat Mitzvah (pronounced Ba*s* Mitzvah) means literally "daughter of the commandment." This is a new tradition among Jews in America and is observed in a limited number of congregations. When a girl attains the age of thirteen, in some congregations twelve, she becomes a subject of the commandment. Since the tradition is a new one, form and procedure of ritual and practice vary with each community.

Some congregations have made the Bat Mitzvah ceremony exactly like the Bar Mitzvah, calling up the girl to read a portion of the Torah on Saturday. Others, unwilling to make so radical a break with tradition, have introduced a variety of ceremonies at their Friday evening religious service. Otherwise, families simply solve the problem by a family festival in the home.

Guests attending services at synagogues or temples follow the same procedure as those outlined for the Bar Mitzvah. Similarly, gifts to the girl should reflect the meaning and purpose of her continuing interest in Jewish life. Non-Jews, who enjoy friendship with Jewish families and are entertained in their homes, will find interesting guidance on behavior and return hospitality in *Your Neighbor Celebrates,* by Arthur Gilbert and Oscar Tarcov, Friendly House Publishers, New York.

Coming-Out Parties

"Coming out" and "debut" are words which are gradually fading from the American home social vocabulary. Changed living conditions, maidless homes, large communities of small houses or cliffdweller apartments all alike as tenpins, higher incomes for unskilled labor, the prevalence of quality cars and station wagons in neighborhoods once referred to as working-class, all combine to strip away barriers between children in the home and everything outside it. In many neighborhoods, children spend as much time outside their homes as in them, from the time they are old enough to toddle through the open front door.

Today there is no need for most young girls to "come out." They are already "out" in the social sense, from the age of thirteen or fourteen, when going steady begins for some. When these first attachments end they date other boys for school dances, parties at their friends' homes, school sports events, and other occasions. Many girls are engaged before they leave high school. Many are married at seventeen, according to the present trend of very young marriages which now average upwards of a million and a half a year.

The purpose of the coming-out parties of the past, which well-to-do families gave their daughters when they reached the age of eighteen, was to introduce the daughter to her relatives from other parts of the country, to young sons of her father's business partners and acquaintances, and to other eligible men. It was a formal occasion planned by social secretaries and experienced caterers. And it signaled a change in the girl's life. Coming out meant that, at last, she could go to dances, the theatre and opera, and to dinners in restaurants with young men. The prestige of the family, a houseful of servants, fabulous catering and floral decorations, an orchestra, the clothes and jewelry made these parties events of such importance that they were described in detail in newspapers and magazine social columns.

Only a few years ago these formal home debuts began to give way to large hotel and country club affairs in which two or three girls, or perhaps the city's entire social listing of eighteen-year-old beauties, were "presented" together at a gala dinner and ball, or at a ball that followed dinners in several homes and clubs.

In some sections of the country, notably San Francisco and Southern cities, these large community debuts are still annual events. Also in New York's Long Island and Westchester County, in Newport, Philadelphia, Boston, Baltimore, Cleveland, Chicago, Denver, some Texas cities, and a few other localities where families of long-entrenched wealth are slow to relinquish social habits, some home debuts as well as the large club and hotel group debuts still occur every year. These debuts are made in spite of the fact that the guests of honor are already "out"—for years they have been going to parties, night clubs, theatres, traveling to Europe and elsewhere with college chums and travel groups, like their older married, or divorced, sisters.

If the term "coming out" can be used today for any lesser occasion, it can apply to the pleasant parties that families in smaller cities and suburban communities, and even in city apartments, like to give a teen-age daughter, a special party at home or in a club, when she graduates from high school or when she turns sixteen. This is usually a dinner or buffet supper followed by dancing in the living room if it is large enough, or in a playroom, or on a big screened porch. Or if budget permits, a party tent is set up on the lawn.

Today the daughter, the guest of honor, has a good deal to say about the planning and giving of her party. She, rather than her parents, decides whom to invite, what to serve because it must be the kind of food her crowd likes, and what kind of fun to plan to keep the party going until late hours. For dancing she may choose a local dance band possibly made up of a few members of the school orchestra. Or the girl and her friends may pool their collections of dance records and at the party her father or brother takes charge of the music to keep things going at a good pace.

Invitations The parents in some cases still issue invitations for such coming-out parties. In other families the daughter may want to give the invitations in person, or by telephone if the party is at home. She may write them on her initialed stationery or a flower-decorated note paper, or a fold-over card keyed to the decoration she is planning for her party. The note might be something like this:

Thursday

Dear Ralph,

Mother and Dad think it is about time we all got together at our house for some fun. So they are giving me a party. Just because I've grown up! Supper and dancing. Friday, June 12th. I do hope you can come.

7:30 o'clock	Sincerely,
R.S.V.P.	(signed)
(Telephone number)	

Menu, the choice of the young hostess and her mother, includes some of the girl's favorite dishes and those she knows her friends prefer. But to add fun, she will surprise them at the end of dinner with a yummy new dessert. If she plans a familiar menu, one the family has used before, then there is less strain in preparation and serving especially if she and her mother must do all or most of the work.

Here's an easy menu for this sort of informal party. Begin with a tomato aspic appetizer salad, followed by stuffed steak roll (easy to prepare, slice, and serve) with baked zucchini, brown-and-serve rolls, plum jelly, and then the surprise dessert, with demitasse for those who take coffee. (See recipes at end of this section.)

The surprise dessert can be ordered from a caterer or local ice cream shop. It might be strawberry ice cream pie. Top each serving with a spoonful of crushed ripe strawberries and whipped cream for a sensational finale to the dinner or buffet supper.

If berries are not in season, use quick-frozen ones, or the caterer can supply frozen chocolate or mocha eclairs. Serve each topped with a spoonful of mocha-chocolate sauce.

If the menu is served buffet, and it will be easier this way for a large party, the supper can be especially comfortable and enjoyable if bridge tables (which can be rented or borrowed) are set up to accommodate all guests. Cover these tables with cloths to match the one on the buffet table. Supply four stools or small chairs at each table. An extra gay touch is to slipcover these with the same fabric as the table-cloths. The whole effect will be a conversation starter.

Color Scheme and Decoration For a summer party use local garden flowers or sprays of leaves from woods and fields as table decoration and elsewhere in the rooms or around the porch. Or, light the porch or garden with glowing Japanese lanterns, now in American shops in beautiful colors. They may be ordered by mail from the Jasmine Gift Shops, 63 E. Fifty-sixth Street, New York 22, or other sources if your local ten-cent store and Japanese shops do not have enough.

From the same shops colored paper butterflies on long, thin wire stems can be ordered for a few cents each—very small ones to add to the girls' hairdos, bigger ones to use in a large cluster as table centerpiece and for decoration all over the room or porch. They are light, airy, and colorful and they guarantee a good start to the party. Small, inexpensive gifts from the same sources make perfect favors for such a party, for example, small round lacquer boxes for stamps or pins for the girls, amusing Japanese kites for each boy in the party. Later, these kites make fine college room decorations.

If the party is given in wintertime, the same Japanese scheme might be used indoors. Or the guest of honor's favorite colors, for example, pink and yellow, can be used in the flowers for the buffet table—pink and yellow gladioli in a low arrangement. Tall yellow and pink candles in flower-trimmed holders add fun and a flattering light.

Favors might be a pink or yellow carnation for each man, or perhaps funny, extra-large paper carnations for them, and a flower headband for each girl.

Make these bands using ten-cent store plastic hairbands; fasten little bunches of artificial or fresh yellow and pink flowers to each. These are very glamorizing for pretty girls and more so for plain ones. Both carnations and headbands can be on the table, holding place cards when guests come in to the dining room.

The party tablecloths can be made of yellow and pink striped chintz or cotton drapery material. Finish cloths all around with a hem band or wide fringe of solid color, matching one of the stripes. Make napkins of the solid-color fabric and hand-hem them, or fringe all around by pulling out about half an inch of threads on each of the four sides.

Use striped fabric to make the slipcovers for the bridge table chair seats or stools; add ties of the solid color fabric on all corners of these covers to hold them neatly in place.

Buffet Table If the buffet table is very large and a family damask linen cloth is the best choice to cover it, a gay touch can be added by a smaller cloth made of striped chintz with a scalloped edge to fit over the top of the white cloth but coming down only a little way on ends and sides (see sketch). These toppers are also amusingly different with their edges cut in large points or squares instead of scallops. Hem all edges, or finish them with cotton fringe or other binding.

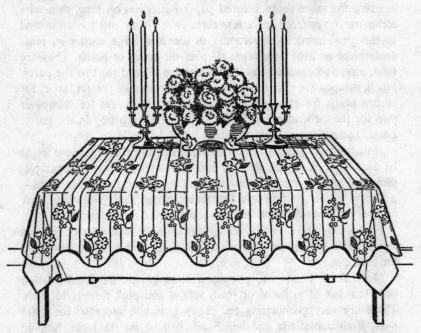

Some smaller parties for this age group are great successes because an autograph tablecloth is used. This is a white sheet bought especially for the occasion. Instead of place cards, the hostess writes a guest's name on the sheet at each place setting. Or asks the guest to write his own name. The date of the party, good wishes, and other comments are written on in turn by guests. Bright crayon is used. Later, the cloth is ironed on the wrong side to set the crayon names. (Better experiment with wax crayons and a scrap of old sheeting to make sure your crayon will "take".) Or the hostess uses a heavy, soft-lead pencil and later the names can be outlined in cotton embroidery yarn in a simple stitch. The idea is to have a gay and individual cloth for the party and a memento of the occasion. It can become a wall hanging for the girl's room at college.

Dinner, served on striped, autographed, or any other choice of cloths, comes to its end with the surprise dessert, and demitasse for those who take coffee. Candy mints in the dinner party colors of yellow and pink are slipped onto the demitasse saucers, or dishes of mints are placed on the table when the coffee is served.

Entertainment Dancing can begin as soon as the music begins. Some hostesses for the sake of good digestion like to show a movie, or plan at least a half hour of just lingering and talking around the table before dancing.

A thoughtful end to the evening includes trays of cold drinks. Provide a large bowl of ice cubes, ice tongs, glasses, bottles of cola drinks and other favorites, or a pitcher of iced tea, and sliced lemons and limes for garnish. And a bowl of spicy cheese dip and a tray of crisp crackers for the hungry.

Sweet Sixteen Party

The Sweet Sixteen Party in some communities is just such a dinner and dance as described above. Elsewhere it may be a surprise luncheon given by the friends of the just-sixteen girl and is similar to a gift shower: everybody brings a gift for the guest of honor. This luncheon is usually for girls only, or girls and their mothers. There is no planned entertainment, just luncheon served indoors or on a screened porch, the menu and decoration being adapted to the season.

Menu This might be chilled fruit cup, cheese soufflé, asparagus with butter sauce, finger sandwiches of ground ham and mayonnaise, and a colorful dessert such as a three-sherbet parfait. Petits fours or other small iced cakes and cookies, iced tea, iced coffee or demitasse complete the luncheon. Or, simply serve a fruit salad, finger sandwiches, beverage, and dessert. (See section on "How to Give a Luncheon" in Chapter 15.)

Invitations can be given in person, telephoned, or written. Any favorite note paper may be used or a small party fold-over card with matching envelope. If addressed to a girl and her mother, the invitation might read:

Thursday

Dear Mrs. Hall and Sally,

For Ellen Clay's sixteenth birthday, Joan Whiting, Virginia Stokes, and Helen Robbins are giving her a surprise Sweet Sixteen Luncheon at my home, Saturday, June 13th. Mother and I are hostesses, but all of the girls hope you both can come. And so do we.

1 o'clock Sincerely,
28 Selby Drive (signed by the girl who is hostess)

R.S.V.P.
Juniper 4685

Color Scheme and Decoration at such a party can be as feminine and imaginative as the occasion demands. For instance, a party for a girl who is interested in dress design and is planning to go to a fashion-design school might be centered around this theme: charmingly dressed dolls of various kinds and sizes are grouped to make the centerpiece on the luncheon table, and a tiny pincushion doll is a favor at each place. Gifts for this guest might include books on dress design, subscriptions to leading fashion magazines, a package containing a few very old French fashion magazines or prints found in an antique shop, a sewing kit, a small sketching outfit, as well as the usual personal gifts of stockings, lingerie, scarves and other accessories, the favorites at this kind of party.

Other themes for this type of coming-out party suggest themselves according to the interests of the guest of honor.

Recipes for Coming-Out Parties

TOMATO ASPIC APPETIZER SALAD

1½ tablespoons unflavored gelatin	½ teaspoon salt
	1 bay leaf
¼ cup cold water	¼ cup chopped celery
2½ cups tomato juice	1 sprig parsley
1 tablespoon chopped onion	1 teaspoon sugar
3 peppercorns	2 teaspoons lemon juice
3 whole cloves	

6 individual molds, in which 1 cup finely-diced celery and
½ cup finely-minced green pepper are equally divided

Soften gelatin in cold water 5 minutes or longer. Mix tomato juice
with onion, seasonings, bay leaf, celery, parsley in glass or enamel
saucepan, cover and simmer for 15 minutes. Strain, add gelatin, sugar,
and lemon juice, and stir until dissolved. Pour into the 6 prepared
molds. Let chill until firm.

To serve, turn out each mold on a chilled small salad plate; garnish
with lettuce or water cress and a small celery heart.

Prepare recipe twice or more often to make right number of servings
for the party. Do not double the recipe and try to make a large amount
at one time. The aspic molds may be prepared the day before the party
and kept lightly covered with waxed paper in refrigerator until just
before serving time. Then unmold and serve as described.

STUFFED STEAK ROLL

1½ pounds thin round beef or flank steak	1½ cups coarse bread crumbs
½ cup French dressing	½ teaspoon salt
3 tablespoons bacon fat	⅛ teaspoon pepper
1 onion, peeled and minced	⅛ teaspoon celery salt
2 (4-oz.) cans sautéed chopped mushrooms	

Ask your meat dealer to give you large, thin slices of steak; or if
2 smaller steaks are used for each roll overlap them carefully. Wipe

meat with wet cloth. Place it in a shallow dish, cover with French dressing and let stand in refrigerator several hours.

Start oven at Moderate (325°F.). Heat 2 tablespoons bacon fat, add onion and mushrooms, and cook 2 minutes. Add crumbs and seasonings, and blend. Drain steak, save its French dressing. Spread stuffing on steak, roll lightly, and tie with string. Heat remaining tablespoon of bacon fat in shallow baking pan; brown meat roll on all sides. Pour drained French dressing over the roll; cover pan. Bake in Moderate oven (325°F.) for 1 to 2 hours, until cooked through and browned. Cut strings with kitchen scissors and remove before lifting hot roll to warmed serving platter. Slice with sharp knife to serve. Makes 6 servings.

Bake 2 or 3 rolls at the same time for a large party. Try the recipe on the family a week before the party to be sure of exact baking time.

BAKED ZUCCHINI

Allow 1 average-size zucchini per serving	Finely chopped bacon
	Salt
Butter	Pepper

Start oven at Moderately Hot (400°F.). Scrub zucchini thoroughly; its sticky surface holds sand stubbornly. Rinse under cold running water. Cut in halves lengthwise, and again crosswise if zucchini are large. Place in shallow buttered baking pan. Dot with butter, pieces of bacon, and season with salt and pepper. Bake in Moderately Hot oven (400°F.) for 20 minutes, or until tender. Serve in warmed dish.

Sweet Sixteen Luncheon

CHEESE SOUFFLÉ

4 tablespoons butter or margarine	Cayenne
4 tablespoons flour	½ pound thinly sliced Old English cheese
1½ cups milk	6 eggs
1 teaspoon salt	

Start oven at Moderately Slow (300°F.). Melt butter or margarine in saucepan; stir flour in until smooth; add milk gradually, stirring continually. Add salt and dash of cayenne, continue stirring until thickened and smooth. Add cheese. Stir until cheese is melted. Remove from heat. Beat egg yolks and add; mix well. Beat egg whites until stiff; then pour cheese mixture slowly into beaten whites. Mix and blend carefully but thoroughly. Pour into 2-quart casserole. Bake 1¼ hours in Moderately Slow oven (300°F.). Take casserole to table at once and serve. Makes 6 servings.

To serve 10 guests, for instance at the Sweet Sixteen Luncheon, 2 soufflés must be made. As soon as one is put in the oven, mix the second one and bake it in a matching casserole. The first one done is served as soon as the luncheon asparagus is passed. Then the second soufflé is brought in and passed. It is a wonderful party dish, but practice making it, at least once for the family, before the party day.

Three-Sherbet Parfait can be made by combining favorite flavors of bought or homemade sherbet. Lemon, raspberry and pineapple sherbets, or lime, lemon and orange, make appetizing parfaits.

Serve in sherbet or parfait glasses: a spoonful of each flavor heaped into each glass and a sprig of fresh mint or a piece of candied cherry on top. Or stand a thin chocolate-covered mint upright in the top of each parfait. One pint each of 3 flavors will make 8 to 10 parfaits. Try the recipe ahead of time to measure amounts needed for your parfait glasses.

Family Reunions

Why have a family reunion? Every family has its own answer to this question. Perhaps a grandfather whose eightieth birthday is approaching has a yen to see all of his children, grandchildren, and great-grandchildren, his sisters and brothers, cousins, nieces and nephews, and all the other branches and twigs on his family tree.

Or, in another family, a son and his wife and children have just come home from Japan or Germany or a job in South America, and they want to see all the relatives right away.

College commencement, a graduation, is another excuse for calling

the family together to attend the school ceremonies and then to celebrate with a dinner and other parties for a day or more before the
graduate leaves for a European holiday. A birthday, wedding, wedding
anniversary, a new baby, the imminent departure of a son for some
faraway job are other occasions when scattered members of a family
come together in a reunion. Also tradition, the feeling of family
closeness, wanting to be together again and to catch up on family
news is the inspiration for many annual reunions.

Automobiles and planes speed today's distant relatives to such a
conclave. And what is equally important, this quick transportation
can carry them off to their homes again, once the celebration ends.
There's no need, as in horse-and-buggy days, to play host to a houseful, with babies bedded down on the parlor sofa, boys and men sleeping on cots, aunts and female cousins crowded into the guest room,
making it a ladies' dormitory for the time being.

The kind of reunion, its duration, size, and the amount of entertaining is an individual matter, and can be determined only by the family
concerned. For instance, a farm or country house setting will offer
different hospitality than a small suburban or city house or apartment.
But no matter what the setting—large home, small house, country, city,
suburb—good food and the time and place for talk are the chief ingredients of this event.

Here is one example: the modern reunion (no overnight guests) in
a small apartment or home might be focused around just one large
company meal, a luncheon or dinner. But this meal should be planned
so that plenty of time for talk precedes and follows it.

Menu for this might start with appetizers such as hot canapés and
chilled juices in the living room or on a porch to allow about half
an hour of talk before the meal is served. Afterwards, the meal can
come to an end with a drawn-out coffee-and-dessert conversation hour
at the table or in the living room, with second rounds of coffee, plus
those traditional after-dinner candies, nuts, and fruits that younger
guests appreciate so much.

Here is another example: if the reunion is in a suburban or country
house it can have a larger scope, such as a week end of festivity with
house guests. The week end might be planned to begin with a Saturday
picnic lunch on the lawn or screened porch, with supper or dinner in

the evening. On Sunday, there is brunch, and at the end of the day, a superb dinner or buffet supper as the finale.

Invitations for any reunion, by telegram, telephone, or letter, must be given well in advance of the date set for the homecoming to allow for the most distant relatives to accept and make the trip or send a letter of regrets.

Planning and Decoration For the greatest enjoyment of those who play host as well as of the guests, all aspects of the event should be carefully planned in advance. Shopping lists must be compiled, shopping done, house cleaned, linens, silver, and all other supplies made ready, possibly extra tables and chairs as well as other accessories hired from a caterer. No matter how simple or how elaborate the meals, flowers add the special touch that says, "Party! Welcome!" So flowers for the table, and for decorating perhaps the mantel and coffee table and small tables in guest rooms, should be ordered. Local garden flowers can be bought from neighbors or a greenhouse, or plants and cut flowers can be chosen from a florist.

Menus Favorite dishes of favorite relatives may highlight the menus; so can new dishes that your immediate family prefers. The freezer and refrigerator help make advance meal-planning effective because some foods can be prepared ahead and frozen until needed. Ice cream, sherbet, pie, other desserts can be ready in the freezer several days before the big party. A large supply of soft drinks, snack crackers, cookies, and sandwich ingredients should be brought in for any teenagers who may be among the guests. Meat, poultry, and fish dealers should have your orders early, well in advance of the day on which you want them delivered.

Perhaps local bakers, food shops, or a caterer can be used for some of the cookery. A neighbor might bake pies, cakes, or casserole dishes; in one suburban community in Connecticut, a housewife whose services are much in demand bakes for her neighbors' Sunday dinners and parties. She drives her car to pick up farm-fresh vegetables for them and gives other preliminary assistance when they entertain, all for a reasonable fee. This kind of help, or extra help in the kitchen, or a caterer who takes over much of the responsibility of supplying, preparing, and serving the food, can save you hours of work, and make the occasion easier for you in all ways.

In Chapter 13, "Overnight and Week-end Guests," and in the sections on How to Give a Dinner and How to Give a Tea Reception, in Chapter 15, "Guests for Meals," also in the chart on How Much to Buy for 50 Persons, there is helpful, detailed information to supplement suggestions given above on menus. A choice of menus and recipes, and guidance on all details of planning and preparation are in these sections, for you to apply to your individual needs and special requirements. Adapt from them the suggestions that will help you, be right for your budget, and harmonize with your personal ideas in planning your family reunion.

It is equally important that when all preliminary planning has been done, you have a schedule of things you will do after the guests arrive so that meal preparation and serving do not keep you from enjoying your visitors. At this point you will probably have plenty of assistance from your guests, because the atmosphere of such a reunion usually induces everybody to pitch in and help. Family and relatives working together provide part of the fun.

Entertainment The occasion, whether one meal, one day, or longer, is not all cookery and work. While planned entertainment of the usual party variety is not called for, a cousin may have brought his movie camera, and group pictures, pictures of everybody, of the house and garden, will be made. An uncle may have brought color films of his home in another part of the country. These must be shown with movies of children, pets, and the trip last summer to Banff.

The playing of a few LP records of greetings and news from relatives who couldn't come to the reunion may be part of the day's events. Maybe a family cookbook is started by the feminine members of the gathering, the favorite recipes of each family inscribed in a notebook. Later this can be typed and inexpensive mimeographed copies made for everyone, with the date and place of the reunion stamped on the cover.

At a country reunion, teen-age and younger children can be shown local places and things of interest: the barn, orchard, nearby stream for fishing and boating. They can be given rides on ponies or farm horses, or put up on a farm machine beside the operator for a ride around a field. There might be swings on the lawn or porch for them, croquet, archery, and games of horseshoes or quoits with some of the fathers and uncles.

At a city or town reunion, while older guests are content to stay in the apartment to talk, youngsters might be taken to a local museum, college campus, the town square, any famous historic buildings, a local sports event, or a new science display. Family interests, as well as the size and location of the house, size of gathering, and the time of year, inspire other forms of entertainment for all in the group.

Wedding Anniversaries

1st Anniversary—Paper A young couple can celebrate their first wedding anniversary, the paper anniversary, with an amusing and yet low-cost party, because paper accessories for table and many other uses are plentiful and inexpensive today. Not only are they in great variety, but are so well designed today that they suggest many ideas for games, gifts, and general decoration of dining room or apartment for such a party. These paper products are sold in five-and-ten cent stores, gift novelty shops, grocery, stationery, and housewares stores.

Invitations to a paper anniversary dinner might be written on note paper or a fold-over card of one color of your planned color scheme. Address envelope to couple or individual. Space the copy to look like an engraved invitation:

Come and Celebrate With Us
Our First Anniversary
A Paper Party
Saturday Evening, September 9th
at 7:30 o'clock

Mr. and Mrs. John Grey   Main 2-2121
42 Sunset Road   R.S.V.P.

Color Scheme and Table Decorations Decide on a color scheme for your paper party, such as blue and yellow, or rose and white, or pink and green. Then buy a paper tablecloth or paper mats and matching napkins in one of the chosen colors. The centerpiece might be assorted paper flowers of exaggerated size, large poppies, roses, iris, sunflowers, daisies, leaves and foliage. Surround their holder with a wide frill of crepe paper and tie around it to hold it in place a paper ribbon of contrasting color. From this ribbon run attached paper streamers of assorted colors, one to each place setting with a place card on the end of each streamer. The card may be white or colored; in addition to the guest's name on it add a huge numeral 1 (for first anniversary). Or, write across each card in ink to match color scheme, "The First Mile", with the date of the wedding and date of this first anniversary.

Also, at place settings arrange paper favors, such as bright colored paper party snappers, always fun and available in the stationery and gift shops as well as in candy stores, toy stores, and pastry shops. Or for each woman, a small paper box of pretty correspondence cards, for each man, a box of decorative paper matches, or a funny paper shaving mug.

You can make these mugs out of waxed (hot liquid) paper cups with handle found in all displays of picnic paper accessories at the stores mentioned above. With brush and ink and watercolors, add a guest's name to the mug and decorate with a huge painted mustache or bouquet of gaudy flowers. Or paste cutouts or decalcomania decorations on the mugs. Decals are on sale in stationery shops, toy shops, and other sources of paper accessories.

Other paper additions to the party include pretty paper towels on the bathroom guest racks. Wear a little paper apron, and if your husband is helping with the dinner, provide him with an apron to match yours. Paper plates in various sizes for first course, main course and other uses, as well as today's paper cups, saucers and mugs are hot-liquid proof. There are also small paper forks and spoons with which to complete the paper place settings.

Menu A first course might be wedges of chilled honey-dew melon garnished with thin slices of prosciutto, the flavorsome Italian ham. Add a small grind of pepper to both melon and ham. Either serve your husband's favorite main dish, or something so good and easily prepared as a beefsteak-and-kidney pie. The pie can be partly prepared in the morning, kept in the refrigerator, and completed at dinnertime. With it serve very small parsleyed carrots, hot rolls, quince jelly. For dessert, have open-face apple pie with a superb Cheddar or Gouda cheese, and coffee. Use a cheese board and knife and let guests cut their own from a two-pound wedge of Cheddar or a whole Gouda cheese. Keep the latter at room temperature for about two hours before serving.

Paper games can be featured at this party, if your guests like games. Here's a paper Who's Who: Clip photographs from magazines and newspapers of famous TV, movie, and stage actresses, and other women in the news. Fasten each picture to a sheet of paper with pin or gummed tape. Number these sheets; there should be twelve of them. Do the same with twelve cutouts of ball players, other sports stars, male actors of TV, movies, and stage, and men in the financial, political, and international news. Be sure all names have been cut off; but keep your own key list of the names of all men and women on the two sets of cutouts.

To play the game, give each guest a pencil and small pad of paper. Pass the twelve sheets of interesting men to the feminine guests, one at a time; allow just two minutes to guess the name of each mystery cutout, and write his name on the paper pad. Then the cutout is passed to the next feminine guest and so on around the party. At the same time, the cutouts of famous women are being passed from one male guest to the next. When everybody has had his and her chance to write down twelve guesses on his paper pad, the host reads off the correct names.

The guest who has the largest number right wins a paper prize, such as a box of fancy paper napkins or towels. The guest who had the fewest correct names wins a paper booby prize, a funny hat to wear for the rest of the evening.

Make A Paper Hat Good fun is sure with a millinery contest. Provide working space, such as bridge tables around which everybody can work. Have a central supply base, such as cleared dining table on which are lace paper napkins in many sizes, plain paper napkins, a roll of waxed paper, rolls of paper ribbons of different widths and colors, lace-edged shelf paper, sheets of gift wrapping paper in many colors and patterns, crepe paper in various colors, colored tissue paper, pairs of scissors, small rolls of gummed tape, a small hand stapler, a few fancy large paper flowers. The contest: everybody makes his conception of the latest fashion in millinery. Paper feathers can be cut and fringed, paper flowers surrounded with paper lace, and many other ideas carried out. This should not be a rush job, but as the creations near completion the host can call out a time limit, such as "Only fifteen more minutes to go!"

The hats are then turned in to the host, a judge is chosen, and a model selected from the ladies present. She must model the hats while they are voted by hand clapping. The best hat receives a paper prize, such as a box of paper sipper straws, or a painted cardboard paper box for cigarettes.

Of course, various games of (paper) cards are just right for this party. Decks for tables of four should be on hand, pencils and score-pads. Old-fashioned striped paper candy bags of jelly beans or candy hearts or other small candies are prizes for these tables.

Paper Gifts Host and hostess gifts for the First Anniversary include various table wares mentioned for house and picnic use, stationery, papier-mâché trays, boxes, bowls, vases, waste baskets and other decorative objects, assorted sizes of monogrammed paper napkins, boxes of paper guest towels, of assorted gift-wrap paper, assorted desk note pads, decorative storage boxes for clothes closets, paper-bound books, magazine subscriptions, decks of cards, other paper games, bathroom boxes of facial tissue, a watercolor drawing, an etching, print, or antique poster.

Recipes for 1st or Paper Anniversary Party

BEEFSTEAK-AND-KIDNEY PIE

1½ pounds round steak
1 pound beef or veal kidney
¼ cup bacon fat
1 onion, peeled and sliced
⅜ cup flour
1½ teaspoons salt
¼ teaspoon pepper
¼ teaspoon thyme
⅛ teaspoon orégano
3 cups water
1 teaspoon Worcestershire sauce
1 (4-oz.) can chopped sautéed mushrooms
Pastry for 1-crust pie

Have beef cut in 1-inch or bite-size pieces. Soak kidney in salt water 30 minutes, drain, slice. Heat bacon fat in large frying pan, add steak and onion and cook until both are lightly browned. Sprinkle flour over, stir to mix well. Add seasonings; stir and brown meat well. Add water, stirring constantly over low heat until mixture thickens and boils. Add kidney. Pour into buttered 2½- to 3-quart casserole. Cover and bake in Moderate oven (350°F.) about 1 hour, or until meat is tender.

Remove casserole, stir Worcestershire and mushrooms into mixture. Cover top with pastry, crimp around edge like pie crust, and make several slits in pastry. Turn oven to Hot (450°F.). Bake until pastry is done and browning. This recipe makes 6 servings.

For a large party, mix and bake as many casseroles as needed. Do not double or triple recipe and bake in one very large casserole.

PARSLEYED CARROTS

Carrots	Butter
Salt	Lemon Juice
Sugar	Parsley

Allow about ⅓ pound carrots per serving. Select small, young, tender carrots. Cut off tops, wash, scrape, leave whole. Barely cover with water in heavy saucepan, add about ½ teaspoon sugar and ½ teaspoon salt for each pound of carrots. Cover and cook 15 to 25 minutes until carrots are done. Do not drain; add light seasoning of salt and pepper. For every pound of carrots add 2 tablespoons butter, 1 tablespoon lemon juice, and 2 tablespoons finely minced fresh parsley. Serve in warmed serving dish.

2nd Anniversary—Cotton For a second anniversary celebration friends or relatives sometimes plan a surprise brunch for Sunday, or a Saturday night supper.

Invitations For either occasion the cotton theme can be mentioned in invitations given in person, or by telephone, with a suggestion that guests wear cotton costumes—the girls' dresses or smocks, skirts and blouses, kerchiefs, stockings, gloves and other accessories of cotton; and cotton shirts, socks, neckerchiefs, jeans, or cotton suits for the men. If the party is large enough to warrant written invitations a small dab of cotton can be stuck on each card or tied on with a bright cotton string through punched holes.

Another way to get cotton onto the invitation: cut a square the size of the invitation card of bright plaid or flowered cotton fabric using pinking shears. Lay the piece over the invitation card, with the top edge sealed to the back of the card with gummed tape. This makes a colorful surprise when pulled from the envelope and keynotes the cotton theme of the invitation. The invitation might be a simple, informal note, or something like this:

It's Cotton Pickin' Time
for Hazel and George Randolph
Come To A Surprise Brunch For Them
Sunday, June 8th
1 o'clock

at the Selwin Smith's R.S.V.P.
18 Gramercy Road Gladstone 4-3100

Decoration A large menu, about 2 feet wide and 3 feet deep, written in bright blue or red ink can be made on a sheet of white

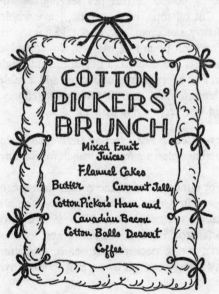

COTTON PICKERS' BRUNCH

Mixed Fruit Juices

Flannel Cakes

Butter   Currant Jelly

Cotton Picker's Ham and

Canadian Bacon

Cotton Balls Dessert

Coffee

wrapping paper or cardboard. Add a border of fluffy cotton, cut in scallops from a roll of cotton batting. The cotton can be glued onto the paper, or held in place around the edge of the menu by loops of bright cotton string or strips of fabric (see sketch).

Hang the decorative menu on the wall of the dining room, big kitchen, terrace, or wherever the table is set up. Headed, Cotton Pickers' Brunch, the menu card should harmonize with red-and-white or blue-and-white checkered cotton tablecloth and its matching napkins, and with a cotton centerpiece such as an old-fashioned sunbonnet with a bowl of cotton flowers in it. These flowers can be the mixed-color cotton corsage bouquets found in the five-and-ten cent stores. Surround the bonnet centerpiece with a circle of small unwrapped cotton gifts, each tied with colored cotton string, such as spools of cotton thread, a package of cotton washcloths in bright colors, a pliofilm package of colored cotton balls for the dressing table, cotton work gloves, gypsy cotton handkerchiefs to wear on the head or around the neck, cotton dishcloths, small hand mop, cotton neckties, cotton socks.

More important cotton gifts from family and close friends might be gift-wrapped and ready on a coffee table for distribution after brunch. These could include such things as matching sets of pillow cases and sheets, bath mats, bath towels, bedspreads, dish towels, aprons, café curtains for kitchen, cotton umbrella for lawn or terrace.

Menu written or hand-printed in large lettering on the cardboard can be:

Mixed Fruit Juices

Flannel Cakes

Butter   Currant Jelly

Cotton Pickers' Ham and Canadian Bacon

Cotton Balls Dessert

Coffee

Recipes for 2nd or Cotton Anniversary Party

FLANNEL CAKES

2½ cups sifted all-purpose flour	1 teaspoon salt
	1 egg, slightly beaten
5 teaspoons baking powder	2 cups milk
1 tablespoon sugar	¼ cup shortening, melted

Mix and sift dry ingredients three times. Combine slightly beaten egg and milk; stir into dry ingredients. Stir in shortening. Pour onto hot griddle in 4-inch cakes. When bubbly, and bottom is browned, turn to brown other side. Makes 18 cakes. Add more milk to batter for thinner, crisper cakes. To serve cakes, top with butter and currant jelly.

Packaged pancake mixes make good Flannel Cakes. Use 2 cups of mix, make batter as directed on package. For Apple Pancakes add 1 cup finely chopped raw apple and ⅛ teaspoon ground cloves. Bake in oiled skillet or griddle as described on package. This recipe makes about 16 cakes.

Fry thin slices of ham and thick slices of Canadian bacon in an electric skillet or table broiler, or in the kitchen. Serve with cakes.

COTTON BALLS DESSERT

Vanilla ice cream	Grated coconut
Ball ice-cream scoop, No. 8 or No. 10	Fresh Raspberry Sauce

Cut balls of ice cream, place on plate covered thickly with grated coconut, turn balls until coated. Work quickly so that ice cream does not melt. Use a wide cooking spoon to lift coated balls to big stem-dish or other decorative serving bowl. Spoon two balls onto each dessert plate as a serving. Pass the sauce. Recipe makes about 8 balls to the quart (with No. 10 scoop, 10 balls).

FRESH RASPBERRY SAUCE

½ cup butter	1 tablespoon cornstarch
1 cup sugar	1 tablespoon cold water
1 cup fresh red raspberries, crushed	½ cup heavy cream

Melt butter in saucepan, stir sugar and berries in. Blend cornstarch and water, stir into berries. Stir constantly and let boil 1 minute. Let cool. Whip cream stiff; stir cooled sauce into cream. Spoon onto Cotton Balls. Recipe makes about 2 cups of sauce, or about 8 servings.

Canned or frozen red raspberries may be used. Ripe strawberries, sliced and slightly crushed also make a delicious Fresh Strawberry Sauce.

3rd Anniversary—Leather Leather being costly as well as unsuited for temporary decorations for entertaining, the third wedding anniversary is usually celebrated in any happy fashion chosen by the celebrants without regard to the leather theme. Leather gifts are welcomed, of course. And generous friends and relatives have a great variety from which to choose, such as small leather match boxes for living-room tables, leather notebooks for purse and pocket, leather-backed brushes, leather desk accessories, picture frames, luggage, brief cases, handbags, gloves, key rings, house slippers, leather-topped coffee and side tables, trays, wastebaskets, and other furnishings and personal gifts.

One young hostess in Philadelphia, famous for her impromptu parties, decided her third wedding anniversary should be danced into the record. She phoned *invitations* to six couples, and to five young women and five bachelors, the idea being she told them, to dance the leather soles off their shoes.

The date fell in late spring. The small garden behind the old house that she and her husband had refurbished and were enjoying was abloom with lilac and other spring flowers. The large porch and adjoining stone terrace made a good dance area for the crowd, which numbered twenty-four with host and hostess. Chinese and Japanese lanterns on tall flexible bamboo poles dotted the garden and others lighted the porch and terrace. The hostess also made provision for the possibility of rain by clearing the living room and hall of the house and rolling up and removing rugs on the morning of the party day. The party could have been held indoors if necessary.

She and her husband hired a trio of college dance musicians famous for their endurance and versatility, so that sambas, rhumbas, waltzes, fox trots, and anything else in demand would be forthcoming. And she hired a part-time maid-cook to help the day before and the night of the party.

She asked guests for 8:30 to midnight. On a buffet (converted garden table) ready on the terrace was a large pitcher of icy punch, glasses, and a platter of small sandwiches for any who hadn't dined heartily at home. Music began about nine.

At eleven, the buffet table was replenished for supper. The necessary, right number of napkins, silver, and dishes were brought out from the kitchen, including two large hot casseroles which were placed on candle-warmer stands, and a covered dish of toast. Guest volunteers carried bridge tables and small folding chairs from the house and placed them around the porch. The hostess added cloths to the tables, assorted solid-color cotton cloths that were matched by the piles of napkins on the buffet.

Menu Here is the menu she and her husband planned: a big tray of appetizers which included thinly sliced cucumbers in fresh dill-flavored French dressing, deviled eggs, stuffed celery, dill pickles stuffed with chive cheese then sliced in thick chunks, strips of green pepper and carrots. The casseroles contained hot curried chicken to be served on buttered toast. The dessert was a finger dessert, assorted small fruit turnovers, served with hot or iced coffee.

Before going on to the recipes for this party it might be suggested for any third-anniversary celebrating necessarily limited to a small city apartment or a small budget that the occasion is a perfect one for "come in for dessert and coffee." For this an invitation is given in person, or by telephone to family and friends, for eight-thirty in the evening. The refreshments are served from a table in the living room, or from a serving cart, or brought in individually on a tray from the kitchen to guests at bridge tables or small tray tables. Besides perfect coffee, or iced tea, iced coffee, or punch, a superb mocha nut pie (it's leather colored) might be served, or a rich brown cake, or any dessert for which the young hostess is already famous.

Recipes for 3rd or Leather Anniversary Party

CURRIED CHICKEN CASSEROLE

5 tablespoons chicken fat or butter	¼ teaspoon saffron
4 tablespoons flour	1 cup chicken stock
¾ teaspoon salt	1 cup milk
⅛ teaspoon pepper	½ cup light cream
⅛ teaspoon nutmeg	2 cups cubed, cooked or canned chicken
¼ teaspoon celery salt	3 tablespoons buttered crumbs
1 teaspoon curry powder	

Melt fat or butter in large saucepan; stir flour in smoothly, add all seasonings and stir until well blended. Add chicken stock, milk, and cream, stirring constantly over low heat until mixture thickens and boils. Add chicken and blend well. Let cool. Keep in covered glass bowl in refrigerator until time to heat for party. To serve, turn creamed chicken into buttered 2-quart casserole. Sprinkle crumbs on top. Heat in Moderate oven (375°F.) for 20 minutes, or until bubbly and browning. Makes 6 servings.

This recipe can be doubled, and reheated in a 3½-quart baking dish, to serve 12. For the anniversary dance with 24 people, the doubled recipe should be made twice, using two identical casseroles.

If chicken stock is not available, use double amount of milk.

ASSORTED FRUIT TURNOVERS

On the morning of the party day, make pastry, cut and fill as described below. After chicken casseroles are heated in oven at serving time, the oven temperature is turned to Hot (475°F.) and a baking sheet of pastries goes in. These little turnovers bake crisp and golden in 8 to 10 minutes. When cooled to slightly warm, they go out to the party table, either on a serving platter or arranged on a cake stand or

2- or 3-tier Lazy Susan, gaily decorated with fresh fruit and flowers (see sketch).

Pastry for two 2-crust pies

Fillings of orange marmalade; cherry, apricot, peach, gooseberry, or plum jam; also apple butter

Use a pastry mix or favorite recipe and prepare pastry in two batches. Roll each out. Cut into crescents, diamonds, and rounds, making 2 pieces alike for each fancy shape. Spread desired filling on one piece and cover with matching top piece. Press edges together with tines of fork. Place on platter, cover each layer with waxed paper, and chill until serving time. Then bake and serve as described. This makes 32 or more small turnovers.

MOCHA NUT PIE

9-inch baked pastry shell or graham cracker shell
1 envelope unflavored gelatin
¼ cup cold water
3 tablespoons cocoa
1 cup sugar

2 teaspoons instant coffee
3 eggs
1 teaspoon rum extract
½ teaspoon vanilla
¼ teaspoon salt
¾ cup chopped pecans

Prepare and bake pie shell or make graham cracker shell. Sprinkle gelatin into cold water; let stand until softened. Mix cocoa, ¾ cup sugar, and instant coffee together in saucepan. Add ¾ cup water. Stir constantly and cook to boiling point; reduce heat and continue cooking and stirring 4 minutes.

Beat egg yolks slightly; pour hot cocoa mixture into yolks slowly, beating vigorously. Transfer to saucepan and cook over low heat, stirring constantly until slightly thickened. Remove from heat, stir in flavorings and the softened gelatin. Mix thoroughly. Chill about 30 minutes or until mixture begins to hold shape.

Beat egg whites and salt together until foamy. Beat in remaining ¼ cup sugar gradually and continue beating until mixture stands in peaks when beater is lifted. Mix into gelatin combination gently with chopped nuts. Pour into baked or graham pie shell. Chill in refrigerator until firm. This recipe will provide 6 servings.

4th Anniversary—Fruit and Flowers, also Silk By the fourth wedding anniversary many young couples have one or more babies and the budget for parties is limited or nonexistent. But a low budget and a busy schedule of baby care need not mean that the anniversary must be ignored. The date makes a good excuse for relatives and friends to plan a party for the couple, perhaps something as old-fashioned and heart warming as a *Bring-A-Dish Supper*.

This kind of party means little or no work for the anniversary celebrants, in advance at least, and no cost whatsoever except coffee for all hands after the party arrives. A surprise party is not recommended under these circumstances, since a young household with one or two small children is seldom prepared for a deluge of guests.

Some close friend or relative familiar with the home of the couple organizes all details. Before she telephones other friends and relatives to ask them to the party, she plans a menu and just what she will ask each guest to bring. The Fruit and Flowers theme of this anniversary gives scope for a number of good dishes of fruit or with fruit garnish, plus bouquets to turn the celebrants' home into a flower-bedecked setting for the dinner.

If eight are invited, the total around the party table will be ten counting the hosts. One guest can bring chilled fruit for the first course, such as cantaloupes or avocados. Another the main course, cold roast turkey or capon garnished with spiced whole peaches. A third guest brings a pan of rice-stuffed tomatoes (love apples) ready to go into the oven at the party. One of the men can bring blueberry, date, or orange muffins from a bakery or his own kitchen. Another can bring the dessert, which may be assorted fruit sherbets or ice creams. And still another guest brings a fruitcake.

This leaves two guests who can bring flowers or share in the cost of buying and preparing the turkey, which is probably cooked by the organizer of the party. The kind and amount of flowers depend not only on the season and what is available at florists, but also on the taste and home of the hosts. Flowering plants to set out in a garden or in window boxes may be welcome, or bouquets for the table and living room, or a corsage for the hostess and a carnation for the host's lapel are possibilities for the two guests to contribute.

Set for an early hour, six or seven o'clock, the planner of this party may have arrived in midafternoon with her cooked turkey already garnished on its platter, to be placed in the family refrigerator. Then she helps the young couple to set a table or arrange the living room for a buffet supper. Being a close friend or relative she may know that their china and linen supply is still low, and she arrives with a box of big dinner-size paper napkins, with some silver from her own supply, with a basket of coffee cups and other things to round out the service. Butter, cream, coffee, perhaps jam or jelly, and relishes can be supplied by host and hostess.

Part of this friend's contribution may be tending the baby while her hostess changes her clothes in the last minutes before the guests begin to ring the doorbell. From that moment on everybody works together, and dinner is ready to serve almost as soon as the last guest makes his appearance.

The fruit and flowers are anniversary gifts. But since silk is also a theme for this anniversary additional gifts for the couple might be scarves, neckties, blouse, handbag, lingerie, sheer curtains, taffeta pillows, lampshades, a silk-quilted comforter for the baby's carriage or various other silk items for the baby such as hood, little jacket, and bootees. Guests might pool funds and give new silk glass curtains for bedroom or living room, or a check for a silk dress for the hostess.

The kind and quality of the gifts depend on the couple, and their needs, as well as the closeness of friendship between guests and hosts.

Recipes for 4th or Fruit-and-Flowers Anniversary Party

The first-course melons or avocados should be washed and chilled before taking them to the party. Cantaloupes can be cut and seeds removed, then pieces put back together and each melon wrapped in waxed paper and put in the refrigerator until time to go to the party.

Avocados should not be cut until just before serving. At the party, the guest who brings this fruit goes into the kitchen, cuts the avocados in half, removes seeds, then fills halves with French dressing made with lemon juice, or any preferred salad dressing she has brought with her.

RICE-RAISIN STUFFED TOMATOES

10 medium-size tomatoes	3 tablespoons seedless
Salt	raisins
1 cup uncooked rice	4 tablespoons butter

Wash tomatoes; remove slice from stem end. Remove center with teaspoon. Sprinkle inside with salt. Invert tomatoes on a platter to drain.

Add rice gradually to 2 quarts of boiling water with 3 teaspoons of salt in it. Boil rapidly for 15 to 20 minutes, until rice is tender when grain is pressed between the fingers. Drain in sieve or colander; rinse with hot water. When rice is drained, stir washed, drained raisins into it. Use to stuff tomatoes. Add dab of butter to the top of each filled tomato. Place in buttered baking pan. Bake in Moderate oven (375°F.) about 20 minutes. Serve hot with the cold turkey. A cheese sauce may be added for extra good flavor.

5th Anniversary—Wood After the first anniversary, the fifth is the most popular with party-givers, until years later when the important twenty-fifth and fiftieth anniversaries are celebrated with large dinners or receptions. Wood, the traditional keynote of the fifth anniversary, and the giving of wooden gifts seem humorous to many so that, for example, fellow employees of the young husband, or his golf companions, or men with whom he bowls may think of the date as an excuse for a good party, with funny gifts all around. This might be a surprise wooden shower for the couple at the home of one of the husband's pals.

Such a party can be fun, even in a small apartment, but the real surprise today is how rewarding it can be for the couple, because wood is enjoying a new popularity in home accessories and furnishings, and many beautiful objects of wood make welcome gifts.

Invitations for this surprise dinner or supper can be in the light mood, which the host hopes will prevail at his party. The size of his apartment determines the number of guests and what they can do as entertainment. Perhaps he can manage twelve for a lively, somewhat helter-skelter supper. Or if the host lives in a house where there is a playroom, or large living room, the supper can be followed by dancing or an evening of music, both of which are ruled out by ordinary courtesy and consideration for tenants below and above the city apartment party-giver.

Here is a typical invitation for the evening:

> Thursday
>
> Dear Julie and Fred:
> *Woodent* you like to help us give Jack and Mary a good party to celebrate their 5th (wooden) anniversary? We hope you will say Yes, and keep it a secret because this is a sur- prise party. Chop up some furniture or something and bring them a wooden gift. Supper at our apartment, Friday eve- ning, November 4th. The time is 8 o'clock.
>
> (signed) Janice and Sam
>
> R.S.V.P.
> High 3-2091

Menu may include dishes that can be bought from a delicatessen as well as others to be prepared in a small kitchenette: chilled vegetable juices and hot sardine canapés, a cold baked ham and potato salad (delicatessen), hot cheese pudding (speciality of the host), hot rolls, strawberry tarts (bought from fine bake shop), coffee.

Since this is a surprise party, there should be no evidence of party plans when the two guests of honor (invited for 7:30) arrive. But al- most on their heels the surprise guests begin to assemble, with gift packages to be heaped on a coffee table, the piano, or wherever there is room. And the fun begins.

At this point the host can bring out the silver, china, and napkins (ready and waiting) needed for the crowd and arrange them on his table. Toasts are drunk, and canapés, hot from the broiler, enjoyed. The host and a helping friend bring out the magnificent baked ham and a platter of delicious potato salad from the refrigerator; then hot, brown-and-serve rolls and the host's specialty, the cheese pudding, from the oven. Guests sit where they find room, on floor cushions, sofa, chairs, hassocks, a bench, with or without small folding tables to hold their plates.

The informality and good food continue through dessert and coffee, and on to the opening of the gifts, which is the peak of the after-dinner period. Handsome wooden bowls, and a set of salad fork and spoon are favorites today. So are carved and polished wooden fruit bowls and serving dishes. Others are a cheese board, tiny lemon-slicing board, bread board, chopping block, chopping bowl and wooden-handled chopper, wooden potato masher, rolling pin, boxes of various sizes and shapes for many uses in kitchen, living room and elsewhere, storage boxes for clothes closets and bedroom, small pieces of furniture such as chair-side tables, book ends, a file box for the desk, wooden sculpture, carved serving spoons and forks from Sweden, wooden jewelry such as cuff links, bracelet, or brooch, musical instruments such as recorder, ukelele, piccolo or more serious woodwind instruments if the guests are musicians.

Also there are countless small wooden objects from which to choose in five-and-ten cent stores as well as gift shops and foreign stores. The host's gift to the guests of honor might be a large wooden utility box, which he turns into a grab bag for the party, filling it with small inexpensive wooden gifts. Every guest draws at least one. Included might be a drugstore package of wooden tongue depressors for the medicine cabinet, package of swab sticks, assorted pencils, small rulers, miniature carved and decorated animals, birds and figures, Government leaflet on how to get rid of termites, ash trays, cigarette holders, miniature pencil sharpeners, pen holder, and similar bits and pieces.

Recipes for 5th or Wood Anniversary Party

HOT SARDINE CANAPÉS

1 (7 oz.) can skinless, boneless sardines	½ teaspoon Worcestershire sauce
2 hard-cooked eggs, chopped	Mayonnaise
	Anchovy butter
2 tablespoons lemon juice	24 small rounds or strips of toast
Salt	

Mash drained sardines in mixing bowl; add eggs, and combine well. Add lemon juice, a little salt if needed (to taste), Worcestershire, and just enough mayonnaise to blend. Spread anchovy butter on toast; heap a spoonful of sardine mixture on each piece, add small dab of mayonnaise. Place on pan under moderate broiler heat until very hot, about 8 to 10 minutes. Makes 24 small canapés. *Anchovy butter:* combine 4 tablespoons butter with 1 tablespoon anchovy paste and mix smoothly.

SAM'S CHEESE PUDDING

12 (¼-in.) slices day-old bread	1½ cups milk
4 tablespoons butter	1 teaspoon Worcestershire sauce
1 teaspoon salt	2 cups (½ lb.) grated Cheddar or American process cheese
½ teaspoon mustard	
½ teaspoon paprika	
2 eggs, slightly beaten	

Start oven at Moderate (350°F.). Cut crusts from bread; butter bread. Use 8 slices, butter-side down, to line bottom and sides of 1½-quart baking dish. Cut pieces to fit. Mix salt, mustard, paprika, eggs, milk, Worcestershire, and cheese, stirring until well mixed. Pour half of cheese mixture over bread in dish. Cut remaining 4 pieces of bread in narrow strips, lay on cheese in dish; add remaining cheese mixture. Bake in Moderate oven (350°F.) for 30 minutes. Recipe makes 6 servings.

To serve 12, make the recipe twice. Do not double it and bake in one larger casserole. When everything else is ready for the party, the recipe can be mixed twice and poured into baking dishes the last thing before guests come. Place in preheated oven just as they begin to arrive.

6th Anniversary—Sugar and Candy, also Iron With so much interest today in low-calorie diets, the thought of planning a party around a sugar and candy theme is too much for many hostesses. But if a young homemaker is determined to plan a celebration for their sixth anniversary, which takes its theme from these sweets, she and her husband might stage a candy-making party in their kitchen, the products to go to a church, school, or club bazaar, or in case the date falls in late December, to a community Christmas tree.

The candy makers might be close friends, two or three couples who can combine time, ingredients, and fun, the anniversary being the excuse for this special get-together. When the candies are finished and cooling, hosts and guests can sit down to grilled cheese-and-ham sandwiches, a green salad, and coffee on the porch, or around the kitchen breakfast bar. Waffles and bacon or pancakes with creamed chicken are alternates for the grilled sandwiches.

Excellent candy mixes are available, especially for fudge. In addition to a selection of these mixes, supplies for the recipes which follow should be assembled and the materials that will be needed for packaging. An *invitation* given in person or telephoned should specify the day, time, and what the guest is to bring—for instance, granulated or brown sugar, coconut, nuts, or some other ingredient of the recipes. Or some of the wrappings, such as pieces of flowery wallpaper or ribbons, colored foil papers, empty commercial candy boxes, waxed paper, fancy labels or decorations for the tops of the boxes, old-fashioned, striped paper candy bags, or waxed paper bags.

The men of the party can make interesting and effective boxes if they are given a worktable of their own, on which the empty boxes as well as wallpaper, other wrappings, glue, gummed tape, scissors, and labels are assembled.

As with any other party, a careful planning of what will be done in the kitchen and what the men will do around the packaging table should be written out ahead of time and detailed lists made, so that all necessary cooking equipment will be on hand and ready—measuring spoons and cups, candy thermometer, wooden spoons, saucepans, all ingredients for the candy and for the guests' refreshments. Specify whether they are in the kitchen or are being brought by the guests, and the same for all necessary wrappings.

The hostess and women guests make the candies and clean up the pans. After refreshments, everybody joins in wrapping and packaging the candies. A bonus of small gift packages of candy might be carried home by each cook and her husband.

If the *iron* theme for this anniversary is chosen as inspiration for a party, it could be especially effective as a barbecue luncheon or supper because much of the cooking and serving equipment for such an occasion is iron.

Iron gifts from friends could add to the supply of barbecue skewers, long-handled cooking forks, portable grills of various sizes and styles, or such decorative gifts for inside the house as fireplace tongs, andirons, candlesticks, trivets, and the iron skillets that are popular for sukiyaki and many other favorite foods. (See section on Barbecue Parties in Chapter 12, "Outdoor Entertaining".)

Recipes for 6th or Sugar and Candy Anniversary Party

BROWN SUGAR FUDGE

1 cup brown sugar (packed)	2 tablespoons butter
1 cup granulated sugar	1 teaspoon vanilla
⅔ cup milk	
2 (2-oz.) squares chocolate, broken	

Combine sugars, milk, and chocolate in saucepan; cook slowly, stirring constantly until temperature of 236°F. is reached on candy thermometer, or when a few drops of syrup dropped into a cup of cold water form a soft ball. Remove pan from heat, add butter without stirring. Set aside to cool. When candy has cooled to 110°F. (lukewarm), add vanilla and begin beating. Continue beating until fudge has lost its shiny look and a small amount dropped from the spoon will hold its shape. Pour into buttered pan. Makes 36 pieces 1 inch square and about ½ inch thick. Most suitable pan is a 6-inch square one, but other small square or oblong pan may be used.

COCONUT KISSES

1 cup granulated sugar	2 tablespoons butter
1 cup brown sugar (packed)	½ teaspoon salt
¾ cup water	4½ cups shredded coconut
1 cup dark corn syrup	

Combine all ingredients except coconut in 2½- or 3-quart saucepan; cook, stirring until sugar is dissolved. Continue cooking, stirring only enough to prevent burning, until temperature of 245°F. is reached on candy thermometer, or a few drops of syrup in a cup of cold water form a firm but not hard ball. Remove pan from heat, add coconut. Mix thoroughly. Drop by spoonfuls on greased surface and shape with hands. Work quickly before mixture hardens. Recipe makes 28 pieces.

If coconut is heated in oven until delicately browned, flavor is improved.

COFFEE PENUCHE

3 cups brown sugar (packed)   1½ teaspoons vanilla
1 cup strongly brewed coffee   1½ cups broken walnuts
2 tablespoons butter

Combine sugar and coffee in saucepan and cook, stirring constantly until temperature 236°F. is reached on candy thermometer, or when a few drops of syrup dropped into a cup of cold water form a soft ball. Remove pan from heat, add butter, set aside without stirring to cool. When cooled to 110°F. on candy thermometer (lukewarm), beat until thick and creamy. Add vanilla and nuts. Pour into an 8×8 buttered pan. This recipe makes 16 or more large pieces, or 32 small ones.

MAPLE CARAMELS

2 cups sugar   ½ cup milk
1 cup light corn syrup   1 cup maple syrup
1 cup condensed milk   ¼ cup butter
½ cup cream   2 teaspoons vanilla

Combine all ingredients except vanilla in 2-quart saucepan. Cook over low heat, stirring constantly, until mixture reaches 248°F. on candy thermometer, or a few drops of syrup in a cup of cold water form a ball of the same firmness desired in finished caramels. Remove from heat, add vanilla, pour at once into greased pan. When cool, cut into small squares with long, thin-bladed knife. Wrap caramels separately in waxed paper or foil. This recipe makes 72 small caramels.

PEANUT MOLASSES BRITTLE

2 cups sugar	1 teaspoon soda
½ cup molasses	2 cups shelled peanuts,
½ cup water	blanched and roasted
6 tablespoons butter	

Combine sugar, molasses, and water in 2-quart saucepan; cook, stirring over low heat until sugar is dissolved. Continue cooking very slowly until temperature of 300°F. is reached on candy thermometer, or when a few drops of syrup dropped into cup of cold water separate into threads that are hard and brittle. Remove from heat, stir butter in, then beat soda in. Add nuts, and mix well. Pour onto well greased marble slab or baking sheet. Smooth out with buttered spatula, thinning out to wide sheet. Loosen from baking sheet while still warm. Let cool. Break into pieces. This recipe makes almost 2 pounds.

7th Anniversary—Copper, also Wool Party-givers who have acquired a number of social debts can make their wedding anniversary the excuse for a big at-home reception to which they invite all the friends and relatives at whose homes they have enjoyed hospitality in the past year. For the seventh anniversary, for which copper is one of the themes, an original background and setting for this party can be worked out without too much expense in an apartment living room, or the dining room and other areas of a house.

Decoration For the coppery accent in decoration, use the glowing copper foil paper found in displays of Christmas wrappings, which can be bought in quantity from stationery and card shops or the manufacturer. Cut a valance of the foil paper (see sketch) for each window of living room and entrance hall or other room where guests will mingle, and fasten valance in place securely over window drapery or curtains. Use pins, gummed tape, or whatever means is most effective for your window. Or for small windows, make café curtains of the foil and fasten to five-and-ten cent store copper rods with copper-rosette café hooks (these are stock items in such stores and hardware and home-furnishing shops).

Make handsome "frames" for all mirrors in the hall and rooms with the copper foil paper (see sketch). Cut the foil in widths to fit over the

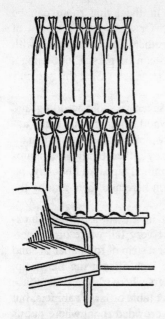

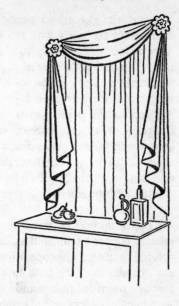

permanent frame; cut fancy edge all around, in outstanding points like sunburst or in scallops, like Mexican tin frames. Fasten the paper frame to the mirror frame with gummed tape, hidden thumbtacks, or any other practical means.

A favorite decorative paneled screen in the living room can be covered for the party with the foil paper. Or make such a screen of three or four panels of plywood hinged together. Cover the panels with copper-striped gift wrapping paper. (Folds can be pressed out using a warm, not hot, iron on the wrong side of the paper.) Coat this screen's hinges with metallic copper paint.

Decorate the paper panels with your seven-year-old wedding and reception invitations, honeymoon menus and photographs, birth announcements of any children and their baby pictures from the first snapshots to the most recent candids, and any other family mementos that can be attached to the panels with gummed tape. Add bouncy, fat rosettes and streamers of copper foil ribbon here and there among the mementos.

Copper decorative wares are plentiful in the shops. Small, inexpensive copper candleholders can support very tall white or copper-colored candles. Swirl copper foil ribbon or a strip of foil paper around each candle from the base to about four inches from the flame tip. Fasten a rosette of ribbon and long streamers where ribbon ends. Place such candle holders on the mantel or buffet table or large cabinets, but avoid putting candles on small tables in a crowded room where guests will be moving about.

Fill small copper boxes with cigarettes, place copper ash trays on the coffee table and elsewhere. Fill copper vases, urns, pitchers with tall bouquets of flowers that harmonize with the copper accents of the room.

In midsummer brown-eyed Susans and cattails from fields and marshes add the right color note. More sophisticated flowers from the garden and florists might be yellow iris, gladioli, marigolds, calendulas, chrysanthemums in yellow and copper tones, or any other available large yellow or golden flowers. For a crowded reception, tall impressive bouquets placed on sturdy tables or chests against the walls are striking and practical (see sketch).

The buffet or tea table pushed back against a wall can be covered with copper foil paper with a beautiful lace tea cloth on top. Or an amusing top cloth of the copper-striped gift-wrapping paper can be made. Press the striped paper on the wrong side to eliminate folds, then fasten several sheets of this paper together smoothly with gummed tape

SAFE LOCATION FOR FLOWERS AT A PARTY.

to make a cover the right size for the table. On the wrong side of the striped-paper "cloth" draw a coarse lace pattern with pencil in the center and around edges. Use curved manicure scissors to cut out the design. Lay this "lace cloth" over the copper foil table cover.

Besides the tall candles in copper holders (described above) on the table, an arrangement of copper-colored fake fruit in a copper bowl or urn can dramatize the color scheme (see sketch). For this buy wax, plastic, or other fake apples, plums, grapes at a five-and-ten cent store, gift shop or wherever artificial flowers are sold. Paint them with copper metallic paint about a week before the party so that it dries and the odor disappears. Arrange the painted fruit in a handsome copper container with decorative fresh green leaves of rhododendron, ivy, or magnolia. Place bowl and candles away from center of table, near wall, or at one end of the table to leave as much space as possible for food and serving accessories.

On the table use fine antique copper utensils, preferably lined with nickel or white metal, or modern copper pieces similarly lined. A coffee or tea samovar borrowed from an antique shop, or one of the many new reproductions makes a useful addition to the table; also a copper teakettle to service the tea tray, and small pieces such as sugar bowl and cream jug, which are available in lined copper today as are various small dishes and trays for nuts, candies, and other foods.

Invitations are given in person, or telephoned, or might be written in brown ink on cards decorated with a small cutout flower or initials of copper foil. Or the most popular form, a simple At Home invitation is written on a fold-over card. Many hostesses hesitate to mention that an anniversary party is an anniversary since it might be misconstrued as a bid for gifts. This is not true of an invitation to a small, intimate family affair, but for a large At Home the anniversary (or birthday) is not always mentioned.

Here is a simple form to follow:

Mr. and Mrs. J. H. Holster
421 Mayflower Drive

At Home
Saturday Afternoon
September 12th   R.S.V.P.
4 o'clock to 7 P.M.   Telephone, Dexter 2-4923

Menu for this kind of reception is tea and coffee, assorted sandwiches, cake that on this occasion is frosted with brown icing such as spice, caramel, or chocolate, small cakes or petits fours similarly iced, and individual ice cream molds of chocolate, mocha, caramel, maple or burnt almond to harmonize with the room's scheme. See the section on How to Give a Tea in Chapter 15 for details of procedure and various recipes.

Another Variation: a big copper-hung country or townhouse kitchen is an ideal place for another kind of copper anniversary party. After dancing, or a club meeting, or some other gathering, everybody adjourns to the kitchen to make waffles and cook sausages to go with them, or to place small, ready-to-bake turkey pies in the oven. A salad is brought out of the refrigerator to be tossed with cheese dressing, and coffee is made. The breakfast bar becomes a fabulous supper bar where talk and good food combine to round out the evening.

For relatives who are gift-minded, the copper and wool anniversary gives plenty of scope. Besides table and cookery utensils, candleholders and trays, hand-wrought copper cuff links, bracelets, flowerpot holders, match boxes and other things of decorative or personal interest are in great variety in gift shops, and advertised in the shopping departments of good magazines.

In wool, there are countless gifts including sweaters and skating caps, mittens and socks, hand-crocheted afghans, neckties, scarves, stoles, and needlework stools and slippers.

8th Anniversary—Bronze, also Pottery Since the two metals, bronze and copper, are somewhat similar in color, the suggestions for the seventh anniversary copper decoration scheme can be adapted for at least one kind of bronze-theme party. The linking of bronze to a wedding anniversary dates back into the years when bronze decorative objects were more plentiful and more in key with the elaborate home furnishings of the period. This heavy, expensive metal, which contains both copper and tin as well as various other ingredients depending on its intended use, today is primarily cast as bells and architectural gates and doors, although some gift and jewelry shop displays include bronze clocks, figures of animals and other sculpture, paperweights, urns, lamp bases, and other objects.

The popular finish of modern bronze is a green patina on dark metal but brown, yellowish, and red-brown pieces of bronze are also in shop collections. While such gifts have less appeal to most modern homemakers than decorative objects of lighter metals and of wood, glass, and ceramics there may be some fond parents and relatives who want to give a bronze gift, such as a fine sculpture, a handsome lamp, or a garden fountain figure as the anniversary present.

Pottery, the other eighth anniversary theme, suggests a party that can have unusual appeal. There is a lively interest today in designing and making pottery as a "more-leisure-time" hobby, as therapy for tired business men and women, and as a creative activity that is rapidly growing in some communities to the popular status of Sunday painting. For an unusual party, which will not be forgotten because it opens a door to future good times together, ask a pottery teacher from a local art school or college art department or some specialist from a local museum to come to your home and give a talk and demonstration on pottery-making—the idea being that prospective students for a neighborhood pottery class will attend the party.

The teacher may bring finished pieces from his school to make a colorful display for the event. But more interesting, he may ask you to provide enough potter's clay and other supplies so that guests can try their hand at shaping pottery. Or he will bring these essentials with him, paid for either by his department or school or by you out of your party budget.

A cleared playroom or living room with carpeting carefully covered with paper or canvas, comfortable chairs for guests, a place for the speaker to stand, small steady tables at which guests can work, and all supplies specified by the teacher should be in readiness when the party begins. Have plenty of paper towels in the bathroom so that your best guest towels are not called into service for the hand washings afterwards!

Instead of the usual invitation to a party, the guests are invited to this one because they are interested in learning how pottery is made, or they want to join a pottery class. Among your friends and neighbors there may be ten to twelve men and women and maybe two or three teen-agers who would enjoy such an evening. You might post a notice on the church bulletin board a week in advance of the party date, which will attract interested potters or tell members of your bridge or P.T.A. group about it.

Invite all comers for 7:30 in the evening, preferably a Friday or Saturday night, or a Saturday afternoon. After the talk by the teacher, would-be potters have fun trying to shape the clay and do whatever else the teacher suggests. The afternoon or evening ends with some such light repast as coffee for adults, chocolate milk shakes or gingerale for teen-agers, and cookies or doughnuts. Or, since this is an anniversary celebration, if the crowd is not too large, maybe you want to offer a more gala repast of make-your-own sandwiches with buttered rolls, sliced meats, followed by cake or pie and coffee.

Another Version of a Pottery Party to celebrate your anniversary might be a casserole supper, or an all-pottery supper at which the colorful primitive Mexican, Spanish, Italian, and other peasant pottery wares are used. Many such plates, cups and saucers and other pieces are sold by mail order through shopping columns in the better magazines, and at gift shops as well as the china departments in large stores. They belong on informal tables in the kitchen or on a porch or terrace. Linens to go with such pottery are bold solid-color or striped linen crash or coarse cotton, hemmed or fringed, with matching napkins.

The colorful, informal atmosphere, which the hand-crafted shapes and rich colors create in combinations with the coarse linens, is heightened by a pottery bowl filled with mixed bright, gaudy garden flowers as the centerpiece. Or, make a tray centerpiece. Set a bowl of flowers in the center of the tray; surround the bowl with fresh fruits, washed and chilled and ready to be eaten as part of the menu. In the center of the flower-filled bowl stands a sturdy, thick candle, either white or in a color to match the pottery.

Menu that is harmonious with this party theme and setting includes dishes to be cooked and served in pottery casseroles: baked onion soup, main dish casserole of stuffed cabbage rolls (see Near Eastern dinner in "How to Give a Foreign Dinner," Chapter 16), a baking dish of scalloped corn and green peppers, with hot French bread, fresh fruit from the centerpiece tray, and a savory cheese-spread, in a pottery jar of course. Mugs of coffee or hot tea with lemon and a cinnamon stick for stirring complete this meal.

Recipes for 8th or Pottery Anniversary Party

ONION SOUP AU GRATIN

4 large onions, peeled and sliced very thin	½ teaspoon salt
	⅛ teaspoon pepper
2 tablespoons butter	6 slices French bread,
5 cups bouillon	toasted
1 teaspoon Worcestershire sauce	6 tablespoons grated Parmesan cheese

Brown onions in butter in 1½-quart saucepan until tender and lightly browned. Add bouillon and seasonings. Heat slowly to boiling. Pour into 6 individual pottery baking dishes. Place 1 slice toast in each. Sprinkle top with 1 tablespoon cheese. Place dishes on baking sheet; set under moderate broiler to brown. Serve at once. This recipe makes 6 servings.

This recipe can be doubled for a larger party. The soup may be baked in a large earthenware soup casserole or marmite, in which case make a layer of toasted French bread in the bottom of the casserole, pour hot soup in, sink 1 or 2 pieces of toast in top of casserole, and sprinkle generously with grated cheese. Set in Hot oven (475°F.) for 15 minutes or until top is lightly browned.

For this type of oven soup the high marmite is preferable to a low marmite or casserole. The high pottery marmites with covers come in 2½-, 3½-, 5-, and 7-quart sizes, for small to large parties. They can be found at foreign housewares stores, restaurant supply stores, and Hammacher Schlemmer, 145 East Fifty-seventh Street, New York 22, New York.

SCALLOPED CORN WITH GREEN PEPPERS

3 tablespoons butter	½ green pepper, finely
3 tablespoons flour	chopped
1 teaspoon salt	2 tablespoons finely chopped
1 tablespoon sugar	canned pimiento
1¼ cups milk	2 eggs, well beaten
2 cups canned corn, cream style	4 tablespoons buttered crumbs

Start oven at Moderate (375°F.). Melt butter in 1½-quart saucepan, stir in flour, salt, and sugar smoothly. Add milk slowly, stirring continually over low heat until mixture thickens and boils. Stir in corn, mix smoothly; add green pepper, pimiento, and eggs. Pour into greased 1½-quart casserole. Cover with buttered crumbs. Set dish in shallow pan of hot water. Bake for 20 minutes in Moderate oven (375°F.). Lower temperature to 350°F. and bake about 25 minutes longer or until top is browned and bubbly. This recipe makes 6 servings.

HOT FRENCH BREAD

Start oven at Moderately Hot (400°F.). Slice loaf of French bread diagonally, not quite through to the bottom. Spread slices on both sides with mustard-horse-radish butter. Place loaf on baking sheet; heat in Moderately Hot oven (400°F.) about 15 minutes, or until hot and crusty. Place hot loaf in a napkin-lined basket or bread tray.

MUSTARD-HORSE-RADISH BUTTER

8 tablespoons butter, softened	1 tablespoon prepared mustard
2 tablespoons prepared horse-radish	

Cream butter and seasonings together smoothly. Makes enough for 1 small loaf French bread. Double all ingredients for a larger loaf.

9th Anniversary—Willow or Reed If the anniversary is a warm-weather date, one obvious party in keeping with the theme of willow and reed is a basket picnic. It is true that present-day food carriers for picnics are more likely to be vacuum containers or insulated metal and plastic boxes and zipper bags. But baskets of all kinds for many uses are more available today than ever before. Imported from many parts of the world, they not only are colorful but well designed handcraft work, interesting, handsome, useful for picnics and much else. Gift shops, mail order catalogues, import shops, and gift departments of big stores feature baskets large and small. Many are hamper or suitcase types equipped with picnic wares.

One such case fitted with equipment and supplies, a covered hamper or two, as well as smaller tote and tray baskets filled with good things to eat give a rustic, old-fashioned air to a picnic. It may be held in the backyard, or you can go far from the maddening crowd by car or station wagon—take folding table and chairs, flowery tablecloth, and a portable record player for bucolic music and country dancing or just lazy listening. (See section on Picnics in Chapter 12, "Outdoor Entertaining.")

Invitations to this picnic are given by telephone or in person by a friend of the anniversary couple, a few days before the anniversary date. Each guest is asked to bring his favorite picnic food in some kind of basket, the basket to be given as a gift to the celebrants. The menu must be discussed when the invitation is given, so that all guests do not show up with little willow trays of chilled deviled eggs or reed baskets holding bowls of potato salad.

Menu Here's a menu that is a picnic favorite of one week-end colony in New Jersey where a wide, quiet river with grassy banks and old shade trees tempt everyone to outdoor feasting: loaves of French bread to cut and spread with seasoned butter, a small baked ham and cold roast chicken or capon or small turkey to slice, mustard, mayonnaise, sliced cucumbers in sour cream with finely-minced parsley, hot covered casserole of sliced frankfurters and noodles, potato salad, deviled eggs, chilled fresh peaches, seedless grapes, cherries, hot coffee or iced tea.

As for any successful picnic, the cold foods must be cold. At least one hot dish should be included for good appetite, and fruit and iced juices for thirst quenchers. Maybe a plump, cold watermelon chilled at home and then wrapped in foil and newspapers is hidden in a hamper as the surprise dessert.

Before placing any of the picnic foods in a basket, the easily perishable meats, salads, and salad dressings should be thoroughly chilled in the refrigerator, then placed in chilled insulated jug or other container, and the container placed in a basket. Less perishable delicacies such as fruit may be chilled, then wrapped in waxed paper or foil, and placed in a basket lined with a bright fringed napkin or colored tissue paper. Bread, cakes, cookies, crackers, and any packaged wafers should be as fresh as possible and carefully wrapped in foil or waxed paper. Decorations of fresh green leaves, flowers, and amusing cards on each basket add to the anniversary party atmosphere of this picnic.

Basket Lunch or Supper on the Lawn A home version of the basket picnic using the same menu can be given in a backyard or on a screened porch or patio. A big garden table, plenty of stools or benches, and nearness to the kitchen make this a comfortable and easy picnic. Or in case of soupy weather, the whole party can be transferred indoors to a playroom, a big kitchen, or a dining room that has been cleared of its usual furnishings and freshened with bouquets of flowers in basket containers.

Paper or bright checkered cotton tablecloths and napkins, paper beverage mugs, plates, cups and saucers give a picnic atmosphere to the dining room. Somebody playing an accordian or records of country songs add to the fun.

Recipes for 9th or Willow or Reed Anniversary

CURRY-CHIVES BUTTER

8 tablespoons butter, sof-   1 teaspoon curry powder
tened
2 tablespoons finely-cut
fresh chives

Blend all ingredients smoothly together. Makes enough for 1 small loaf French bread. Ingredients can be doubled for larger loaf.

CUCUMBERS IN SOUR CREAM

1 pint commercial sour cream	2 tablespoons finely-cut fresh parsley
1 medium cucumber	

Wash cucumber; use tines of fork to score the green peel from one end to the other. Use thin-bladed, sharp knife and cut in thinnest possible slices. Blend with cream, add parsley. Chill thoroughly. Delicious on cold meats or as sandwich spread in place of butter or mayonnaise. This recipe makes about 2½ cups.

FRANKFURTER AND NOODLE CASSEROLE

1 (8-oz.) package noodles	Salt and pepper
¾ pound frankfurters	1 (10½-oz.) can condensed
3 tablespoons butter or margarine	tomato soup
2 small onions, peeled and chopped	⅛ teaspoon Worcestershire sauce
2 cups diced celery	½ cup buttered crumbs
1 small green pepper, chopped	

Start oven at Moderate (325°F.).

Cook noodles as described on package; drain, rinse. Slice frankfurters; brown in hot butter or margarine with onions, celery, and green pepper; cook until vegetables are tender. Season lightly. Pour layer of noodles into deep 3-quart casserole; add layer of frankfurters and vegetables; repeat until all is used. Make top layer noodles. Pour soup mixed with Worcestershire over all; sprinkle crumbs generously over top. Bake in Moderate oven (325°F.) for 45 minutes, until brown and bubbly. Makes 8 servings.

Cook this dish the last thing before picnic time. When done, cover warm casserole and wrap in thick layers of newspaper before taking to the picnic.

10th Anniversary—Tin and Aluminum; 11th Anniversary—Steel; 12th Anniversary—Silk or Linen; 13th Anniversary—Lace; 14th Anniversary—Ivory Fashions come and go in celebrating wedding anniversaries. The present trend, which has developed in the last few years among young marrieds in many communities, is to celebrate only the first three or four anniversaries with parties. After five or six years their celebrating is more likely to be a quiet home dinner with the youngsters. Or, the couple goes out for dinner and the theatre or some other favorite, and rare, indulgence.

When parties are planned for the tenth anniversary or later ones, they follow the general pattern of those described for the early years, or they take some favorite local form of entertaining. This may be a pizza party (young marrieds of Minneapolis) or a barbecue (many far western states) or a cookout (New England shore states). The party is a family and neighbor affair ending, maybe, as a square dance or a big sing with family guitarists and fiddlers.

Gifts for the anniversary are in order, of course, and these have become casual or humorous and less and less expensive in most communities. They are usually token gifts: for the steel anniversary, one steel knife with a penny included in the gift package so that "friendship is not cut"; for the linen anniversary, one amusing linen kitchen towel; a ten-cent store package of *lace*-paper shelving for kitchen, a small ivory figure, a tin pan, and similar articles. Taste in some localities now frowns on elaborately contrived anniversary parties and heaps of expensive presents. These restrictions have come about because, in families of young children, budgets for entertaining are almost nonexistent, and in maidless households there is so little time to plan and give parties.

15th Anniversary—Crystal This anniversary seems universally popular and the occasion for a very special dinner. Many department stores and gift shops recognize the fifteenth anniversary as a party date, and encourage celebrating it by their displays of crystal and glass wares on carefully decorated tables. For celebrants of this event the happiest solution is a dinner planned by a relative or friend, the guests all adults, with the children having a party of their own elsewhere for the evening.

Invitations are given in person or telephoned to six or eight friends, about ten days before the anniversary date.

Menu is planned to be sufficiently different from the usual home dinners of the guests so that the atmosphere is unmistakably "Party" and the evening will be remembered with special pleasure. Here is a favorite party menu of a Pennsylvania hostess: first course, asparagus with Mousseline sauce; followed by sweetbreads Gaston, zucchini San Remo, French bread, Finnish lettuce salad, coffee-chiffon pie, and demitasse.

Decorations Using the crystal theme to its utmost, the table can sparkle with new glass and crystal pieces. It is lighted by crystal candelabra, with the centerpiece a glass or crystal footed bowl or epergne filled with glass fruits, and small glass animals and other figures grouped around the base of the bowl. For color contrast the table is covered with a cloth of yellow, blue, or favorite color linen, or with flower-printed place mats.

Glass baking dishes and serving dishes are called into use on this table. Most of these utility pieces as well as the decorative pieces are gifts for the two guests of honor and are given them at the end of the evening.

This party, and a chinaware celebration of the twentieth anniversary, are popular in communities where families are making home alterations and additions, or redecorating and furnishing twenty-year-old houses. Also in many households in recent years, the many parties given by the teen-age children have steadily depleted the glass and china supply. For either party, gifts that are basically useful evoke the most heart-felt thanks.

Recipes for 15th or Crystal Anniversary Party

ASPARAGUS WITH MOUSSELINE SAUCE

3 pounds fresh asparagus (about ¼ pound per serving)
Boiling water

Salt
Sugar
1½ cups Mousseline Sauce

Wash stalks under running cold water, scrub with brush to remove scales and sand. Rinse under running cold water. Cut off tough ends. Tie stalks securely in bunches, stand in large asparagus steamer in about 2 inches of boiling water. Add about 1 tablespoon salt and 1 teaspoon sugar to water, and cover steamer. Cook for 15 to 20 minutes or until tips are tender. Drain, remove string, arrange on hot platter to serve. Pass Mousseline Sauce with asparagus. Recipe makes 10 servings.

MOUSSELINE SAUCE

1 cup butter	6 tablespoons heavy cream
4 egg yolks, slightly beaten	Paprika
2 tablespoons lemon juice	

Divide butter in 2 portions and put 1 piece in enamel or glass double boiler with slightly beaten yolks and lemon juice. Lower part of boiler contains hot but not boiling water. Stir constantly until butter is melted. Add remaining butter and stir until sauce thickens. Remove from heat, beat in cream gradually. Pour into warmed sauce server. Dash top lightly with paprika. Serve at once. This recipe makes about 1½ cups of sauce.

SWEETBREADS GASTON

5 pairs sweetbreads	5 tablespoons melted butter
2½ tablespoons vinegar	1½ cups Almond Butter
Salt and pepper	Sauce

Wash sweetbreads thoroughly in cold water. Cover with boiling water, add vinegar and salt. Let come to boil, cover saucepan and cook gently at almost simmering for about 15 minutes. Drain sweetbreads, plunge into cold water, then drain them again. Remove membranes and tubes. Pat dry with paper towel.

Preheat broiling oven for 5 minutes. Split pairs of sweetbreads in halves lengthwise. Brush with melted butter, sprinkle lightly with salt and pepper. Broil 3 inches from high heat until golden brown, about 10 minutes. Turn pieces occasionally. Serve with Almond Butter Sauce. Recipe makes 10 servings.

ALMOND BUTTER SAUCE

¾ cup butter	1 tablespoon lemon juice
¾ cup chopped or shredded almonds	

Melt 1 tablespoon butter in small pan and sauté almonds over low heat until lightly browned. Add remaining butter and lemon juice. When hot, serve with sweetbreads. Recipe makes about 1½ cups, 10 servings.

ZUCCHINI SAN REMO

10 medium zucchini squash	5 pieces bacon, half cooked
5 tablespoons butter	
2 (3-oz.) cans sautéed chopped mushrooms	

Start oven at Moderately Hot (400°F.). Scrub zucchini thoroughly; cut in halves lengthwise, then crosswise. Arrange in greased baking dish, dot liberally with butter, and sprinkle with salt and pepper. Scatter mushrooms and finely-chopped bacon over all. Bake in Moderately Hot (400°F.) oven for 20 to 25 minutes or until vegetable is tender. Makes 10 servings.

FINNISH LETTUCE SALAD

3 heads Butterhead or Boston lettuce	10 small pieces stuffed celery
French dressing	
½ cup commercial sour cream	

Use only the tender, curly, very small leaves from the heart of the lettuce. Wash, drain, and chill thoroughly. To serve, toss lightly with a little French dressing blended with sour cream. Garnish with stuffed celery on small salad plates. The secret of the good flavor is the coldness and delicacy of the lettuce. Recipe makes 10 servings.

COFFEE-CHIFFON PIE

1 envelope unflavored gelatin	1 cup heavy cream
1 cup strongly brewed cold coffee	3 eggs
	1 teaspoon rum flavoring
1 cup sugar	¼ teaspoon cream of tartar
½ teaspoon salt	1 9-inch baked pie shell
¾ cup strongly brewed hot coffee	2 tablespoons powdered instant coffee

Soften gelatin in ¼ cup cold coffee. Combine ½ cup sugar, salt, remaining cold and hot coffee, and ½ cup cream in saucepan. Stir over low heat until scalding point is reached. Beat egg yolks and add hot mixture slowly to yolks. Return to saucepan and stir over low heat until boiling point is reached. Stir softened gelatin in. Chill until partially set, then beat until smooth. Add flavoring. Whip remaining ½ cup cream until stiff and fold in. Beat egg whites until they stand in soft peaks when beater is lifted. Add cream of tartar. Add remaining ½ cup sugar slowly, beating well after each addition. Fold coffee mixture carefully into this meringue. Spoon into pie shell. Garnish with light sprinkling of powdered coffee. Chill. Makes 6 servings.

Make the recipe twice to serve 10 or 12.

25th Anniversary—Silver Traditionally this anniversary is celebrated with almost as much ceremony and family awareness as the fiftieth anniversary. Usually a very special dinner party marks the event, either at the home of the celebrants or of a married daughter or son. Relatives and old friends are invited to make this a memorable occasion. The kind of house and family customs influence the style of this important gala dinner. An Italian-American wine-growing family of California will celebrate this anniversary differently from a New England college professor's household; a city couple living in a small apartment will enjoy a different kind of party than a suburban family. No matter what the setting, the importance of the occasion in most homes is shown in careful planning, superb food, a handsomely set table, abundance of flowers, and the special quality of enthusiastic hospitality that dressing up always contributes to a dinner.

Gifts Silver gifts need not be costly and large. Small personal tokens such as initialed cuff links, a tie clasp, charms for a bracelet, a cigarette box, picture frame, or pencil, and similar pieces are often more appreciated than more expensive objects. The gifts, in any case, should be suited to the taste and needs of the couple who are celebrating their twenty-five years of marriage.

Menus Here is one dinner menu served in a well-equipped home at a silver anniversary dinner in Columbus, Ohio. Of course, this elaborate party was easy for this family because they have a cook and serving maid regularly employed by the family. And for the party, which numbered twenty-five guests besides the celebrants, a second waitress, a cloakroom maid, and another to answer the door and to help wherever needed were hired from a local caterer. The kitchen in this home is geared for large parties because the family has to entertain a great deal. It includes a large gas range, an electric range, serving pantry space for big refrigerators in which to chill foods and make frozen desserts, and a supply of extra-large cookery utensils.

The recipes for this menu, to serve 27, can be adapted for a smaller number of servings.

The large dining-room table seated 12. Four guests sat at each of 3 small tables in the glassed-in sun porch and the remaining 3 guests were given a gay little round table in the center (see sketch). The family's best silver trays, platters, and vegetable dishes were used and silver candlesticks lighted tables as well as the big living room and library and the sun porch. Silver bowls full of white and red carnations were everywhere in the rooms.

Menu Jellied Madriléne with avocado garnish, and caviar in small pastry shell; boned rolled roast leg of lamb, lima beans cooked with mushrooms, French bread, mocha mousse, chocolate cake, demitasse. The mocha mousse in flower molds was ordered from the caterer. The chocolate cake was baked in single sheets in oblong pans, thickly frosted with chocolate icing and cut in squares. Here are recipes:

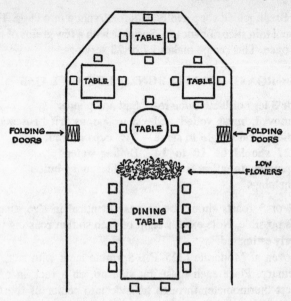

Recipes for 25th or Silver Anniversary Party

CAVIAR SPREAD

2 (2-oz.) jars caviar
2 or 3 tablespoons thick sour
cream
1 small onion, peeled and
minced

4 tablespoons finely minced
parsley
27 tiny toast or puff paste
cases

Combine caviar and sour cream. Chill. Just before serving add onion and parsley. Fills 27 tiny pastry cases. Serve with the chilled soup.

JELLIED MADRILÉNE WITH AVOCADO GARNISH

14 (12-oz.) cans consommé
Madriléne
2 or 3 lemons

1 avocado
Paprika

Chill cans in refrigerator overnight and until serving time. Slice lemons paper-thin and place 1 slice in the bottom of each chilled bouillon cup. Break jellied soup gently with fork, spoon into cups. Top each with a small thin slice of avocado. Sprinkle with a few grains of paprika. Serve at once. This recipe makes 27 or 28 servings.

ROAST ROLLED BONED LEG OF LAMB

2 or 3 legs of lamb bone removed, meat rolled and tied; total weight to serve 27 should be 10 to 14 pounds to allow second helpings	Salt and pepper 3 teaspoons dried rosemary 1½ cups currant jelly Boiling water 3 tablespoons butter

The 2 or 3 roasts should be as near identical in size, shape, and weight as possible. Note exact weight of each so that roasting time can be properly estimated.

Heat oven at Moderate (325°F.). Sprinkle meat with salt, pepper, and rosemary. Place each roast, fat side up, on a rack in a shallow pan. Insert thermometer through fat side into center of roast. Don't add water, don't cover, and don't turn lamb during roasting. Leave 2 or 3 inches between each pan in the oven. Allow 30 to 35 minutes per pound for roasting to well done. If meat thermometers are used, the final reading should be 185°F. for well done. During last hour of roasting, baste each leg of lamb with ½ cup of currant jelly mixed with ½ cup of boiling water and 1 tablespoon of butter.

Plan roasting time so lamb is done about 30 minutes before serving. Start carving about 20 minutes before serving; the roasts can be sliced more easily if they have stood for 10 minutes or so. Stack 10 to 12 servings in heated shallow pan, place pan in warm oven with heat low and door open. Serve on hot platter. Makes servings and second helpings for 27 or more.

LIMA BEANS WITH MUSHROOMS

9 (10 to 12-oz.) packages quick-frozen lima beans 3 (3-oz.) cans sautéed, chopped mushrooms	Salt ¾ cup butter

Cook beans as described on packages. Add drained mushrooms in last few minutes of cooking. Add butter, about 1½ tablespoons per package of beans. Makes 27 or more servings.

For best results, use 2 kettles instead of 1 very large one.

50th Anniversary—Gold After the silver anniversary and before the golden event, some families celebrate the various anniversaries which follow the silver, for example, the *30th—Pearl, 35th—Coral, 40th—Ruby,* and *45th—Sapphire.* A family luncheon or dinner, or larger affair with guests, such as a reception, elaborate buffet supper, picnic, barbecue, cookout, beach sing, or almost any favorite form of entertaining can be adapted to these occasions. Significant as these dates are to the family, they are in general less often celebrated than a few decades ago.

For the fiftieth anniversary, which usually brings the family and its distant connections together in a reunion, the easiest and most effective entertainment for the elderly couple as well as the young, middle-aged, and old guests is some form of reception. This may either follow a big luncheon or dinner, or it may be an afternoon or evening open house with no guest meal involved. The reception or open house is easier on the guests of honor, since it provides only light refreshment (their preference!) and brings the greatest number of friends and relatives together in one room, with time for greeting all of them and catching up on their family news.

Invitations for this are given in person, or telephoned, except for distant guests to whom letters are sent well in advance of the date.

Refreshments Serve any delicious light repast, such as iced tea or punch, sandwiches, double-ring cake, and ice cream. An alternate menu is: hot tea and coffee, a golden wedding cake (3-tier wedding cake frosted with orange-gold icing), and golden (custard) ice cream in wedding-bell molds. The double-ring cake, which will serve up to 30 people, is actually 2 cakes set together, frosted and decorated with silver and gold dragées. Each cake of this pair is baked in a 10-inch tube or ring pan.

Tablecloth A metallic gold lamé cloth on the buffet table, covered by a smaller, open-work lace cloth. Gold-rimmed glassware and china, gold-decorated china candlesticks and decorative figures as center-piece around flowers.

Flowers All the golden flowers, garden marigolds, asters, yellow and orange lilies, zinnias, calendulas, nasturtiums, chrysanthemums and the florist's yellow roses and gladioli in vases and jars in the reception room and elsewhere in the house. A corsage of golden roses for Grandma, and a boutonniere of a single gold rose for Grandpa.

Gifts Gold pencils for purse and pocket, key ring, charm for bracelet, gold lamé spectacle case, gilt-edged playing cards and writing paper; jewelry; gold-painted telephone for bedside table.

The 55th Anniversary—Emerald This and the 60th, and 75th called the Diamond Anniversaries, follow much the same pattern of entertainment as the 50th. They should be planned for the ease, comfort, and enjoyment of the elderly couple, avoiding the fatigue of elaborate meals, or long, drawn-out receptions.

2

ENGAGEMENT AND BRIDAL PARTIES

Engagement Luncheon

This important luncheon is given by the mother or an aunt, a sister or older female relative, or a close friend of the engaged girl for her and her best friends and favorite female relatives. Any delicious favorite menu, simple or elaborate, can be served, depending on the season and the facilities of the home of the hostess and whether she must prepare and serve the luncheon or whether there is a cook and waitress or some other helper.

It is planned and served like any other luncheon party. Near its end the hostess tells her guests the engagement news. Some indirect and amusing means may be employed to announce the engagement: the dessert might be miniature 3-tier wedding cakes, each no bigger than a cupcake iced with white frosting and with initials of the engaged couple in pink or yellow frosting on the top. (Bake cake in single sheet; use 3 sizes of cookie cutters.)

Or, as dessert and coffee are served, a record of the wedding march (from Mendelssohn's Incidental Music for *A Midsummer Night's Dream*) is heard playing in another room and the hostess walks around the table, placing tiny bride-and-groom doll favors on the table before each guest. Small heart-shaped cards are tied to the dolls, the girl's initials or name on the card fastened to the bride doll and her fiancé's initials on the groom.

Another charming way of telling the engagement news: as soon as coffee is served, place small nosegays of fresh flowers at each place setting, with names of the engaged couple on two cards tied to each bouquet.

Or, a centerpiece, such as a low bowl of flowers, might hold the announcement news. From this bowl, narrow flower-embroidered ribbons are laid to each place setting. As dessert and coffee are served, guests are told that there is a secret on the hidden end of the ribbons. They pull the ribbons from the centerpiece bouquet and each ribbon has a tiny spray of artificial orange blossoms tied to it and a card with the names of the engaged couple on it.

Decoration Since the engaged girl is the guest of honor, it is especially gracious to use her favorite colors and flowers on the table and elsewhere in the house. And, of course, the choice of guests is hers on this occasion.

Invitation For the announcement luncheon, the hostess telephones or writes a note about two weeks before the party date, asking the special list of the engaged girl's friends to come to the luncheon. She does not mention the engagement since its announcement is to be the surprise of the party.

> Monday
>
> Dear Hildegarde:
>
> I hope you can come to luncheon Friday, April 10th. I'm asking a few other friends of Jerry, to make ten around the table. So please do come, for I know Jerry would feel badly if you are not among our guests. One o'clock is the time.
>
> Affectionately,
> (signed)
>
> 602 Rose Place   Monte 4-2121
> R.S.V.P.

Menu See Girl's Birthday Luncheon (in Chapter 1) for a delicious menu with recipes for main dishes. Also see Flower of the Month list at end of Birthdays section for suggestions as to color scheme and flowers.

Engagement Dinner

A dinner to announce an engagement is a more serious occasion than the feminine luncheon. But it is flexible as to the size of the guest list and the degree of formality observed. It is given by the parents of the engaged girl in their home or at a hotel or club, so that her immediate relatives can meet her fiancé. If his family lives in the same city, his parents and other members of his family are usually included in this dinner. But if they live in another part of the country, it is not necessary to include them if the cost of traveling and possibly staying at a hotel is involved. The parties that include them are usually only those affairs immediately preceding and following the wedding. The guest list for the announcement dinner also may include young friends of the couple as well as older friends of their two families.

Ideally the engaged girl's father and mother are hosts for this dinner. But if her father is not living or cannot be present, then an older brother, a grandfather, or favorite uncle or some other male relative acts as host with her mother. If her mother is not living or cannot be present, an older sister or grandmother or favorite aunt serves as hostess.

Since most of the guests probably know why the party is being given, the announcing of the engagement is very informal and usually is made before dinner while pre-dinner appetizers are being enjoyed and toasts can be drunk to the couple.

If the girl's father or some other member of the family prefers to be more formal, the announcement can be withheld until the coffee and dessert are served. There is no hard and fast rule about how the announcement should be made, by whom, or when, since these depend on the degree of formality in which the family lives and entertains, family tradition, and the personalities and preferences of the couple.

If a buffet supper is easier to prepare and serve, and this is the case in a maidless home, there is no reason why such a supper should not replace a dinner, especially if the guest list is large. It is the preferred form of entertaining for most people today.

Invitations Like the dinner or supper, the invitation for this occasion must be adapted to the family concerned. It may be telephoned, given in person, or written to relatives at a distance about two weeks before the date of the dinner. Formality of phraseology is usually absent from it since this is a family affair. A mother might write, using her stationery which has her name, address, and telephone number on it:

Friday

Dear Grace,

George and I are having some friends of our Gene and Scott Freeman into supper on Saturday night, May 5th for a very informal announcement party. We want very much to have you and Phil join us. Please do phone and say you will be here. The time is seven-thirty.

Devotedly,

R.S.V.P.   (signed)

Decoration Usually the dinner or supper table reflects the engaged girl's personal taste in flowers and color scheme. One gay Boston announcement dinner, which was the envy of all the girls who attended, was pink and white throughout in decoration. Pink organdy mats and matching napkins were used on a long mahogany table. Three shallow, rose-pink antique glass bowls placed down the center of the table held low arrangements of pink roses, white tulips, babies'-breath, and white freesia. Pink-bordered white china was used for all courses except the dessert, which was served on rose-pink antique plates matching the flower bowls. Pink and white candles in tall silver and glass sticks were used on the table and elsewhere in the room.

The same color scheme can be adapted to a buffet supper. Use a large pink organdy or linen cloth on the buffet table, or leave it bare except for a few pink mats used under the piles of plates and to cover hot-dish pads. The small tables to seat four guests, placed around the room or porch, add pretty color if they are covered with matching pink linen cloths, with a small bouquet of mixed pink and white sweet peas as centerpieces.

Menu This depends on the size of the guest list, whether there is a cook and waitress and other help, and whether the meal is served buffet or at the dinner table. With canapés and juices served before the meal, almost any favorite family menu is adaptable to this dinner or supper. One suggested menu is: roast veal or veal Provençale, baked stuffed potatoes or potato puff pudding, new peas or string beans, hot rolls, warm cherry tarts made with large black cherries or strawberry ice cream in a large meringue shell.

The veal and potato recipes are given here. See sections on How to Give a Dinner and How to Give a Buffet Supper (in Chapter 12) for details of planning, preparing, and serving.

Planned entertainment after dinner is hardly necessary at this kind of big family party. But if there is space for dancing, this always makes a good ending to the evening. Showing a travel film of some place the couple may go on their honeymoon would make an interesting finale. Also, the camera fans among the guests will want to make movies of this occasion.

VEAL PROVENÇALE

4 pounds leg of veal cut scal-
lopine style as thin as possible
½ cup flour, sifted with
2 teaspoons salt and
1 teaspoon pepper
4 tablespoons butter
¼ cup olive oil
2 small onions, peeled and
chopped

½ clove garlic, peeled and
minced
2 (No. 2) cans tomatoes (5
cups)
1 teaspoon dried basil
½ teaspoon sugar
1 teaspoon salt
¼ teaspoon pepper
3 tablespoons finely cut fresh
parsley

Start oven at Hot (425°F.). Pound veal slices between sheets of waxed paper with mallet or cleaver until thin. Dredge meat lightly with seasoned flour. Heat 2 tablespoons of butter and the olive oil in a flame-proof, 3-quart shallow casserole; brown meat lightly on both sides. Sauté onion and garlic in remaining 2 tablespoons butter in skillet; cook and stir until the onion is transparent. Add tomatoes, basil, sugar, salt, and pepper; continue cooking and stirring until the mixture thickens. Pour over veal in casserole. Cook in Hot oven (425°F.) for 15 minutes or until the sauce bubbles. Sprinkle with parsley and serve. This recipe makes 8 servings.

For a larger party make the dish twice or more often, using matching casseroles if possible.

POTATO PUFF PUDDING

8 medium potatoes	2 green peppers, chopped
⅝ cup butter (1 stick plus 2 tablespoons)	1½ teaspoons salt
	½ teaspoon pepper
½ cup light cream	4 eggs
2 large onions, peeled and chopped	⅓ cup grated Parmesan cheese

Cook scrubbed potatoes in boiling, salted water until they are tender, about 35 minutes. Drain, peel, and mash potatoes thoroughly. Gradually beat in 6 tablespoons of butter and enough cream to make potatoes light and fluffy. Melt remaining butter in skillet. Add onions and green pepper and sauté until tender. Add to whipped potatoes. Season with salt and pepper. Let cool.

Start oven at Moderate (375°F.). Beat egg yolks into cooled potatoes. Beat egg whites until stiff but not dry. Fold into potato mixture. Spoon mixture into well-greased, deep 2½- or 3-quart casserole. Sprinkle top generously with cheese. Bake uncovered 15 to 20 minutes. This recipe makes 8 servings.

For a larger party, make the recipe twice or more often, use matching casseroles if possible.

Bachelor and Ushers' Dinner

This relic of the days of gay blades, wild oats, and horse-and-buggy romancing has changed considerably. Just as there are many young men who do not know what this traditional dinner is, and would not want one in any case, there are others, young executives and professional men, especially in the larger cities, who enjoy entertaining their friends in their apartment. They may cook and serve dinner themselves or have a part-time maid who cooks for special occasions, or a favorite caterer who prepares meals and brings them in and serves them.

Such a host can provide a modern version of the bachelor dinner, a good get-together for his own or a friend's last fling as a single man, and for the ushers and other men of the wedding party.

Invitations are given by telephone or in person about a week before the dinner date. The guest list may include the engaged man's close men friends as well as those who will be best man and ushers. The time set for the dinner depends not only on what hour the host comes home from the office but also on the crowded schedule of the wedding-party members, who may have to help decorate the house and church, or meet trains and planes of arriving relatives. Once the time is set, the host can manage if he prepares and shops in advance, even if the apartment is small and time is limited.

Menu, which pleases most men and is easily prepared, is broiled steak, baked potatoes, hot rolls, tossed green salad, and for dessert delicious warm apple pie with a fine cheese. The meat, salad greens, brown-and-serve rolls, and any basic necessities such as fresh coffee and cream can be bought the day before. Greens for the salad can be washed the night before the dinner, wrapped in a towel, and placed in the refrigerator. This not only makes them cold but crisp. The pie can be bought at a good bake shop or from a favorite restaurant or club.

If serving facilities are cramped, as they usually are in a small apartment, and if one sufficiently large table is not available, two bridge tables can be used to seat six or eight. These tables should be covered with attractive cloths, and places should be set with silver, water goblet, and napkin.

If the meal is cooked in a kitchenette, it is easier to serve the warmed plates with the meat and vegetables right at the small range or electric rotisserie-broiler. Salad greens are then taken from the refrigerator, quickly broken into the salad bowl, and tossed with dressing. The salad is served onto cold plates, at the table. Heat-and-serve rolls can be buttered before serving, which does away with bread-and-butter knives and plates. The tables should be cleared before dessert and coffee, and all used dishes carried to the kitchenette and out of sight.

If the host lives with his family, and his mother or a family cook prepares the meal for the bachelor dinner, she can leave the kitchen to him for the serving and final touches and take herself off to the movies or elsewhere, since the idea of this occasion is *no women* even to serve the table.

Alternate Menu For warm weather, a cold baked ham, potato salad, stuffed celery, olives, radishes, French bread spread with herb butter and heated in the oven, strawberry tarts, iced or hot coffee. Another summertime menu is: cold roast beef, mustard sauce, jellied tomato aspic with chopped raw vegetable salad, buttered whole-wheat rolls, hot or iced beverage, wedges of watermelon and honeydew melon served in a huge bowl of cracked ice.

Gift Showers for Engaged Girls and Married Couples

No matter what kind of a gift shower you would like to give a girl who is about to be married, it is wise to consult her mother or family about what she needs or would like to have. She may have an overabundance of the very furnishings you and other friends had originally planned to shower her with. Her mother or close relative can give you her list of things still to be bought, and this can provide the theme for the shower.

Bath Shop Shower A Bath Shop Shower, once you have planned it with the engaged girl, can outfit the couple's bathroom superbly and generously with accessories in the color scheme they like best. There can still be a surprise for the guest of honor at the shower in the way you and other guests present the gifts.

Invitation Select a date agreeable to the busy bride-to-be. For the invitations, draw an old-fashioned bathtub the right size to fit on your correspondence cards or note paper (see sketch). Use heavy paper or cardboard, cut bathtub out, and use it as a pattern for drawing on cards or note paper. Use blue crayon for this, or one of the engaged girl's favorite bathroom colors. Fill the sketched tub with roughly drawn gift packages and with big soap bubbles floating above it and off the page. Below the tub, write in blue ink:

A Bath Shop Shower
for Helen Grayson!
Luncheon at my house, 1 o'clock
Saturday, May 8th

Esther Longman   Main 2-4137
4041 Dawson Drive   R.S.V.P.

Helen's new bathroom color scheme is blue and orchid. She needs everything! Please telephone me so we can discuss before you buy a gift for the shower.

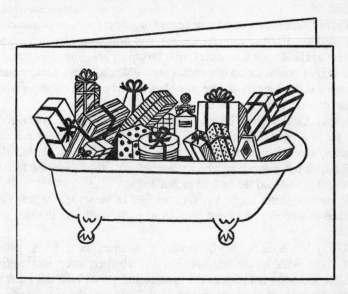

Decoration In a sun porch or somewhere not visible to guests, set up the Bath Shop. Use mirrors for the background to increase apparent size of the display. Make shop tables and shelves by covering whatever small household tables and shelves are available with blue or orchid tissue paper, crepe paper or gift wrapping paper.

Hostess and guests work the day before the party to arrange the display and to make signs and cards and all decorations to look as much like a shop as possible. A hamper, standing metal towel rack, stacks of folded bath towels might be included. Other gifts left in opened boxes as in store displays might be shower curtains and matching window curtain, bath rug, bathpowder, oil, bath salts, and a bottle of her favorite toilet water. Make the display area lively with bouquets of fresh or artificial flowers and large sale signs. Each sign bears the name of the guest who brought that gift: Solid Gold Bath Hamper, only $99.00 sold to Bessie Wales; Diamond Embroidered

Bath Towels, only a few left, $1,000 each, sold to Sally Grey; and similar fun on large and small cards, attached to all gifts. Use cardboard of orchid and blue or cover white cards with tissue paper in these colors.

Table Decoration Use blue or orchid organdy, linen, or cotton cloth and napkins. For the centerpiece, use any blue, lavender and purple flowers available, such as asters, iris, larkspur, anemones, hydrangea, blue ragged robins or cornflowers, sweet William, sweet peas, violets, arranged in low long bowl. Use pale blue, orchid or pink china, or white china decorated in any of these colors.

Menus Cold shrimp bisque, served in a bouillon or cream-soup cup set in a bowl of ice; crisp crackers seasoned with celery salt and paprika; chicken breasts sautéed with mushrooms, tiny curried rice croquettes; for dessert, raspberry sherbet with thin sticks of frosted white cake, and iced tea or iced or hot coffee.

A simpler menu might be: thin wedges of honeydew melon with crushed blueberries, creamed chicken in patty shell, the sherbet, and coffee.

A tray luncheon is also quite simple: assorted sandwiches, jellied fruit salad with lemon mayonnaise, the sherbet, cake and coffee.

After luncheon is finished, the hostess and guests take the guest of honor "shopping" to their special Bath Shop on the sun porch or wherever it is set up. If there is no porch or extra room for the shop, the gifts and shop can be displayed ahead of time all around the dining room. Luncheon served as in a store tearoom on small tables or tray tables, two or more guests at each, adds novelty when the shop setting is in the dining room. For these, small paper tablecloths and matching napkins in blue or orchid add the right color touch.

Book and Record Shower for Couple Gift showers for an engaged *couple* are as popular today as those for a bride-to-be. Such a shower gives an excuse to men and women friends of the pair to entertain them in some easy way, such as a buffet or barbecue supper or a kitchen party, and to give them gifts that they will appreciate. A Book and Record Shower is especially appropriate for some couples. Books about a hobby in which they are interested, or some profession of one or both are welcome, such as gardening, fishing, decorating, cooking, stamp collecting, bridge, photography, travel, dress designing, biography, poetry, music, art, animals. Some records can be chosen by the guests to fit in with a library started by the man in his bachelor days, others selected to please his fiancée and her musical taste.

At one such party, the guests gave records of wedding music as part of the shower gifts. These included "Wedding Bells," with chorus and soloists from Victor Herbert's *Red Mill;* the beautiful *Wedding Day at Trollhagen,* a lyric piano piece composed by Grieg for his own wedding day (the Walter Gieseking recording of this is especially charming); "Through the Years," theme song of Vincent Youmans' musical by the same name; "If I Had A Cow, A Plow, A Frau" from *Arms and the Girls,* wonderfully sung by James Melton; "Marrying for Love," Ethel Merman's solid rendition of the hit song from Irving Berlin's *Call Me Madam;* and Jerome Kern's "Will You Marry Me Tomorrow, Maria." There are many other records of wedding music listed in record catalogues as well as selections of dance music for the couple's own at-home entertaining after the honeymoon. Or friends can give special albums or collections, which they know definitely that the couple want.

Invitation After a date is decided on by the hostess and the engaged couple, the invitation can be given in person or by telephone about ten days before the event. The hostess consults with the couple and makes a list of books and records they would like to own. When giving the invitation to their men and women friends, she mentions the list and lets each guest select the book or record that he or she wants to bring. This way duplications are avoided. The gifts, wrapped and giver's card inside, are delivered to the hostess's home a few days in advance, so that she can plan the decoration and other details of the party.

Decorations If there is room on a screened porch, or perhaps in a large, cleared garage, a Silver Platter Tree can be set up using either a small dead tree cut down in a nearby woods, or a tree can be made starting with a florist's tub or a good-sized wooden keg. Insert a pole or hollow metal curtain rod (cut and sold any desired length in drapery departments) in the keg as the trunk of the tree. Fill the keg or tub with earth, cinders, or sawdust. Make branches out of wire coat hangers and picture frame wire, using pliers and wire-cutters to shape them.

Fasten the branches securely to the trunk using heavy, wide electrician's tape. Put the short branches near the top, the wider ones near bottom. All branches should be firm. Paint the trunk and branches with aluminum paint. Let dry thoroughly a day or so, and add second coat of paint if needed. Hang gifts on some branches, place heavier packages near trunk on lower branches. Fasten a large, loosely mixed bouquet of gay artificial flowers in the top of the tree—tulips, roses, sprays of lilacs, green leaves, or whatever is available.

Here and there on the platter tree, fasten big gaudy flowers and brightly colored plastic, wooden, or papier-mâché birds bought from five-and-ten cent stores or novelty shops. Or cut bird shapes out of bright colored paper, and with gummed tape attach long feathers for tails. Set birds here and there among the gifts (see sketch).

Menu Since this event is a platter party, even those friends who hate puns will forgive you if you make the platters interesting enough. Pancakes as well as records are called platters, so one menu idea is stacks of "platters" served with either creamed chicken or creamed chipped beef topped with crisp bacon. Serve glasses of chilled vegetable juice first, and cold shrimp in a bowl set deep in cracked ice, with cocktail-sauce dip. After the pancakes, serve large, open-face blueberry tarts with vanilla ice cream as a topper, and iced or hot coffee.

Your interpretation of a platter supper might be a one-plate meal, always a good idea when there is an informal crowd. The platter for each guest might contain: a serving of hot meat loaf garnished with chutney relish, baked acorn squash, a hot corn muffin. Dessert is in the same key—a big pan of warm deep-dish peach pie right out of the oven, each serving topped with vanilla ice cream. Coffee follows.

Here is a warm-weather platter supper: individual jellied grapefruit-ring salads filled with chopped cucumber, green pepper, radish, and mayonnaise; small ham sandwiches in assorted shapes; ice cream cones in assorted flavors, hot or iced coffee or tea.

Dancing to platters is the logical finish to the evening.

Clean-Up Shower The art of cleaning a house, and keeping it clean, is so specialized and important to today's homemakers that manufacturers have produced hundreds of useful products which play a role in this department of housekeeping. The displays of these in grocery and

housewares stores inspire a cleaning-closet gift shower, one of the most welcomed by any bride.

The hostess for such a shower begins her plan by listing various necessities from the many available. The prospective guests choose the gift that they want to bring to the shower. These include silver, brass, and other metal cleaners and polishes, a cleaning kit for the bathroom, a book on how to clean house, chemically-treated dustcloths, wet mops, dust mops, dish mops, scouring brush, scouring powder for kitchen pots, soap flakes and can in which box fits, cake soap, floor wax, rubber and plastic gloves, whisk broom, fluid cleaners for mirrors, window glass, and glass-topped furniture, furniture polish, Venetian blind cleaners, a vacuum cleaner (this might be the gift of a well-to-do family or relatives).

Invitations are given by telephone or in person in order to guide the guests in what to bring. A little later, a few days before the party, the hostess might send a small card to each guest, with a drawing of dish mop or scrub brush in one corner, as a reminder date, time, and other essentials.

Decoration If grocery and home furnishing stores will lend, give, or sell posters—the bigger the better—of various cleaning products, put these up as background decoration in the dining room or living room or wherever the party will be centered. Run a streamer of bright-colored crepe paper or ribbon from each poster to a mop figure of a woman sprawled in tired sleep on a coffee table. A sign on the figure says: Here Lies Poor (name of guest of honor) Who Had No Cleaning Closet.

This figure is made with a twist-cotton mop, the type used for wet mopping. Use water colors or crayons and paint a tired sleeping face on paper and fit it under the mop "hair," or use a tired-looking Halloween mask. Dress the mop in a new-style cotton house dress, stuff it with tissue paper to fill out the figure, and tie a large cleaning apron around the figure. For hands, stuff tissue paper into a large pair of men's cotton work gloves, and fill badly worn, old house slippers with tissue paper for feet. Make the figure as realistic and comic as you can. Pile wrapped gifts on the floor around the coffee table. The gifts include the mop, house dress, apron, and gloves.

Menu A shower given at teatime may be more appreciated than a luncheon party, because of the engaged girl's schedule of things she must do before her wedding. Menu suggestions: tea sandwiches, hot tea and coffee, a delicious lemon layer cake, sherbet-topped fruit cup; or, waffles with stewed black cherries and vanilla ice cream topping, hot tea and coffee; or, toasted cheese sandwiches hot from a table broiler, baked apples, hot coffee or tea; or, coconut cake baked in wedding-bell-shaped pan, peach ice cream, coffee.

Clothes Closet Shower This shower party of gifts for the clothes closets in the bride's new home can be copied in style, menu, and other details from the Bath Shop Shower. The shop idea is one of the most effective ways of displaying an assortment of such gifts and adding some fun to the presentation. As with other gift showers, it is best to consult the engaged girl about her preferred color schemes. Shelf edging, garment bags, covered or painted hangers, hat boxes, garment boxes, covered sets of utility boxes come in solid-color plastics as well as many fabrics in various colors and sizes. Knowing her preferred color scheme, guests can select furnishings in the desired colors.

A Fix-It Shower A shower of tools for house, laundry, garage, and garden can make a good party for the engaged couple who are going to move into a house. If weather permits, this might be staged in a cleared garage or barn and the area around it, or in a cleared playroom, laundry, or back porch or terrace.

Invitation Host and hostess send an invitation about ten days before the party date to a few couples as well as unmarried women and men.

Anything Need Fixing?
Everything from electric irons to Model-T Fords
can be fixed with the right tool.
Bring your repair jobs and bright, shiny new tools
to do the job to our
Fix-It Shower
for Lillian Brant and George Harris.
We'll all work on the repairs. But the tools are
shower gifts for Lillian and George.
Saturday Afternoon, May 19th, 4 o'clock and Stay
for Supper

The Browns   Colby 5-2110
Colby Road   R.S.V.P.

When their friends telephone to accept, the hosts can suggest tools already on the gift list, and let each decide what he wants to bring— anything from screw driver, hammer, or a box of nails to garden shears, trowel, electrician's tape, roll of electric cord, cords with plugs, extension cords, and similar accessories. A large tool cabinet for garage or basement, the gift of two or three guests who combine their funds, makes a much appreciated gift. It might be painted a bold color, such as bright pink. At the party every guest autographs the cabinet with his initials in black paint or some bright color, and the hosts add the date. The cabinet will be a longtime reminder of a good party.

After the repair jobs are finished or put aside, a barbecue supper or porch buffet is served. In cool weather if the playroom or laundry has been the scene of the party, a hot dish is featured in a simple menu served buffet or cafeteria style.

Menu Barbecued steak or chicken halves, potatoes baked in foil, tossed green salad, garlic bread, watermelon, iced drinks. For a porch supper, serve baked beans cooked with sliced frankfurters or smoked sausages, buttered Boston brown bread, cottage cheese, gooseberry jam, angel cake baked in ring pans and iced with white frosting, vanilla ice cream and raspberry sauce. For a cooler night in playroom or laundry, serve shrimp with rice prepared earlier in the day and reheated in chafing dish or table skillet; or a tangy cheese pie, green bean and onion salad, compote of sliced peaches and bing cherries, and hot coffee.

Recipes for these dishes are in large basic cookbooks, but here is one host's recipes for his favorite cheese pie and shrimp with rice.

THE BEST CHEESE PIE

3 eggs
1 tablespoon flour
1 can condensed tomato
    soup, undiluted
¼ cup light cream
¼ cup finely chopped peeled
    onion
1 teaspoon prepared mustard
1½ teaspoons Worcester-
    shire sauce

⅛ teaspoon cayenne
¼ cup finely chopped green
    pepper
½ pound process Cheddar
    cheese grated (2 cups)
1 cup chopped ripe olives
Deep 9-inch pastry shell, un-
    baked

Start oven at Hot (450°F.). Beat eggs in large bowl; stir flour in smoothly, then add remaining ingredients one at a time, mixing them well. Bake pastry shell about 5 minutes. Then pour the cheese mixture into shell. Lower oven temperature to Moderate (350°F.) and bake pie for 15 to 20 minutes, or until top begins to brown. Remove from oven and let cool slightly. This pie should be served warm, not hot. Makes 6 servings.

To serve a large party, make two or more pies. Pie shells can be kept ready in refrigerator. Ingredients can be measured, ready to combine at serving time. Mix and bake just before mealtime.

CHAFING DISH SHRIMP AND RICE

3 tablespoons butter	About ½ pound uncooked,
1 onion, peeled and sliced	de-veined quick-frozen
1 green pepper, coarsely	shrimp, partially thawed
chopped	½ teaspoon salt
2 (8-oz.) cans tomato sauce	Grind of black pepper
½ bay leaf	2½ cups cooked rice

Melt butter in 2-quart chafing dish or saucepan. Add onion and green pepper. Cook slowly, stirring occasionally until tender. Add tomato sauce, bay leaf, shrimp, salt and pepper. Simmer 15 minutes. Add rice. Stir to heat through. Serve at once. Garnish with chutney, minced parsley, or rings of raw sweet onion. Recipe makes 4 large servings.

This recipe can be doubled, and made in the kitchen in a large enamel kettle. To serve, reheat in two large chafing dishes at the table. It can also be cooked in a 1-gallon kettle, and the kettle then placed on a candlewarmer stand or electric warmer on the buffet or cafeteria table, so that hungry guests can help themselves.

Games Shower If your engaged friends have all the home furnishings essential to a happy start in their new house, there is still a good gift-shower party for you to give them. This one can provide them with some of the accessories for leisure, especially games of various kinds to enjoy together and others to use when they entertain.

A games shower can be planned around an evening of bridge, or some other game such as Chinese checkers, backgammon, darts and mixed games, or some other pastime that your crowd particularly enjoys. Guests for two or more tables of bridge make a good number for a surprise shower.

Invitation Guests are invited by telephone or in person to come and play bridge on a convenient evening. All but the engaged couple are told that this is a surprise shower party, and they are asked to bring card games and other game gifts for the bridal pair. Stationery, toy, and novelty shops sell not only bridge decks but other playing cards and various card games, score pads, gift packages of score pencils, backgammon sets, Chinese checkers, Scrabble, chess sets and many other familiar favorites as well as new games. Books on backgammon, bridge, chess are welcome in this assortment of gifts. All should be gift-wrapped, the giver's card enclosed, and all packages kept out of sight until suppertime.

If the party is planned for eight o'clock, the hosts may want to provide cold drinks during the evening for the players but withhold more serious refreshments until later. As ten or ten-thirty approaches, the hostess can bring out supper accessories to a buffet table. She may supply covers and napkins for the bridge tables, or she can bring in decorative supper trays for each guest. This is the time to request the engaged girl to go to the kitchen and bring in the cart of good things she will find there. Instead of food for the party, the cart is stacked high with gift packages. Her surprise and the pleasure of opening them with her fiancé are part of the evening's fun.

Menu Serve your favorite cake baked in three square pans, small, medium and large, and put together as a tier. Frost smoothly and add the names or initials of the engaged couple. With it serve caramel ice cream or pineapple sherbet and coffee. Or serve deviled-ham sandwiches toasted on a table grill, ice cream in molds of diamond, club, heart, and spade with petits fours of the same shapes in assorted icings.

Home Decorating Shower A do-it-yourself shower for a young couple who will live in an old house, or an apartment in an old-style residence, is fun and sure to please the engaged pair, especially if they are furnishing with hand-me-downs from their families and pieces bought second-hand, or at auction sales and antique shops. The idea of the shower for them is that every guest brings a small piece of furniture, such as a box, stool, small table, lamp, tray, and the means of refinishing it effectively. The refinishing is started at the party and the refinished pieces are the shower gifts.

One such party was given near Katonah, New York, for a couple who had just acquired a reconditioned barn as their new home. They had bought beds and a few large pieces, and a complete bathroom and new kitchen were installed but they needed many small furnishings. Friends and neighbors staged an all-day home decorating shower.

Invitations were given by telephone or in person by one of their neighbors acting as host, with a list of the kind of furnishings that would be welcome: small chair-side tables, larger end tables for bedroom and living room, book shelves, mirror frames, work table or desk, chairs of every kind from metal ice cream parlor chairs for the tiny stone terrace to Windsor chairs and others from farm sales, lamp bases, useful boxes and chests for living room, dining room and elsewhere.

The time set for the party was from 10 o'clock until 5 on a Saturday in early summer. Each guest was to bring whatever he or she wanted to give the couple, with whatever refinishing supplies were needed for putting the gift in good condition.

One man cleaned two handsome oil lamps, removed wicks, and mounted each on a wooden base which he cut with the host's power saw from scraps of an old teakwood table. He wired the lamps, and they were ready for shades and a place in the living room.

One girl sandpapered an old painted chair—it turned out to be cherry—and wiped it down with a wet cloth, and after lunch waxed and rubbed it to shining beauty. Sanding, painting, scraping, and polishing jobs filled the host's big porch and cleared garage. At 1 o'clock the host and hostess rang their brass dinner bell and work stopped for an hour or longer, while the party feasted, as in the early days of this country, at a big table set up under the trees on the lawn.

Menu Iced lemonade to cool hot brows and savory small hot pizzas as appetizers. Then cold fried chicken, country salad of sliced cucumbers and tomatoes in seasoned vinegar, a loaf of fresh cheese bread to slice and butter, a pan of warm gingerbread fresh from the oven and ice cream to top it with or served plain, hot coffee. A big, wooden bread-dough bowl of summer fruit was placed on the table for afternoon snacks.

Preparations for the luncheon were made the day before. The pizza topping was mixed, put in a covered jar, and stored in the refrigerator. Chickens were fried, cooled, then placed in refrigerator to chill. The pizza appetizers were made of English muffins, split, toasted, and spread with the reheated pizza mixture and served hot. Final preparations for the luncheon went smoothly and easily, with one or two guests helping the hosts. After the leisurely meal everybody went back to work to finish the gifts. At the end of the afternoon, before guests departed, cold lemonade and grape juice refreshed them for the road.

This kind of shower, with limitations, can be given in the cleared basement, laundry, playroom, or garage of a house in town. It is important that only useful and decorative, worthwhile things be brought to the shower and that guests with experience in refinishing, painting, or other repairs be willing to guide the amateurs. The result is attractive and useful pieces, which save the couple some of their furnishing funds, and please them besides with the generosity and good taste of their friends.

Variation of Home Decorating Shower can be given as a luncheon in a small apartment or any home. Instead of refinishing old pieces, the engaged girl's friends bring some small furnishing such as a pair of candlesticks, book ends, tray, wastebasket, framed print, chair-side table, jug or vase for flowers, candy dish, or similar accessory. Good gifts in this group are books on home decoration, and subscriptions to home decorating magazines.

In addition, guests are asked to bring samples of new decorating fabrics from their favorite shops, samples of wallpaper, paint color cards, pictures cut from decorating magazines of interiors, rugs, furniture, table settings, and all else of interest. After luncheon, these are sorted out on the cleared dining table or a living-room table, so that the engaged girl can compare, discuss, and exchange ideas on color schemes and furnishing.

Invitations This shower can be a surprise party, the invitation given in person or by telephone to women friends of the bride-to-be. A folding doll house—many large and small ones are in the toy, stationery, and novelty shops—makes an amusing and appropriate centerpiece for this luncheon table. A bride and groom doll about to enter the house are followed by a long parade of toy dogs, cats, horses, and other pets, which wind around the house. Four small bouquets of garden flowers in small matching jugs or tumblers are placed, one at each corner of the setting.

Menu Any good luncheon menu (see Bath Shop Shower) is suited to this party.

Kitchen Cutlery Shower One of the most popular showers from an engaged couple's point of view is a party that brings in all the small kitchen gadgets they forgot to buy. The large kitchen equipment and obvious utensils, even a few fancy pans, casseroles, a teakettle and the coffee maker usually go onto the bride's own kitchen list. But cutlery and small grinders, graters, can openers and similar things, although essential, often are omitted.

Invitations Friends who plan a cutlery shower for a bride-to-be can make it a surprise. An invitation can be given to her to come to luncheon or tea with a few friends on a suitable date. The hostess and friends plan a list of gifts. In keeping with the old superstition that a knife or scissors or any gift with a cutting edge must be accompanied by a penny so that "friendship is not cut," bright new copper pennies fresh from the bank should be attached to each piece of cutlery. To add to the fun, ask guests to wrap their gifts so as to disguise the contents. At the party the packages are heaped in the center of the luncheon table or on a handsome serving cart, the cart itself being a group gift, and at the end of the luncheon, the guest of honor must guess the contents of each package before opening it.

Here are some of the things most brides forget to add to their kitchen: a French pastry whisk for beating egg whites, sauces, and cream; a good strong large corkscrew, various knives, from paring size to bread knife; poultry shears, an easy-to-use can opener, rolling pin, cutting board, wooden salad set; wooden spatulas; slicer-boards for potatoes, fruits, vegetables; pastry bag and tubes; skewers, both wooden and long decorative metal ones; chopping bowl with curved, fitted chopper; cheese grater; wire skimmer; long handled, heavy cooking spoons and forks; pancake turner, potato masher. A few minutes' shopping in five-and-ten cent stores and in kitchenware stores will suggest many other useful gifts in this small gadget category.

Menu and Table Decoration for this shower depend on the season. Fresh flowers for the table, a pretty corsage for the guest of honor are always in season. Or decorate a very large straw beach hat with small kitchen gadgets such as tiny gelatin molds, very small cookie cutters, and other shiny, small pieces. Fasten these on with gummed tape or thread. Fill the hat with artificial flowers and suspend it like a chandelier over the center of the table. Dangle other small gifts from it—

these may be wrapped in bright tissue paper and fastened to the hat on the end of colored ribbons or cords of various lengths to make a shower of small, bright packages (see sketch). The menus suggested for the Bath Shop Shower are adaptable to this shower.

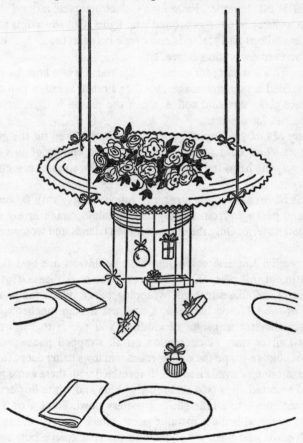

Kitchen Utensil Shower Kitchen utensils may be included in the cutlery shower, and the party then is simply called a Kitchen Shower.

Decoration With a cleared playroom, laundry, or basement room, a lively evening party for the engaged couple can be given, using the gift utensils as decoration. Suspend pots and pans from the ceiling on wires of different lengths, so that the upper part of the room seems full of shining aluminum, bright enamel, copper and other wares.

Make bouquets of gadgets and tie them with bright red ribbon—for instance, a wheel egg beater, cooking spoon, and wooden spatula tied together as one bouquet. Fasten the gadget bouquets around the room on side walls or in clusters around wall lights. Cut silver-foil wrapping paper in scallops and garlands and drape between the gadget bouquets and wherever decoration is needed.

Menu This is a party for dancing, followed at a late hour by a supper of scrambled eggs and sausages, toast or French bread, a pan of warm open-face plum tart, and coffee. Or, if the season is right, serve fresh strawberries for dessert.

Plenty of fancy wrapping paper should be on hand for the gifts, and ribbon or silver cord to tie packages for the ending of this shower, when everyone helps the two guests of honor wrap their presents.

Lingerie Shower is usually a surprise luncheon, gay with flowers, good food, and packages from every guest containing some lovely piece of trousseau lingerie. Only the closest women friends and women relatives are invited.

Decoration Lingerie colors and delicate flowers are best suited for decoration at this party. Or use an up-in-the-stars theme. Cut a large star out of metallic silver gift wrapping paper. Place the star in the center of the table on bare wood, and use a blue luncheon mat set. Or place the star in center of cloth, if you prefer to use one. Add gummed silver stars as decoration on all wrapped packages.

If possible, re-drape the dining-room windows using deep, full swags of blue tarlatan or dyed cheesecloth sprinkled with these same gummed stars of assorted sizes (see sketch). Use blue and white flowers for the table centerpiece in a blue glass or pottery bowl. Paint 4 or 5 slender wooden sticks with silver metallic paint, attach a silver star to the top of each stick, and poke the sticks into the centerpiece bouquet. They should be tall enough to stand above the flowers.

Roll the table napkins and slip them into napkin rings made of silver paper fastened with a star. To make the rings, cut strips of paper about 2 inches wide and 8 to 10 inches long, depending on the size of the napkins. Fasten ends together making loose ring; attach the gummed tape on the inside of the paper, to hold smoothly. Decorate each ring with gummed blue star.

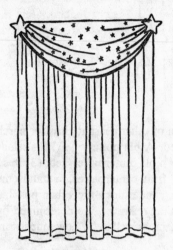 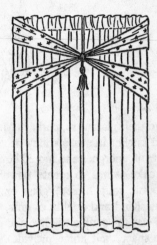

Pantry Gifts Shower is more timely if given after the couple have moved into their apartment or house, since it is a shower of packaged foods, especially delicacies for impromptu meals. Gifts can be various mixes, specialties such as rarebit, canned and powdered soups, appetizing smaller canned and packaged foods such as imported sausages, pâtés, anchovies, spreads, olives, sandwich fillings, fine crackers.

This shower is effective if given the same treatment as the Book and Record Shower. A Pantry Tree can be lively and decorative.

Refreshments for this party should be made of pantry-type foods— a canned spaghetti supper, for instance, with tossed green salad, a dessert from cans or freezer such as superb home-style peaches, with cookies and coffee. A kitchen counter or playroom bar is the setting for this kind of supper.

Table Setting Shower should not be a surprise unless the young bride has registered her choices of patterns at local stores and the shower gifts match her selections. For instance, serving pieces in the silver or china patterns, dessert plates of some harmonizing pattern, and, to ex-

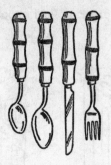

tend their glassware, perhaps Mexican or other peasant glass for porch and kitchenette meals may be selected. A big pottery bowl for salads or fruit, epergnes and footed bowls for table centerpieces, sets (3 sizes) of cake stands to create flower and fruit centerpieces, a handsome ceramic soup tureen, glass or silver candlesticks are other possible gifts. Kind and quality of gifts, as for any shower, are determined by the way the couple will live and entertain, as well as by how much storage space their home provides.

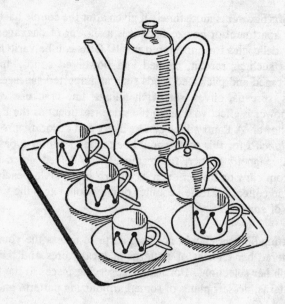

The Stork Shower Close friends of an expectant mother can provide a wardrobe for the baby and many useful furnishings for the nursery in a Stork Shower luncheon or tea. Nursery supplies, thermometer, washable basinette accessories such as pillows and coverlets, soft towels, a baby scale, and other essentials are welcomed by most young mothers because they help her stretch the budget for the new member of the family. Flattering overblouses for herself and countless little gifts including socks, bootees, and toys for the playpen create a happy atmosphere at such a party.

Menu In deference to the expectant mother, the menu should be simple but delicious, and served in an atmosphere of leisure and happy conversation rather than the high jinks that sometimes dominate this kind of shower. An umbrella-shaped cake makes an amusing final touch to the menu (see sketches). Here is the recipe and directions for making it:

UMBRELLA CAKE FOR SHOWERS

1¼ cups sifted cake flour	⅓ cup hot water
1½ teaspoons baking powder	1 teaspoon vanilla
½ teaspoon salt	½ teaspoon lemon flavoring
3 eggs	9-inch round pan, greased
¾ cup sugar	and floured

Start oven at Moderate (350°F.). Sift flour, baking powder, and salt together three times and set aside. Beat eggs until thick and lemon colored; beat sugar into eggs gradually; blend in slowly (*low speed* on blender) hot water, vanilla, and lemon flavoring. Quickly and thoroughly blend in dry ingredients. Pour into prepared pan. Place in oven immediately. Bake for 25 to 30 minutes or until cake is done according to test. Let cool.

Cut off one quarter of the cake in one piece. Make a scalloped edge along straight side of remaining cake with a biscuit cutter. Cut straight side of quarter-cake to make handle. Cut handle base and triangular tip from rounded edge. (See sketches.) Place on flat serving tray covered with waxed paper.

CHOCOLATE GLAZE FOR UMBRELLA CAKE

1 cup semisweet chocolate pieces (1 6-oz. package)	3 tablespoons light corn syrup
1 tablespoon butter	2 tablespoons milk

Melt chocolate pieces and butter over hot, but not boiling, water. Remove from heat, and blend in corn syrup and milk. Spread over cake and handle while still warm. Decorate with ornamental frosting ribs (see sketch).

Ornamental Frosting Combine 1 cup of sifted confectioner's sugar, 3 to 4 teaspoons of evaporated milk, and a few drops of red food coloring to make mixture pale pink. Press through the smallest tube of your cake decorating set to complete the umbrella, as described.

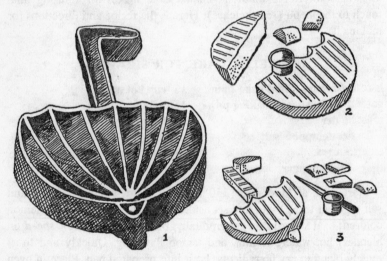

Wedding Breakfast and Reception

The wedding breakfast and reception cannot be discussed in the usual terms of party planning and party giving, since all aspects of the wedding ceremonial, and the entertainment for family and friends that surround it, are steeped in tradition, controlled more or less as to form and even the details.

The traditional procedure for the breakfast and reception have been established and followed through the years according to almost unbreakable rules. Whether the rules were made by some long-ago etiquette specialist or how they evolved, probably no one knows. One guess might be that the early American heiress copied the formal wedding receptions of titled British and European girls and set a pattern in America which, though modified, is still encouraged by bridal consultants and etiquette authorities.

Most brides-to-be want to conform to the popular formula. If you are one of these, a guide to the planning and presenting of a home wedding, the breakfast and reception, complete with all details, you will need to consult an etiquette authority, such as *Amy Vanderbilt's Complete Book of Etiquette.*

Using such guidance to the solid structure of tradition on which to plan, you may want to take some liberties and let local or family customs and personal preference vary the suggested menus and other activities. This can add a sense of freedom and pleasure to the day, providing the sequence of events is not changed. The reception, if there is to be one, takes place after the ceremony, when family and friends gather to toast the bride and groom, and when a luncheon is included it must be carefully planned.

In every large city as well as most smaller centers, there are florists, entertainment bureaus, decorators, and caterers who specialize in weddings. Some of these specialists have large staffs and they can take over all planning, preparation, food, decoration, music, and service with trained maids and butlers and other helpers for every detail. They will set up a gay, beautiful tent on the lawn for bridal luncheon or reception or dancing, and their kitchen staff works in another tent away from the party tent and away from the house, so that all sounds and odors of cookery are removed from the house.

They decorate country house or city home using your garden and local flowers, or have garlands, bouquets, and other arrangements made in their own workrooms. They do not need suggestions and help from the bride's family as to what to do, what to serve, how to decorate, but they take such suggestions as their working plan and develop every detail for the day with care and according to the budget agreed upon with the family.

This sort of professional service is not necessary in some families where experienced, imaginative, and creative planning for all entertaining is the rule, and where a staff of helpers in the kitchen and household ease all entertaining. For a family with a very small budget for the wedding, professional assistance is ruled out. The simplicity or elaborateness of a reception is the bride's decision.

Planning, shopping, and cookery for a wedding breakfast and reception are no different than for any other important entertaining. But since the family of the bride is also in the wedding party, it is almost imperative that some outside help be on hand for cleaning and arrangement of the rooms the day before, to set tables, help with decoration, and especially with the cookery on that day and the wedding day, to help with serving, and later with cleaning up and restoring the house after the wedding. Sometimes a neighbor or two will gladly help when there is a wedding in the family, or maids and cooks who work on a part-time basis can be hired by the hour or day.

Whoever is in charge of plans must use whatever help is available to clear space for the reception, the living room and any rooms which adjoin it, removing small furniture and most of the accessories. The reception area should be bright with flowers, garlands, greens, or any favorite decorations. For a summer wedding in a suburban or country house, garden flowers, especially white ones or mixed garden roses are used. The flowers should be added last, probably on the morning of the wedding day while the family is still at the church.

If the plan includes dancing after the reception, rugs should be taken out and the floors made ready for dancing the day before. Prepare the room according to your plan of what you want the reception to be. The object of the rigid clearance is to provide space for the receiving line, for reception guests, for a buffet table, for the bride's table and possibly other tables for guests.

The receiving line will stand just inside the entrance to the reception room. The line consists of the bride's mother, the groom's father, the groom's mother, the bride's father, the bride, groom, maid of honor, and the bride's attendants. Usually the two fathers walk about and act as hosts, as do the best man and the ushers.

The Bride's Table as well as reception buffet table and comfortable places for guests to eat and chat must be ready and waiting when the reception begins. As soon as all guests are greeted, the bridal party goes to the bride's table and is served. It may be a small table, with places for the bride, groom, and their attendants, bride at groom's right, ushers and bridesmaids alternately around the table. Or the bride's table may be large enough to seat the entire bridal party including parents of the bride and groom together, the clergyman and his wife, or the parish priest, men and women alternating.

The bridal table may be set up in a room, screened porch, or sun parlor adjoining the larger room where the reception is held. The table may also be set in a special place at one end of the reception room, or in the center, with smaller tables for guests placed around the room. At a country or suburban wedding, the bridal table may be in a cooled dining room, or in a party tent set up on the lawn, and the reception guests served at small tables on a screened porch.

Decorations The reception buffet table and small tables traditionally are covered with white linen cloths, the table decorations in the same color with garlands of smilax (any florist can order these) and white flowers, or for a summer wedding in the country, mixed bouquets of garden roses. For a second wedding the color scheme may be any favorite colors of the bride. If there is music it should be lively and gay but not so obtrusive that it drowns out conversation.

Tradition calls for a toast to the bride and groom. The punch may occupy the center of interest on the reception buffet table or on a separate table, or on a garlanded, decorated cart (see sketch). The iced bowl in any case should be on a large tray, trimmed with smilax, or orange blossoms, or white flowers and their foliage. Someone, not a member of the wedding party, should be in charge of the punch and serve it to everyone for the toast before guests begin to serve themselves

from the dishes on the buffet table. Someone else is hostess at the reception table to see that the bride's table is served first, and all small tables served immediately afterwards (with help of waitresses) or that the guests help themselves.

If the menu is prepared in the home kitchen and served by the family without trained help, most of the traditional formalities of bridal reception service are not even attempted. But in any case, the bridal table must be served before the wedding guests are served.

Traditional Menu, usually called a breakfast, is actually a luncheon. This begins with hot chicken or clam bouillon usually topped with seasoned whipped cream, or, if the day is warm, jellied Madrilène or some other iced soup. There is a main dish, such as delicate creamed chicken or sweetbreads-and-mushrooms in patty shell, with new peas and tiny parsleyed potatoes. Sometimes included is a green salad or a jellied salad, an aspic, lobster mousse, or any other delicate fish or meat mousse. Dessert is ice cream in fancy molds, such as wedding bell, double ring, heart, with petits fours and coffee.

In some families, their own traditional wedding dishes are served in place of such a menu and their own historic wedding customs prevail, especially in the decorations and music. It is a bride's privilege to modify the conventional plans to please her family and herself.

Bride's Cake Throughout the reception and during luncheon the Bride's Cake has been the centerpiece on the bride's table, or it is brought in at the end of luncheon on a decorated cart to the bride's table. It is cut by the bride and served to the groom and then to the rest of the bridal party at her table, and if there is a second table for parents and close relatives, the bridal cake is also served to them.

This may be a caterer's or home-made cake of rich, delicate white layers in tiers, decorated with or without clusters of frosting flowers, with or without bride and groom dolls on top. But nothing is written on this cake (as on a birthday cake).

Wedding Cake, which is usually dark fruit cake, may be cut, wrapped in foil, put in white boxes and tied with white ribbon to be given to all members of the bridal party as well as to reception guests.

As soon as the bride cuts and serves her cake at the end of luncheon, she and the groom may excuse themselves and leave to dress for their departure. All guests stay until the couple have said their good-bys, the bride has tossed her bouquet to her waiting bridesmaids, and the happy pair has rushed away to a waiting car to begin their honeymoon trip. With a large reception and music, their friends may stay for dancing. At simpler weddings guests may linger after refreshments for conversation and coffee late into the afternoon.

Smaller Weddings When there is no room for a reception or for other reasons only the immediate families attend the wedding, a family luncheon may follow the church or home ceremony. At such a luncheon there is usually only one table with bride and groom and their families seated informally around it. The menu for this occasion is whatever the bride and her parents prefer. They may serve the traditional wedding breakfast menu, or something quite different. For example, a country luncheon of honeydew melon, broiled chicken, new asparagus, hot rolls or biscuits, the Bride's Cake, and homemade lemon ice cream. The cake may be the centerpiece on the luncheon table, or it may be brought in at the end of the luncheon to be admired, then cut by the bride and groom and served to everybody. It may be homemade or a caterer's cake, 3-tier, or simply a large layer cake, the top decorated with frosting flowers. And, as at the larger affair, there should be punch in which to toast the bride and groom, before the luncheon begins.

The same sort of luncheon is a favorite of families who live in city apartments and who prefer a home luncheon after the wedding to a club or hotel affair. If the traditional menu is not served at this home luncheon, any simple but delicious combination is suitable. But it should include a Bride's Cake, and sherbet, ice cream, frozen mousse, or parfait to go with it, and punch in which to toast the couple.

Late Afternoon and Evening Weddings are sometimes preferred to a morning ceremony. In small homes, or when for any reason the wedding has been kept small, a dinner or buffet supper for the wedding party may follow the wedding. In a larger home with facilities for a reception, guests may be invited for dancing and late supper after an evening wedding. All such entertaining follows the usual rules for buffet supper evenings with the exception that there should be some beverage in which to toast the couple and there should be a bridal cake.

Menus for these suppers include sliced turkey in aspic garnished with pimiento and capers, ham mousse, small assorted sandwiches of anchovy, cheese, and cucumbers, small tomatoes stuffed with celery salad, small buttered rolls, the Bride's Cake, fruit sherbets, and coffee. Or, chafing dish of lobster Newburg, herbed French bread toast, lemon gelatin ring filled with fresh grapefruit, white seedless grapes, and sliced avocado salad, the Bride's Cake, ice cream bombe, coffee.

Decorations for these afternoon and evening weddings should be white flowers, with smilax or other greens. Tablecloth and cloths for small tables around the room should be white. Or for a second wedding, in the bride's favorite color. Candlelight, especially in silver or crystal candlesticks, should be used as lavishly as possible as decoration and to light the table. The bride's bouquet might be laid in the center of the table and surrounded by candlesticks holding lighted candles.

Another centerpiece arrangement for these tables is mixed bouquets of white flowers in crystal or silver epergnes or other footed containers, used as a pair on the table with candles between. Place cards, small gifts for members of the wedding party, or small packages of wedding cake are sometimes added to the place settings.

3
HOLIDAY PARTIES

Spring

St. Patrick's Day One of the first spring holidays that party-givers seize upon as an excuse for entertaining is St. Patrick's Day, March 17. It is a fine, meaningful date on which to have a few friends in for supper, a Shamrock Chowder Supper planned to satisfy the hungry, tickle their ears with Irish tunes, and end the evening with reels, jigs, or more modern versions of the dance.

Invitations can be given in person, by telephone, or mailed out about ten days ahead of the party date. It will be in harmony with the homeland of the saint if you use cards or notepaper decorated with bright green edge or a small shamrock or a Paddy hat and pipe.

Decoration of your table depends on the degree of formality you prefer. In store displays of paper tablecloths and napkins there are green ones and also white paper cloths decorated with shamrocks and other Irish emblems, in sizes to use on the buffet table as well as on small tables around the room. Paper decorations and favors in Irish green, such as small clay pipes, Paddy pigs, and jaunting cars, are plentiful at novelty, stationery, and five-and-ten cent stores. So are large Paddy hats for guests to wear. By mail order, the Dennison Party Bazaar, 411 Fifth Avenue, New York 16, New York, can supply all, including note paper for the invitations.

A large green Paddy hat makes an amusing centerpiece for the paper-decorated buffet table. Place a bowl or vase inside the hat and fill it with green carnations. If your florist can supply tiny pots of fresh

Also see "Children's Parties," Chapter 4

shamrock, as most of them can around this holiday, use these as favors. Tie green ribbon around the pots, attach green-edged place cards to the ribbons and set them on the small tables to show guests where you want them seated.

For a more formal table use a green glass flower holder or bowl centerpiece and fill it with green leaves and white carnations. Use green glass accessories, such as candy and nut dishes, salt cellars, and water goblets; a cloth of white linen, organdy, or lace, and large bold green linen napkins, or a green linen cloth and large napkins of white and green striped linen. Silver, pottery, or crystal candlesticks with tall green and white candles add sparkle to the table with either the paper decorations or the more formal linen cloth. Green and white china gives another fitting touch.

Menu, as indicated in the invitation, begins with a delicious chowder. If possible serve it from either a very large tureen or a deep marmite or soup casserole kept hot on an electric warming tray. New England clam chowder and Maryland corn-and-crab chowder are universally popular as well as delicious and filling. With either one serve large, seasoned chowder crackers (one brand, which comes in a tall round can, is called Sea Biscuits): spread crackers with butter, sprinkle with celery salt or a mixture of dried herbs, such as basil, orégano, and marjoram, and crisp in hot oven for 5 to 10 minutes. Serve warm.

Since the chowder is the main dish, servings should be larger than usual and in deep soup bowls. Your best green salad might follow the chowder and a generous cheese tray, with coffee. Or omit the salad and simply serve an especially good party dessert, such as a chocolate roll cake and coffee. In some families, the one and only dessert served after chowder is deep-dish apple pie with Cheddar cheese.

Entertainment Your guests may want to relax and listen to Irish tunes, and after a while, to dance. There are many unusually fine Irish records to be had through Folkways Records & Service Corporation, 117 West Forty-sixth Street, New York 36, New York. These include an LP "Irish Popular Dances" recorded in Ireland with Irish pipes, violins, bagpipes; it includes jigs, reels and hornpipe. Other LP records from the same source are "Jigs, Reels, Hornpipes," an LP "Traditional Irish Songs" sung in Gaelic and the beautiful "Songs of the Irish Rebellion of 1798," folk melodies with lute accompaniment. Among other record labels Epic 10-inch "Irish Melodies" and two 10-

inch and 12-inch LPs in Imperial Records of "Famous Irish Folk Dances." Also "Irish Folk Music" in two 10-inch London records and "Irish National Airs." Other fine new LP recordings of Irish music are available from time to time; consult your record shop catalogues, and don't miss the Decca record of "The Little Gaelic Singers of County Derry" sung by an adult voice with a children's choir.

Recipes for Shamrock Chowder Supper

NEW ENGLAND CLAM CHOWDER

4 slices lean bacon

4 small onions, peeled and chopped

4 medium potatoes, peeled and cubed

1 tablespoon salt

Grind of fresh pepper

3 cups water

4 10½-oz. cans minced clams (or 1 quart cleaned clams and their liquor)

1 quart milk

4 tablespoons butter

16 soda crackers

Chop bacon coarsely, heat in large soup kettle and fry until almost crisp. Add onions, cook and stir for 5 minutes. Add potatoes, salt, grind of pepper, and water, and cook for 10 more minutes. Add canned clams or chopped, cleaned clams and their liquor to the kettle, then add milk and butter and cook for 3 minutes, until steaming hot and at boiling point. Sprinkle crushed crackers into chowder, stir but do not boil. Pour into warmed marmite or deep soup casserole, and place on buffet table warmer. Makes 6 to 8 servings.

MARYLAND CORN-AND-CRAB CHOWDER

2½ cups small raw potato cubes

1 cup thinly sliced onions

2 cups hot water

1¾ teaspoons salt

4 to 5 cups milk

2 6½-oz. cans crab meat or same amount quick-frozen with bones removed

2 17-oz. cans cream-style corn

2 tablespoons minced parsley

Combine potatoes, onions, water, and salt in large soup kettle. Bring to boiling and cook about 10 minutes. Stir in milk, then cleaned crab meat and corn. Cook over low heat until steaming hot. Pour into hot tureen or deep soup marmite. Sprinkle top with parsley. Place tureen or marmite on table warmer. Makes 6 to 8 servings.

CHOCOLATE ROLL CAKE

1½ cups semisweet choco- late bits	5 eggs
⅓ cup sugar	2 teaspoons vanilla
¼ cup water	

Melt chocolate in the top part of a double boiler over hot water; add sugar and water. Stir until smooth. Remove from heat, let cool, stirring from time to time. Beat egg yolks until they are thick and lemon colored, then stir them into cooled chocolate, adding vanilla. Beat egg whites until they stand in points when the beater is removed. Add chocolate-yolk mixture to whites and beat just long enough to blend. Chill to spreading consistency, that is, for about 3 to 4 hours in refrigerator.

6 tablespoons cake flour	4 eggs
6 tablespoons cocoa	¾ cup sugar
¼ teaspoon salt	1 teaspoon vanilla
¾ teaspoon baking powder	Confectioner's sugar

Start oven at Moderately Hot (400°F.). Prepare shallow jelly-roll pan, 10-by-15-by-½ inches; grease, and line it with waxed paper, then grease the paper.

Sift flour, cocoa, salt, and baking powder together three times. Beat egg whites until they stand in points when the beater is removed. Fold in sugar a little at a time. Beat yolks until they are thick and lemon colored. Add vanilla and fold in egg white meringue. Fold in sifted dry ingredients. Pour into prepared pan. Bake in Moderately Hot oven for 13 minutes. Turn out on dish towel sprinkled thickly with confectioner's sugar. Quickly cut off crisp edges of cake. Roll up. Let cool on rack. Unroll, spread generously with chilled chocolate filling. Roll up again and chill in refrigerator 1 hour or longer, until serving time. This recipe makes 8 servings.

Other St. Patrick's Day Parties The same color scheme and decoration suggestions, as well as menus, can be adapted to a luncheon for bridge club, sewing club, or other group, to supper after bowling club, supper for poker enthusiasts, supper for older teen-agers who enjoy folk dancing, supper for welcoming new neighbors, supper for school music director and small glee club or choral group interested in Irish music.

A Green Menu Some hostesses like to serve a green menu on this holiday. Here are some foods that come ready-tinted for this color scheme: honeydew melon, seedless grapes, avocado, limes; such vegetables as peppers, asparagus, water cress, salad greens, cucumbers, unbleached celery, brussels sprouts, cabbage, peas, chives; many versions of the pickle family, and olives; garnishes of fresh mint and parsley. For dessert, a mint sherbet, ice cream mousse, parfait, bombe, or individual molds of delicious pistachio in the same frozen desserts. Cake icing can be tinted with a drop or two of pure food coloring.

Candy mints of several kinds are available in green; green nuts for topping cake frosting are the small, good-tasting pistachios; green paper frills for the crown roasts and chops add still another bit of color. *Erin go bragh!*

Arbor Day

Another spring holiday, which inspires family and community parties, is Arbor Day or Plant A Tree Day. First observed on April 10, 1872 in Nebraska, an Arbor Day is now observed in every state in the Union, the District of Columbia and Puerto Rico but on various dates. It is a legal holiday in Florida the third Friday in January, in Nebraska April 22, in Utah the second Monday in April.

In order to promote the good purpose of Arbor Day, several organizations have been urging that the last Friday of April be selected as National Arbor Day in the northern, middle western, and western states and that families, communities, schools, churches and organizations make it an occasion for planting trees.

Young families with new homes as well as those whose older yards and gardens need refurbishing can plan their own Arbor Day ceremonies. Professional advice on selection of trees and how to plant them is free for the asking from state agricultural colleges; in some states trees are obtainable free through the same source. The job of digging the holes and setting the young trees in place, the watering and other care are family chores in which all members including the youngest toddlers can participate. The setting out of one or more trees in your garden or yard with the promise of shade, beauty, and blossoms in years to come is an event important enough to give it special attention, an occasion for an impromptu party for participants and onlookers: make lemonade or punch in which to toast the new trees, cookies or brownies all around for those who labored.

Following a larger, community or school Arbor Day program, committee members might gather in the family playroom or kitchen for coffee and crullers, or pizza and coffee. Sandwiches made at the table and toasted on a table grill are an alternate. Use the blender to make chocolate milk drinks for young committee members, serve coffee or tea to refresh the grownups.

Easter

Easter Brunch In some sections of the country, the one-time large Easter Sunday dinner after church has given way to a lighter midday meal, a brunch. Brunch is simpler than a luncheon or dinner, more easily prepared and served. In addition to the family, the parish priest or the clergyman and his wife may be invited as well as youngsters home from college for the holidays and perhaps one or two of their friends to this informal meal, which is in keeping with the relaxed atmosphere of the ending of Lent.

Invitations are given in person or by telephone one week or ten days before Easter, the time set about half an hour to an hour after church. The exact time depends on how long any clerical guests may be delayed by their duties following the service and how much time the hostess may need after church to complete the brunch preparation.

Decoration of the table and dining room for this party will be light and refreshing if spring flowers such as mixed bouquets of daffodils, jonquils, or tulips, and freesia are placed around the room and on the table. If you own a handsome pottery tureen in the rooster, setting hen, rabbit, duck, or recumbent lamb design, this is the time to use it as a centerpiece. Fill the tureen with assortments of candy Easter eggs, large and small, to be nibbled at the end of brunch, or wrap the candies in bright pliofilm or foil and tie in little packages for favors. Or, for the centerpiece, fill a pretty basket with home-colored Easter eggs, decorate the basket with a toy rabbit and a big bow of pink or yellow ribbon. Table linen in yellow and white, and china in the same colors or other spring tones are just right for this table.

Serving the brunch is simplified and the informal atmosphere encouraged if guests help themselves English-style from dishes placed on electric or candle warmers on a buffet, sideboard, or serving table. The brunch table is ready with place settings of silver, water goblet, service plate and napkin. The first-course fruit is in place when guests enter the dining room. The hot dishes, muffins, and coffee are brought in to the sideboard or buffet when guests have nearly finished eating their fruit. When the guests have finished their fruit, they go to the sideboard and serve their own plates with whatever they prefer.

Also see "Children's Parties," Chapter 4

Since this is the first meal of the day for some of the guests, they will want their coffee with the main course. A second pot should be made to serve later with coffee cake. A delicious, freshly baked coffee cake or one bought from a fine pastry shop makes a conversation-piece finale, while guests linger over their coffee.

Menus One well suited to this occasion is a coupe of assorted chilled melon balls for the first-course fruit, scalloped eggs and tomatoes, broiled lamb chops with fresh mint garnish, and pan-browned potatoes as the hot dishes, and small hot muffins, strawberry jam, cinnamon cake, and coffee. Lamb chops may be omitted and crisp bacon served on the eggs.

An alternate menu for brunch might be: a section of chilled cantaloupe garnished with pitted black cherries, eggs Gruyère, broiled thin slices of Easter ham, brown-and-serve biscuits, gooseberry jam or apple butter, pancake pie and coffee.

Here are the egg and pancake pie recipes:

SCALLOPED EGGS AND TOMATOES

1 ripe tomato for each person to be served	Salt and pepper
1 egg for each person	Butter
	Grated Parmesan cheese

Start oven at Moderate (350°F.). Cut tops off tomatoes, scoop out centers, and place in well-buttered, shallow baking dish. Break fresh eggs, one at a time, into a saucer and slip egg into the hollow of each tomato. Sprinkle with salt and pepper, dot with butter. Bake in Moderate oven (350°F.) about 15 minutes, or until eggs are well set. Remove dish from oven, sprinkle generously with cheese, brown under broiler. Then place dish on table warmer on buffet. Serve with curl of crisp bacon on each tomato, unless lamb chops are included in this menu.

EGGS GRUYÈRE

1 slice bread for each person to be served	**Butter**
	Salt and pepper
1 thin slice Gruyère cheese for each person	**1 egg for each person**
	Grated nutmeg

Start oven at Moderate (350°F.). Cut slices of bread and cheese into rounds of the same size. Fry bread rounds in a little butter, one side only until lightly browned. Season lightly with salt and pepper. Place round of cheese on each round of bread. Place these, cheese side up, in buttered shallow baking dish. Break eggs, one at a time, into a saucer and slip egg onto each round of cheese. Season with salt, pepper and nutmeg, dot with butter. Bake in a Moderate oven (350°F.) about 15 minutes or until eggs are nicely set. Place hot dish on table warmer on buffet.

PANCAKE PIE

Make 14 to 18 very large, thin French pancakes. Sprinkle shaved maple or brown sugar and pieces of butter over each. Stack, sprinkle top with confectioners' sugar. Bring into brunch table warm from the kitchen. Cut into pie-shaped wedges. Serve warm with maple syrup or syrup made with brown sugar and orange juice. One pancake pie serves six.

If there are more than six at the table, serve something else, such as a favorite cinnamon cake, or panetone, the Italian Easter bread that is sold in all Italian bake shops. It is delicious with coffee, super-delicious if you cut it in thin slices and spread with cream cheese thinned with orange juice.

Easter Dinner Some families who do not entertain during Lent like to have a dinner party on Easter Sunday. Whether dinner is served in the early afternoon or in the evening, the traditional spring lamb roast or baked Easter ham is usually the featured dish. Tiny new potatoes, at least one green vegetable such as peas or asparagus, and some special dessert, possibly the current favorite of the college youngsters home for vacation, are traditional in such dinners.

Decoration and color scheme for this family event usually develop almost without a special plan on the part of the hostess. In the country or suburbs in many parts of the land forsythia is in bloom, and the first garden flowers such as tulips are ready to cut and arrange on the table and throughout the house. City hosts have no such resources, but they may receive a box of Easter flowers from a florist sent by some relative invited to the dinner, or they buy flowers from the corner stands and flower shops.

A corsage worn to church that morning might be re-arranged in a silver or glass goblet or mug as a small centerpiece and flanked at sides and ends with small dishes of yellow and white mints and toasted almonds and filberts.

Another fitting decoration for this table is made with colorful Easter eggs arranged high in a pair of tall, stemmed bowls, placed at ends of the table. The center area can be crowded with chocolate rabbits and fluffy chicks as favors.

Menu might begin with a wedge of chilled honeydew melon with a section of fresh lime, or with a broiled half grapefruit, or sliced fresh nectarines with chilled orange juice poured over them. Fresh mint sauce accompanies the roast lamb, and a delicate mustard sauce is served with the ham. The tiny new potatoes may be pan browned with the roast or fried in deep fat. New peas have special flavor if cooked French style: three or four lettuce leaves, butter and salt and pepper are put into the saucepan with the peas with a little water. The peas should be cooked to tenderness. Another delicate spring flavor in this dinner is a salad of water cress with finely chopped capers and sliced radishes.

The Easter cake can be baked in a lamb-shaped cake pan and frosted with white icing and thickly sprinkled with shredded coconut; add raisins for the lamb's eyes and nose.

Another dessert is a large coconut angel cake, brought to the table with a few fresh freesia blossoms or other small spring flowers on top. Or, bake a chiffon cake and serve it with sweetened whipped cream and crushed red raspberries or strawberries.

Passover and The Seder To be invited to a Passover (Pesach) Seder is a great tribute to a guest, for it is a religious festival celebrated by Jewish families in the sanctity of their homes. The services are of deep meaning and beauty, and the rituals follow closely those observed in ancient times.

Passover is celebrated in the spring of each year. Sometimes the date occurs at the same time as Easter. According to tradition, Christ was crucified before sundown on the fourteenth day of Nisan in the Hebrew calendar, the date of Passover. Early Christians and Jews observed Passover and the Easter season at the same time. When Christians adopted the Roman calendar, which was based on the solar year, the observance of Easter became a variable date, the first Sunday after the first full moon following the vernal equinox (March 21st in our calendar today).

The observance of Passover commemorates the Exodus, or the deliverance of the Jews from bondage in Egypt. According to tradition, the name comes from the event that prepared the way for the Exodus, the sparing of the Hebrews in Egypt: God smote the first-born of the Egyptians, but passed over the homes of the Hebrews, which had been marked, according to God's command, with the blood of the paschal lamb.

The Seder marks the beginning of Passover. It is held on the first and second nights of the eight-day observance, when the entire family gathers at the dinner table. This has been beautifully set, with flowers, ceremonial wine cups, and special dishes and objects uncontaminated by use during the rest of the year. These dishes (and cooking utensils used for this meal) are used only during the Passover holidays. The traditional Seder is both a meal and a service of worship, celebrated with prayers, songs, and blessings performed in the order which has been followed for centuries; Seder means "order." Almost always there are guests at the table, for it is a custom to share the blessings of the holiday with friends, neighbors, and even strangers.

Among Orthodox and Conservative Jews the Seder is held on both the first and second nights of the eight-day holiday. Reform Jews, who observe a seven-day Passover, usually hold their Seder on the first evening.

The ritual for the Seder ceremonies is in the ancient book, Haggadah, which relates the Biblical Exodus of the Israelites from Egypt, led by Moses. Haggadah means "telling" and the Seder reflects the Biblical injunction, "Thou shalt tell thy son in that day saying, 'It is because of that which the Lord did for me when I came forth from Egypt.' "

The youngest child present at the Seder asks four traditional questions of his father, beginning with, "Why is this night different from all other nights?" The answers from the Haggadah unfold the drama of the Exodus.

At the Seder various foods are present which symbolize the hardships the Israelites suffered during their bondage in Egypt and praise given for their deliverance. Matzah (matzoth), unleavened bread, is eaten in memory of the fact that the Jews, escaping from Egypt, had no time to leaven their bread. Bitter herbs (maror) symbolize the embittered existence of the Israelites during their enslavement in Egypt. The shank bone of a lamb is on the table, a reminder of the paschal lamb. Roasted or hard-cooked eggs are served, symbols of the free-will offering that accompanied the sacrifice of the lamb.

Haroseth, which is a paste made of pounded apples, raisins, and nuts mixed with cinnamon and wine, is served because it resembles the mortar used by the Israelites when they labored on the walls of Pharaohs' buildings. Salt water is also served, to symbolize the tears shed by the Israelites. Parsley or water cress on the ceremonial platter reminds everyone of the continual rebirth of growing things, and is a symbol of gratitude to God for the products of the earth which come to life each Spring.

Since Pesach is known as the Festival of Freedom, wine is drunk at the Seder (if desired, unfermented raisin wine may be substituted) and when, during the reading of the Haggadah, the plagues decreed by the Lord upon the Egyptians are named, drops of wine from the cups are spilled to show that no one is gladdened by the suffering of enemies, and therefore, the cup of salvation cannot be full.

One cup of wine is left standing, usually in the center of the table, for Elijah, and at one point during the services, the door is opened to express faith in the coming of the Messiah, and that the Prophet Elijah will be the bearer of the good tidings of eternal peace.

In many homes the person conducting the Seder wears a white robe (kittel). This is to remind all present of the sanctity of the Seder ritual, and to recall the white vestments worn by the Priests. It also symbolizes the color of freedom.

It was the traditional custom for the celebrants at the Seder to recline on couches, and today, in some homes, this may be symbolized by the placing of cushions at the host's back. The men present wear a head covering, either their own hat or the skull cap called the yarmulke.

At one point in the service one of the three matzahs on the platter is broken in half, and a piece hidden, while the children keep their eyes tightly closed. Later they search for the piece, and the finder gives it up only when he is promised a gift in exchange. This piece of matzah is called the afikoman; after it is eaten, no other food is served. Songs, poems, and stories follow the meal, the children taking part in all. These songs and stories teach faith in the future and encourage a reliance on God's promise of freedom. A final benediction of the Seder ends the evening.

Menus suggested by Jewish hostesses for the festival of Passover: half grapefruit, celery and olives, gelfilte fish (stuffed baked fish) with beet horse-radish, meat borsch, roast chicken, fresh asparagus, potato kugel (baked potato pudding), a lettuce salad, Passover macaroons (made with matzah meal, almond paste, egg whites and sugar) and candies and nuts usually bought at kosher candy shops (candies and cakes made under supervision of a rabbi) with matzah and tea or black coffee.

A seasonable melon may replace the grapefruit and a chicken soup with knaidlach (Passover dumplings) the borsch. An alternate main dish is pot roast with vegetables, served with honeyed carrots and cole slaw. For dessert, sponge cake, matzah, fresh fruit, tea or black coffee.

Certain foods are forbidden during Passover. Leavening (yeasts and similar products) may not be used. Jewish cookbooks usually indicate dishes especially suited to Passover meals.

May Day

Many suburban, village, and small-city women who belong to church sewing groups, garden clubs, and assorted community welfare organizations have long since adopted the first day of May, May Day, as their own for a variety of kindly deeds. They have borrowed the charming childhood custom of leaving a flower-filled basket at a neighbor's door.

But the doors are the doors of shut-ins, of lonely old people, sick men and women, hospital wards, veterans' hospitals, and similar institutions.

The most likely entertainment for themselves, after their rounds of collecting their own garden flowers and free flowers from local nurseries, arranging them in baskets, and driving around the community delivering them, is to stop in for luncheon or tea at the home of one of their group. Usually this is a pick-up luncheon, eaten from trays, or around a kitchen counter, or carried out to a porch table if the day is warm enough. The hostess for the day must plan the menu and service the day before, and prepare foods in advance so that it literally is a pick-up meal.

Menu One of the simplest and most satisfying for such luncheons: the hostess for the group the day before prepares a large lemon gelatin mold filled with mounds of cooked peas, green beans, asparagus tips, and sliced radishes and cucumbers. It is ready in the refrigerator, and so are sour-cream mayonnaise and cold cuts, such as boiled smoked tongue and bologna or salami to slice and serve with pickle relish. While one of her guests takes these from the refrigerator, and everybody works together to arrange the trays with the necessary plates, forks, and napkins, she pops brown-and-serve rolls into a hot oven and puts water on for coffee or tea. Dessert for her hungry friends is orange cupcakes or squares of cake iced with lemon frosting and served with sliced, quick-frozen peaches ready in a frosty bowl in the refrigerator.

The nicest silver and handsomest linen napkins, always a pleasure to use, add piquant contrast to a pick-up meal. Or, it is the perfect occasion on which to get out the bamboo-handled stainless steel cutlery, fringed checkered cotton napkins, and those big, garish pottery plates your daughter brought home from Italy last year.

Also see "Children's Parties," Chapter 4

Child Health Day also falls on this date by Presidential proclamation and school, and community and various organizations may be involved in speeches, meetings, exhibits, and other activities concerned with the purpose of the day. Any home entertaining—a luncheon, tea, or supper—for these committees, speakers and visitors might be shared by neighbors. (See Chapter 8 for details on community entertaining.) But the pick-up luncheon described above is well suited to this occasion also.

Tray Luncheon is popular for this sort of semi-official entertaining, since it is easily served and its informality creates just the atmosphere needed. A tray luncheon can be decorative as well as delicious. Matching Italian papier-mâché trays, rattan trays, or brightly lacquered Japanese trays, or a set made in the school carpentery shop add interest to the party. So do novelty stainless steel knives and forks with colored plastic or wooden handles in place of your best silver.

A tray luncheon also gives you free reign in the matter of napkins, anything from large flower-printed paper napkins to fringed cotton or embroidered and hemstitched dinner-size linen. They should harmonize with the tray, however. Embroidered linen goes with the rococo Italian trays, bold solid color napkins are good with Japan lacquer, fringed cotton or paper with rattan and wood trays.

Menu for the trays might be: hot chicken or beef pie baked in individual casseroles, mold of tomato and chopped raw vegetable aspic on lettuce leaf, raspberry sherbet and cookies, and hot coffee. The same menu can be served as a buffet luncheon or at the dining-room table.

Memorial or Decoration Day

May 30th, Memorial Day or Decoration Day, is a legal holiday in all states except Alabama, Georgia, Mississippi, and Texas. And while it is celebrated as a legal holiday in Virginia, it is called Confederate Memorial Day. Another Confederate Memorial Day is celebrated in both of the Carolinas on May 10; in these two states May 30th is a legal holiday only for Federal employees.

In any community a memorial day, by its origin, is not a day for gala celebrations and merrymaking. But in countless cities, towns, and villages, school children, school bands, and other young as well as older citizens participate in memorial services at a local soldiers' monument or military cemetery, veterans' hospital or community center. When the services are concluded, officials and the onlookers follow an old American custom and go home to a holiday lunch. In some parts of the country a picnic is traditional, since this is the first holiday of the summer. In others, a church luncheon or lawn luncheon is served to honor the speakers and other guests.

A Home Luncheon on this occasion might be planned to entertain a guest speaker or committee member, school band leader, or family marchers in a parade, or visiting relatives. Only the most informal type of invitation, that is, by telephone or in person, is indicated.

Decoration In honor of the day, use a color scheme related to the flag's colors. For the table centerpiece, put clusters of small American flags in two matching vases, and place one at each side of a bowl of whatever red, white, and blue flowers are available—red peonies, white peonies, blue iris, or red roses, white iris, blue larkspur (see sketch). Set the table with straw mats, with bright blue, solid-color

linen napkins, or a white cloth or white mat set, and blue and white china.

Menu Serve chilled tomato juice cocktail first, crisp cheese crackers;

then chilled shrimp salad in lettuce leaf garnished with sliced stuffed olives, onion rings and tiny tomatoes filled with horse-radish flavored mayonnaise, and hot popovers as large as possible. For dessert, serve raspberry tarts, with hot or iced coffee or tea.

Another menu is: mixed fruit juice cocktail with anchovy canapé, chicken croquettes with cheese sauce, herbed lima beans, hot biscuits and apple jelly, stewed dried apricots with whipped cream, and iced coffee or tea.

A third suggestion for this menu: iced grape juice, celery, radishes, curried rice ring filled with creamed tuna and chopped green pepper, tiny raisin muffins, orange chiffon pie, and hot or iced coffee or tea.

Feeding the School Band In place of this kind of luncheon, the family may be feeding the school orchestra after its morning's duties. Either playroom or backyard barbecue service will please these teen-agers. A favorite menu consists of hamburgers on toasted buns, milk drinks made in the electric mixer (red-white-and-blue sipper straws for these), and ice cream sundaes. Fixings for the sundaes, in bowls on a tray each with its own spoon, should be chocolate and butterscotch syrups, chopped nuts, whipped cream, maraschino cherries. Consult the band member of your family on whether a big layer cake or cupcakes or cookies is preferred with the sundaes. The proper oblong sundae dishes could be bought or borrowed from a soda fountain for the party. These are a good investment in a teen-age household.

Summer

Fourth of July, Independence Day

Stars and Stripes Terrace Supper Besides picnics, barbecues, clam-bakes, and various community social events on Independence Day, the hot holiday encourages even the city-bound hostess to give some kind of a party, for example, a Stars and Stripes Terrace Supper. This might be nothing more strenuous than a cold buffet supper served on the terrace of a small apartment, or if a summer storm descends, in an air-cooled living room.

Menu for a Stars and Stripes Terrace Supper is extendable. In its smaller form it is just right for the city apartment with a kitchenette and rooftop terrace. Enlarged, it can be prepared in a country or suburban kitchen and served buffet or as a sit-down dinner on a large screened porch, terrace, or patio. Small version: ham or lobster mousse on a cold platter set in a bowl of cracked ice, tossed green salad, cheese finger sandwiches, iced watermelon shell filled with chilled watermelon balls, fresh pineapple cubes, honeydew or cantaloupe balls, pitted cherries, seedless grapes, and berries. Enlarged menu: Add one hot dish, such as chicken or meat turnovers with mushroom sauce, or a casserole of hot veal birds, and hot, herb-buttered French bread instead of the sandwiches.

Decoration For buffet or dinner table, use a boldly striped red-white-and-blue linen or cotton cloth with solid-color blue napkins. Other combinations are a white cloth with both solid-color red and blue napkins, or a solid-color bold blue linen cloth with white napkins bound with red edge.

Put tall hurricane lamp shades around low candlesticks, with blue or red candles; between these lights on the table, have a bouquet of small American flags in a jar. Wrap the jar with white crepe paper, flute top and bottom edges of paper, and tie red-white-and-blue ribbon around it with streamers reaching out in all directions from the jar across the tablecloth (see sketch). At place settings, if it is a sit-down dinner, put small liberty-bell-shaped paper cups, or red-white-and-blue paper drums filled with pecans or almonds or red and white mints.

The same good foods can be served on a Fourth of July paper tablecloth, in paper plates and with paper mugs. For favors at this party as well as added decoration, there are imitation firecrackers, some filled with candies, others with salted nuts, or tiny American flags standing on small wrapped boxes of candies.

If ice cream and cake are preferred to the watermelon dessert, bake the cake in a bell-shaped pan, cover it thickly with white frosting, and decorate it with a rosette of red-white-and-blue ribbon. Ice cream in bell-shaped molds is one more way of adding the Liberty Bell theme to the menu. If you make a freezer of vanilla ice cream, roll it out to the

Also see Picnics and Barbecue sections, Chapter 12, and "Family and Community Parties," Chapter 8 terrace or porch when you are ready to serve it, and scoop out generous portions for everyone. Top the servings with either crushed fresh red raspberries or blueberries for holiday color as well as superb summer flavor.

If this supper is given in the country, in addition to fireworks for the evening, dancing to records or radio is in tune with the day, or a few games of croquet and horseshoe pitching before dark falls.

The city party-giver on the Fourth of July evening with her guests on a tiny terrace can watch across the dark rooftops the scattered remnants of showy fireworks that modern Fourths produce, and listen to new records, the latest from favorite dance bands here and in Paris.

Drop-In Guests on July Fourth Have an icy cold watermelon on hand, or tall glasses of cold lemonade, or iced tea, iced coffee, gingerale with lemon peel in it, cola drinks with piece of fresh lemon or lime in each glass. Serve ice cream with strawberries, if you have these summer favorites in the kitchen. Don't forget red-white-and-blue sipper straws.

Autumn

Labor Day, the first Monday in September, is either the first holiday of the fall season or the last holiday of summer, according to your calendar of entertaining. By any calendar the Labor Day week end is a time for hospitality. In some families it is the time for a cookout with the children, or a bicycle picnic (see the Picnic section in Chapter 12). In town, Labor Day may be the occasion for friends coming back from Europe and the country and other vacation places to get together to catch up on the summer's news.

Come In for Coffee and Dessert Party One of the easiest and most pleasant evenings of this kind for this holiday. The invitation is telephoned or given in person, for 8 o'clock or any suitable hour soon after dinner. The dining-room or living-room table is arranged for buffet service of coffee and dessert with small plates, forks, spoons, cups and saucers, and napkins. Or, in a very small apartment, the refreshments and accessories are assembled in the kitchen on a tray and brought in to be served from a coffee table in the living room.

Menu Coffee should be almost ready when guests arrive, and should be served as soon as they have removed their wraps and settled themselves in the living room. Favorite combinations with the coffee are: sumptuous cake, such as chiffon spice cake with caramel icing, or Lady Baltimore cake, or coconut and lemon layer, or tender marble cake with marble frosting, or an angel cake baked in a ring pan, left unfrosted, and served with its center filled with crushed fresh peaches and whipped cream or with peach ice cream.

Other combinations: coffee and pecan pie, or mocha chiffon pie, or a warm, deep-dish pie, such as plum, apple, peach, or cherry. A Linzer torte or any other open-face jam torte is always in season. Or, if you are famous for an especially good dessert, such as a family pudding, or mountain high lemon meringue tarts, or French pancakes made at the table, serve your speciality.

Men appreciate the sweetmeats tray that some hostesses provide with this kind of coffee-and-cake evening, as well as after dinner. This is especially true if the tray includes such good things as homemade fudge, candied orange and grapefruit peels, nougat, freshly roasted filberts or large pecans, and little pine nuts for nibbling.

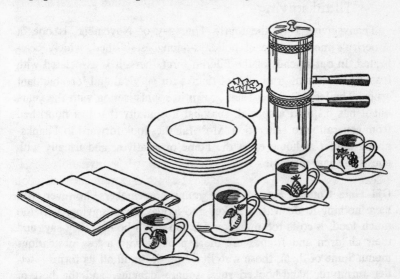

Coffee and Cheese Another pleasant version of the evening coffee party presents fine cheese instead of a dessert. The familiar popular American Cheddar is always appreciated on a cheese tray, but the less well known Gouda, or Edam, or a properly soft Camembert, and any local or family favorites should be there, too. So that they can be cut easily, and easily spread in the case of the Camembert, let all the cheeses stand at kitchen temperature two hours or more before placing on the tray.

A cheese knife should be supplied with each cheese on the tray. Your guests will need small plates and butter spreaders or other small knives. To go with the cheese, provide warm, crisped crackers of interesting flavor and various shapes as well as freshly made, thin toast. One last gourmet touch to this feast is a bowl of chilled ripe pears and apples. Camembert fans know that this cheese is at its best when spread on a freshly cut, ripe pear. The good McIntosh apples and other fragrant eating varieties awaken the flavor of any cheese when combined with it in a hearty bite.

Winter

Thanksgiving

Thanksgiving Day, the fourth Thursday of November, is one of America's most significant holidays—long established, widely celebrated. In our legends of the Pilgrim forefathers, it is associated with feasting, a feast of gratitude, of thanks for survival and for abundant crops. The legendary feast has grown in sophistication with the years but it has inspired a special, seasonal hospitality that has flourished from generation to generation. Most families look forward to Thanksgiving dinner at home or at the home of relatives, and usually with guests to share the table.

Old-Time Country Supper Some young homemakers, however, will have nothing to do with a turkey-and-fixings Thanksgiving. It is too much food, it costs too much, and is too much bother, they say, and their children and friends are more pleased with a less pretentious menu. Some of them, those who like Americana in all its forms—settler furniture, hand-hooked rugs, square dancing, and the best of Colonial cookery—prefer an Old-Time Country Supper on Thanksgiving Day. The supper fits into their scale of living and entertaining and their guests praise them for their originality.

Decoration For this kind of supper or dinner, the decoration also is inspired by settler days and by antiques they have collected or inherited. A kitchen table scrubbed bare or covered with a homespun type of linen cloth, and set with antique pewter plates and candlesticks, early English bone china, stoneware, ironware, or Dutch blue or the modern reproductions of these wares express this theme. For the centerpiece, fill a large wooden mixing bowl with autumn fruits—apples, pears, quinces, grapes. Or, use a pewter platter with gourds and red and golden ears of corn banked around a fine pumpkin or mighty squash.

Other accessories to consider as a centerpiece: brass candlesticks and an antique, decorated sugar box, or wrought iron candlesticks and a wooden bowl or tray. One young Massachusetts hostess uses an old iron kettle as a centerpiece. Scrubbed clean and rubbed with a little olive oil to darken it, it is filled with red apples and autumn leaves on her Thanksgiving table.

Menus for the Old-Time Country Supper consist of early New England, midwest, and southern dishes, such as roast spareribs, scalloped potatoes, pickled beets, coleslaw, hot rolls with cherry chutney or jam, pumpkin pie or tarts, and coffee.

Another menu is meat loaf, baked stuffed onions, succotash, hot corn bread and apple butter, floating island or baked caramel custard, and coffee. A bowl of apples, and nuts to be cracked, belong on this table. Around Lancaster, Ohio, where there are some fine chestnut groves, part of any Thanksgiving celebrating is roasting, shelling, and eating the good chestnuts.

Traditional Turkey Dinner Another type of hostess, one who prefers the Traditional Turkey Dinner can delight her family and guests with the New England version, which begins with oyster stew, then calls in

superb roast turkey with sage-flavored bread stuffing, cranberry sauce, buttered squash, creamed onions, hot rolls, quince or beach plum jelly. Dessert is mince, apple, or squash pie, with coffee, of course.

Or, she may prefer the southern version, which adds to this menu a baked ham, spoon bread, and a black chocolate cake or a rich steamed pudding with hard sauce.

From such dinners as these, the hostess with a small apartment can select favorite dishes and combine them in a more limited menu to suit her cooking and serving facilities: turkey, or roast capon or duck, one green vegetable such as peas, potatoes baked or scalloped, brown-and-serve rolls, and a dessert that in her case can be bought from a good bakery.

Thanksgiving Night Buffet A dinner of any size may be too much for an apartment hostess to undertake, because of lack of kitchen and dining-room space or for other reasons, and yet it is still possible to have a few city bachelors and other small-apartment dwellers in for Thanksgiving hospitality.

For this hostess, a Thanksgiving Night Buffet is easily put together, using the special services of big-city food purveyors and her own kitchenette equipment. She might let a catering service prepare all of the dishes and deliver them ready to serve on Thanksgiving afternoon. Or, a turkey can be ordered several days before the holiday at a rotisserie, delicatessen, or restaurant, to be roasted the day before Thanksgiving and delivered or picked up by the hostess. The cooked turkey is kept in her refrigerator until time for the party. Sliced and served cold, it can be garnished with savory relishes such as chutney and corn relish. A green vegetable, such as peas or asparagus, zucchini, or braised celery, can be cooked in a saucepan on an electric grill and served hot, or be replaced by a crisp green salad. Potatoes au gratin and brown-and-serve rolls can be made hot at the last minute in a table broiler-roaster or on a grill with an oven cover.

Dessert, such as a pumpkin, pecan, or mince pie, can be ordered from a bakery or restaurant well in advance of the holiday and picked up the day before. Or orange ice cream can be ordered in turkey or pumpkin molds and one of the famous French many-layer chocolate cakes served with it.

To add Thanksgiving color to city or country dinner or supper, use golden yellow, orange, or curry color in tablecloths and candles; for the centerpiece, a large paper or pottery turkey, or a pumpkin shell filled with autumn leaves and yellow chrysanthemums, and for each guest at a dinner table or small tables around the room, small paper pumpkins or turkeys filled with salted nuts or raisins and small candies.

The Thanksgiving buffet evening is the night for bridge or canasta, or tables for backgammon experts, and Chinese checkers, or any other games popular with your crowd—perhaps dominoes, using the giant-size dominoes on a low table or the floor. If there is room enough, guests might dance to new records or radio, or just listen to them.

Christmas Entertaining

One of the pleasant, smaller Christmas parties develops around the trimming of the tree. This may take place two or three nights before Christmas or on Christmas Eve, although the night before Christmas is more likely to be a family time filled with midnight church service, last-minute gift wrapping, and preparations for Christmas Day entertaining.

Trim The Tree and Sing Carols Party For this friends are invited by telephone or in person for a convenient hour after dinner. Besides boxes of trimmings at hand and new records of carols or a book of carols waiting on the piano, have light refreshments that are easy to serve and made ready ahead of time.

Coffee and doughnuts or cookies are sufficient for some crowds. Or, if guests have come from a distance, perhaps without having had dinner, something hot, such as pancakes or waffles, can be made and served in the kitchen as the evening draws to a close. A casserole of spaghetti with tiny meat balls and Parmesan cheese topping, cooked and ready in the refrigerator, can be made hot at the end of the evening. Pizzas, especially small ones made quickly on toasted English muffins, are always welcomed for their good flavor. The pizza mixture can be made ahead of time and kept in a covered jar in the refrigerator; reheat, and serve on the toasted muffins. Sliced salami, bologna, and

Also see "Children's Parties," Chapter 4

cheese, with buttered rolls for guests to make their own sandwiches, are also easily assembled and served.

Serve the refreshments after the tree trimming and before carol singing, which should be the last pleasant episode in what is always a happy evening, the trimming of the tree.

Pancake Breakfast A special Christmas morning breakfast is necessary when there are house guests. One solution is a tray breakfast sent up to the guests' rooms. On the tray, put a pale green or white tray cloth and napkin, a sprig of fresh holly or pine, and, in covered dishes, warm toast, a scrambled egg and small serving of broiled ham, a small pot of coffee, cup and saucer, and necessary silver. If the guests prefer a juice and coffee breakfast, send up just that, in as decorative a fashion as possible. Since it is Christmas Day, one of the children may volunteer to take up the trays and be the first to say "Merry Christmas!"

But an early breakfast with children, family, and guests around the Christmas morning table is fun. It is part of the day's enjoyment, because gifts may be opened at the table, if they have not been opened Christmas Eve, and the atmosphere of holiday jollity beginning with this meal sets the pace for the whole day of family activities. The table should be set the night before ready with china, silver, glassware, napkins, and a coffee tray. Fresh holly or pine can be used for a small centerpiece.

The breakfast menu should be generous if there is to be no regular meal that day until evening dinner. It should be a classic winter breakfast of fruit juice, cereal, pancakes or waffles or French toast; or pan broiled ham and mashed potato patties, with brown-and-serve biscuits or corn muffins, and coffee.

The fruit juices can be defrosting in a glass pitcher in the refrigerator over night. If pancakes or waffles are to be featured, the batter can be mixed the night before and kept in a covered pitcher or jar in the refrigerator, or quickly combined at breakfast time from ready mixes. Dry cereals or a quick-cooking hot cereal with brown sugar and top milk to serve with it are easily assembled for serving. If the ham and potato patties are served in place of pancakes or waffles, the patties can be shaped the day before and kept ready on a covered platter in the refrigerator for pan browning at breakfast time. Coffee can be made and served at the table by a guest or one of the family.

Besides good, sustaining food for a long day, the purpose of this breakfast is to provide a pleasant, leisurely morning for family and guests. A neighbor may drop in with small gift packages and join the coffee drinkers. Breakfast should last as long as children and guests want it to last, ending only when the children go off to play with their new games and toys, and adults go off to walk or drive around the neighborhood to see the door decorations and community tree and other sights.

Grownups left behind wash breakfast dishes and help decorate the dining room and make other preparations for the late afternoon or evening dinner. If dinner is not to be served until evening, a snack of sandwiches and milk should be available about noon in the kitchen for youngsters and grownups.

A Family Christmas Dinner Any good dinner can be served on Christmas Day and be called a Christmas dinner. But certain festive dishes, through association and traditional preference, contribute to the holiday atmosphere which Christmas deserves.

Menu for one such dinner: chilled cranberry juice and stuffed celery; roast duck or capon with pecan stuffing, casserole of sliced sweet potatoes with orange, creamed small onions, corn pudding; small toasted and buttered rolls, peach jam; fruitcake, ice cream bombe of vanilla, raspberry sherbet, and pistachio ice cream, and coffee.

Decoration Use a white linen cloth and napkins, your finest. A low arrangement of fresh holly and pine is the centerpiece, or a snowy toy Christmas tree decorated with brilliant miniature balls and garlands in mixed colors or all one color, such as red, green, star blue, chartreuse, or pink. A Santa in his sleigh might be used, the sleigh filled with striped candy canes of assorted sizes for favors. Tie narrow green ribbon of different lengths to the canes, and a card that says Merry Christmas on the end of each ribbon, straighten the ribbons out so that they trail behind the sleigh across the table. Tall white candles in your best candlesticks belong on this table, no matter what the centerpiece is.

If the dinner is served in the evening, bed time for tired Christmas children follows close on the dessert, or even before the dessert is finished. And adults have the rest of the night to themselves for talk, dancing, or carol singing.

Come to Christmas Night Supper and Listen to Records A Washington, D.C. newspaper woman and author has become famous through the years for her teas and her Christmas Night Supper. She lives alone. The few remaining members of her family live in Europe and their own family duties prevent them from joining her at holiday time. She knows other women and men who, like herself, live alone and cannot be with their families in other cities for Christmas. Her first Christmas night supper years ago was given out of her kindness and thoughtfulness for these friends.

The party has grown through the years until now no less than twenty are invited but usually thirty or more come, friends of friends, who call up and ask if they may drop in. Drop in to this hostess means come for supper and the evening. This party is not simply a crush of guests who mill about. They are all friends who appreciate her hospitality, enjoy her good food and the opportunity to be in the company which gathers at her home.

Her old-fashioned apartment, which is the main floor of a Washington house, is always fragrant with country pine and holly for the party. She uses candles everywhere for light, the most unusual ones being a very tall pair of Italian altar candles, which stand on the floor at the ends of the mantel and a dozen or so tall tapers in a many-branched, Mexican ceramic candelabra, which she places in the center of the buffet table. She uses her most beautiful embroidered Italian linen napkins and family silver; the table is bare except for huge Swedish straw hot-plate mats.

Menu always includes one or more roast boned turkeys, capons, or ducks in aspic, because this kind of roast slices economically and easily and is delicious. With it the hostess serves a hot casserole of southern corn-and-pimiento pudding, hot casserole of scalloped oysters and noodles, small hot rolls, pickle relish, and raisin chutney. Her dessert is always the same—small, open-face apple tarts, the pastry very rich, the sliced apples glazed with brown sugar and butter just before baking.

Her apartment is too small for dancing. But invariably there is someone from among her radio and TV friends who sings or plays the piano, or a friend back from an assignment in the Himalayas who shows a film made among the snows. One year a Bengalese attaché came early and stayed late and sat on the floor after supper and sang very sad, very funny Indian songs. Everybody sits on the floor, after the sofas and the chairs are full to listen to new records and old ones especially Christmas music from all over the world. One year it was a collection of records made with children in many countries singing their native Christmas songs, not only endearing but amusing because so many of these foreign-made records of tiny, eager voices and strange instruments included "I'm Dreaming Of A White Christmas."

Many other hosts and hostesses, in large or small cities and towns, can follow this same plan of an open house on Christmas night, for friends who are away from their families. The menu can be as simple as sandwiches, fruitcake, and coffee. A more elaborate menu might be: a huge, English-style veal-and-ham pie, served cold with hot spoon bread and a green vegetable such as stuffed zucchini; for dessert, Christmas fruitcake and brick ice cream, or ice cream molds in bell, star, wreath, or other Christmas shapes, with coffee.

More Decoration Ideas Fill a large copper or silver bowl with pine branches and red apples. Or, make a Renaissance centerpiece with a handsome wide vase or epergne. Fill it with a gorgeous pineapple, the tips of its spikes gilded, large bunches of pale green and deep blue or black grapes, oranges, kumquats, crabapples, and luxurious pears, with gilded walnuts and Brazil nuts here and there. Let grapes trail onto green leaves arranged around the vase on the table.

Paint old candlesticks white. Place tall red candles in them. Surround with matching low bowls containing red carnations, white carnations, holly. Use two of each, the flower bowls alternating with holly bowls.

Gild pine cones, and do the same with artificial grapes, apples, pears, oranges. Make a long centerpiece of pine branches and the gilded fruit and cones. Use gold-painted candles in tall sticks on this table.

Fun To The Last Moment Hang a Christmas grab bag on the inside of the house door *after* your guests have arrived. Filled with small, wrapped dime-store gifts and wrapped candies and cookies, it extends any Christmas party to the last minute of the evening. Guests pull out a gift before leaving. Or hang miniature filled red and green stockings in a bunch on the inside of the door. Each guest receives a stocking the last thing before he leaves your party. Wrapped candies, nuts, nonsense gifts add fun to these.

New Year's Eve

The Watch Night party can be almost any kind of party you want to give—a dinner followed by dancing, a costume dance and midnight supper, a quiet or noisily gay reception and open house for a mixture of young and old friends, a small come-in-for-coffee party. These are familiar traditional New Year's Eve parties all over America. But something different?

Family Song Fest If you are interested in music, you can give a musical party, a wonderful party to celebrate the outgoing old year. Let it be music of many moods, for the spirit of the last night of the old year is both sad and happy. One party for a musical New Year's Eve is a Family Song Fest, singing and holiday fun made by the members of the family and their friends.

Invitations A few days before Christmas give the invitations by telephone or note for your New Year's Eve party, to friends who sing perhaps in a church or school choir and others who play the piano, guitar, cello or some other instrument. Include the school, church, or glee club director or someone else experienced in group singing. If no such person is available, let the evening of music develop as it will on suggestions from guests.

Music In your early planning include the buying or borrowing of song books, sheet music, and music racks from friends, school, or musical clubs. Arrange to have plenty of comfortable chairs, benches, and hassocks, as well as good lighting around the piano and music stands. Sheet music of the easily singable songs of the Twenties, now revived, might be borrowed from friends or bought. Old English ballads, madrigal collections, local school songs, American mountain songs, songs of childhood, western songs, and many others are available through music stores, public library lending service, and from the collections of choral and glee groups. Or if your music stores cannot supply what you want, write music publishers for catalogues and prices in time to order music and have it mailed to you for the party.

Since the musical party is meant to salute the midnight hour, it should not begin too early—nine o'clock at the earliest. By eleven, tired singers and instrumentalists should be refreshed with food and drink, then provided with a cold sparkling punch in which to toast the New Year and each other.

Menu After a week of holiday feasting the menu for supper on this last night of the old year need not be elaborate. Hostesses in your crowd may usually serve sandwiches and coffee or cake and coffee— either combination is suitable for this occasion. If you may want to make a more gala New Year's Eve feast, serve something hot from a big

Also see "Teen-Age Parties," Chapter 5

chafing dish on the buffet table, such as, jambalaya on toasted crackers, with tiny rice croquettes reheated in a casserole in the oven, then brought to the table and placed on a table warmer. With these, serve a dessert of special cinnamon apples, fruitcake, and coffee, and a little later, the punch for midnight toasts. If supper is served at midnight, begin with the punch and toasts.

Decoration Like the assembling of the sheet music, the decoration and accessories should be planned and bought or made well in advance of the busy holiday season. For the buffet supper, large paper napkins with Happy New Year and the date stamped in gold on them can be ordered through department stores, novelty shops, and stationers.

Buy gay paper party hats, one for each guest, and group the hats in the center of the table as decoration until supper time, then distribute them to be worn for the toasting to the New Year.

Silver and gold foliage (green branches of various kinds dipped in or sprayed with silver and gold metallic paints) can be ordered from a florist. These make handsome effects if used in two or more large arrangements with pine on mantel, chests, and elsewhere in the room. To go with these, gold, silver, and red candles in tall candlesticks on the buffet table. The table can remain bare or be covered with a metallic gold paper cloth. For this buy rolls or packages of gold Christmas wrapping paper; press paper on wrong side with warm, not hot, iron to remove folds and creases; seal together enough strips of the paper on the wrong side, using gummed tape, to make a covering for the buffet table. With small sharp scissors cut a scalloped or other decorative edge around it.

The gold and silver theme can be echoed in the bright brass of a coffee warmer, casserole trivet, and other table accessories. You can also use handsome silver accessories, such as chafing dishes, coffee service, holders for casserole, platter for fruitcake, and serving dishes for cinnamon apples.

Here are recipes for the jambalaya and special cinnamon apples. See the Index for the quantity punch recipe.

JAMBALAYA LOUISIANA

2 onions, peeled and diced
½ pound ham, cut in narrow strips
½ pound bulk sausage
1 tablespoon bacon fat
½ cup chopped tomatoes
½ clove garlic, peeled and mashed
Small piece red pepper pod, chopped fine

1 tablespoon minced parsley
¼ teaspoon dried thyme
2 cups stock or bouillon
¾ cup washed, uncooked rice
1 dozen drained oysters
Salt and pepper

Cook onions, ham, and sausage in bacon fat in large saucepan until sausage is well browned; add tomatoes, garlic, the red pepper pod, parsley and thyme. Cook 5 minutes; remove garlic and discard it. Add stock or bouillon; bring to boiling, add rice. Cover and simmer about 18 minutes, or until rice is tender but not soft. Remove from heat. Let cool, and keep in covered bowl in refrigerator until suppertime. Reheat in a large chafing dish or two smaller chafing dishes; when hot and simmering, add drained oysters and cook only until their edges curl. Serve jambalaya at once on toasted crackers. This recipe makes 8 or more servings.

Without a chafing dish, the final stage of this cooking can be done in a casserole in the oven while crackers toast. As soon as oysters are hot and edges curled, bring casserole to table and place on candle warmer or electric warmer for buffet service. This recipe can be doubled—cook in a large kettle, then finish in two large chafing dishes, or in two matching casseroles as described.

SPECIAL CINNAMON APPLES

12 tart apples	3 cups water
Cloves	Small glass apple jelly, about
2 cups sugar	1 cup
6 tablespoons red cinnamon candy drops	

Wash, pare, and core apples; stick 2 or 3 cloves in each. Cook sugar, cinnamon candies, and water together for 5 minutes in large, shallow saucepan or kettle. Carefully place apples in syrup, simmer until apples are tender but not mushy. Baste often with the syrup. When apples are done, lift each with a wide shallow spoon to serving platter. Stir jelly into remaining syrup until it melts. Pour over apples. Let cool.

Serve plain or with whipped cream. If all syrup is used up in cooking apples, make fresh amount, stir jelly in as described, and pour over warm apples. Let cool, and serve. Recipe makes 12 servings.

New Year's Day

Guest Luncheon on New Year's Day College students home for the holidays are the excuse in some families for a luncheon on New Year's Day. They invite their friends. The family invites one or two people, a man or career girl who couldn't go home for the holidays. This is also a day when the city career girl or a gourmet bachelor likes to serve luncheon to two or three friends in their own small apartments.

The secret of a relaxed, easy holiday luncheon for any hostess is: keep the menu small and very good. Serve it in an informal or unusual setting, for example, the playroom lunch counter. In very cold weather serve on trays or small tables around the living-room fireplace or on a bridge table in a sunny window. Other suggestions are the dining-room table set with amusingly different wares, such as Swedish pottery and a big Swedish straw figure for the centerpiece, or Mexican peasant wares, or a large French soup marmite on a table warmer, with French Quimper or other peasant bowls and wares. A coarse linen mat and napkin set goes with any of these, and so do woven straw mats and mats of cork with hand-printed linen napkins.

Menus Here are two for this kind of day: oyster stew, toasted crusty French rolls, apple pie, cheese, and coffee. Or, start with tomato juice, then beefsteak-and-kidney pie, endive and grapefruit salad, corn sticks, baked caramel custard, and coffee.

New Year's Day Eggnog Party On the first day of the new year it is an old custom in many parts of the world to go calling in the afternoon, or to stay home and open the house to other folks who are out making calls. Eggnog has come to be the libation associated with this hospitality.

Eggnog was probably originated by some inspired English physician or housewife as a builder-upper for frail, anemic, and puny children. It is delicious as well as filling and strengthening, and it is no wonder that it emerged from the nursery into the social scene as an English winter holiday drink. It appeared on the Christmas dinner tables in southern Colonial America, especially in Virginia, and is still found in large Thanksgiving and Christmas menus. Today it is also the most popular beverage to offer New Year's Day callers.

Eggnog should be thick, rich, smooth, and very cold and it should be served in punch glasses, or any relatively small glass.

A good eggnog tastes even better if tasty sandwiches are served with it, such as very thin anchovy sandwiches, others of water cress or chopped ham, smoked turkey, smoked tongue, sliced olives, smoked salmon and sturgeon. Avoid serving cookies and cake with eggnog, except very black, fruit-filled fruitcake.

One Southern hostess always serves small, hot corn sticks and beaten biscuit with eggnog at her New Year's open house. Another hostess, a New York painter, serves an assortment of delicious toasted crackers and tiny pretzels with eggnog. A Florida college teacher who has open house for her senior students on New Year's Day is famous for the thin toast strips lightly buttered and delicately seasoned with mixed spice, which she serves with mugs of eggnog. She serves one round only, because her once-a-year hospitality menu includes, besides eggnog, a supper of grilled sandwiches, Caesar salad, and coffee which the students prepare themselves, in the patio if the weather is fine.

Eggnog, like tea, may be served from the dining-room table or a cleared table in the living room on which small napkins, small plates, sandwiches, and spoons are arranged as for tea. The spoons are needed because a properly made eggnog is too thick to drink. It is sipped, but a spoon makes it easier to get the last third of the glass's contents. It can be also served in the kitchen into glasses or mugs, and passed on a tray to guests, with small folded napkins, sandwiches, and spoons.

The eggnog punch bowl or pitcher should rest in a larger bowl of cracked ice as long as there is any of the egg mixture left.

Here are recipes for two non-alcoholic eggnogs:

EGGNOG 1.

4 eggs	2 cups light cream
½ cup sugar	2 tablespoons rum flavoring
⅛ teaspoon salt	1 cup heavy cream
2 cups milk	Freshly grated nutmeg

Beat eggs, sugar, and salt in the top of a 2-quart double boiler. Add milk and light cream slowly, stirring, and mix well. Cook over hot water, stirring, until mixture barely coats metal spoon. Chill. Stir in flavoring. Whip cream stiff and fold into mixture. Pour into cold punch bowl set in a larger bowl of cracked ice. Sprinkle the top with grated nutmeg. Serve at once with punch ladle into glasses. Makes about 10 servings.

EGGNOG 2.

1½ cups sugar	1 quart light cream
6 eggs	2 tablespoons vanilla or
Salt	sherry flavoring
1 quart milk	Nutmeg

Beat 1 cup sugar into egg yolks in 3-quart double boiler. Add ½ teaspoon salt. Stir in milk and cream slowly. Cook, stirring, until mixture coats metal spoon. Let cool. Add ¼ teaspoon salt to egg whites and beat stiff; add remaining ½ cup sugar. Beat well. Mix into chilled yolk mixture with half of the vanilla or sherry. Taste, and if not sweet enough add remaining vanilla. Chill 4 hours in refrigerator. Pile lightly into punch cups. Serve with a dash of grated nutmeg on each. Makes about 12 to 14 servings.

Lincoln's Birthday

The birthday of Abraham Lincoln, February 12th, is more often the inspiration for serious school, political club, and community meetings than for home entertaining. But if you plan a tea or some other party for the date and want to link your affair with the memory of the great president, you can do it by using various small favors and table accessories designed with this special seasonal and historical atmosphere.

The novelty and stationery stores display many ideas inspired by the Lincoln birthday anniversary: flags of various sizes and kinds, flag-decorated favors such as small boxes to hold candy or nuts, place cards, cardboard log cabins, tiny spinning wheels (for Lincoln's homespun clothes), small stovepipe hats and other such items. Use the best you can find of such accessories on the table for any party on that day.

Backwoods Supper For the entertaining idea suggested below, a bouquet of mixed, old-fashioned garden flowers, if you can find them at this time of year at the florist, belong in a squat pottery jug on the table for authentic color. If you own homespun or hand-woven tablecloths and napkins, this is the time to use them, as well as any antique pewter, wrought iron, and early American china and pottery. Of course, you can use any simple, attractive table ware.

Menu To carry Lincoln-period atmosphere into any menu for the day, the dishes of his part of the country and his era can be featured with good effect. They include sausage cakes, baked smoked pork butt with mustard greens, bacon, game, such as quail or pheasant as well as duck and turkey, corn bread baked as a thin pone or in sticks in iron stick pans, baked hominy, hominy croquettes, creamed hominy, chutney, tomato-pickle relishes, baked apples or apple pie, poundcake, and coffee.

Several English desserts were known and served in that part of the Middle West—flummery, floating island, and similar custards, usually decorated with jelly and served with poundcake. But it is doubtful if the Lincoln cabin knew them.

But tea and poundcake or coffee and a plain cake suggest themselves as pleasant refreshment for any simple tea given on this holiday.

A Backwoods Supper menu made up of some of the dishes listed above might be served on this date to a political campaign discussion group or any other guests. One suggested combination: baked smoked pork butt with sauerkraut (in place of greens), small hominy croquettes, corn bread and peach butter, baked apples, and coffee.

St. Valentine's Day

The lighthearted, colorful, decorative accessories of St. Valentine's Day add feminine prettiness to any party at which they appear. Many hostesses deliberately postpone a bridge luncheon or some other form of entertaining for their women friends until February 14th in order to use the charming Valentine's theme of flowers and hearts, light colors, and sentimental verse to spark their table and enliven the atmosphere. This theme also is especially appropriate for engagement luncheons, showers, teas, dinners, and other parties connected with marriage plans.

Decoration in the St. Valentine's theme is no problem for any party of that date, because the designers who create the world of paper novelties for such use seem especially devoted to the third century saint for whom the day was named. Birds are supposed to begin their spring mating on St. Valentine's Day, and the world of elves and flowers and woodsy people, the fairy world, awakens to the sounds of spring, still unheard by human ears until some weeks later.

To celebrate these events valentines of lace paper, flowers, birds, ribbons, hearts, and verse are in plentiful supply; so are paper hearts in pink, red, blue and other colors, heart-shaped boxes large and small, heart-shaped candies wrapped in beautiful new foil papers, paper tablecloths covered with hearts or with valentine verses or flowers and paper napkins to match are in the paper goods departments, novelty, and stationery shops. For the kitchen there are heart-shaped biscuit and cookie cutters, large heart cake pans, heart-shaped molds of various sizes for gelatins, ice cream, and mousse.

St. Valentine's Day Bridge Luncheon A bridge luncheon for serious players is not elaborate and long drawn out and the dishes are prefera-

Also see "Children's Parties," Chapter 4

bly simple rather than rich and heavy. A menu formula many bridge hostesses follow is a salad as a main course, delicate but delicious dessert, with hot or iced beverage.

For this luncheon the decoration can be pink paper or linen tablecloth and napkins. Buy white lacepaper shelf edging and outline a large heart in the center of the cloth-covered table (see sketch). Inside this outlined heart place small, red heart-shaped boxes, one for each guest. Fill boxes with old-fashioned heart candies with messages on them, or if your candy stores can't supply these, use any other good heart-shaped candies.

At one side of the heart, stand upright a fancily decorated, larger heart-shaped box of red or pink satin or cardboard. It should be thickly decorated with sequins, lace rosettes, rosebuds, and ribbon bows, all in pink, white, and red. This is easily made, using a heart-shaped candy box, of which many styles are available at this time of year. Glue or gummed tape will hold the decorations in place; scatter sequins can be bought at novelty and stationery shops. Fill this gay box with a prize for the players, such as handkerchiefs, a pretty scarf, stockings, or a heart-decorated glasses case.

Menu Serve a Waldorf salad on crisp lettuce with jellied cranberry heart. Garnish the salad heart with a mixture of cream and Roquefort cheeses smoothly blended together; use your pastry decorating tube to place the swirl of cheese on the gelatin heart. Have heart-shaped biscuits with red currant jelly, and for dessert, white chiffon cake baked in a heart-shaped pan and thickly iced with pink frosting. Decorate cake top with small red candy hearts, or serve strawberry ice cream in heart molds, garnished with whole fresh or quick-frozen strawberries. Hot or iced tea or coffee.

Idea for St. Valentine's Dance Buy an assortment of different lace-paper valentines. Have on hand two large silver, glass, or pottery bowls. Cut the valentines in half, drop one half in one bowl, the other half in the second. To choose partners for the first dance, let men draw from one bowl, women from the other, and find their partners by matching the halves together.

Menu for St. Valentine's Tea Serve heart-shaped cookies iced with white frosting and decorated with small pink candy hearts; white layer cake baked in heart pans, frosted with white icing and coconut; heart-shaped sandwiches, such as white bread with cranberry jelly filling, currant jelly, sliced chicken, cucumber, water cress. Have hot tea and coffee, with their accessories of sugar, milk, cream, cloves, sliced lemon, and small heart candies.

Washington's Birthday

The personality and housekeeping of Martha Washington have been an inspiration to generations of American hostesses. The first president's wife knew how to dispense hospitality. Good food, good conversation, pleasant surroundings combined to make her fame as a hostess at Mount Vernon. In the succeeding years, on February 22nd, the birthday of George Washington, many American homemakers serve the same kind of dishes that were enjoyed by Washington and his family and guests. Afternoon coffee parties were popular in his day, and his wife served delicious foods with the coffee.

Washington's Birthday Coffee Party Modern coffee parties have long been popular as February 22nd entertainment for club, committee, sorority, alumnae reunion, and other groups, and for afternoon at-homes. Enhanced by some of the Martha Washington foods, they take on special significance and interest.

Decoration For this, there is the usual abundance of paper novelties in small cherry trees, ribbon-decorated paper hatchets, small military drums to hold candies and nuts, from which the best can be chosen to use on a buffet table. Red, white, and blue flowers, whatever is in your florist shops, belong on the table as a centerpiece. The buffet table may be left bare or covered with a handsome cloth. Napkins may be of tea size or larger to match the cloth, or they may be assorted paper napkins, some in red, others white, some blue, or white decorated with the date and a little Washington tricorn hat or hatchet or drum.

Menu Besides coffee serve tea, also, and perhaps a frozen trifle, which is cake and ice cream together, or cider sherbet, a white nut cake, and gingerbread. All of these were offered on the Mount Vernon table.

This menu is sweeter than the modern taste for afternoon coffee foods. You may want to add tiny hot cheese canapés or assorted savory sandwiches, such as cucumber, water cress, anchovy, thin ham or smoked tongue, to round it out for present-day taste.

Here are the modernized recipes from the original cookery note-book at Mount Vernon. The delicious gingerbread was the one served by Martha Washington to Lafayette on his visit to Mount Vernon a few years after the end of the Revolution.

SPICED GINGERBREAD

½ cup shortening

2 tablespoons grated orange peel

½ cup brown sugar (packed)

3 eggs

2¾ cups sifted all-purpose flour

1 teaspoon soda

½ teaspoon salt

2 tablespoons powdered ginger

1 teaspoon *each,* powdered cinnamon, mace, nutmeg

1 cup dark baking molasses

¼ cup strained orange juice

¼ cup brewed coffee

Start oven at Moderate (350°F.). Cream shortening, beat orange peel and sugar in until smooth and light. Beat eggs in gradually, mixing well. Sift dry ingredients together three times. Add dry ingredients alternately with molasses, orange juice, and coffee to shortening mixture, and blend well. Pour into well greased pan 8-by-12-by-2½ inches. Bake for 30 to 35 minutes in Moderate oven (350°F.). Let cool. Recipe makes 24 or more servings.

CIDER SHERBET

2 tablespoons plain gelatin	2 cups sugar
1 quart sweet cider	¼ cup lemon juice
2 cups water	

Soak gelatin in ½ cup of the cider. Boil sugar and water together for 10 minutes in a 2½-quart enamel saucepan. Remove from heat; stir in soaked gelatin until dissolved. Add remaining cider and lemon juice and stir. Pour into refrigerator trays and freeze with refrigerator turned to coldest point, for about 1 hour or until of mushy consistency. Scrape mixture out into chilled bowl and beat. Return to trays. Freeze about 2 hours, or until firm enough to serve. Recipe makes 2 quarts, 8 to 12 servings.

FROZEN TRIFLE

2 egg yolks	½ cup orange juice
⅜ cup sugar	½ cup chopped toasted
1/16 teaspoon salt	almonds
1 cup milk	½ cup or more raspberry or
1 cup heavy cream	strawberry jam
1 slice plain butter cake 1 inch thick, cut to fit refrigerator tray	

Beat egg yolks, sugar, and salt together in saucepan. Scald milk and pour slowly over egg mixture, stirring. Cook slowly, stirring constantly until it coats a metal spoon. Chill. Whip cream stiff. Place cake in refrigerator tray. Pour orange juice over the cake slowly so that it absorbs the juice. Sprinkle with ¼ cup almonds; spread with jam. Combine whipped cream with egg mixture, pour over cake, nuts, and jam. Cover top with remaining nuts. Freeze about 2 hours or until firm enough to cut. This recipe makes 8 servings.

CHILDREN'S PARTIES

General Planning

• Indoors or out, the secret of a successful party for children is to keep them busy, but not long at any one game and not necessarily all doing the same thing.

• *Outdoor Play Equipment* can make young guests from four to eight happy for part of the afternoon. Small barrels, stumps, a tent, large boxes to climb on and crawl through are examples. Toy departments and manufacturers have new educational climbing equipment and jungle gyms of various shapes, teeter-totters, and rope swings.

• *Outdoor Games* such as croquet, toss the ring (child's quoits), and other familiars are favorites with children from six to ten. Archery, running games, three-legged games are fine for slightly older children. Twenty minutes to half an hour of doing something they like and have done before dissolves children's shyness and puts them at ease for the rest of the party, which may take place indoors or on a porch and not include active games.

• *Costumes for Parties* can be made using patterns shown in all large pattern companies' magazines and quarterlies. Or costumes can be bought in toy departments of large stores, in many shops, and from party services and costume companies.

• *Table Accessories* Paper plates in various shapes, mugs, and other containers, as well as tablecloths and napkins, paper hats small enough

Also see "Family and Community Parties," Chapter 8; "Family and School Parties," Chapter 9; "Folk Dance Parties," Chapter 11; and "Outdoor Entertaining," Chapter 12 for the tiniest birthday celebrants as well as larger ones for older children, flame-proof crepe paper, paper favors of great variety and interest—decorations of many kinds are sold in stationery and toy shops, in paper goods departments of stores, or can be ordered from catalogues of the Dennison Company, 411 Fifth Avenue, New York 16, N.Y. This company also publishes *Party Ideas,* a magazine full of detailed instructions for making favors and decorations for many kinds of parties.

• *All Wares* on the party table for children should be easy to handle, a mug with handle, instead of large glass, for milk or lemonade, small plastic and paper containers, plates large enough to hold everything at once, fork and spoon light in weight and smaller than adult silver.

• *Refreshments* should be familiar foods, especially for very young children, need no cutting, and should be regular meal dishes, since ideally a children's party menu is served as luncheon or supper. (Note menus that follow.)

• *Table and Chairs* should be of comfortable height and size for children, different sizes for different ages. The toddlers like their own very small furniture and feel at ease with it; older children resent too-small chairs and prefer to be uncomfortable on adult chairs. Between toddlers and sub-teens there are medium-size chairs and medium-height tables, which are ideal for play and meals.

• *Put Breakables and Small Objects Away* in all rooms where children will play, eat, or be entertained.

• *For Any Children's Party* a book such as *Singing Games* prepared by the National Recreation Association, Department G, 8 West Eighth Street, New York 11, N.Y., is a great asset. It contains twenty-six songs, each with description of a game that children from four to eight years can enjoy playing. Order by mail, fifty cents by check or money order.

• *Invitations and Decorations* For Western and outdoor parties, write to National Wildlife Federation, 232 Carroll Street, N.W., Washington 12, D.C. for sheets of their beautiful, colorful gummed stickers. These are usually free, but a small contribution, ($1.00) is sent by many to help the work of the Federation. Birds, fish, flowers, animals, outdoor scenes, sportsmen are subjects. Use them on invitations. Or tape one of the stickers, picture side up, to outside bottom of child's drinking glass, then cover bottom of sticker with gummed tape.

• As for all other entertaining, plan well in advance for the children's parties. Discuss with your child or children what kind of party they want. Include in your preparations all they can do to help, such as making invitations and decorations and helping to clear and arrange rooms.

Plan the menu, consulting with them; make or buy favors, centerpiece, prizes and gifts well ahead of party date. Wrap the prizes and gifts in advance before party day. These gifts as well as those the guests bring either should be opened at the beginning of the party or placed on the table as favors to be opened when the birthday child opens his. Plan games, buying or making any accessories needed for them. Order new records for game music, or for some other phase of the party.

The day of the party should start early for you, with the final clearance of the rooms in which the children will play or be entertained, placing final decorations, arranging party table, preparing a place for children's wraps and for those of the mothers who come to help or simply to escort their children. One or two mothers, as suggested in various party plans which follow should be asked to help with games, and whatever else is needed.

• *Party Services* plan parties, provide invitations which you or your child address and send, supply foods and party wares, prizes and favors (gifts) without which a child's party is a failure, costumes if you want them or at least gay paper hats for various ages, leis of artificial or fresh flowers and other accessories, and even such delights as a live donkey or pony to ride, or a magician with a live rabbit in his hat, or a clown who plays wonderful tunes on an accordian, or a puppet show or a story teller or reader. All this is available, at a price, for mothers who work and have no time to plan parties, and for parents who would rather spend money than time, or who haven't the strength or ingenuity for entertaining but still want their children to have parties like other children.

Their services can be still more costly if these professional entertainers set up amusing party tents in the yard or garden or redecorate your living room to look like a zoo. They can also supply gay covers for party tables, and all sorts of delightful devices in which the birthday cake or favors are concealed.

They will provide at least two or three directors or party managers. These patient, skillful, firm, and experienced men and women are party craftsmen who take charge of every detail, so that a busy or bored parent has only to look in from time to time during the afternoon to see that joy is unrestrained and that there is no fighting, or lone brooding on the sidelines.

If you want to use such services for the whole job or for parts of it, consult them two or three weeks before the party date. They need time to plan, shop, and work out your ideas and theirs. In large cities consult the telephone directory for names and addresses. You can also get information about such services from children's departments of large stores, at toy stores, caterers, and florists. In smaller cities, ask at the local newspaper office, florists, and caterers.

Birthday Parties

The most important parties in a child's life are his birthday parties. At a birthday party he is the center of things. It is *his* birthday. And at the same time he is giving his friends a good time. That's quite an ego build-up, and usually he reacts as the psychologists predict: he is happy at his party, outgoing, and enjoys every minute of the games, refreshments, blowing the candles, and opening his presents as well as giving small gifts to the guests. He is still happy as he says good-by to his friends, when their parents come to gather them back into their own clans.

The Toddlers Some mothers say that the age at which children are conscious of the meaning of their birthday party is five or older. Others say that even their youngest of two, three, and four not only have fun wearing paper hats and counting the candles on their cake, but also that they understand the meaning of the celebration.

To take care of the child who isn't so precocious, as well as his more advanced host of three or four years, the toddler party must be very simple. Mothers bring these children at an hour for which you have asked them. This is preferably late afternoon, so that there is half an hour of social activities to be followed by refreshments.

Decoration Bright balloons added to the room in which the children are entertained, and perhaps little leis (wreaths) of bright artificial or fresh flowers for both boys and girls to wear and to keep, of course, may provide sufficient entertainment as well as decoration.

If you can give these young children a very brief, lively, noisy puppet show, with not too complicated a plot, or seat them in a circle on the floor or in little chairs and give them a simple story by an experienced story teller, that's enough. Supper comes next, then home to bed.

Menu Supper should be about what they would have at home—for example, chicken hash, finely cut green beans or baked zucchini, small buttered biscuit, small glass of milk, the birthday cake cut in small pieces and served with ice cream.

The cake should be bright and colorful with pink icing and pink candles, or a mixture of several colors of candles on white, pale yellow, or orange-juice frosting. The table should be lively with color; a pink or blue paper cloth and napkins, pink or blue wares, pink sipper straws for the milk—or use rainbow colors, pink, yellow, green, blue all together. The centerpiece may be a group of small-children's party hats, very glossy and pretty. These are handed to the children as soon as they are seated at the table.

In addition there should be small favors or gifts for every child, such as bright snappers to open and blow, or favor balls which open and reveal several small gifts inside. Or small home-wrapped gifts such as tiny animals, dolls, engines, for boys and girls. These are sold in pastry shops, florists, stationery, and toy shops.

For the Family That Likes to Plan Things This report from a young Minneapolis mother contains many ideas for parties for children from two to the teens. Here are her party formulas:

"We have five children, which means five birthday parties every year. Our youngest's recently celebrated second birthday was no problem, simply a matter of adding a little sparkle to the evening meal and explaining to her that the pretty color was for her birthday. She loved it. We brightened our usual dinner time (no guests) by hanging pink and silver balloons from the dining-room chandelier, using pink paper napkins and serving a pink cake (from the freezer) adding two pink candles to it. Balloons and candles are so exciting for young children that plenty of party excitement was created just by having them at our evening meal.

"We've had a rule for some years that the birthday child could invite to his party *only the number of children he has years*. It has worked wonderfully. But our seven-year-old boy prefers, instead of a party, to have his one closest friend for the day, and take a trip to the zoo, or a train ride to St. Paul, or a visit to a local fire house, then his choice of the foods he likes best in dinner at home.

"Balloons were important in our nine-year-old's birthday in January. After lunch for him and nine of his friends, they were to go skating on the big lake near our home. Because I felt responsible for the children while they were our guests, I had to have some way of identifying them in the crowds on the lake. Helium-filled balloons, white with red and blue stars, were tied to their chairs at luncheon on long strings, which permitted the balloons to float to the ceiling. When the children went out to the lake, each child had his balloon tied onto one wrist. It was a gray, cold day but it looked warmer and brighter with the children racing around on their skates, their balloons flying after them.

"Party-giving without help in the house is a challenge. We've solved it partly because the older children love to feel they are helping, by setting the table, leading the games, and planning a treasure hunt, which is a popular feature of their parties. Our nine-year-old planned a treasure hunt of the simplest sort for his six-year-old sister's birthday party. He hand-printed each child's name on a slip of paper, tied it to a long ribbon with a prize on the other end, hid the prizes under furniture, and let each child find her own. It wasn't very neat but it wasn't complicated, and the children loved it.

"Children under the teen years are not very demanding in parties. The important thing is having their friends come to the house. Every party is either lunch or supper, to avoid, in the middle of the afternoon, the type of food that sends a child home too full of sweets to eat his regular evening meal. Their mothers are grateful.

"The favorite menus for our children's luncheons and suppers, no matter what the theme of the party, is something filling such as a casserole of chopped chicken hearts cooked with browned rice, inexpensive, easy to serve, delicious. Gradually they have accepted other new things (instead of hamburgers, frankfurters, and spaghetti). Shrimp, lobster, and steak are favorites. They are expensive, yes, but we do not serve them often. I'm glad to feed the children a good protein meal, and a vegetable; spinach is popular again, thanks to the return of the old "Popeye" cartoons on TV; raw carrots, celery, cucumbers are eaten in strips; lettuce is eaten without dressing, out of hand—everyone wants to be a bunny. Dessert is standard: cake with candles, and ice cream, the cake served in small portions because I find that children don't care for large pieces of cake.

"Party Invitations Are Simple We like the children to do as much for themselves as possible. Sometimes they telephone their friends a few days in advance—not too early, because children get impatient, or forget. And they now know that they must remind their friends to ask their mothers for permission to come to the party. Other times they write notes, which they distribute by hand, simply asking their friends to come to a party, giving date, time, and our address. They make up their own guest lists. We interfere only when all the little boys except one in the Cub Scout group are invited, or all the little girls but one in the block; we remind them that someone's feelings might be hurt and they usually take that into consideration.

"One of the most successful birthday celebrations any one ever gave around here was planned by a neighbor who wanted to take her little boy and his friends of six to eight years on an outing. It had to be something different. It was arranged for them to visit a scrap iron company, where they had a chance to watch fabulous machinery at work crushing whole automobiles! Afterwards they had treats at an ice cream parlor sort of place, and then home. No work and no mess for mother, and a wonderful time for the children.

"One other thing we have tried to observe in birthday entertaining, and that is, we like the birthday child to give his guests some kind of present. Part of his planning of his own party is deciding on a gift for each guest. Usually it is a ten-cent store pinwheel, or one of those wonderful, match-box-size automobiles, and similar small items, which the child wraps and has ready days before the party.

"Some of our parties are dress-up, depending on the season and activity. The Christmas party always is and so are little girls' birthday parties—pity the child who doesn't have party shoes. All little girls seem to be born with fashion consciousness, and they examine each other's clothing in detail before party fun can begin.

"One Christmas, and also a birthday party, was based on a Mexican legend of the Christmas donkey, which bears a great bag of good things for poor children. In Mexico on Christmas a giant, gaily decorated bag of toys and goodies is thrown into the middle of the floor and beaten with sticks until it bursts and the goodies roll out for all present.

"For our Christmas afternoon open house the neighbor children were invited for 4 to 5 o'clock. (Their parents came at the same time to drink eggnog.) Our boys decorated a huge, heavy paper grocery bag with crayons, strips of crepe paper, and bits of bright ribbon. They drew funny faces on all sides as well as on the bottom of the bag. They filled it with wrapped candies and little trinkets, such as whistles and penny dolls. The bag was hung on a bright cord from a living-room rafter. Each child was blindfolded and given a go at the bag with a stick decorated with bright ribbon streamers. After several swats, he had to pass the stick to another child, and blindfold her or him. One finally succeeded in breaking the bag, then everyone scrambled to fill pockets with the treats.

"It was funny, lively, and without the children knowing it all went into a movie, which was being made by the family camera fan. Christmas cookies and lemonade were passed. Then with their parents they trotted off home. End of party."

Children's Parties in City Apartments There is little room in most city apartments for games. City mothers appreciate the kind of birthday party, which consists of a trip to see something of interest, then back home to luncheon or supper. For such trips, keep the guest list small, and always have a guest mother or two along to round up the stragglers who want to be last on the bus, or last into an elevator.

Besides the obvious pleasures, such as seeing a new children's movie, there are museums, public buildings, art galleries where children's work is shown, zoos, small-children's pet zoos, a ride on a sightseeing bus or boat, visit to a big market house, to docks where boats are loaded and unloaded, and many other things and places. In most cases, permission must be obtained before even a small group of children can be shown around a dock or building; in some instances a company police-man or guard can be asked to act as guide.

The trip should not last long, the actual sightseeing part of it about half an hour, especially if children are under eight. Luncheon or supper should be ready when they return to the birthday child's home. This means that all preparations for the meal were completed earlier in the day, and that a kitchen helper is on hand. And the luncheon or supper should be bright with centerpiece, party hats, gifts, noisy blowers, and a cake with candles.

Costume Parties for Children

You can omit some of the suggested decoration and entertainment from these parties and still please young guests.

Circus Clown Party This is a costume party for children six to eight years old.

Invitations Use child's small note paper with clown or circus tent or some other circus motif on it, or a clown-party printed card. Your child might use plain, bright pink note paper and with crayon or paint make a clown on it. Then he or she writes something like this to seven friends, four boys and three girls, or three boys and four girls, so that there are eight at the party, equal numbers of boys and girls.

> Dear Teddy: Please come to
> My Circus Party
> Saturday Afternoon, April 7th, from 4 to 5:30 o'clock.
> Be Sure to Wear A Clown Costume
>
> (signed) Dodey Brown
> 16 Hilltop Road

After invitations are mailed or delivered, you can telephone the mothers and assure them that the party refreshments will be the chil-dren's supper. Also ask one or two of them to help you with games and other chores at the party. Discuss these with them in detail as soon as your plans are complete.

Decorations Clear the playroom, family room, or living room for games. In the dining room make tent top by using strips of red and yellow flame-proof crepe paper about 12 inches wide and long enough to reach from chandelier or center of ceiling to side walls. Alternate the strips, one yellow, one red, around the room, until entire ceiling is hidden. Put a cluster of bright red and yellow balloons where strips start at the center of the ceiling or chandelier. Slant the strips downward to the walls, and fasten the ends to the walls with gummed tape (see sketch).

Use two bridge tables or round folding-leg tables for supper; place the tables with legs folded under them on low boxes with benches, stools, or little chairs around them. Cover the tables with bright striped cloths or circus paper tablecloths or use mats as shown.

The centerpiece on each table is a bought toy paper circus tent or one made by your child from colored paper and decorated with animals and clowns cut from magazines. Under each tent place two small stuffed circus animals, such as an elephant, horse, tiger, or seal. Have one of these for each girl at table, and add two small clown bean bags, one for each boy. Tie a narrow, striped ribbon around the neck of each animal and clown, and run the ribbon from the centerpiece out to the child's plate, with his or her name on a little card decorated with a circus clown or tent on the end of the ribbon. Or use clown centerpiece.

Use brightly-patterned pottery plates with large flower, animal, dot, or stripe pattern, or decorated paper plates. Have sturdy, not too large, goblets or mugs for beverage, bright yellow or orange sipper straws, and large yellow or orange paper napkins printed with circus figures.

Games Provide two toss-the-ring (children's quoits) sets or some other outdoor action game, which your child likes and which both boy and girl clowns play for the first part of the afternoon. One of the guest mothers can help keep score on this.

Circus Noise Game After twenty minutes or half an hour, they may come indoors and play this. Children sit on the floor or low stools or chairs in two rows facing each other. The first child at the beginning of one row starts the game. He is told to make a noise like a circus animal (roar like a lion, or bark and clap like a seal, etc.) but he must not tell which animal he is. The other children must guess which animal he is imitating. A hostess-helper writes down the name of the first child to guess right. The game continues down one row and up the other until all have roared, barked, neighed, etc. The child guessing right most times wins a prize, a clown doll for a girl, a book on the circus: *Children of the Big Top,* by M. Murray (Little, Brown), or coloring book of circus drawings for boy.

Supper Menu Individual casseroles of scalloped chicken-and-rice on serving plate, with buttered, small roll or jelly sandwich; milk or chocolate milk drink made in blender and served in a glass or mug, with brightly-striped sipper straws; ice cream in clown-shaped molds or a ball of ice cream with a clown face on it, made with raisins and a thin strip of candied cherry for a smiling mouth (see sketch); clown-face cookies, which are soft cookies, iced with pink, with the face made on each by using a wooden pick dipped in chocolate frosting.

As parents come to pick children up to go home, put a record on such as "Day of Fun at the Circus" (R.H. 4001, Schwann LP record catalogue).

Cowboy Roundup Party This is a costume party for seven- to ten-year-olds.

Invitations Use large folded note paper in tan or beige color. Let your party child write the invitations on it. On first page of folder he or she writes something like this, or whatever he wants to say to seven friends, four boys and three girls, or three boys and four girls, so that there are eight at the party, equal numbers of boys and girls:

Cowgirls and Cowboys!
Ride This'a Way
for the Roundup!

On inside of folder he or she writes:

At My House
Saturday Afternoon, September 10th
4 o'clock to Half past 5
Wear your Cowgirl (or Cowboy) Costume
Trail Rider, Pioneer, and Indian Costumes Welcome, Too.
Park All Guns At The Door.

(signed) Bobby Evans
504 Closter Street

(Invitations to girls say Cowgirl Costume, to boys, Cowboy Costume.)

As soon as invitations are mailed or delivered, you can telephone the mothers of the guests and explain that refreshments will be the evening meal; also, you will want to ask one or two to help with various jobs of the afternoon.

Decorations Use a cleared playroom or living room. Decorate with cowboy and Western photographs cut from magazines, posters or large Western travel pictures from local travel bureau offices, or large cowboy and horse drawings by your child.

Use screens or hang up a curtain to make a movie theatre with chairs for the audience and a money-taker at the entrance. Place signs outside the "theatre" giving the name of the picture, actors' names, and other details. Give children wooden pennies or buttons and charge admission according to height or age—so much for each inch or each year. If possible show them a movie of Western travel, such as Yosemite, Grand Canyon, California, or ranching country with plenty of horses. Or, borrow or rent a lantern and colored slides of the West showing ranch life, travel, and famous sights. The father of the birthday child, or a high-school student, or the film operator from local movie house can show movie or slides and tell the children about each scene.

If neither movie nor lantern slides is available, have a guitarist to play and sing Western songs, the children singing with him. If this isn't practical, let them listen and sing to records. They all sit in a circle, on the floor, and listen to cowboy and Western songs, many of which are available in LP recordings for children (lists available from Folkways Records, 117 West Forty-sixth Street, New York 36, N.Y.).

Here are favorites: "Cowboy Ballads," "Music of the Sioux and the Navajo" (notes for children on this), "Adventure of the Lone Ranger" (Decca), "American Folk Songs for Children," or any one of several records in the series called "Birds, Beasts, Bugs, and Fishes" and "Who Built America" folk songs. And of course, "Get Along Little Dogies" and "Home on the Range," both 10-inch LP Decca.

Chuck Wagon Decorations for dining room or wherever supper is served should include a chuck wagon. Use table and chairs of comfortable height for the children. Fasten a tall, slender pole to each corner of the table, wind the poles with a strip of orange crepe paper, then with a narrow strip of yellow. Fasten long streamers of both colors at the top of the poles.

Let the party child go to work and make a large sign to fasten either on the wall above the table or to fit between two of the poles. He can use a strip of yellow paper the right length and about a foot wide, and use deep orange crayon, or Magic Marker (from Dennison or a stationery shop), or water color or poster paints, and print CHUCK WAGON on it.

The Table He can also print a menu on the same kind of paper and hang it on the wall near the table. Leave the table bare, or use bright paper cloth and Western paper napkins with brands, horseshoes, cowboys and other scenes, and either decorated paper plates or bold pottery plates. The centerpiece on this table can be a toy horse complete with saddle, or a covered wagon complete with horses and drivers, or group of toy guitars, one for each guest, surrounded by small packages for each child containing a cowboy scarf and miniature toy horse or some other small Western toy from the ten-cent store.

Tie packages with rope (twine) loop, one end over centerpiece horse's saddle or neck or over covered wagon, and trail out other end to the guest's plates with a Western place card on it. This card may have a brand (initials of the guest) or a horseshoe with guest's initials or name inside it. Your party child can make these cards with your help.

Menu Chuck Wagon Stew (lamb or beef); Ranchers' Biscuits (small buttered soft rolls); Roundup Ice Cream (vanilla with nuts or dates in it); Sunset Cookies or Cake (orange frosting); Pardner's Drink (milk flavored with chocolate or mashed banana from blender, or hot cocoa). Include bright sipper straws for the cold drinks.

The record mentioned in the Circus party ("Fun at the Circus") has a "Roundup" on its other side, to play as the supper comes to an end and children prepare to leave.

Gypsy Party This is a costume party for eight- to twelve-year-olds. The success of this party depends on its music, and hiring or finding someone who will contribute his services as a gypsy violinist. You may also feature a story teller (hired), or someone from the local library, or a high school girl who expects to train for play-school teaching—someone who will read up on gypsy lore and tell simple, short stories of how the gypsies live and travel in their wagons, eat around a campfire, dance, sing, and play the violin.

Invitations Let the party child cut jagged edges around orange and yellow correspondence cards or folders (see sketch). And write on them:

Come To My Gypsy Party
Friday Afternoon, September 9th, 4 to 5:30 o'clock.
Wear A Blue Gypsy Handkerchief on Your Head
and Big Gold Earrings.

(signed) Sammy Field
203 Harris Street

(On girls' invitations, write Wear A Red Gypsy Handkerchief on Your Head.)

When the invitations have been mailed or delivered, telephone to the mothers of invited children and explain that a bright cotton (man's) handkerchief will do for the gypsy headdress. Large brass curtain rings or ten-cent store loop earrings should be sewn on the head kerchiefs at the right place to dangle below the ears. Menu will be supper; and ask one or more mothers to be guest helpers.

Let children play a short time at the beginning of the party—any popular outdoor games that your child and his guests like, such as, croquet, toss the ring, and drop the handkerchief. As soon as all have arrived, the music or stories can begin.

Decorations Use a cleared playroom, or living room, or the big, cleared room over the garage, if there is one. Decorate with fresh branches and greenery and make it as woodsy as possible.

In the center, arrange a gypsy campfire. For this, use large black iron kettle with legs. Fill it with brightly wrapped gift packages, small dolls, fiddles, harmonicas. Make an imitation fire under the kettle, using orange and red crepe paper cut in flame-shaped strips.

Children sit in a circle on the floor around the kettle. The story teller tells one very short story; then the violinist or song leader plays or sings a gypsy song to go with the story and leads the children in singing. Or, all listen to gypsy records between the bits of story telling. Neither stories nor music should be of long duration. Ten to fifteen minutes is as much as the children will take without a change-over to something new.

Part of the fun is dancing around the gypsy fire, to the violin or records. Show the children a simple dance step: they join hands, boys and girls alternating, to form a circle, and dance 3 steps around in one direction, turn, dance 3 steps in opposite direction, then dance all the way around the kettle twice, singing "Gypsy Oh!" Repeat. Then all sit down again in a circle around the gypsy kettle.

Records for gypsy dancing and listening include "Folk Songs of Hungary" (a guitarist and singer including children's songs), "Songs and Dances of Yugoslavia," and "Songs and Dances of the Basques," all available from Folkways Records (see preceding section on Cowboy Party).

Menu Serve the children at one large table in the dining room or a room other than the one in which they played. Decoration of the table, like the play area, should be woodsy. Use a green cloth and fresh branches or leaves, with either bright pottery or paper dishes and bright paper napkins. For the centerpiece remove wrapped toys from kettle and place in the center of the table.

Write out menus on jagged cards like the invitations and place one in front of each plate with the child's name on it. The dishes: Gypsy Roast (meat loaf with small whole, buttered carrots and mashed potatoes); Gypsy Pudding (baked corn pudding); buttered small rolls; Gypsy Ice Cream (three layers, chocolate, vanilla, strawberry); Gypsy Cake (marble cake, chocolate frosting); Gypsy Brew (milk drinks, cocoa, or lemonade).

The gypsy fiddler or singer dances the children into supper with music, and after supper he dances them out the door when their parents call for them to go home.

Holiday Parties

St. Patrick's Day This is a good day for a party for six- to ten-year-olds. Children of almost any age, but especially the six-to-tens, like a St. Patrick's Day party for its bright green decorations and the fun of Paddy's pig, Paddy's pipe, and shamrocks for good luck.

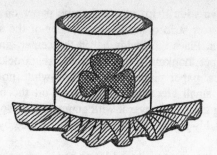

Invitations Buy children's note paper decorated with shamrock, or Paddy hat, pipe, or other Irish motif. Your child can also make his or her own invitations, by cutting a Paddy hat shape from green paper (see sketch). On the note paper he or she writes in green ink, or on the Paddy hat in white ink:

It's A Foine Time You'll Have
at my Irish Party
St. Patrick's Day, March 17th.
Come at 4 o'clock and Stay for Supper at 5:30

(signed) Mary Sullivan
56 South Lane

Decorations Make or buy a large Paddy hat for the centerpiece (see sketch). To make it, use a small hatbox or any round box, or cut a strip of cardboard and shape it into a hat, and fasten with gummed tape or hand stapler. Cover with bright green crepe paper. Make a frill of the same paper for the brim of the hat, use white and another shade of green to make the hatband. Add a big shamrock cut from dark green paper to front of the hat, as a decoration. Leave the top of the crown open, and fill the hat with favors, such as bought paper novelties with shamrock decorations or small packages of green mints, spicy green gum drops, or green-striped bubble mints wrapped in green foil and cellophane.

For the table, use a white paper tablecloth with Paddy pigs or shamrocks on it, or any other with St. Patrick's designs. Or leave the table bare and lay two wide strips of green crepe paper on it from end to end, with a narrow strip of white crepe paper of the same length on top of the green. Place the Paddy hat in the center, and set the table with white paper napkins decorated with shamrocks or other St. Patrick's figures, paper plates, or green-and-white pottery or plastic plates. Stick a small green paper shamrock on the bottom of each child's drinking glass and cover it with gummed tape so that it stays in place. Small Paddy pigs for place cards can be made by your child, or bought.

In playroom, basement, cleared living room, or where children will play, hang clusters of green and white balloons, some with white clay paddy pipes fastened to the balloon strings. The latter are given to guests the last thing before they leave for their homes.

Games As soon as a few of the children have arrived, start them to playing "Find The Tail of Paddy's Pig." Show them a big green cardboard pig, which you or your child cut out following a careful line drawing or a picture in a magazine. The tail and part of the pig's rear end are cut off in one piece. This you and your child have hidden somewhere in the playroom, behind a drapery, in a cupboard, in a wastebasket, in a box on a low shelf, under a rug, or any other place that a child can reach but not find too easily. Let everybody hunt for it, including late comers, but not much more than fifteen minutes. As soon as the pig's tail is found, the finder gets the first prize of the afternoon, a ten-cent-store soap bubble-blowing pipe set, not like Paddy's pipe but still a pipe. It should be wrapped in green-and-white striped paper.

The next game is "Catch Paddy's Pig." Use the same green cardboard pig but fasten his tail end on securely with plenty of gummed tape or staple it. Have a stick ready, about 3 feet long, wrapped spirally with strips of green-and-white crepe paper. Hang the green pig on a short string from one end of the stick. Children sit in a large circle. One child is blindfolded, he or she stands in the center of the circle, and slowly waves the stick with the paper pig on it around the circle. A party helper must guide the waving so that it is fast enough for the pig to go by most of the children but not too fast for some child to catch it.

Each child must try to catch the pig as it flies past. The first one to catch it goes to the center of the circle, is blindfolded, and now is the one to wave the pig around the circle. The first stick waver steps outside the circle and counts to 10 slowly, while the stick and the pig go round the ring. The next child to catch the pig goes to the center of the ring and replaces the second stick waver. Stick wavers No. 2 and No. 1 now count 10 together. Continue, until everyone has caught the pig.

"Matching the Shamrock," a sit-down game, is next, which the children play at any low table around which chairs can be placed.

For this game, buy or make as many large green paper shamrocks as there are children at the party, and one extra. Cut all but one of these into three different shaped pieces each. Mix the pieces together in a green hat box or bowl. When the children are ready around the play table, pour the cut shamrocks out on to it. Mount the uncut shamrock on a big sheet of white paper and hang or pin up above the table where all can see it.

The game: each child must find the three pieces that make a complete shamrock. They should not hurry. The first one to finish gets a Paddy Pig Penny Bank, wrapped as a gift in bright green paper and tied with white ribbon. The second child to complete his shamrock gets a tiny St. Patrick's Day novelty gift from the dime store. A party helper can keep this from becoming a scramble and casually help the slowest to find the right pieces.

Menu Supper comes next. Sandwiches cut in shamrock shapes filled with chopped lettuce, pickle, olives mixed with a little mayonnaise; baked stuffed peppers (ground beef, lamb, or chicken in cream sauce with rice or macaroni and a little cheese); cloverleaf rolls spread with a little butter and jelly; shamrock cookies frosted with white and sprinkled lightly with finely chopped green mint candies; ice cream with slice of candied green cherry on top; milk, with green sipper straws.

Easter

Easter Egg Coloring Party For five- to ten-year-olds. The Saturday before Easter is a perfect time for this kind of party, which does not call for games or decorating the house. It will delight many children because they can play with color and make something. Let your child invite five or seven friends to come Saturday morning at 11 o'clock. The day before, hard-cook enough eggs (and put in refrigerator) so that each child has at least four to decorate for his Easter basket. Provide a comfortable worktable, or two smaller tables, making an area large enough for everybody to sit around and have room on which to paint and decorate eggs.

Have on worktable: paints or dyes ready-mixed in bowls and dishes with small brushes and swab sticks (from the drug store) to be used for daubing on color.

Provide an assortment of gummed stars, dots, little gold decalcomania figures, sequins, hearts, birds, tiny paper butterflies, strips of gummed gold paper, colored gummed tape, Duco cement and Sobo adhesive. These are all available in good stationery shops, dime stores, and notion counters.

Also needed are several small scissors to cut spirals, strips, zigzags, bow knots, and other figures from colored gummed tape.

One or more mothers or an older brother or sister should be on hand to offer guidance. Each child should paint or otherwise decorate four eggs.

Also needed (but not put on the worktable) are small dime-store decorative baskets for each child with green tissue paper cut in strips making the nest in each. Tie bows or rosettes of yellow ribbon on the baskets and attach a small Easter card with name of the guest on handle of each basket. Keep the baskets out of sight until after lunch. Everybody works at least an hour. Then while eggs dry, luncheon is served.

Decoration The table centerpiece is a ring of fresh flowers or leaves and in its center a china, glass, pottery, or stuffed hen-on-nest or toy rabbit, surrounded by candy eggs. Use bright straw or plastic place mats and Easter-printed paper napkins, with yellow, pink or blue plastic, paper, or pottery plates.

Menu Creamed, finely chopped dried beef with chopped, hard-cooked eggs on split soft buns; small blueberry muffins with marmalade; egg-shaped cookies frosted with golden yellow icing and decorated with chocolate dots, bowknots, and swirls; strawberry ice cream; milk or hot cocoa to drink.

After lunch, the children return to the worktable to find a surprise— the gift baskets with their names on them. Each fills his or her own basket with the eggs he or she decorated, and with candy eggs from the luncheon table. End of party.

Egg Hunt Party This appeals to children anywhere from four to ten or more. It is a charming custom that has been growing in popularity in many communities in recent years, to serve Easter brunch or luncheon to a few friends and their children after church, with the egg hunt the exciting and rewarding finale to the children's afternoon.

Decorated eggs, gay and beautiful, must be bought or made ready a day or so before—at least three for each child, and preferably four or five for each. On the morning of the party, some time before the children arrive, the eggs must be hidden in bright colored straw, raffia, or grass nests all over the garden, weather permitting, or all over the house if the weather is bad.

Favors for the children at the luncheon or brunch are bright baskets of various shapes and colors, each decorated with a small Easter rabbit or ribbon bow. While parents sip coffee after lunch, the children enjoy the hunt, filling their baskets as they go from nest to nest.

This kind of combined adult and children's luncheon is easy to serve buffet from a colorful table, parents helping their children to the dishes.

Decorations Turquoise blue cloth and napkins, centerpiece a big folded-paper hen or rabbit. Place a few candy eggs under the hen, or around the rabbit. Table wares include your prettiest china for this party, such as plates of pale grey, lime, or a lighter tint of turquoise than the cloth, with deep purple, rose, or green demitasse cups and saucers, crystal goblets for adults, punch cups or mugs for children.

Menu This begins with orange juice for everybody. Then, for the adults, individual casseroles of curried lamb with chutney, and scallions and chopped green pepper as garnish; deviled eggs, asparagus vinaigrette. For the children, creamed chopped roast lamb on split soft roll; small baked stuffed potato; milk to drink. Dessert for both grownups and children, a cake baked in an Easter lamb mold with coconut frosting, lemon ice cream in egg molds garnished with ruffle of whipped cream. Coffee for grownups.

Easter Afternoon Party for Children The Egg Hunt need not be a luncheon. Guests may be invited for 4:30, the eggs and nests prepared as described above, one nest for each guest and the small host or hostess, hidden in the garden, around the yard and even in the house. Be ready to transfer the egg hunt indoors to the playroom, living room, and elsewhere if weather is bad.

First comers must wait until all guests have arrived before the hunt can begin. They can be entertained briefly, taking turns looking into 1 or 2 handsome vista eggs. These old-time novelties have been revived, many now coming from Europe. Some contain simple scenes of flowers and rabbits, others have landscapes full of flowers, trees, a village, people, animals. They are for sale at fine candy and gift shops.

After all guests are on hand, each is given a small empty but pretty Easter basket, someone blows a whistle for the Easter Rabbit, and the hunt begins. As soon as a child finds a nest, he brings it in to a worktable and there is about half an hour of basket decorating for everybody. For this provide short pieces of pastel colored ribbons, tissue paper, crepe paper, fresh and artificial flowers, little stuffed rabbits, chicks, and hens. The children will need scissors, pins, gummed tape, and someone, mother or older brother or sister, to make suggestions and help.

When all baskets are finished, they are placed in a row on the worktable. The children vote for the prettiest by clapping, and then clap again for the next prettiest. The prettiest wins a prize, a small bright bag of candy Easter eggs tied with ribbons. Prize for the second prettiest is a small fluffy chick (dime or novelty store) wearing an Easter bonnet.

Supper is served about 5:30, the same menu as the children's portion of brunch described above.

May Day

May Day Party One kind of May Day celebration, for seven- to twelve-year-olds, is Filling The May Baskets, a party popular with rural and suburban mothers, especially in California and the Southeastern states, who have well filled flower gardens or nearby woodland with spring wild flowers in bloom.

Invitations Your child can invite friends in person or by telephone, asking five to seven or more to come for a May Day party lunch on the porch, then to fill baskets for shut-ins or sick children. She tells her prospective guests the time, 12:15 P.M., and the day.

Prepare a worktable in one section of a screened porch or in a basement playroom, or cleared garage, a table around which all can sit. Also needed are small, deep baskets in which a cheap water tumbler will fit, cutting shears with which to trim stems, short lengths of raffia or green cord to tie flowers in position, and blooms from the garden. Choose those which last longest, such as daisies and small tulips, as well as jonquils, daffodils, narcissus, and whatever is available. A few branches of laurel in bloom, small azalea branches from the woods, and wild flowers make welcome additions to these bouquets. There should also be small, flower-decorated cards on which children can write their

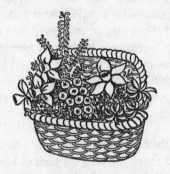

greetings or names. The traditional May Basket was an anonymous gift, but children like to put their names on what they give.

Decorations For the luncheon arrange each child's food on a pretty tray, with a paper napkin printed with spring flowers, birds, bees. Trays can be decorated a few days earlier by your child. They can be dime-store papier-mâché, metal, plastic, or fiberboard. Using water colors, she can paint flowers and butterflies. As soon as they are dry, she can brush them with colorless, quick-drying varnish, to preserve the color and make them washable. These trays are useful for all kinds of parties.

Menu Each plate contains three small sandwiches, one of white bread with chopped egg-salad filling, one of Boston brown bread with cream cheese and jelly, one of nut bread with thin slice ham or chicken. For the beverage, a glass or mug of milk, cup of hot cocoa, or glass of lemonade. Give the children bright striped sipper straws for the cold drink. For dessert, small molds of orange gelatin filled with cubed canned peaches, canned seedless cherries, cubes of orange, and a dab of whipped cream on top; flower-shaped cookies, some iced in pink, others white or yellow, decorated with swirls of chocolate frosting.

After lunch, the children work at the table to fill the baskets. Each child selects the flowers she wants and arranges them with small pieces of fern, mulberry, or other green leaves in the water-filled tumbler in her basket. Here guidance from a mother or other party helper may be needed.

When baskets are finished—this should take no more than half to three-quarters of an hour—each child fastens a little name card on the handle of her basket. Then they go in a group with one or two mothers or party helpers to leave their baskets at homes where there is a shut-in elderly person or a sick child, or they take them to a hospital for old people or children. All go home when they have distributed the last basket, the young hostess and her mother going along until the last child is seen home.

Maypole Party For the family with a pleasant yard, an afternoon party for children from six to ten can take the First of May theme as inspiration, and it can give them games and fun.

Invitations can be written by your child on any party note paper, or she can paint flowers on little cards and write invitations on them:

> Dear Drusie:
> Please come to my May Day Party
> Friday, May 1st, at 4 o'clock.
> Mother says we'll have Supper at 5:30.
>
> (signed) Betsy James
> 12 Poplar Street

If the making of a Maypole and the supervision of its dance are too complicated for your plans, a tiny Maypole can be made as a table decoration. Or both large and small poles can be featured as described below.

This May Day party can also be nothing more than a pretty, flower-decked supper, with tiny maypole favors for everyone. To add the touch of drama which children love, dress up a tea cart with flowers and streamers (see sketch), put a small record player on the cart and

wheel the music around for singing games, such as "London Bridge," "Musical Chairs," and other favorites. Then load the cart with their supper, wheel it to a terrace, patio, or screened porch, and let the boys play waiter. They help you lift the dishes from the cart to the decorated party table, and assist you in other ways.

A much more detailed party plan must be worked out for the Maypole Party. A small pole, not more than 6 feet tall, can be made using a stout curtain rod or a heavy bamboo rod, such as those which come in rolls of new carpet. Paint the pole pale green. Fasten three or four plastic, dime-store pinwheels at the top, so that they do not interfere with each other and will spin in the breeze. These pinwheels are usually in two colors, such as white and red, pink and blue, etc. Use the same colors for a huge bouquet of extra large, artificial flowers. Arrange flowers below and around the pinwheels, fastening flowers securely to the pole with tacks and winding with wire. Pinwheels should show above the flowers at different heights so that they spin freely (see sketch).

Use a length of ribbon which, when fastened under the flowers at top of pole, will hang down to the ground with about 1 foot to spare. Fasten ribbons securely on top of pole, under flowers, a ribbon for each guest, in pink, yellow, green, blue. Let them hang free. When pole is set up in the yard, it should be pushed deep in the earth for steadiness. The loose end of each ribbon should have a little nosegay of fresh or artificial flowers fastened to it.

Winding The Maypole This is the first game of the (good weather) afternoon. For this play guidance or directing by a mother or older sister is needed. Children take their places around the pole, in pairs

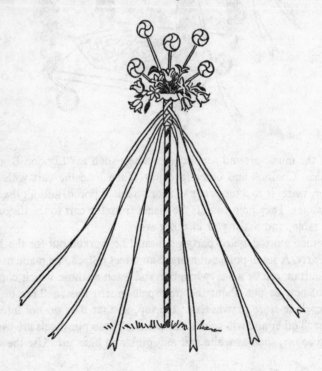

facing each other, one faces one direction, her partner the opposite; that is, every other child is facing the same direction. They sing to the tune of "Here We Go Round the Mulberry Bush": "Here we go, up high, down below, round the Maypole, round we go." The song is repeated until the pole is wound with the ribbons. As they sing, each child carries his ribbon over or under the ribbons of children going in the opposite direction. When the Maypole is wound, each child fastens the end of his ribbon to the pole, with a brightly colored thumbtack. Hang a colored string and a little card with child's name on tack just before it is pushed clear into pole. Now everyone has signed the Maypole.

The Flower Guessing Game This is a sit-down game and a good one to follow the singing and dancing. It is popular with suburban and country children. Children sit around a play table or two smaller tables. Each one is given a sheet of paper and a pencil. On each paper are numbers from 1 to 10, down the lefthand side. Children must name flowers, which are shown by a mother or other party helper.

Drama is added, the suspense wonderful, if the flowers are brought in from another room, only one at a time. Display an easy one first, such as a big sunflower kept fresh in a bottle of water. Explain to the children that they must be silent, and write down No. 1's name. They must not speak the name out loud. When No. 2 is shown, they do the same. This one should be easy, too—a rose in a small vase. No. 3, a daffodil, kept fresh in a glass of water. No. 4, violets in a little vase. No. 5, apple blossoms, a spray in a jar. No. 6, dogwood, short sprig in glass of water. No. 7, hyacinth, growing in a pot. No. 8, tulip, in a vase. No. 9, carnation, in vase. No. 10, a single iris in vase.

Only a few minutes are allowed for guessing each flower (helper should gauge the time by the children's reactions). Then it is carried away to the other room, and the next flower brought in. When all have been shown, and the children have written down names, all flowers are brought back into room and placed around the table together. The party helper names them, No. 1 sunflower, etc., and the children grade their own papers, marking *right* or *wrong* beside their guesses. The child with the most right gets a May Day prize, a child's book on flowers, or a record of children's songs. The child with next highest number of right guesses, a little framed flower print for his room.

Supper If weather is fine, the children put on their coats or sweaters and sit outdoors around the Maypole for their supper. For this, the dishes are arranged on trays, or the supper table has been set up near the pole while the flower game was played indoors.

Fresh flowers and bright but light colors should be the theme of the decorations. Use a paper tablecloth printed with spring flowers, paper napkins to match, and plastic, paper, or pottery plates in spring colors, such as yellow or pale green. The centerpiece may be a small Maypole standing in a yellow cake. Cake may be baked in a funnel pan and iced with yellow frosting. Have yellow and green ribbons of the little Maypole hang down around the cake. Favors: small wreaths of fresh or artificial flowers for girls to wear on their heads, party hats for the boys with a flower fastened on brim or crown.

Menu Small meat balls in very little brown gravy; creamed potatoes; bread-and-butter sandwich; carrot sticks; cooked prunes (cold) stuffed with cream cheese; glass of milk; the cake with peach or apricot ice cream in flower molds.

Halloween Lantern Party The night of Halloween is the best possible time for a party for your children from seven to twelve, and their friends. It will keep them away from the streets and trick-or-treat nuisances, ringing doorbells, and rat-ta-tatting on windows. It is the time for a big, fun-filled evening, and it should be planned for a later hour than most of their parties, so that they feel they are really having a night of celebrating.

Dinner away from home with other children at a lively, decorated table is party enough for many youngsters. For others, the challenge of new games adds excitement. You and your children decide which kind of Halloween party to give. For either, ask one or more mothers to help with the new games and other chores of the evening.

Invitations Let your children design the invitations, such as big pumpkins cut out of orange paper, a pumpkin-lantern face painted on one side, and invitations written on the other in black crayon or ink:

For information on Fourth of July entertaining, see Picnics and Outdoor Family Parties

Come To Our Halloween
Lantern Party
Friday Night at 6 o'clock
Supper and Fun

(signed) Sally, Jeff, and Bob Granger
1600 Hillcrest Street

Decorations Buy paper-pumpkin lanterns or make them, using ripe pumpkins, for all guests and your children. Cutting a pumpkin calls for a strong hand, so an older brother or the man of the house has a job. There should be grinning lanterns in the windows to greet arriving guests, another inside the entrance, lanterns around the playroom, cleared living room, basement, or wherever the children will play. In the dining room put the biggest pumpkin lantern of all, in the center of the table. Other lanterns are placed on buffet and elsewhere in the dining room.

For a tablecloth, use a wide strip of orange crepe paper from one end of table to the other. Have paper napkins printed with pumpkins or witches, large paper, plastic, or pottery plates, and on a small table just inside dining-room door, witches' hats for the girls and party hats with black cats or goblins on them for boys.

Games As soon as all guests have arrived, they play "Who Are You?" This is a getting-acquainted game. Halloween masks are needed, a different one for each child. To play the game, all the boys go into one room and close the door. Girls sit on the floor in the first room in a half-circle facing the door through which boys went. On the door put a sign, "The Boo Who? Room."

A party helper or one or two mothers of guests help boys to put on masks and tell them what to do. The door opens, the first boy steps into the room where the girls sit, and yells, "Boo! Who am I?" Girls must guess who he is. If they guess right or wrong he keeps mask on, tells his real name and sits down on the floor with girls. Game continues until all boys have come out to be guessed. Then girls go into the "Boo Who? Room," put on masks, come out one at a time, and boys must guess their names. When all girls have been guessed out of the room, boys and girls still wearing masks join hands, form a circle and dance round the room to the song, "Who's Afraid of the Big Bad Wolf?" As music ends everyone must try to be the first to yell, Not Me! Then they all pull masks off, or push them back on their heads.

For the next game the party helper now hangs up a large paper on a wall. On it, she points out, are the names for Slow Pokes in the "Witches' Musical Chairs" game. Names are: Big Black Shadows, Wicked Witches, Pumpkin Heads, Horrible Ghosts, Hooting Owls, Terrible Dark Nothings.

Before they start, party helper explains game which is a version of Musical Chairs. Children arrange play chairs in a large loose circle, each one choosing a chair as his own. Music starts: this may be any of your children's favorite march or ballet records. Children march, not too fast, around outside circle of chairs. The music stops unexpectedly. Children who aren't quick enough to get to their own chairs when the music stops for the first time become Big Black Shadows. A party helper writes their names on paper on the wall opposite "Big Black Shadows." Next time around, when the music stops again, the slow ones are Wicked Witches, and their names go up on the wall. Next time, Pumpkin Heads, then Horrible Ghosts, then Hooting Owls, and finally Terrible Dark Nothings. This ends the game, and the Terrible Dark Nothings get consolation prizes, small boxes of licorice and orange gum drops, to take home with them.

After this game the children go into supper, to music if there is another new or favorite old record to play. They leave masks and candy boxes on a table outside the dining room, because, as they go in, girls are given witches' hats and boys Halloween hats to wear at the table.

Menu Orange juice; meat-filled turnover with a little gravy on it; scalloped sweet potatoes with marshmallows; buttered biscuit with jelly. For dessert, a dish of three small balls of ice cream, vanilla, chocolate, and orange, with a witch-shaped cookie standing up in the middle. Milk or hot cocoa is the beverage.

Later, as children prepare to leave with parents who have come to see them home, each is given a pumpkin lantern to light the way.

Thanksgiving

Young Children at the Family Dinner If relatives and in-laws are invited to bring their children to your home for Thanksgiving dinner, it is easy to give the children a holiday party of their own without making much extra work for yourself. For three or more children ranging in age from five to ten years, provide a separate small-fry table of suitable size, height, and the right number of small chairs. Place it in the dining room if there is plenty of space, or just outside the dining room door, so that the children feel that they are part of the family celebrating, yet are having their own party.

Decorations Make the children's table gay with party decorations, of which there are unlimited varieties at this season in the Thanksgiving theme, at stationery, candy, and novelty stores and gift shops. Use an orange paper tablecloth, or a white one printed all over with Pilgrim Fathers pursuing turkeys, or with bright corn and harvest fruit. Have paper napkins to match. The centerpiece can be a big hollow cardboard turkey, or a painted wire or wicker basket, filled with favors, such as snappers and small toys, all wrapped in orange crepe paper or gold foil. Party hats for all add just that much more party spirit, fun, and satisfaction. Bobbing over the table, a bright orange balloon for every child; each long balloon string is carefully tied around a good eating apple on the table heavy enough to keep the balloon from rising to the ceiling. Balloons and apples are given to children after dinner, but during the meal the apples and their balloons surround the centerpiece.

Menu Serve the children small portions of the grown-up menu, omitting soup and one of the vegetables. Turkey for their table should be sliced and cut in bite-size pieces, with very little gravy; small serving of dressing; sliced or scalloped sweet potato or mashed potatoes; buttered soft roll with cranberry jelly; small piece of stuffed celery. For dessert, a small piece of pumpkin pie or a ginger-cookie man, with ice cream served to them in pretty dessert dishes from a big mold of vanilla and chocolate ice cream being passed at the grownups' table.

If dinner is at noon, small children nap afterwards and later take a walk with a grownup, or visit some special museum or a new building or children's movie. If dinner is served at a later hour in the afternoon or early evening, youngsters can play for a while afterwards, preferably their favorite indoors games, such as Chinese checkers, dominoes, and others which they like, then early to bed.

Christmas

All over America, school Christmas parties begin about a week before the holiday. Youngsters make decorations for these, paint cards for their parents and friends, and make many small, inexpensive decorations for their own Christmas trees at home. They begin the holiday vacation full of party talk and party expectation, all focused toward the excitement of Christmas eve or morning in their own homes. Later there are parties with their friends, mostly to see their decorated trees, and times to play with their new toys and games.

Carol Singing Party This is one of the most satisfactory Christmas parties for young children a few days before Christmas. It should be given in the early evening after children have had supper at their homes.

The party is nothing more than a group of children from five to twelve or older with someone to lead the carols, play the piano, or oversee record selections. After about an hour of singing, refreshments, such as Christmas cookies and hot cocoa or a milk drink, are served. After this, the visiting youngsters are picked up by parents, or escorted to their homes.

Come See Our Tree Party is another, not too contrived, party for two or three days after Christmas, when the effects of too much Christmas dinner, too much candy, too much excitement are beginning to wear off.

For this party children from eight to twelve are invited for 6 o'clock supper. Your own children give the invitations in person or by telephone. First comers listen to new records and look at the new toys. When all guests have arrived, supper is served.

Decorations Use a white paper tablecloth sprinkled with silver stars of various sizes—gummed stars from stationery and dime stores—

with white paper napkins with a star on each. Have a small toy all-blue Christmas tree as a centerpiece and around it, small brightly wrapped gifts for each child—a tiny doll, animal, or toy. Buy or make Christmas party hats silver, gold, blue. Use plates of pale blue pottery, plastic, or paper.

Menu Mashed potato nests with creamed turkey or chicken, or combination of chicken and ham; cranberry jelly sandwich; small lettuce leaf with small square of tomato aspic in it. For dessert, Christmas cookies cut in star shapes, ice cream in blue or pink frilled paper cup with a little Christmas bell candy or cutout on it, hot cocoa or a milk drink.

After supper, the family tree is lighted. All sing carols until parents come to take them home.

For ideas for an easy and inexpensive Christmas afternoon party for children see page 171.

Hanukkah Children's Parties In December, Jews observe a festival called Hanukkah. It is a joyous, eight-day holiday celebrating the first great victory for religious freedom won by the Jews more than two thousand years ago. Today children love the Hanukkah festival not only for the beautiful family candle ceremonies each night, but because it has become a time for the exchange of small gifts on each of the nights, and because it is a traditional time for playing games.

Children of other religious denominations invited to an afternoon Hanukkah party should take wrapped gifts for the party grab bag. Delicious cakes and other refreshments are served and the grab bag yields several gifts for each child present.

New Year's Day

Snow Man Party The snow man theme can provide a good party for five- to ten-year-old children who live where winter coats the landscape generously with white. This party if given on the first Saturday of the New Year can be considered a celebration of the New Year as well as a Snow Man Party. With changes in games and table decorations, it can be modified to become a New Year's party for children who live in warmer parts of the country where snow is a rarity or is never seen.

Invitations Let your child buy snow man cards, or cut snow men out of drawing paper and make a face, buttons, hat and pipe on him with crayon or ink. On the back of each snow man he can write something like this:

> Dear Jimmy, Please come to
> My Snow Man Party
> Saturday morning, at 11 o'clock
> and stay for lunch.
> Mother says wear your snow boots,
> warm snow suit, and mittens.
>
> (signed) Charley Waite
> 321 11th Street

As soon as invitations are delivered or mailed, telephone mothers of prospective guests and tell them to bundle children up for about half an hour of outdoors play in the snow. Also ask one or two to help with games.

On Friday, the day before the party, your husband and children with the help of any teen-agers in the family make a fine, big snow man in some part of the yard where the children can play next day. Before party time on Saturday, add the final touches to snow man, such as pipe, red necktie, tall black hat or any funny hat.

When children arrive, they begin their play in the snowy yard. They work in pairs. Each pair makes a smaller version of the snow man. Each is given a box containing pieces of coal or wood for buttons and eyes, a strip of red wool or an old red necktie, old stocking cap, red beret, or hat for their snow man. Your husband, or some other party assistant, helps any who need guidance in rolling the snow for the first chunky lower half of the snow man or other parts of his anatomy.

This can't be a rush job. But as soon as all pairs of children have finished their snow men, everybody lines up as a Judging Committee. Father, party helper, or some adult manages the judging, explaining that each pair's work deserves applause. The children clap for each pair of contestants. The snow man getting the most applause is the best, and the two children who made him receive First Prize, which are small bought snow man favors containing candy boxes filled with assorted candies. Or each winner receives one of those glass or plastic balls in which there is falling snow no matter which way the ball is turned, or little bags of assorted spicy gum drops. A second prize is given for the funniest snow man, which children choose by clapping.

Then everybody goes indoors to a playroom or hall where they are helped to remove boots, snow suits, and mittens and make themselves ready for luncheon.

Decorations Since this party takes place near New Year's Day, the New Year's theme can be carried out in the table decorations. Push

table against one wall. Hang a big calendar of the month of January on the wall. Your child can make this, using a large sheet of drawing paper and adding black crayon numerals in ruled spaces to look like a calendar. With a red crayon he makes a ring around January 1st, New Year's Day. From that date, narrow, twirled streamers of red crepe paper trail out to guests' plates, each with small place card bearing the child's name and Happy New Year! Favors wrapped in matching red paper are small calendars or small dime-store note books containing a calendar page. The centerpiece is a bright red bowl or basket filled with snow ball favors, which contain assorted tiny toys.

For the table, use a white paper cloth with New Year's symbols on it—calendars, Father Time, baby New Year—white paper napkins printed with New Year's designs, and bright red pottery, plastic, or paper plates.

Menu Individual casseroles of broad noodles cooked with small meat balls; small soft buns split and spread with cheese; carrot sticks;

green pepper rings; individual baked caramel custards; soft ginger cookies in snow man shape iced with white and decorated face, buttons, and hat of chocolate frosting; hot cocoa or milk.

Guests go home after luncheon.

For children in warmer areas the same decorations, table settings, and menu (with minor changes) can be used for a New Year's Party. Children are invited for 4 o'clock in the afternoon. Invitations can be telephoned or given in person, or your child can paint a big January 1 in bright red on cards and on the other side write something like this:

> Dear Jimmy, Please come to
> My New Year's Party
> Saturday afternoon, 4 o'clock
> and stay for supper at 5:30.
>
> (signed) Charley Waite
> 321 11th Street

Before supper, the children dance to children's records and songs. Or if this group has not been going to dancing class, seat them in small chairs and show a movie. Or play children's records from other countries with someone to tell them little stories about foreign children, how they live, and what games they play. "Christmas Songs of Many Lands" (Folkways) sung in English with guitar accompaniments, notes and texts is ideal for this kind of party. So is another Folkways record called "Folk Songs for Children," voice with banjo; it contains short, singable songs which children quickly pick up and can sing along with the record. From the same source there is the school-age number in the series called "Birds, Beasts, Bugs, and Fishes," which has a singer with banjo, story song, and adventures. See the section on Cowboy Party in this chapter for information about Folkways Records.

While table decorations remain the same as for the Snow Man party, colored favor balls should replace the snow balls in the centerpiece. Strawberry or peach ice cream can replace the custard, and cookies should not be snow man but some other shape such as animal or flower and iced with strawberry frosting.

This party ends with supper.

February

Lincoln's Birthday Supper A school play or a church, school, or club celebration in honor of Abraham Lincoln's birthday makes a good prelude to a party supper for children from six to ten on this holiday or a day preceding.

Invitations can be given in person or by telephone a few days before the entertainment. Ask one or two mothers to help shepherd the children to your home from the school or wherever entertainment has been given.

Decorations Let your child or children make the centerpiece for their party table. This can be a log cabin of cardboard, the walls, roof, and chimney put together with gummed tape then painted with water colors or colored with crayon copying a picture of Lincoln's birthplace. Leave the supper table bare except for cork, raffia, or plastic place mats. Use paper napkins decorated with log cabin, or the date, or some other Lincoln memento, and pottery or paper plates stamped with the date or rail fence or other timely design.

Favors for boys and girls are small toy-store puzzles wrapped in bright paper, and small bags of old-fashioned molasses candies or peppermints, not to be opened at supper but to be taken home. A special prize for some child, *Lincoln's Animal Friends,* by R. P. Randall, (Little, Brown).

Menu Small bowl of corn chowder; small hamburger sandwich on soft buttered bun; relish, ketchup, or mustard; warm gingerbread with small ball of ice cream on it; cocoa or milk to drink.

St. Valentine's Day

Make A Valentine Party
For 7 to 10 years

This is a rewarding and easy party to give for seven- to ten-year-old children, since in it they entertain themselves. It should be given on the Saturday morning before February 14th, St. Valentine's Day, or as an afternoon party a few days before the holiday.

Invitations Let your child or children take care of these by cutting hearts about 4 or 5 inches wide out of red paper. Using white ink, the child writes on one side of the heart:

Come to Our House
Saturday Morning at 11 o'clock
and Make Valentines.

And on other side he writes:

Mother Says We'll Have
A Party Luncheon at 12

(signed) Mary and Lee Brown
768 Parkway Street

Prepare a worktable for the children around which they sit. Have on hand sheets of red, pink, white, and blue papers. Other necessary supplies: various sizes of gummed hearts in red and other colors; lace paper shelf edging and small lace paper doilies, with which to make edges and frills on valentines; tiny decalcomania and other gummed pictures of birds, flowers, girls and boys; Duco cement and Sobo adhesive; gummed tape in colors; short lengths of narrow ribbon in red, pink, blue; several pairs of small scissors. Some mother or a party helper should guide the shy ones and show them how to start. Children make valentines for about an hour.

Decorations Several days before the party, your children make the decorations for the luncheon table. Suggestions: large red heart to hang down from the chandelier or ceiling, on red ribbon right over the center of the table; large red paper hearts to serve as table mats, on which plate, glass, fork and spoon go; pretty white paper napkins on which they stick a large gummed, red paper heart in one corner, then with white ink write a child's name or initials on the heart. Use plates of white pottery, plastic, or paper. For favors, buy small heart-shaped boxes filled with heart candies.

Menu Individual meat pies baked in small heart-shaped pans; au gratin potatoes; currant jelly sandwiches; strawberry or cherry ice cream in heart molds, heart-shaped sugar cookies, hot cocoa or glass of milk.

After lunch, the finished valentines are displayed around the work-table. Children vote for the prettiest by clapping and it wins First Prize, a heart-shaped box of mints. Second prize, if it is won by a girl, is a heart-shaped pin cushion or little red apron. If the winner is a boy, award him a package of luncheon cookies to take home with him.

Washington's Birthday

Patriotic Supper Party The school and community events inspired by Washington's Birthday usually satisfy most children's social needs for the holiday. But if your children between six and ten want to invite a few friends home for games, outdoors and in a playroom, and a party supper after a school play or community parade or speeches, this supper can be their final party of the winter.

Invitations These can be red-white-and-blue cards made by the party child or folders cut in the shape of a drum and decorated with red and blue water color paints. Invitations may be telephoned as well.

Decorations may be brought home from school where children have cut or painted cherry trees, military drums, rows of soldiers marching, flags, and other patriotic emblems. Use any of these on the supper table. Or you will find in dime and novelty stores an abundance of paper novelties in red, white, and blue: shields, flags, flag-decorated favors to be filled with candies, drums to be used as centerpiece, military paper hats, streamers, decorated tablecloths and napkins.

The supper table may be left bare except for red, white, and blue place mats with white paper napkins on which a cherry tree, or the date, or a red-white-and-blue drum is printed. The drum theme always pleases children. A large one as centerpiece can be filled with smaller drum boxes full of goodies, or toy soldiers and flags, two favors for each guest. This is the party for balloons in patriotic colors, fastened in a cluster above the table to be untied and distributed to parting guests. For added decoration, hang more balloons on walls with bow-knots of red-white-and-blue crepe paper and long streamers hanging down from each cluster.

Menu Sliced frankfurters and noodles in individual casserole; slice of baked stuffed green pepper filled with chicken or beef hash; small lettuce sandwich. For dessert, half an orange hollowed out and filled with cherry-flavored gelatin in which are a few red seedless cherries and two fresh cherries with stems on top. If fresh cherries are not available, use two candied cherries and a small mint leaf. Cookies, iced with white and decorated with sliced candied red cherries, and hot cocoa or milk complete this supper.

Unusual and Interesting Parties for Children

Doll Sewing Party
For girls 8 to 12 years.

Many schools and Sunday Schools encourage children to share their toys and dolls with needy children of other countries. In some communities, groups of girls led by a teacher or one of their mothers meet regularly to make doll clothes for such children, or for a local hospital and similar charity. This is one kind of doll sewing party.

Another is a less serious afternoon party to which a little girl asks a few friends to bring their dolls and sew. Six or seven besides the hostess is a good number for this party.

Invitations For either party invitations given in person or by telephone are sufficient. Guests are asked to bring their dolls and sewing bags for an afternoon of sewing.

If the invitation is for luncheon and sewing afterwards, guests should be asked to come at 12:30 and stay until about 4 o'clock, or whatever is convenient.

If guests are invited to come for sewing and "tea," they should be asked for 1 o'clock to 4 or 5 in the afternoon.

For either group, comfortable chairs around one large table or small tables of appropriate height are necessary. While guests are supposed to bring with them thread, needles, scissors and fabrics or trimmings in their sewing bags, the hostess and her mother should see that plentiful supplies of these essentials are on hand.

For the community sewing group, ask mothers of the guests for scraps from their own sewing bags of silk, ribbon, old and new fabrics.

For your child's private sewing party, provide these from your own supplies or buy small remnants and pieces of silk, chintz, and other easily sewn fabrics.

For either party, supplies can be spread out on a table so everyone can help herself. Cutting, sewing, and finishing advice should be at hand from the mother of the hostess.

Menu If the party begins with luncheon it can be: a small appetizer of fruit salad, such as hollowed out half an orange shell filled with seedless white grapes, small pieces of orange, sliced strawberries or banana; followed by salmon or tuna croquettes with cream sauce, garnish of beet relish, brown-bread-and-butter sandwich, glass of milk, small meringue cookies.

Serve luncheon on trays at the sewing tables. Or serve at your child's favorite lunching place, which may be the kitchen counter, the dining-room table, or bridge tables. Let her decide on the color scheme for the trays, such as yellow napkins and a fresh rosebud or little bouquet of artificial flowers on each tray. If she prefers the dining-room table or bridge tables, cotton or paper tablecloths and simple but pretty china can be used to carry out her favorite colors.

If the party is sewing followed by refreshments at tea time, you can serve brownies and lemonade, which are favorites of many children, or chocolate milk drink from the blender or hot cocoa, with assorted small cookies made by your party child. These refreshments can be served right at the sewing tables. But add a pretty paper napkin covered with brightly printed butterflies or rosebuds, or some other decoration preferred by your daughter.

At the end of the community party, which sews for a local hospital or for dolls to be sent to a child welfare organization, photographs of the seamstresses, their dolls, and their instructor might be made by the local newspaper photographer in a small community or a photographer for the school paper. This makes a fine, exciting ending to the afternoon.

Magic Party
For 5 to 7 years.

Fun and pleasurable excitement for children can be provided by a professional magician, hired through a party service, who comes to your party prepared to pull a rabbit from a hat and other wonderful tricks. He may also be a high school or college boy who has mastered old familiar tricks with cards, the famous one with colored handkerchiefs and the United States flag, and that of pulling a rose from behind little girls' ears or a half dollar from the ears of little boys.

Let your children invite their guests by telephone or in person to come to a magic show at 4:30 o'clock on a Saturday afternoon. After the magic, serve supper on a table made pretty with bright blue, yellow or rose paper tablecloth and napkins. Use as a centerpiece a musical cake holder which when wound up turns slowly, playing a tune as it turns. Load cake holder with wrapped favors, such as toy planes, freight cars, bright plastic floating fish, small doll dishes. Serve any of the party menus described in this chapter.

If older children are included in the Magic Party, let all youngsters play together one or two games after magician has finished and before supper is served. The first game will appeal to the older children—a question and answer game with the magician or a guest helper. This should not last more than fifteen to twenty minutes. Every child is asked how he thinks the magic tricks are done, the party helper keeps score on answers. Best guesser or child who makes best answers is given a copy of *The First Book of Magic* (published by Franklin Watts).

Then everybody plays Floor Basketball. Place a waste basket or any deep, not too wide basket on the floor. Divide children into two teams with paper tags of two different colors, such as red and blue. Children stand in two rows, Red team in one row, Blue team in one row, facing each other with the basket between. A party helper keeps score. First Red player tosses bean bag, then first Blue player, followed by second Red player, second Blue player, etc., until all have tried to throw bean bag in basket. The team with the most winners receives special prizes, such as decorative bean bag for each or Japanese fish or bumblebee kites. Losing team members are given small, brightly colored wooden bugs or animal favors. (A Japanese store in your community can supply these or write to Jasmine Shops, Inc., 63 East Fifty-sixth Street, New York 22, New York.)

Porch Party After Pet Show Let your children invite their friends who have shown pets in a local community pet show to come to your house, after they take their pets home. Have lemonade and cookies for all, or if it is summer, serve watermelon or strawberries and cookies, at a big table on the porch so that everybody can talk about the show.

Puppet Show Party For All Ages

One version: If your children are interested in puppets and marionette shows, their play time for weeks can be devoted to making a marionette stage, complete with puppet dolls on strings, and to preparing a show with dialogue. Finally, they are ready to practice the manipulation, acting, and dialogue of the puppets. When they have rehearsed the plays for you, and they feel ready for a performance, then make plans with them for setting up the stage and a curtain or screen behind which they work. The time has come when they can have a puppet show party.

Invitations These they send or give to their friends for a Saturday afternoon at 2 o'clock. The cleared living room or playroom should have chairs arranged like a theatre, with puppet stage placed so that all can see, yet where the hidden puppeteers can easily manipulate their actors and speak the dialogue.

After the performance and the thunderous applause, serve a snack "tea," such as cheese sandwiches and apples, or ice cream sodas or milk shakes from the blender with cookies.

Second version: You, or a school teacher, librarian, or other local puppeteer can start a children's group in puppet making. Let your children invite friends of six to twelve years for the first meeting, for a Saturday afternoon. The experienced puppeteer will know what supplies should be on hand to start some children working on the first steps in designing and constructing the theatre, and to help them with the first steps in creating puppets, their costumes, and the mechanisms to operate them, and other details.

At the end of the first class, serve the children little sandwiches and hot cocoa, or in warm weather, lemonade or a cold fruit punch and cookies. This is the time to discuss the next meeting of the group, whose objective can be a community marionette theatre, and a fine big opening performance some time later in which all the children will have some part, with other children and parents as audience.

Painting Party If you have a large playroom, or cleared room over a garage, or some other place where children can meet and paint, not only for one party but for succeeding times, you can provide them with fun and many hours of quiet play in painting. To start the children at the first painting party, use materials recommended by your children's art teachers. Finger painting and the use of small sponges, daub brushes, and feathers, as well as regular brushes, are now popular in most schools, and so is the use of big, thick pastels. Homemade easels, tilted tables, or other surfaces on which the painters can fasten paper are needed.

Talk with the manager of a local art store, and then suggest to the children invited for the party what they should bring with them, besides a smock or apron. Some will wear old jeans and a sweater for the painting. It is messy, and some place to wash hands is essential in this studio.

If the group works well together after several Painting Parties, spark the next one by announcing that they must begin to get ready for an art show. Let them invite mothers and other guests for a date one week later. Let a school art teacher or two act as judges. Eventually an outdoor art show of the children's work can be part of some community, church, or school fair.

Since most children do not enjoy long, unbroken periods of any kind of play, the painting parties should be scheduled for Saturday mornings at eleven, and at the first signs of disinterest on the part of one or more, luncheon should be offered. This menu can be their favorite hamburgers on a buttered bun, milk or chocolate milk shakes from the blender, and cookies or small iced cupcakes.

If some children want to paint again, after lunch, set a time limit on their stay, restricting them to only half an hour more so that they do not get bored with this new game.

5

TEEN-AGE PARTIES

• To begin with, here's an aside to parents from two famous psychologists. There is one vitally important thing to remember if you are a parent whose fifteen-year-old son or daughter is planning to give a party: he, or she, will want to do most of the party planning, most of the party arranging, and most of the party running himself. He will welcome concrete help with the refreshments, but for the most part it is *his* party.

Recommended by parent groups in junior and senior high schools, and for use in church and community centers, is the *Handbook of Co-Ed Teen Activities,* by Edythe and David DeMarche, published by Association Press, $7.95. Another guide is the mimeographed "Adult-Youth Relationship in Planning and Chaperoning Teen-Age Parties," available for 10 cents from the Berkeley, California, Recreation Department, City Hall Annex, 1835 Allston Way, Berkeley, California.

Here are eight party ideas contributed to this book by teen-agers in different parts of the country. They also suggest that some of their best times are in school theatre activities, community parties, and in big outdoor events, such as sailboat racing, hay rides, golf, skating, archery and other field tournaments, and picnics.

All-One-Color Party One-color theme parties are very popular in parts of Florida and California for birthdays and other occasions. The hostess decides on a color as a party theme, asks all guests to wear clothes or accessories in that color, and provides refreshments to match.

For instance an Orange Dance in either of these states comes easily. But the idea is just as good anywhere else in America. If it is summer time, girls wear orange cotton prints or solid-color orange chiffon or linen dresses, or white skirts with orange blouse, sashes, or other accents. Boys wear orange neckties and a big orange boutonniere such as zinnia or calendula. Invitations, table decorations, and favors are all in this color.

For menus for this and other parties, besides a standby general cookbook teen-agers use the teen-age magazines continually. These regularly publish new dishes which teen-age cooks have contributed to their party pages and suggestions for meals and parties for many occasions.

For a color party or any other, do not add food coloring to main dishes since too much doctoring of food makes it unappetizing and hungry guests resent its unnaturalness. Instead give color accent to the menu using foods which Nature has provided in the theme color.

Menu for the Orange Dance: tall glasses of iced orange juice as appetizer with hot cheese canapés; buttered torroncini, which are little Italian pasta corkscrews cooked like spaghetti, seasoned with butter, salt, and pepper, and mixed with finely ground carrots, which give it the orange color (delicious); small chicken-and-mushroom pastry patties with cream sauce. Tossed salad may be omitted, but dessert is essential—orange layer cake with thick orange-juice-flavored frosting, and orange sherbet. Or serve an orange gelatin mold filled with tangerine sections and sliced kumquats with whipped cream topping. Offer a choice of beverages, and don't overlook iced tea with big, paper-thin slices of orange in it.

(See Color Chart, in Chapter 17, for help in planning other one-color parties.)

Bowling Party The American Junior Bowling Congress has started many teen-agers on bowling and good times with bowling parties. There may be an A.J.B.C. teacher at your best local family bowling alley. If not, write the Bowling Congress (1913 West 103rd Street, Chicago 43, Illinois) for free leaflets on how to improve your bowling and get more fun out of it. Then if you and your friends are beginning

Also see "Costume Dance Parties," Chapter 6; "Folk Dance Parties," Chapter 11; and section on Picnics in "Outdoor Entertaining," Chapter 12 to bowl so well that the proprietor of your favorite bowling spot doesn't wince when he sees you come in, it's time to plan a party.

This could be a Saturday morning of bowling followed by lunch at someone's backyard barbecue. The menu might be grilled Canadian bacon cut as thick as ham steaks, a big pot of baked beans warmed on the back of the grill, buttered buns, tossed salad with Roquefort dressing, and sundaes or open-face butterscotch tarts.

Or you may bowl on Saturday afternoon and invite the crowd to your home afterwards. Serve supper at the kitchen counter, or around a kitchen table: grilled beef, onions, green peppers and bacon on skewers, or a big omelet with tomato sauce; bread and butter; milk shakes made in the blender; devil's food cake.

Or, it's good fun on a cold Saturday night after bowling to go to somebody's house and have a big clam chowder or oyster stew. Crackers go into the stew, but serve sliced French bread toasted and spread with lemon butter (butter mixed with grated lemon peel) with it. If your crowd are big eaters, also have ready a platter of sliced cold meat such as homemade beef loaf or boiled ham, bologna, and sliced cooked franks, and let them make their own sandwiches with more of the toasted French bread. A caramel layer cake, or frosted cupcakes, brownies, or individual baked custards are good desserts for this party.

Box Social and Square Dance Teen-age employees of one of New York's largest magazines are square-dance enthusiasts. None of them has much money to spend on entertaining but by combining funds—the girls provide the supper, the boys pay for the music—they have evenings that they and friends from school and other offices all enjoy, with little cost to any one of them.

Hosts for the parties are usually the same two young men, because one of them lives in a ground-floor apartment with access to a large backyard so the dancing doesn't disturb neighbors. His obliging family goes out for the evening after stripping their big studio living room for the party. The other boy is a fine dance caller.

Here's exactly what the invitation to one of their best evenings said. It was one large sheet of cheap white paper printed in black, using old-time country newspaper type:

Allemande Left to Blossom Street
And Dance with Your Honey, Nice and Sweet
Grand Right, and Left to 289
And Come To A Party that's Country Fine
Swing Your Partner in Gingham and Plaid
Come Dressed Country Style, Fancy or Mad

We're giving a Square Dance Party at 7 P.M. Saturday,
 March 15.
Caller: The Blue Eyed Bombshell from Beacon Hill and His
 Joy Street Jugglers.

Here's the Set-Up:
 You Girls: Bring a fancied-up Box Supper
  We'll auction it off at 9:30
  You'll eat with the fella that bids highest for it.
 You Boys: Bring a bit of cash.
 We'll provide Coffee, Prizes, Fun and Music
  plus full instruction for Square Dancing

Since Square Dancing is done in sets of 8, it is important for
us to know how many of you are coming, so please call:
Chelsea 3-1186.   Fred Santry
Y'ALL Come! Hear!   Pete Colvin

Box Supper Suggestions Not only should each girl's box supper be
amusingly different and gay in wrapping and tied with ribbons to attract bidders, but the food inside the box should be fresh and appetizing and consist of a good supper for two. Line the box with
several layers of waxed paper and wrap each sandwich and every piece
of food separately in heavy waxed paper or foil. Add a fresh flower,
spray of leaves or sprig of fresh herb here and there to wrapped foods.
 It's a good idea to have two different kinds of sandwiches, such
as sliced ham with mustard on buttered soft roll, and another of tangy
cheese spread on whole-wheat bread cut in squares for easy handling.
Potato salad in small covered paper cups is always welcome (with

wooden picnic forks); or deviled eggs; two good breast pieces of cold fried chicken; small raspberry jam turnovers or a chocolate cupcake with thick fudge frosting. And ahead of time girls should ask the hosts to provide refrigerator space or some other cool spot for the boxes so foods keep fresh until suppertime. (Boys seldom think of such things.)

Square dancing has become so popular that your community probably has someone who can teach the dances, do the calling, and supply the right kind of old-time music. Advertise in your school or local paper if no other detective work brings them forward. Here are some square dance records, 10-inch LP's, available from Folkways Records (see page 177 for address): *Square Dances,* Piute Pete, contains the calls and dance instructions for Easterns, Westerns, and instrumental, descriptive booklet included; another is *Country Dance Music,* Washboard Band, recommended for square-dance accompaniment, beat, speeds, and timing given.

Come-and-Bring Party Spur of the moment parties are sometimes more fun than those planned weeks ahead. One of the best, according to teen-agers in New Mexico, Texas, and California is a Come-and-Bring Party. The party-givers telephone their best friends to come on Friday or Saturday evening and bring games, or dance music, or a guitar and a good singing voice. Someone brings four chairs, one girl brings cups and saucers or the dessert, such as an ice-box cake she likes to make. A girl may be asked to bring two extra boys, and one boy is asked to bring his big ice tub to hold ice and bottles of soft drinks.

Depending on what guests are bringing with them, the hostesses provide the rest of the refreshments, entertainment, and decoration, or whatever they know their crowd likes.

Menus are no problem for this crowd. They make use of such edibles as oven-crisped (quick-frozen) fried onion rings and potato chips served with a good cheese and mustard dip; a hot casserole of something sustaining and filling, such as noodles or macaroni with meat sauce and crumb topping; toasted soft rolls or thick slices of Italian or French bread for those who want bread with every meal; a dessert, wonderful sundaes for the boys (which they make themselves) and fruit compote or honeydew melon for girls who are figure-conscious; cold soft drinks, milk, or milk shakes made in the blender.

Fun depends on what the guests bring in the way of entertainment. One such evening began with dancing (a boy brought a large collection of dance records), ended with supper served at 10 o'clock, and everybody home before midnight, according to the teen-age and parents' schedule observed in that community.

Another Come-and-Bring afternoon party turned into an archery contest. One of the crowd, newly interested in this ancient game, brought a target and all else needed, taught his friends all he knew, and they spent an afternoon practicing. Then they planned a serious archery tournament for a few weeks later, when all hoped to be experts. The supper, which followed on a big porch, was a pan of meat loaf with tomato sauce hot from the oven, a loaf of homemade bread on a slicing board, a jar of jam, and peach ice cream homemade in a freezer. Everybody helped himself to everything.

They spent the evening singing to guitar and banjo, improvising and doing their local version of songs and flamenco.

Come for a Swim and Lunch A swimming party is one of the easiest ways to get acquainted with a new boy or girl in the neighborhood. A pool, lake, or river may be your favorite swim spot, or even an irrigation canal, which in some parts of the Southwest are wide and deep enough for swimming and where good picnic swimming parties line their banks during summer. And of course, boys and girls who live near a bay on the seacoast or beside the ocean make good use of swimming parties for their summer fun.

A swim followed by lunch around the pool, or on the beach, or under shady trees on a river bank calls for no special planning, except good food and invitations to the crowd you like best. (If you don't know how to swim, start learning. If there isn't a boy to teach you, join a class at school, or go to the "Y" or a Red Cross training center. Around private pools and beaches there are usually swimming instructors.)

Menu The good swimmers say, swim first and eat afterwards. Then rest at least an hour before swimming again. If you invite your crowd for 11 o'clock on a sunny Saturday morning and everybody swims and plays around the pool or on the beach for an hour, lunch tastes good afterwards. It should start with a cool-off drink, such as fruit punch

full of orange and lemon juice, or iced grape juice. If som...
shivering with cold from the water give him a glass of hot tea...
the cold or hot drink, serve big, juicy hamburgers or cheesebu...
broiled on a portable grill barbecue or brought out from the kitchen ...
a serving cart. Other favorites are frankfurters with mustard, cheese,
and pickle relish on split long rolls, or hero sandwiches made of giant
slices of Italian bread or big hero rolls, buttered and spread with
everything you like, such as lettuce, anchovies, crumbled cheese, sliced
dill pickle and ripe tomato, a thin slice of boiled or baked ham, sliced
hard-cooked eggs, and maybe mustard relish.

Anyone want dessert? A bowl of washed, chilled black cherries with
stems left on, or strawberries ditto. Dip the latter into powdered sugar
in a green grape leaf held on your palm. Some boys like cookies or
another sweet with every meal. Bring out a large, covered cooky jar
full of assorted cookies and let them help themselves.

Games Talk may be slow if new friends have just met for the first
time at this party. There's nothing like a guessing game to keep things
going. Try the "National Park Quiz Game" based on the names of the
less known National Parks. The famous ones don't count in this game;
there are nine others few people know. For this give everybody a pencil
and paper. Each boy and girl writes down as many names of less well-
known National Parks and their location as he can remember. Those
who know all, or the most, get prizes, such as a new beach ball or
swim cap. Here are the nine parks: Mesa Verde National Park, Colo-
rado; Big Bend, Texas; Isle Royale, in Lake Superior; Acadia, Maine;
Olympic, Washington; Zion, Utah; Bryce Canyon, Utah; Wind Cave,
South Dakota; Lassen Volcanic National Park, California. An excellent
book for this is *America's National Parks* (Doubleday).

Another quiz that's fun because there is at least one amateur astrono-
mer in every crowd is "How's Your Heavenly Bodies?" Ask everybody
to write in a column from the top of the paper downwards, the
words Star, Planet, Comet, Meteor, Meteorite, and opposite each name
write a short definition. When all have finished writing ask the astrono-
mer to give the correct definitions and let each guest grade his own
paper. Winners' prizes are star maps, on sale in stationery and book
shops, or a copy of *Careers* game.

Here are the heavenly facts:

Star: a huge mass of glowing vapors and gases, which shines by its own light. The sun is a star.

Planet: solid body, which revolves around the sun in a fixed orbit and shines by reflecting the sun's light. Stars twinkle; planets shine steadily.

Comet: moves about the sun on elongated orbit; may be visible once in a hundred years or a thousand years or some other measure of time established by astronomers. Consists of many small, meteorlike particles surrounded by envelope of gas. It may have a gaseous tail, which stretches out for millions of miles; shines by reflecting the light of the sun, partly by absorbing and re-emitting it.

Meteor: shooting star, composed of solid particles most of which are iron and stone. When one enters the earth's atmosphere, friction generated makes it glow brightly, and often burns itself up. Most meteors are visible only a few seconds. Meteorites are meteors that reach the earth's surface.

Time to swim again, or go home. This same kind of party is a favorite for tennis players, young golf crowds, and for the lawn or grass bowling devotees.

Costume Dance—Come As The One You Want To Be This party brings out some surprising secrets about the boys and girls in your crowd. At a dance given by a teen-age brother and sister who did all the decorating and cooked the supper, too, a chef turned up— he happened to be the boy they liked best in the next block. With him was a hula dancer, prettiest girl in the community, wearing a grass skirt over her bathing suit and fabulous fresh real flower leis around her neck which she made with zinnias, marigolds, daisies, violet leaves, and asters from her mother's garden. A red-nose hobo came next, wearing battered old derby, raggedy clothes, real live toes sticking out of his shoes; his date was a cowgirl, terrific hat and bright red shirt her brother had sent her from Wyoming, and no spurs.

A sailor brought a ballet dancer. An artist wearing a paint-smeared smock and sad mustaches hanging down to his collar brought an interior decorator wearing a very funny little hat, dozens of bracelets and necklaces, carrying swatches of decorating fabrics, a package of wallpaper samples, and a paint color card. A farmer arrived in faded blue overalls, big red handkerchief in hip pocket, and an enormous straw hat with a few pieces of hay sticking through a hole in crown. His date was a city slicker model in the latest-fashion-from-Paris dress which she and her mother made from some old draperies, with a hairdo out of this world, eye make-up out to there, an emerald ring as big as a door-knob.

Setting for the dance was the basement playroom, cleaned up and freshly painted by the host and hostess. They followed the modern idea of different colors on different walls, one white, one bold bright blue, the other two pale yellow. They added blue wall seats and blue-painted legs to the big built-in buffet table. They waxed the floor for dancing which began about 8 o'clock. A huge, yellow-painted wooden tub was filled with ice and bottles of soft drinks, glasses stood ready on a tray. Music was records, interrupted for a couple of radio programs which featured dance bands that evening.

Supper at 10:30 was buffet style. A stack of small tray tables provided one for each guest. Plates, napkins, silver were brought from the kitchen on a big tray. Then two large casseroles of delicious shrimp creole. They were cooked earlier in the day and kept in refrigerator, then topped with buttered crumbs and reheated in oven. (Hosts' mother put the casseroles in the oven about 10 o'clock so that they would be hot for supper.) With them were plenty of hot saffron rice (freshly cooked by their mother) and buttered toast.

Dessert was marvelous cheese cake with stewed black cherries on top. Milk to drink, or coffee for anyone who wanted it. Everybody started home before midnight, and two tired hosts did the cleaning up. Their mother helped with dish washing and putting things away.

Girls' Pajama Party According to statistics compiled by two psychologists, on fourteen- and fifteen-year-old girls, the party they like best, next to a dance, is a pajama party. (Their grandmothers and great-grandmothers called them slumber parties.) The hostess invites four or five girls of her age whom she especially likes to come to supper or dinner and spend the night.

This usually means that they eat early and go to the movies. Then, back at the hostess' home, changing into their sleeping clothes and spend the night giggling and talking about boys, eating, and playing pranks on each other. There is little or no sleeping. Whenever the spirit moves them, they raid the family refrigerator by previous arrangement and planning between the hostess and her mother. They change beds from time to time, or everybody piles into one bed room to eat and talk there for a while.

The food supply usually includes sandwiches made earlier in the day, wrapped in waxed paper and ready in the refrigerator for the foragers, bottles of milk and chocolate-flavored milk drinks, fruit, mixed cheese dip and packages of fresh potato chips to eat with it. Cookies, small fruit tarts, brownies, and frosted cupcakes may be available, even ice cream from the freezer. Candy and nuts are among the hostess' request to her mother for the night's supplies.

The dinner that precedes the pajama party may be anything the hostess and her mother want to provide the guests. Usually it is the family evening meal, a roast or casserole of meat and vegetables, tossed salad, dessert such as lemon meringue pie, and beverages.

Of course, the hostess may want a gala party in which she decorates the dining room and table with her favorite color. One Ashland, Kentucky, fourteen-year-old loves yellow. She says the best pajama party she ever gave started with a yellow-and-white dinner. She used a yellow tablecloth and napkins, and yellow-and-white china, and made a centerpiece, and other bouquets around the house, of carefully arranged, mixed yellow flowers.

Menu began with broiled half grapefruit; then broiled chicken breasts with lemon butter; steamed yellow squash; baked, stuffed potatoes; lemon layer cake frosted with yellow; lemon ice cream served in yellow paper frilled cups inside dessert dishes; milk for girls and coffee for father and mother.

Most girls omit records and radio from these all-night talkathons, because elsewhere in the house the parents of the hostess and the rest of the family are trying to sleep. And while there may be a pillow fight or two, breakage and destruction are usually kept to a minimum or entirely avoided.

Let's Travel Dinner or Progressive Dinner One of the best ways to give a dinner dance, and keep it moving from the time dinner begins until the last goodnight on the girls' home doorsteps, is to divide the dinner among three or four or more hostesses. Four girls, all of whose homes are in a suburban area near Indianapolis, gave a Let's Travel Dinner, which has been much copied in their crowd because it was lively and good fun. The families helped them prepare and serve the food but the girls chose the menu and planned all the details.

Invitations were given by the four girls to two additional girls and six boys for dinner, to begin at 6:30 o'clock at Betty's house.

Menu was divided into four parts. The first course served at Betty's: chilled mixed vegetable juice with appetizers of hot creamed lobster and Parmesan cheese in scallop shells, with toast points, stuffed celery, and ripe olives. Betty used the family living room for this, setting up three bridge tables with blue cloths and napkins, blue plates, and forks and water glasses on each. When her date and the other five couples had arrived, she served the tables and then sat down with her guests to enjoy their delicious first course.

They were due at Helen's house at a little after 7 P.M. for the main course of the dinner. This was a superb ham loaf (ground ham, hard-cooked egg, crumbs) with mustard sauce, tiny rice croquettes with currant jelly in center, buttered lima beans, and buttered hot rolls. Helen's home was chosen for this course because her family has a large dining room. Her mother opened the dining table out as far as it would go and set twelve places using the family's prettiest lace dinner mats and linen napkins, candlesticks and silver accessories. The centerpiece was a bouquet made up of small nosegays of fresh flowers, which at the end of the dinner were given to the girls.

About 8 o'clock they were due at Sally's house. She and her mother live in a small apartment. They arranged the living room for buffet service, setting up three bridge tables and covering them with flowered chintz cloths. They turned a living-room table into a buffet lighted with candles in tall pottery sticks, and arranged forks and napkins on it, ready for the salad course. Her mother made a tossed green salad of Boston lettuce, endive, water cress and cucumbers, had it very cold and ready to finish when the guests arrived.

While they took off wraps, Sally's mother tossed the salad with a fine Roquefort cheese dressing and placed the big salad bowl and chilled salad plates on the buffet. Boys and girls helped themselves to salad, and Sally went to the kitchen to bring in a tray of open-face sand-wiches, which she and her mother had made earlier in the day. They were narrow strips, small squares, circles, and triangles of toast and buttered bread, some covered with anchovy fillets, others with the thin-nest possible slices of smoked salmon or baked ham. This is a wonder-ful combination of flavors with salad.

It was nearly 9 o'clock, and right on schedule, when the couples got to Barbie's house where they were to eat dessert and dance. Her family, which includes 5 children, have a large basement playroom. It was hung with Japanese lanterns and big Japanese kites. Two large tables were left bare except for the piles of dessert plates, forks, and bright paper napkins on each. When the twelve traveling diners arrived, Barbie's young brother and sister, aged ten and eight, escorted couples down stairs to the playroom with music of piccolo and small drum.

Dessert followed the last ones down. It was a big melon-shaped mold of strawberry, vanilla, and pistachio ice cream and a platter of petits fours in the same colors. Everybody sat around the tables to eat des-sert. Coffee was offered those who wanted it.

Dancing began not too long after 9 o'clock to special local radio dance bands, and continued later with records.

6

COSTUME DANCE PARTIES

• Patterns for a large variety of popular fancy-dress costumes for men, women, and children can be bought at pattern and notions counters.

• Theatrical and costume rental services in large cities, as well as in many smaller ones, can supply almost any kind of costume for boys and men, girls and women.

• And if you have time and imagination, and can sew, you can make your own costumes. For materials, haunt the dime stores, foreign shops, mill-end fabric outlet stores, theatrical fabric companies, antique shops, auctions, and the family attic. Use mail order ads for unusual accessories, side-street manufacturers who supply the millinery and fashion trades, and many other sources.

Part of the fun of a costume party is making the fancy-dress that you will wear. If it can be concocted out of things you already have—beach hat, gaudy scarves, costume jewelry, Japanese kimono, old evening coat—so much the better, for your budget and your creative genius.

Also, the wear-what-you-have idea is the basis of one of the most popular costume parties.

Come-As-You-Are Dance One interpretation of this idea appeals especially to young marrieds, because it costs less than a fancy-dress

Also see "Children's Parties," Chapter 3; "Teen-Age Parties," Chapter 5; "Folk Dance Parties," Chapter 11; and "Foreign Dinners," Chapter 16 costume party yet is just as much fun. For this, guests are supposed to wear what they have—anything from lounging pajamas to jeans, hostess gown to office suit.

In a second version of the Come-As-You-Are Party, guests wear costumes that reveal what each thinks he really is or would like to be.

Invitations For either dance send invitations about ten days before the party date. For the first version, which is a dance for your close friends in the community, use fold-over informal cards either with your name, or both your name and your husband's name, and your address on the first page. Write on the inside something like this:

> Dance and Supper at Our House
> Saturday Evening, February 9th
> 9 o'clock
>
> Come As You Are   Joan and Bill
> Costumes!   R.S.V.P.

For the larger dance, with what-you-think-you-are or would-like-to-be costumes, young marrieds as well as single men and women are invited for New Year's Eve, or some other important holiday or occasion. Use the same kind of invitation cards, but with your name and your husband's name and the address on the cover. Inside write:

> Dancing and Supper
> Saturday Night, February 9th
> 9 o'clock to Midnight
> Please Wear Costume of
> The One You Think You Are
> or Would Like To Be
> R.S.V.P.   Crystal 4-6213

In either of these parties your budget and your taste guide you as to the kind and amount of decoration and refreshments. The party is conditioned by the space you have. In the small, intimate home dance, the budget goes for music and food with no special decoration attempted. A local dance trio or collection of dance records provide music, cold drinks are served through the evening, and the party ends with a supper for which the main dish may be the specialty of the host or hostess.

Decorations Hosts for the larger party may spend a considerable amount on decorations, by turning a cleared-out living room or a playroom into a gala ballroom. A Long Island family that gives a dance at the drop of a hint from any friend converts their children's big playroom into beautiful settings. For one dance they hung the walls with draperies of rose colored tarlatan (flame-proof), used the same fabric at all windows and added deep swags of flower garlands (artificial flowers in many colors) over the windows and as side drops hanging down to the floor (see sketch).

Supper tables in this festive ballroom were covered with the same tarlatan to the floor, over white tablecloths. They rented ten tall, electric Florentine torchères from a theatrical warehouse to light the room and garlanded these floor lights with flowers like those in the window treatment.

Guests danced to a small dance band until 10 o'clock when supper was served. Iced punch was served throughout the evening and after supper until the band stopped playing, at midnight.

Menu The supper for either party: hot creamed crab meat on Parmesan cheese toast, sliced baked ham and ripe olives in aspic, and a salad of Belgian endive on water cress with chopped beets and orange peel added to French dressing; small, hot croissant rolls; apricot mousse; coffee. For economy, the salad or the aspic may be omitted.

Favorite Americans Costume Dance This is a good party for any patriotic holiday when you want to entertain school or college club friends, or merely a mixture of (older) teen-agers and other guests who like to dance.

Invitations Send these about ten days to two weeks before the party date. Use a card with a red-white-and-blue border or some patriotic symbol, such as shield or flag on it. Write:

You Are Invited To A
Favorite Americans Costume Dance and Supper
Friday Night, February 22nd.

9 PM to	Mr. and Mrs. Charles Budge
Midnight	4 Campus Street
R.S.V.P.	Temple 2-2641

Please dress as your favorite American.

To close friends, omit Mr. and Mrs. Charles Budge and write Mary and Charles and add "Do come!" or some other personal message.

If guests telephone for help in choosing a costume, you might suggest such names as Uncle Sam, George and Martha Washington, Abraham Lincoln, Daniel Boone, Teddy Roosevelt, Gen. Custer, Stephen Foster, Robert E. Lee, Betsy Ross, Pocahontas, Charles Lindbergh, Paul Revere, Sam Houston, Benjamin Franklin, William Penn, Priscilla and John Alden, "Buffalo Bill" Cody, Annie Oakley, Ethan Allen, Susan B. Anthony, Jane Addams, Lucy Stone.

Decorations are what you like, in red, white, and blue. Balloons are festive and gay, bouquets of flowers always effective. Flags are used for more serious occasions. Decorate the supper room in the same theme as the dance room. Cover small tables with white cloths, and place a red-white-and-blue favor, such as a snapper or noisemaker or little box of candies or some funny little wrapped-up animal, on each folded white napkin. Guests serve themselves at a buffet table. Or, filled supper plates can be brought in from the kitchen and placed before guests who have sat down at the tables (without place cards) where they please.

Menu Supper dishes served at Mount Vernon to guests of Martha and George Washington included chicken pie. Baked in individual casseroles, little chicken pies are easily served to a large crowd. Place the small casserole on a plate, and add a narrow slice of fresh pumpernickel spread with savory cheese mixture, a spiced peach or Seckel pear. Serve frozen eggnog and devil's food cake for dessert, with coffee.

Or, since oyster stew was a favorite at the Washingtons' supper table, your holiday dance menu might be simply a superb oyster stew and delicious open-face sandwiches of ham, chicken, cheese, anchovies, followed by coffee and cake.

Mardi gras Costume Dance The old name for the three days preceding Ash Wednesday, the beginning of Lent, is Shrovetide. Of these, Shrove Tuesday is also called Mardi gras Day (literally, fat Tuesday) and Pancake Day from an ancient custom of eating pancakes or Shrove cakes on this last day before the long period of fasting begins. It is a public holiday in Alabama, many Florida cities, and many places in Louisiana, with festivals, dancing, and merrymaking in organized celebrations. New Orleans has been famous since early in the eighteenth century for the carnival of feasting, music, and fun in homes and in the streets, known as The Mardi Gras.

The Mardi gras theme makes a colorful and lively costume supper dance. Here is the way one such party is given annually by a former New Orleans family now living near Philadelphia. For a less expensive party and one easier to give, the special decorations and some of the luxurious menu can be omitted. And it is not essential that guests come masked, although part of the Mardi gras fun is in the masking and unmasking.

Invitations should be sent about two weeks before the date of the party, on fold-over cards or note paper decorated with a little mask or a domino (a half mask). This is similar to the invitation used for the Philadelphia party:

You Are Invited
To Come To Our Party
Mardi Gras Night
Dancing and Supper
Tuesday, February 17, 9 o'clock

Please Wear Costume and Domino

Mr. and Mrs. Stephen O'Hare   Castle 8-2431
Old Cottage, Castle Road   R.S.V.P.

When guests telephone to accept, they may ask about appropriate dress. Any of these traditional Mardi gras costumes will be in the spirit of the occasion: old Spanish and French costumes for men and women, pirates, sailors, monks, nuns, ballet dancers, devils, Pierrots and Pierrettes, jesters, clowns, gypsies, Creole beauties with elaborate turbans. At unmasking time, which should be when supper is announced, it adds fun to have one or two prizes ready to bestow for the best costumes.

Decorations If there is a playroom, basement, or garage space for dancing, make it bright and lively with balloons in pink, purple, lime, turquoise, orange. If possible, have colored lights to play on the dancers from time to time. A hired dance trio or band may bring these lights with them to use for certain dances.

But the chief decoration for this party is in the supper room. This may be the cleared dining room and living room opened up together to make one large room, or any other large space which can be turned into a carnival midway, along which at supper time the hungry dancers can find good New Orleans food.

Teen-age and other family carpenters and designers take charge of the decorating. Cut cardboard fronts about 6½ to 7 feet high (see sketch) for carnival booths. Decorate them with big, colored Halloween masks, streamers, balloons, flowers, musical instruments. Use orange, red, warm pinks, rich purple paints, poster inks, and tempera to color them.

These fronts should be shaped to fit in front of and around the two ends of kitchen tables. Arrange them and the tables that are behind them close to a wall, leaving room for placing and removing the platters or containers of food and for someone to stand and serve at suppertime. Three such booths are enough.

Rent or borrow small tables and chairs. Cover the table tops with bright, solid-color orange, pink, purple, lime, or turquoise paper, cut to fit and smoothly turned under all around the table top and tacked on under side to hold firmly. Make simple, straight slipcovers for all chair backs of double-thickness crepe paper or inexpensive cotton fabric in same colors as the table tops. Mix chairs, using assorted colors at each table.

In each booth there must be someone to serve the food. It adds to the carnival atmosphere if these servers wear chef's tall hats and white coats.

Menu Guests go from one booth to the next as at a buffet table. In each booth, in addition to the foods, there should be the necessary plates and silver for that course. At the first booth a guest chooses from a whole cold baked ham or turkey, pan of hot baked oysters, hot rolls, and quince preserve. His plate served, he picks up a knife, fork, and folded napkin and passes along to the next booth. Hot shrimp Creole on fluffy rice and small stuffed tomato salads are served in the second booth. When guests are ready for dessert, the third booth offers pecan pie and coffee.

Guests sit down where they please at the bright tables, which are grouped around the room in front of the booths. They return to the booths for seconds, for more coffee or whatever they want.

For a simpler menu, serve only pancakes (for Shrove Tuesday) with creamed crab meat, or creamed chicken, turkey, or ham on them, and the dessert and coffee.

As a finale for this party, it is fun to show a colored travel film of the real New Orleans Mardi Gras. Or, make color movies of this party at supper around the gaudy booths as background.

Out-Of-This-World Costume Dance Space men and women, of course, come to this party. The long tights some skin divers wear are suitable costumes because, oddly enough, they look like cartoonists' ideas of space men. So are any amusing conceptions of modern-minded men and women as to what our neighbors on other planets wear, the funnier the better. This is a wonderful children's party idea, too.

Invitations should be written on flying-saucer-shaped paper, which you can cut from blue note paper:

The Saucers Have Landed!
Space Men and Women Are Coming To
Dance and Stay for Supper
Saturday, March 21   9 o'clock
Wear Your Best Space Costume
Betsy and Will Watson   Center 4-8230
29 Main Street   R.S.V.P.

Decorations Decorate the playroom, or wherever the guests will dance, with stars. Cut out or buy large and small paper stars, dozens of them, and cover them with bright metallic foil or paint with metallic silver paint. Suspend them from the ceiling on silver Christmas cord at different heights, using mixture of many sizes so that the top of the room is full of bright stars. If there is a chandelier, hang clusters of stars from it on blue cords.

Place big silver stars over any windows, and if possible drape windows with white and blue cheesecloth or tarlatan. (Buy flame-proof fabrics from theatrical supply stores.)

Instead of tables, use trays. Buy dime-store metal or plastic trays, and paint flying saucers and stars all over them, using pale blue paint. When dry, coat them with colorless varnish and let them dry thoroughly. A good souvenir of your party is to add date and name of party to each tray and present it to the guest who eats his supper from it. *This Tray From The Watsons' Flying Saucer Party,* and the date. Use water-color paint brushes for lettering, or Magic Marker (sold in stationery and art shops) in light blue.

Menu If you have kitchen help or can prepare enough chicken soufflés for the crowd, this airy dish is just right for an interplanetary party. If soufflés are too difficult to manage for your crowd, serve a light, well-seasoned chicken loaf with mushroom sauce, small hot buttered rolls, deviled eggs in aspic with garnish of water cress and mayonnaise; for dessert, mocha tarts with very high, light meringue topping, and coffee.

National Costume Dances Most popular of all costume dances are those in which all guests wear costumes of one country, such as a Brazilian Costume Dance, a Ceylonese Costume Dance and others inspired by China, Cuba, Greece, Hungary, India, Italy, Ireland, Japan, Mexico, Peru, Spain, Thailand, Turkey. Of these, Japan is especially popular because of a growing interest in America in Japanese architecture, decoration, foods, and theatre. Mexico is probably next in popularity because many Norte Americanos visit the land below the Border and are enthusiastic about the fiestas, foods, colors and the way of life there.

Such national dances are planned by returned travelers, or a member of a language study group or of an international club and similar organizations, or simply because a special costume party can be fun for hosts and guests.

Information on national costumes, songs, dances, decorative dolls (which show costumes), and much else is available from various foreign information services and embassies in the United States. A list of such offices and their addresses is sent on request if you write Public Inquiries Unit, Visitors' Service, Department of Public Information, United Nations, New York.

Your own local library is a source of books and possibly photographs and films showing various national costumes as well as books of foreign cookery. Local music shops carry, or can order, records made by orchestras, singers, and other musicians in many countries.

National costumes can be copied in inexpensive fabrics from pictures or museum garments, or bought from import shops where foreign wares of many kinds are available. Japanese, Chinese, South American, Mexican, Government of India and many other such shops are in large and small cities all over America. Many of them advertise in the fashion and home furnishings magazines and their interesting wares can be ordered by mail.

Once a national theme is decided on, such as a Japanese Costume Dance or Mexican Costume Dance, proceed as for other described costume parties. Use colors and products of the foreign country to decorate playroom or wherever guests dance, and add to the national atmosphere by decorating the supper tables with native wares and serving a menu of that country for the dance supper. (See "How to Give a Foreign Dinner," Chapter 16.)

Large foreign restaurants can help you plan such menus; many foreign foods are sold by mail order through advertisements in fine magazines. Your book stores have books of foreign cookery and can order others for you. The women's magazines describe many foreign dinners and give the Americanized version of the cookery; their service departments will send such recipes to you. (For more suggestions, see the next dance described below.)

Round-The-World Costume Dance Some hosts like to mix several countries together at a costume dance, making it a round-the-world affair. For this party ask guests to come in a costume of their favorite foreign country, such as Italy, Spain, Mexico, China, Japan, India, or our newest state, Hawaii.

Decorate with mixture of wares and themes from several countries, such as Japanese lanterns, lovely Indian saris and Spanish shawls hung as wall decoration (in some instances, these might be borrowed from a museum or local collection). Use Indian and Spanish travel posters, Mexican straw and tin figures, tall ceramic candlesticks from the same country, or an Italian or Sicilian donkey cart, which you can make. Paint a small wooden cart with flowers, landscapes, angels, and anything else which appeals to the artist, then decorate with fresh or artificial flowers and fruit. Use this cart when serving supper, or for the bowl of iced punch that you make available for thirsty dancers. Use Hawaiian leis of fresh or artificial flowers on tables or as supper favors for the guests.

Menu Serve foreign foods. Here are some suggestions. Italian: supper of large hot pizzas, tossed green salad, spumone, coffee. Spanish: casseroles of chicken with saffron rice, tomato salad, frozen custard, coffee. Mexican: chili con carne, or roast turkey, bread sticks, green salad, chocolate mousse, coffee. Japanese: sukiyaki made at the buffet or supper tables in electric skillets, hot rice, tea, ice cream and cookies or chilled melon. Indian: curry of shrimp on rice, condiments such as chopped green pepper, shredded coconut, chopped salted peanuts, chutney; tea or coffee, honeydew melon or mixed fresh fruit platter of melon, fresh apricots, peaches, apples, seedless grapes. Hawaiian: deviled crabs in shells, or casseroles of deviled crab, herbed toast, mixed fresh pineapple and grapefruit salad, tall glass of guava sherbet, coconut cake, coffee. (Also, see Chapter 16, on foreign dinners.)

Other Costume Dances

All-Sports Costume Ball. Guests come in costumes for yachting, baseball, football, golf, tennis, riding, swimming, skating, hunting, smallcar racing, horse racing, skin diving, flying, mountain climbing, cricket, croquet, bowling.

Artists and Models Costume Dance. Ancient and present-day painters, famous models, present-day models.

Country Boys and Girls Costume Dance. A favorite with grownups in cities.

Costume Party on Skates. See Chapter 12, on "Outdoor Entertaining."

Different States of the Union Costume Party. Costumes are based on famous men, historical facts, products.

Favorite Heroes and Heroines of Novels. These can be from the past or present-day.

Favorite Opera and Musical Comedy Stars. Choose old-time or present-day figures.

Rue de la Paix Costume Dance. Plan an evening of Edwardian and the Twenties elegance. Ladies wear their (funny) idea of the latest Dior, Balmain, Chanel, Balenciaga, and other famous fashion designers. Gentlemen wear dress-up evening clothes of the Twenties, with fake mustaches, military decorations, royal ribbons and orders. The dances are elegant waltzes, two-steps, and fox trots. Decorate rooms with many large mirrors, borrowed or rented, and fresh and artificial flowers in lavish bouquets.

Supper should be in the same key: pâté and caviar on thin toast points; cold stuffed lobster on ice; cold smoked salmon in aspic; tiny hot rolls; lime or lemon gelatin with artichoke hearts previously marinated in French dressing; superb coffee mousse; demitasse.

Sailors and Their Sweethearts Costume Dance. Ancient, present-day, all ranks from admirals to gobs, girls from "every port."

Sciences and Arts Costume Dance. (Favorite in college towns.)

7

FAMILY AND CHURCH ENTERTAINING

Some of the social pleasures of old-time, small-town church going are being revived today, not only in small towns but in suburban churches near large cities, in housing-development communities, and in many city churches as well. The trend today in places of worship of various denominations is toward a closer relationship with the immediate neighborhood, which existed in America's early years when the local meeting house was a center of village life as well as a place of worship.

After-Service Coffee Hour One of the simplest and most popular of these old-time, church-social occasions is the After-Service Coffee Hour, now observed in churches of many denominations. Hot coffee is served in the community or social room of the church immediately after the religious service, as a welcome to strangers in the congregation and as a pleasant, informal time for talk amongst members and clergy.

This kind of coffee hour is also popular in congregations where a clergyman, priest, or rabbi cannot make personal calls on all of his parishioners. It provides an opportunity for members and leaders to become better acquainted.

To provide a coffee hour in your church, a sum is needed from church funds or a donation from members of the congregation to

Also see "Family and Community Parties," Chapter 8; and "Outdoor Entertaining, Chapter 12 provide the necessary cups, saucers, and other supplies. One or two members volunteer, or are asked by the clergyman, to be responsible for making and serving coffee. They must have facilities to produce a fresh, hot brew quickly after the service ends. But not before! The appetizing aroma of coffee should not mingle with the Benediction and the Amens.

If the church is small and there is no community room, the After-Service Coffee Hour might be held in the parish house, or in turn at near-by homes of members of the congregation.

Church coffee hours need not be limited to the after-service period. They may be held on one afternoon or evening each week in the church social room, perhaps with a short program of music by some local musician. Various members of the congregation act as host and hostess, in turn.

Serving coffee is also a simple and pleasant way of entertaining a few new church members invited to your home to get acquainted with each other and older members. At the Home Coffee Hour or Coffee Klatsch, additional refreshments, such as cookies, pound cake, or doughnuts or open-face sandwiches might be served with the coffee. (Also, see the Index for various references throughout this book on entertaining with coffee-and-dessert.)

Bazaars and Fairs Fund raising for various church needs goes on continually in the community through the generosity and hard work of church members. Some church Ladies' Aid groups hold monthly sales in the church social rooms of home-baked cakes, breads, cookies, and other products, or larger sales such as a Church Bazaar or Fair. All of these can be money-makers if they are well organized. Organization starts with a committee and a plan. (See the section on committees in "Family and Community Parties," Chapter 8.) Careful planning carries the idea through to success.

A Church Bazaar or Fair is a sale of donated merchandise to bring in funds for some church need, such as a new roof, a paint job, a new bell, organ, carpet, awning, or general repairs. It is given in the church social room, or if the church lacks space, a bazaar can be given in a school gym or other public room, or in a large playroom, basement, or other space of a home. In fine weather it might be given on a church terrace or lawn.

Advertising and Publicity The plan for a bazaar or fair should include notices sent one week before the bazaar date to local newspapers and women's programs on local radio stations, and repeated the day before the bazaar opens and on opening day. Posters commercially printed or made by children and teen-age artists should be placed in friendly shop windows, the local library, and at bus and railroad commuters' stations. On the day of the bazaar, additional posters should be tacked on lamp posts and fences along nearby highways to attract tourists as well as local customers. All such notices and posters should give name of bazaar, location, date, hours, and any additional important information.

Soliciting Merchandise After the advance publicity, a committee to solicit merchandise for the bazaar goes to work telephoning or calling in person on church members and neighbors. Arrangements are made to pick up donations, and to receive those delivered by donors. All items should be listed and priced for the auditing record of the bazaar, then sorted, classified, and grouped for the sale tables, which are usually folding tables borrowed from homes of church members and other tables from the church's social rooms.

Arranging the Tables A simple layout of the bazaar is sales tables arranged in two rows facing each other, the center aisle between kept free of displays and wide enough for customers going from table to table. Saleswomen behind each table need chairs and a till or covered box in which to keep money for change and from sales.

If eager teen-age artists want to hang gay decorations, such as crepe paper streamers, banners, and large sales posters to brighten up the room, such color is welcome and adds to the gala atmosphere. But a church bazaar is a simple undertaking, with no budget for decorations. All effort of committees and helpers should be concentrated on collecting enough suitable, donated merchandise to bring in a sizeable sum of money and on attracting customers who will come in and buy.

Sales Items The most popular sales items in a church bazaar are the traditional homey gifts. Homemade stuffed dolls, animals, and toys for babies are typical. Hand-hemmed towels, oven mitts, pot holders, and other useful kitchen accessories always sell. So do crocheted jackets, mittens, socks, knit things for older children and grownups.

A "Yours-and-Mine" table is a money-maker because it displays white-elephant donations, such as used lamp shades, a pair of window draperies, table linens, pillow covers, and other furnishings no longer needed by the donor but useful to someone else. Decorators and young homemakers like such tables at bazaars because many "finds" are possible, which can be turned into useful, desirable furnishings.

At every church bazaar, tables of home-baked cakes, rolls, bread, and pies bring in cash; homemade candies are good sellers at another table; so are jars of homemade pickles, relishes, jams, and chutneys. Good second-hand books should be displayed on one table; the church Scout troop can collect these and bundles of old magazines and donated phonograph records. If the bazaar is held near the winter holidays, Christmas and New Year's cards, gifts, candies, ornaments, and other timely merchandise are sure to attract customers. At this season, too, commercial toys and games, gift stationery, and many other inexpensive gift items sell readily. The bazaar organizers buy these wholesale and sell them marked up at reasonable retail prices.

Besides committee members in charge of various jobs at the bazaar or fair, volunteers should be on hand to help wrap, clear away empty cartons, perhaps serve hot coffee to the workers, run errands and help in cleaning up and restoring the room or garden afterwards. As with any other money-raising activity, when all financial reports are complete, the publicity or press committee should send a notice to local papers on any interesting facts about the bazaar and state the amount raised for the church.

Sewing For Church Funds The Sewing Bee, Quilting Bee, and Hooked Rug Bee are pleasant social, home-church occasions. Originally a bee was a neighborly gathering of people "to engage in united effort, as practical assistance," such as harvesting a crop before a storm, building a barn, making clothing. Later some bees became competitive such as the husking bee and spelling bee.

The old name has lingered and is still used by neighbors, members of the church who meet to sew for an orphanage or hospital, or for a stock pile of children's warm clothing, which the church can use in emergencies for families when there is sickness or unemployment. Or the group of sewing women may make aprons and other accessories, hooked rugs, quilts, and other merchandise to sell at their bazaars and fairs.

Entertaining Such Groups in Your Home need never be lavish. The first essential is a comfortable and suitable place for all to work, a large, cleared dining-room or playroom table, good light, and comfortable chairs. Supplies of scissors, needles, yarns, and whatever may have been forgotten by various members of the sewing group should be available. Usually one member is responsible for these and they are purchased out of a budget. The budget may have been accumulated through a bazaar or church fair or from donations.

Meeting to sew, knit, or make rugs may occur once a week or less often in the home of the members in turn. Since most of the group are usually homemakers, an afternoon hour is easier for them than morning or evening bees.

Refreshments served at tea time or just before they hurry home to their families should be something as simple as hot tea or coffee, or in summer, a tall cold glass of lemonade or orangeade, with macaroons, fruit cake, or cheese straws, or some other small, light cookie or cracker.

Socials and Lawn Festivals Socials and Lawn Festivals have been a part of the American scene since small communities began building churches so that the circuit-riding preachers could give up their horseback journeying, settle in villages, and hold regular Sunday meetings. The socials helped to pay for the church bell, the first pews, eventually for an altar and small organ in these early meeting houses.

Socials and lawn festivals are still helping to pay for such essentials and many other necessities in the neighborhood church. Today the community is larger, and among the committees for the affair is one to cope with the crowds that attend. But the social itself has changed little. Still high on the list of the most popular are Ice Cream, Strawberry, and Watermelon Socials. Almost as popular, in some sections of the country are Peach, Blueberry, Cherry, and Raspberry Socials.

A large lawn, park area, or paved plaza is needed for this pleasant event. Since a fine lawn is difficult to achieve and costly to maintain, the modern trend for outdoor events is away from such precious landscaping around a church or residence and toward some area not quite so vulnerable to racing children and the damaging effects of table and chair legs and the footsteps of even the most orderly customers. A large paved terrace, a dead-end street closed to traffic for the evening, a paved area of a neighborhood park are suitable for a social.

The location should be easily accessible to customers who come in cars as well as to the neighbors who stroll over from nearby homes. The name Block Party is applied to such a fete or social when given in a roped-off street. A Block Party may also include dancing, and a bazaar as well as refreshments.

Those in charge of the social arrange for the space, for clearing and making it ready for tables and chairs, and cleaning up afterwards. A committee plans and puts up decorations, such as Japanese lanterns or other gala lighting. Other volunteers are responsible for table linen, china, and silver, or the paper equivalent of these accessories. Another committee purchases supplies and foods, prepares them to be served and sold, oversees the serving, and cleans up kitchen areas afterwards.

It is important that someone take charge of advertising the event. There must also be someone to sell tickets before the date and to arrange for money and tickets to be taken at the entrance of the grounds, or in some other convenient way collect money from customers for the food served them.

At least a week in advance of the social, a notice should be sent to local newspapers and the women's programs on local radio stations. Colorful, pretty, or amusing posters help to bring in customers. School children or volunteer artists of the church membership can make these, which, like the press story, must state date, place, hour, kind of social and its price and purpose. An early-evening hour is usually the most popular for this kind of party.

At an Ice Cream Social three or four kinds of ice cream may be served, the most popular being vanilla, chocolate, strawberry, coffee, or caramel-nut. If cake is served, there should be a choice of at least two kinds of homemade favorites. What to charge? Costs of food and other essentials vary in different parts of the country. Work out a price based on costs of your supplies for a generous serving of ice cream, with and without cake. The prices at the social should compare favorably with local soda fountain prices.

At a Strawberry (Blueberry, Cherry, Raspberry) Festival or Social the berries are served in as many ways as the ingenuity and cookery skill of the women of the church make possible. Favorites are berries with cream or ice cream, berry shortcake, and strawberries served whole with stems left on to be dipped into powdered sugar and eaten out of hand. Also berry-flavored ice cream is served at berry socials, or some local specialty such as a berry frozen pudding, or berry pies, or mixed fresh berries in bowls, with or without cream.

A Watermelon Festival or Social calls for male help in the kitchen area to handle and cut the ripe, juice-heavy melons into serving pieces.

Hot or iced coffee or tea is served at some of these summer-night festivals. For these and the suppers that follow, see the Index for quantity cookery charts, which help you to estimate what and how much to buy. Large, general cookbooks also contain quantity cookery information.

Suppers as Fund Raisers Popular church suppers today in many sections of the country include the old favorites, Oyster Supper, Chicken Supper and, added in recent years, the Covered Dish Supper because of its ease of preparation and serving.

The success of a modern church supper depends largely on its being *one of an established series* and on having a well-equipped kitchen and an uncrowded, pleasant community or social room in which to serve it. Families or individuals who come to the church for their evening meal expect not only good food, and it must look and taste like home-cooked food to satisfy them, but they want it nicely served.

This kind of food and service are the products of experience, and are seldom found at the once-in-a-while, unorganized church supper. A series, planned and put on by women who are experienced home cooks, good managers, and who give their time and effort either in the church kitchen or in their home kitchens to produce dishes of high standard, will produce suppers that bring in considerable revenue for the church fund, and that also stimulate interest in other activities at the church.

The Most Popular Menus include favorite local foods, familiar dishes for the most part, with novelty added in a new salad or dessert. For such suppers, the plates as served should look as they do in a comfortable home, without the use of, for example, an ice cream scoop to measure mashed potatoes, turnips, rice, cottage cheese and other foods. Servings should not be obviously small. One of the pleasures of eating a church supper is that it is different from restaurant food, and its quality, flavor, and appearance suggest a good, old-time, bounteous meal. It should be priced at about the level of local tea room meals.

Experienced supper committees know that careful planning of every detail is necessary. They must buy fresh, good-flavored, high-quality foods, use tried and successful cookery methods, and serve on attractively set tables in a well-lighted, comfortable room. These are essential to the success of each supper and build a reputation for good suppers, so that a large repeat, paying crowd is always assured.

As with other fund-raising events, newspaper and radio notices and posters are necessary to bring the supper to the attention of as many people outside the parish as possible to insure a worth-while crowd.

New England Church Suppers are popular and include traditional dishes, such as codfish cakes, crab cakes, baked fish, baked beans, Boston brown bread, coleslaw, apple pie and cheese, and coffee.

So is an Oyster Stew Supper or a Clam Chowder Supper, which includes not only large bowls of steaming stew or chowder with crackers but, after the stew, meat or fish loaf, scalloped potatoes, coleslaw, hot rolls, cranberry relish, mixed homemade pickles, blueberry pie or tarts, and coffee.

Middle-Western Church Suppers usually include either baked or fried oysters, coleslaw, scalloped potatoes or corn pudding, hot rolls, ice cream and cake, or apple pie with ice cream, watermelon in season, or strawberries and cream, and coffee.

Or they are Fried Chicken Suppers with mashed potatoes and gravy, biscuits, jellies, peas or lima beans. Relishes include mustard pickle, deviled eggs, chow chow and sweet pickles. Ice cream and cake for dessert, and coffee.

Or they are Chicken and Turkey-pie Suppers, the pies usually baked in individual casseroles, vegetables included in the pie, with a small baked, stuffed potato extra, warm cornbread, relishes, jellies, preserves, coffee. For dessert, a choice of pecan, chocolate chiffon, or lemon meringue pie, and coffee.

In some sections of the Middle West where Swedish families have lived for several generations, Smörgasbord Church Suppers are regular occurrences in the community. The Smörgasbord includes the traditional hot and cold Swedish dishes in a display large enough to satisfy the appetite of teen-agers as well as grownups.

Usually there are three or four salads, such as red cabbage, potato with anchovy or herring, lettuce salad (small heart leaves only), herring salad; two or three kinds of cheese, including local favorites flavored with caraway and other seeds and homemade schmierkäse (similar to cottage cheese); cold baked smoked ham and venison, cold boiled smoked tongue, other cold meats; pickled herring, lobster or fish in aspic, and such dishes as these kept hot on warmers: scrambled eggs and anchovies, little meat balls in brown gravy, scalloped potatoes, mushrooms and lambs' kidneys in browned butter, scrambled eggs with mushrooms, mushroom or asparagus omelet.

Also on the table are deviled eggs, pickled beets, sliced pickles, pickle relishes, radishes, carrot sticks, stuffed celery, scallions, sliced or quartered tomatoes sprinkled with fresh parsley, sliced cucumbers sprinkled with fresh dill. There may also be cold sliced roast game, smoked salmon, cold boiled fresh salmon with mayonnaise, and various pâtés in aspic, and cold meat loaves garnished with sliced potato salad, the potatoes marinated in vinegar dressing and sprinkled with fresh dill.

Supper guests help themselves as at a buffet party, to cold foods first, later to hot dishes, then to cheese. A dessert, such as Swedish apple cake or a fruit pie, is included in the cost of the supper, with coffee. The price may be modest because most of the foods are donated by local growers or merchants.

Pennsylvania Dutch Church Suppers serve the traditional dishes of that area. They are so bounteous that they attract tourists from as far away as New York City. These meals feature stewed chicken and gravy, pork sausage or flat sausage cakes, or a beef sausage sliced and sautéed; mashed potatoes with chopped onion, celery and herbs shaped into cakes and sautéed in butter; lima beans, beets, new corn, noodles, egg salad, coleslaw, seven sweet and seven sour pickles and relishes, a variety of home-canned fruits from which to choose, large sweet rolls white-iced, shoo-fly pie, which is a brown-and-white, lightly-spiced crumbcake, doughnuts, plus several other kinds of pie and cake.

The pies and cakes are served from a buffet, but usually all the main dishes are put on large tables, and guests, seated around the tables help themselves or are helped by waitresses.

There are other local favorite dishes which may be on the Pennsylvania Dutch table. Whatever the selection offered, it is enough to crowd large tables, to stuff the customers, and to delight cookery connoisseurs. The secret, of course, is for each guest to help himself only to the most appealing dishes and not try to sample all. But Pennsylvania hospitality usually weakens the resistance of even the most disciplined.

Western Church Suppers include Steak Suppers and Roast Beef Suppers. Other favorites are Roast Pork Suppers and Spareribs Suppers with sweet potato pudding, a green vegetable, and the sweet frosted, hot breads of local Norwegian and German tradition.

These same kinds of suppers are served in the northern areas of the Midwest, where Dutch and Scandinavian descendants of early settlers still prefer specialties their ancestors knew so well how to cook.

Wisconsin and Michigan Church Suppers may include a great variety of homemade breads, especially those made with rye flour, fruit-flavored breads, such as pear and prune breads, and numerous sweet rolls, muffins, biscuits, doughnuts and Hungarian coffee rolls. There are usually superb beef stews with a great variety of wonderful dumplings, Dutch ham potpie, noodles with veal and pork, ham and chicken shortcake, barbecued pork chops with prunes, many main dishes made of apples as well as desserts, especially apple dumplings, many cheese main dishes as well as a variety of cheeses from which guests help themselves. Winter church suppers in this area are sure to include fruit puddings, cobblers, and dumplings with superb berry sauces.

The pies and cakes are among the best in America, and like the Pennsylvania Dutch church suppers and luncheons, the Wisconsin and Michigan parties attract tourists from a distance, from Chicago and many other cities to the south as well as across the Canadian border.

Many Seaport Area churches serve Church Seafood Suppers. These may be Fishermen's Platter Suppers, which are selections of several kinds of hot or cold seafood served on one plate with condiments and salad dressings, rice or potatoes, a green salad, cottage cheese, fruit salads, fruit tarts, and coffee.

Or Shrimp Suppers with this shellfish cooked in several different ways so the diner may eat his fill. These usually include a shrimp salad garnished with green pepper and hard-cooked eggs, hot shrimp creole, shrimp fried Japanese style, all with hot rice, a green vegetable, and a fruit salad or warm fruit pie for dessert, and coffee. Or a Lobster Supper, Oyster Supper, Clam Supper are popular with seaside local residents as well as visitors.

Covered Dish Suppers are favorites in all parts of the country today as church suppers. They are easily served because the hot covered dishes brought from their homes by the supper committee and neighbors are placed on a big decorated buffet table ready to serve. Warmers and electric grills and hot trays are used to keep hot dishes hot, other dishes are placed on bowls of ice to keep them chilled, and as at a home buffet party, plates, necessary silver, paper napkins, and trays are available. At these suppers, guests pick up a tray, plate, and silver and help themselves to the array of good foods.

The hot dishes include the home favorites of casserole cookery, such as baked beans, macaroni and cheese, macaroni with tomato and meat sauce, shrimp creole, spaghetti and meat balls, chicken and noodles, baked corn and green pepper pudding, cheese- and rice-stuffed green peppers, meat- and crumb-stuffed baked onions, baked lima beans and tomato sauce, meat loaf, salmon or tuna loaf, vegetables baked in cheese sauce.

Cold dishes, such as sliced ham in aspic with a garnish of deviled egg halves, or tomato aspic mold garnished with raw vegetables and served with mayonnaise are good additions to a covered dish supper. So is a large bowl of tossed chilled salad greens properly dressed with a good French dressing. A covered dish of hot rolls, or one of hot spoonbread, or a big pan of warm cornbread add much to this feast. Dessert can be deep-dish plum or berry pie, or finger desserts, such as cookies, cupcakes, fruit tarts. And coffee.

Seasonal Church Suppers In some parts of the country seasonal church suppers are so popular that there are requests from the community to repeat them each year. The most successful are spring and autumn suppers; midsummer in many areas is too hot for this kind of entertaining, and also many possible patrons are away on vacations. Winter church suppers are of course frequent and popular. See Holiday suppers, below.

The Spring Church Supper, put on as a fixed-price buffet, gives guests their choice of foods that are refreshingly lighter than the dishes most families have been eating during the past winter. Salads may be the chief attraction, or huge platters of melon slices and filled fruit-cocktail glasses. Green salads, a chicken or tuna salad with a choice of dressings, and one hot dish, such as creamed chicken-and-mushrooms to serve on toast or creamed chipped beef to serve on split and toasted English muffins, are favorites. Desserts are cake, chocolate meringue tarts, or ice cream, with a choice of hot and cold beverages. The first blooms from neighbors' gardens used on the tables and around the room in bouquets add spring color.

Harvest Church Supper Early in October is the time to serve this seasonal buffet supper of the traditional harvest dishes: baked acorn squash, creamed cabbage, baked stuffed onions and green peppers, casseroles of orange-flavored sweet potatoes, and scalloped potatoes. Oven-cooked spareribs, hot sausage cakes, baked fresh or smoked ham are popular meats for this dinner. Desserts are pumpkin and mince pies, deep-dish fruit pies, chocolate pudding, doughnuts, warm gingerbread with ice cream. Cider and hot coffee are popular beverages.

This supper room can be festive with decorations of ears of yellow and red corn, squash, pumpkins, stalks of corn and autumn leaves, bowls of fruits and colorful vegetables.

Holiday Church Supper A church supper planned for Lincoln's or Washington's Birthday, St. Valentine's Day, or some other holiday (except Thanksgiving and Christmas, which are home festivals) is usually a success, especially if there are local celebrations in community, school, and other centers. The supper attracts the crowds who have had a day of leisure and want to go out for their evening meal. Decorations for these holidays can reflect the spirit of the date, and the menu can include specialties associated with the day. (See "Holiday Parties," Chapter 3, for decoration and menu suggestions.)

Home Entertaining Besides these suppers, which church members frequently plan and serve, in the church other church-home entertaining includes such widely divergent occasions in the home as a party for Children's Sunday School Class. See "Children's Parties," Chapter 4.

Party for Men's Bible Class. See the Index for suggestions under Mens' parties, Coffee, and High tea.

Luncheon or Tea for Clergyman and Wife. See Christenings in Chapter 1, also How to Give a Luncheon, and How to Give a Tea, in "Guests for Meals," Chapter 15.

Luncheon for Ladies' Aid Society. See section on How to Give a Luncheon, in Chapter 15, and various luncheons throughout the book.

FAMILY AND COMMUNITY PARTIES WITH A PURPOSE

When family entertaining extends into the community and takes on responsibility, so that the entertaining becomes a party with a purpose, the busy-sounding word, committee, makes its appearance. For no matter how eager and how many the volunteers for the many duties connected with making a community function a success, organization and direction are essential to smooth procedure and to obtaining the hoped-for results, such as funds raised, membership increased, or whatever objective inspired the occasion.

For a sizeable event, even something as relatively simple as a big lawn supper, the working committees of volunteers should include Reception, Food Preparation, Serving, and Straightening-Up. Others, such as Publicity or Promotion, Entertainment, Donation, or Ticket Committees may be needed.

To decide what committees are necessary and what each will do, there must be a committee chairman, perhaps the man or woman who suggested the affair, or someone who has had experience in guiding social or community events to success. He or she must be able to define the responsibilities of the various committees clearly, so that there will be no conflict of duties, and with such enthusiasm, steady guidance, and strength that everyone sees his duty and does it—happily.

A Reception Committee is responsible for such assorted jobs as receiving delivery packages, handling of guests' wraps, seating, advance

Also see "Family and Church Entertaining," Chapter 7; and "Outdoor Entertaining," Chapter 12 ticket sales, and selling admissions at the door. This committee is also responsible for name tags to be worn by guests and committee members, and it is the committee that makes introductions of speakers and arranges for seating speakers and guests of honor at their special tables.

A Food Preparation committee plans menu, shopping, cookery, and kitchen and dining-room work schedules, and either cooks the food or oversees other cooks. In short, this committee is responsible for a good meal properly prepared and served.

A Serving Committee plans table decorations and place settings, the amount and kind of linen, silver, china, glassware, flowers needed, possibly place cards. It also plans both kitchen serving and dining-room handling of filled platters and used dishes.

A Straightening-up Committee schedules the work and methods of advance cleaning up and arrangement of the dining room or the place where the party is served, as well as cleaning and straightening up after the party. It is responsible for used linen, silver, china, glassware, and kitchen utensils, and the cleaning and returning of these items to their proper places.

The size and kind of function determines the number and kind of committees. It is better to have too many than too few, providing all committee members live up to the demanding job with which they have been honored.

After-Town-Meeting Parties When a party of community interest takes place in a home instead of an auditorium, school, or other public place, the "committee" more often than not is simply the head of the house and his wife, with perhaps a neighbor or two to help. Such a party is the get-together of neighbors who have been to a town meeting. Throughout America, town meetings are growing in popularity every year. And while many questions of local public or political interest are raised and settled at the meetings, there often remains unfinished business, which enthusiasts feel is worth another hour or more of earnest consideration.

This is an excuse for a pleasant evening at somebody's house. These guests, after a hectic or tense meeting, should be fed before any further discussion is begun. Whatever is served should be simple but delicious. Essential silver, plates, napkins should be available, chairs around a kitchen table, counter, or dining-room table, or small tables and chairs around a fireplace. Before the day of the town meeting, plan for the party to follow it as for any other home entertaining. Invite guests ahead of time in person or by telephone, and perhaps a few others as the meeting comes to an end.

Menu If the crowd is very large, refreshments as simple as coffee, doughnuts or pie, and cheese are sufficient. For smaller groups, make-your-own sandwiches and coffee is a welcome supper. Or, serve a fish or corn chowder or oyster stew, with crisp crackers and coffee.

Cracker Barrel Theme is popular for these parties because its name suggests the old-time, leisurely, village store discussion of local and national questions of importance. For a big Cracker Barrel Party after a town meeting, planned as a discussion to follow the meeting, buy a large, clean barrel from a market or grocer and paint it white inside and out. Stuff the barrel three-quarters full with crumpled paper, and place opened boxes of crisp, fresh crackers—salty, cheese flavored, whole-wheat, many varieties—in the top of the barrel, their open tops level with the barrel top. Set the barrel on the floor at one end of a serving table.

Place a tray of cheese on the table, holding a big piece of Cheddar, any popular local cheese, a large wedge of blue or Roquefort, a jar or wedge of Old English or Smoky, and a bowl of onion-flavored cheese dip. Add a grocer's basket of eating apples, washed and polished, a condiment tray of dill pickles, small sweet pickles, whole pickled small green peppers, and pickled walnuts. Hot coffee or cider are the beverages for this help-yourself menu.

This same easy but effective party can be given for the preliminary meeting on fund raising for a political candidate, or to introduce a local candidate to a neighborly group. In some communities the women's political club supplies refreshments for such gatherings, bringing cold cuts, rolls, and dessert to the hostess who provides the house, the condiments and spreads for the sandwiches, the coffee, and a leisurely atmosphere. Hot coffee and good food are conducive to relaxed good talk and the political club and hostesses have found the results helpful to their candidates.

Other forms of fund raising on a larger scale are discussed below under Fund Raising Parties.

Father-Son Parties Various fraternal organizations, chambers of commerce, booster and business clubs hold Father-Son Luncheons and Dinners as part of their membership development program, or as a contribution toward local adolescent and teen-age welfare and good family relationships. Such parties are also held to sponsor and work up new community projects, such as a golf course, swimming pool, tennis courts, junior baseball club, annual salary for life guard at pool, new safety markers for school streets and other areas.

These parties when held at noon are usually in a business men's club or public restaurant, the evening parties in a home where the son of the house and his father act as hosts. Besides a good supper there should be some entertainment of interest to both men and boys, such as showing films of travel, sports, and other subjects. Films of various lengths and unusual interest are available at low rental from many Government agencies. For example, there are several on wildlife preservation: *Traplines,* 16mm, sound, part color, 30 minute film. Rental fee, $5.00 plus postage and insurance both ways. *Northernaire's Ginger and her Woodland Orphans,* 40 minute, sound film in color: Ginger, a cocker spaniel, with her adopted orphans, a bear, porcupines, raccoons, foxes, beaver. Rental fee, $5.00 plus postage and insurance both ways. For all ages. *Adventures of a Baby Fox,* film by Swedish photographer Arne Sucksdorff presents a trip through the woods following the antics of a baby fox. Accompanied by original dialogue and musical score. For all ages. Rental, $2.50, plus postage and insurance both ways. For any or all, write *Defenders of Wildlife,* 3310 Dent Place, N.W. Washington 7, D.C. Send 70 cents to Superintendent of Documents, Washington 25, D.C. for a pamphlet called *A Directory of 3,300 16mm. Film Libraries.* Also a *Film Society Primer* is available from the American Federation of Film Societies, 110–42 69th Avenue, Forest Hills 75, New York. Cost per copy, $1.00, listing all sources for films and film information.

In place of a movie, or in addition to it, the chief attraction of a father-son supper or dinner may be a guest of honor such as a returned local boy who has made a name in national league baseball, or in golf, tennis, swimming, in Wall Street, as author of important book, as a movie or television actor. He talks about his youth, career, work.

Menu For a supper preceding any business talk and films or a guest speaker, or both, a barbecue meal is always relaxing and satisfying to boys and men, weather permitting. But this is true only if the host is an experienced barbecue cook. There is much misuse of barbecue setups, in which showmanship replaces cookery and results in charred steaks raw inside, smoke in guests' faces, and hunger rampant.

A barbecue supper can be delicious and satisfying in the hands of a good cook, and under right conditions. For such a party, the experienced cook-host and his son can offer their guests hot, deliciously cooked chops, steaks, hamburgers, or skewered combinations of meat, mushrooms, and vegetables; potatoes baked in foil, or a dish of scalloped potatoes baked in the kitchen and carried out to the barbecue.

A salad expert may be present and he should be encouraged to mix his favorite. For him have ready washed, chilled greens, a few red-ripe tomatoes, green pepper, cucumber, and ingredients for salad dressing, or good, bottled dressings. Crusty rolls are heated in a covered pan in the kitchen or on back of barbecue grill. Dessert is a must for this crowd. Depending on the season, it can be watermelon, or a freezer of homemade ice cream, or freshly baked apple or peach pie from the kitchen.

Instead of outdoors, the whole dinner might be done in a big kitchen or family playroom, father cooking the steaks or chops on the grill or range and his guest helpers lending a hand on salad and setting the places around the kitchen table or lunch counter.

Or, if the man of the house is not a cook, the party fare can be prepared like any other guest meal and served to the men and boys in the dining room at one large table or small tables. But girls and women of the family should not join the party either for dinner or any entertainment which follows. For this, see How to Give a Dinner, How to Give a Buffet Supper, in "Guests for Meals," Chapter 15.

Mother-Daughter Parties Many women's clubs and women active in church organizations, hospital, and charity leagues share their organization and social activities with their daughters in Mother-Daughter Luncheons and Teas. While these functions are largely social in their over-all style and the effect on the young guests, some are organizational and concerned with community fund raising for church, library, hospital projects, and others on which father-son combinations also work.

To give such parties, see the descriptions of various luncheons and teas throughout this book, for color schemes and menus. Then plan the occasion to include at least one important, interesting speaker, or someone to talk and show a movie or colored slides. Or, an author of a book on a subject of interest to mothers as well as daughters, such as home decorating, or planning city and town improvement, in which local girls and women can co-operate in a campaign to keep parks and streets clean and to improve home lawns and houses.

Local political speakers or others interested in securing more playgrounds for the community, in planning play areas and other help for underprivileged children, or in starting a little theatre group, or in improving public parks and planting more trees are logical speakers for these occasions. So are men and women who want to stir up interest in starting junior art shows, summer theatre, and musical and sports events.

Not only are teen-age daughters helpful and useful in the leg work and errands in such undertakings, but for girls with talent and imagination this community activity may be the beginning of a career.

Fund Raising Events

Art Show of Children's Drawings and Paintings can go on display in a large home playroom, large, cleared garage, school gym, or club house. In fine weather it can be an outdoors show set up around a church or library lawn. Funds from sales go toward any community need such as playground, swimming pool and winter skating pond, puppet theatre, or something else of use to children.

Committee members for this show send announcements to local papers about one week ahead of the event, giving date, location, and name of committee member and address where paintings are to be delivered. Some committee members also make, or have made, posters to place in store windows and other public locations. The same committee has labels made for each painting with artist's name, title of picture, and price. Others hang the show on opening date, handle sales, dismantle the show after it closes, and restore the show space to its original condition. After the show, the publicity committee member writes a newspaper story about the sales, amount of money taken in, names of artists who sold pictures, and other facts. This is sent to local papers on the last day of the show.

Auction of Pictures by Local Painters and Owners is another art show for community benefit. Included are old and modern paintings, selections from neighbors' attics, old houses, from warehouses where family furnishings have been stored for years. This event might be organized to raise funds to help build a music auditorium, concert hall, workshop for junior painters, or for funds to add to community Christmas chest, hospital flower fund, and similar objectives.

Committee members must take care of an advance announcement to local papers, giving name of event, date, place, opening hour, and duration of show. This publicity should include any other interesting information about what will be in the auction, the names of painters who donated pictures, and names of donors of old paintings. A local newspaper may contribute small ad space for some such committee request as:

Give Us Your Old Paintings!
From Attics and Cellars
Auction, Saturday, June 4th, 1 o'clock, sharp!
Greely's Park
Committee for Swimming Pool Fund
Telephone Main 3-4269 and
We'll Call For Your Donations

Other committee members for this auction make personal calls or telephone to painters and picture owners and any sources from which paintings might be donated. A local women's radio program might make daily announcements of the auction. Some committee member may qualify as an auctioneer, or a fee can be set aside from the proceeds to pay a famous local auctioneer.

The event can take place outdoors in a big lawn or park in fine weather, or indoors in a large, well-lighted room or barn, where there is space for chairs for the audience of buyers, and a table or easel on which the auctioneer's helpers can display pictures as each is put up for selling. All entries in the sale should be hung or be on view for one day, or at least for several hours, before the auction, so that prospective bidders can examine the paintings. As with all events, the committee member who takes care of publicity should send a final story to local papers, reporting any amusing or interesting events at the auction, as well as the total amount of money raised by the sale.

The Box Lunch Supper or Social is popular as a fund raiser because it is not too much work for individuals or committees, and it provides fun for young couples, whole families, school, church, and other groups. Given for almost any worthy cause, this old American favorite can provide an evening of fun and food, with square dancing, folk dancing, movies or any other interesting program depending on the group giving the party.

A date is chosen and announced in local newspapers. The supper can be planned for outdoors in fine weather on a lawn, in a little park, or in a group of backyards that can be opened together. In winter, a large, cleared playroom, warehouse, restored barn, community hall, or other space can be used.

A committee makes the arrangements for the place, for the clearing and decorating, and in some cases, for assembling tables and chairs as well as linen, china, glass, silver. Some box parties are lap suppers, eaten out of the boxes. People sit on the floor, or around one large communal table, or anywhere in conversational clusters.

Another committee decides what price of admission to ask, and how to guide the auctioneer to make as much as possible on the supper boxes. Someone must plan to make and serve hot or cold beverages for grownups and provide milk and other beverages for children if they are expected.

Women guests prepare boxes in their home kitchens, wrapping them prettily in bright, colorful combinations of paper to stimulate bidding. Each box should be lined with several layers of waxed paper and contain a good supper of not easily perishable foods, for one person. Avoid fish in salads or sandwich fillings, custards, and custard-type desserts. Wrap all foods in waxed paper or foil. Have cold foods thoroughly chilled before putting them in the box, then wrap with cold foil to retain freshness. Pack boxes just before taking them to the party.

In some communities, favorite restaurants may contribute a number of boxed suppers to a fund-raising party or the equivalent of the suppers in a money donation. A food market may give a basket of fruit or five pounds of coffee. A dairy company may give several gallons of ice cream or quarts of milk. Such donations are usually solicited by a member of the fund-raising committee, or the restaurateur or grocer may be on the committee.

The fun begins when the boxes are auctioned to the highest bidders. A committee member is the auctioneer, or by demand, some popular personality of the community, such as police chief, teacher, singer, or head of a political club, does the selling. Buyers take their boxes and sit in family groups or with friends around tables. In summer they sit on the grass or a terrace. Hot coffee and other drinks are on the house or sold. The entertainment follows—dancing or whatever has been planned.

Or, if the party is a family affair, adults may linger and talk, children play together around low tables and chairs, or play bought games such as "Wide World" travel game (two to six players at a time). Equipment in this boxed game includes six planes, six dice, destination cards, travel agent cards, and folding map of the world. The old Rook card game, for two to four players is popular, as is "Derby Day" in which any number of players can participate. This boxed game includes an extra large folding game board, six smoothly enameled horses, three large dice, hurdles. If there is floor space, a toss-the-ring quoits game is fun. And, of course, tiddlywinks makes a good game for restless children. A new boxed tiddlywinks set contains four felt pieces, four elephant tiddlywinks, twelve baby tiddlywinks, and a plastic cup that fits into the big playing square.

Menus for boxes containing supper for one person: at least two sandwiches, one of white bread with sliced ham, one of whole-wheat bread with ground-up, seasoned cheese; fresh fruit, such as a peach, a small bunch of washed grapes, or an apple; covered paper cup of potato or chicken salad; two brownies or a piece of good layer cake. Another menu might be: a meat pie in individual casserole, foil wrapped; two pieces of stuffed celery, two olives; Boston brown bread and butter sandwich; covered paper cup of chilled orange gelatin filled with chopped orange and seedless grapes.

A third suggestion is: cold fried chicken—two pieces, one of them half a breast; covered paper cup of vegetable salad; two fresh bread sandwiches of smoked boiled tongue or of cream cheese with currant jelly; individual pecan tart.

A final suggestion: two or three pieces of sliced cold turkey or ham, bread-and-butter sandwiches, little covered paper cup of pickle relish; covered paper cup of cold baked beans; apple turnovers. For more ideas also see "Teen-Age Parties," Chapter 5, for square dance or box social Supper.

Carnival A permit from city authorities or the police may be necessary for a carnival or fair of any kind to raise funds for church, club, college, or any other community cause. The carnival may be such a big under-taking that the local college theatre workshop is called in to help, as well as chamber of commerce members and other responsible civic and business organizations, and men, women, boys, and girls from assorted clubs and groups are asked to volunteer.

A community carnival, large or small, is fun for all concerned. It can be fun for the general chairman or manager who is responsible for the scope, size, and character of the carnival and who, with a planning committee, decides on the kind and number of booths, side shows, and other entertainment. There is fun for the college and art school designers, volunteer carpenters, electricians, and local artists in making various structures for the midway and booths. There is fun, finally, when the carnival opens for the pitchmen selling their wares, fun for the barkers who mingle with crowds in the midway urging them to buy, fun for the crowds who come to spend their money to help a good cause.

Suitable Location Long before the busy gay midway is open, the committees essential to running a large carnival work on all details. The first is a suitable location, such as dead-end street, old disused alley, a plaza area in the community park, the alley of an old carriage house, studios, side street, large armory or drill hall, community hall, or other available space where two rows of gaudy booths can face each other with a midway for the visiting crowds between. (See sketch.)

Design and Makeup The next problem for planning committees is the overall design and makeup of the carnival which is first plotted on paper, worked over and completed in its paper stage before other committees go to work. To gain the maximum financial benefit from the undertaking, the booths should contain products donated by local merchants, manufacturers, and householders. The committee responsible for soliciting and collecting merchandise must make careful records of all gifts and their sales value in order to price them for booth selling, and for the accounting records of the event.

There should be several booths selling light refreshments—coffee and doughnuts in one, in another cold drinks and ice cream sticks, cones, or other frozen desserts to be eaten out of hand. Another booth sells home-made pies, cakes, and fruit tarts. One booth can contain donated, salable white-elephant merchandise at bargain prices. One booth offers rebuilt toys and dolls, another sells attractive nonsense, such as giant beach hats, butterfly nets, sun glasses, false-bottom drinking glasses, balloons, Japanese kites and lanterns. There may be a booth for fresh and artificial flowers; another, for hot buttered popcorn and homemade fudge.

In one booth a game of darts or toss the ring is continuous, the players paying for the privilege of playing and winning inexpensive prizes, such as a noise-maker or candy bar. There may be a booth where fortunes are told with cards or tea leaves by some local woman with a flair for this, but check with the police authorities for permission. A fish pond is always popular: you pay your money and fish for a package. Much the same idea is carried out on gaily decorated peddlers' carts, which are pushed along the midway full of wrapped (donated) gifts; customers choose a package—no peeping first—and pay a quarter or half dollar for it.

Many other carnival attractions are possible depending on locality, talent, and space. Dancing is always a good money-maker, especially in the evening; this calls for a floor and music. More hot foods can be served, such as waffles, pancakes, and plate suppers; be sure to find out if food permits from local health department are necessary for these. Amateur circus acts, pony-and-cart rides or donkey-back rides for children, and a magician's booth may be along the midway.

Once plans are made for the shape and scope of the carnival, the various committees set the designers and carpenters to work. The possibility of rain may have to be considered in the plans, unless the carnival is indoors. What to do? What is the cost of renting a giant tent top? Is there other protection? The local design experts have or discover the answers. Other committees make lists for the ordering of supplies. Others discuss and order what is needed to decorate booths and make them attractive as well as effective sales spots.

Other committees go over in detail what is needed for serving the public, handling money from sales, replenishing food supplies which give out in the middle of the carnival, selecting helpers to relieve booth attendants, and countless other problems, which should be delegated to enough committee members and listed in orderly, workable plans to insure their accomplishment.

A press or publicity committee sends out the first announcements of the carnival to newspapers as soon as the location is decided on, date set, and preliminary work under way. If the budget permits, hire a printer to run off carnival posters on cheap yellow or white paper. These should be posted in shop windows all over the community about

a week before carnival day. These bills should be about 12 by 24 inches, printed with old-time poster type in red and black something like this:

Stupendous!   Wonderful!
COME TO THE CARNIVAL!
in Parker's Lane
To Raise Funds for The New Gymnasium
Beautiful Girls   Handsome Men
Fabulous Foods   Games   Music
Novelties from All Over The World
Toys   Gorgeous Fashions   Flowers   Teacup Readings
Begins Saturday, May 24th, at 12 o'clock noon
Closes 10 o'clock Saturday
Night
Come One   Come All
Prizes   Gifts   Fun

Other committees round up volunteers, women and teen-age boys and girls, who will help outside the booths in various ways, giving each a special job and rehearsing him in it before the carnival day.

An important local personality, such as the president of the chamber of commerce, the mayor, or some other official should be asked to

open the carnival. His speech should be carried on local radio and TV programs.

Besides the color and comedy of the decorated booths, the salesmen inside them, as well as the outside helpers in the midway and barkers at the entrance and elsewhere, should wear bright carnival costumes. These include clown suits, circus-master riding breeches with fancy boots, tall hat, bright silk shirt, and gaudy waistcoat; cowboy costumes; women and girls wear spangled and sequin-trimmed shawls, scarves, blouses, and gypsy skirts.

Committee members responsible for sales should plan to take care of all cash taken in by the booths. It should be collected every hour or so and turned into a prearranged, safe place. Background light and dancy music for the carnival as a whole adds to the atmosphere of gaiety. Records can provide this, from a booth at the center of the midway with two responsible teen-age boys or girls in charge to relieve each other from time to time.

If heavy crowds are expected and if there is a possibility of rowdyism or troublemakers, arrangement must be made with the town police for representatives to be on duty throughout the day. See also Costume Parties for suggestions on costumes.

Good-Fellow Parties This is a name given to a great variety of fund-raising events by men's civic and business organizations. Many American towns and cities are famous for the generosity, charitable work, and warm-hearted response of their business and civic leaders to calls for help from Red Cross and other welfare groups. In some parts of the country, some clubs, lodges, church groups, and political groups have a policy of spur-of-the-moment fund-raising parties for emergency needy cases, such as destitute families, the sick and aged, or for aid to a Community Chest in a current crisis. The name Good-Fellow Parties for these events has grown in importance and meaning through the years as the results from these parties have increasingly aided communities and individuals.

Besides spontaneous fund-raising inspired by an emergency or crisis, Good Fellows also organize many kinds of entertainment to keep a backlog of funds with which they can service various charitable needs including scholarships for local boys and girls. The most popular parties are seasonable and easily accomplished, such as an Evening of Dinner and Dancing at a country club, hotel, or someone's home, at a fixed price, all profits going to their reserve fund or for a special charity.

Or they organize a Golf Tournament between rival business men's clubs or employees of local firms, a Swimming Meet, Baseball Game between local amateur teams and other sports events well planned, well advertised in local newspapers, radio, posters, and mailed announcements with moderate admission fees.

Or the Good-Fellow group may collect funds regularly from their monthly or weekly business men's luncheons or dinners, to which paying guests are invited by announcements, invitations, and solicitations to hear a speaker on some timely subject. All profits from these go into the group's fund for emergency cases.

There is no limit to the scope of such entertaining. Locale, season, and public taste influence the group of men in their choice of the easiest and most popular fund-raising effort. Also Good-Fellow groups may help other fund-raising activities, such as a carnival, church or town supper, or school bazaar, either by giving a sum from their reserve or aiding in the management, promotion, or other work of the fund-raising affair.

Silver Tea A Silver Tea so called because it is used to raise funds and because you pay to come to the tea, is popular with women's clubs, church and garden clubs, and other feminine organizations as a pleasant, social way to raise money for various charity needs, or the redecoration of club rooms, and other outlays. A tea for money-raising can be given in a home, church social room, club house, library, or other place where a large crowd can be entertained.

See the section on How to Give a Tea in Chapter 15, "Guests for Meals," for help in advance planning and the details of preparing and serving tea to a crowd. Add to these plans the work of a publicity or press committee, which is necessary for the advertising and promotion needed to make a Silver Tea a financial success. These promotion efforts should include announcements in the local papers about one week ahead of the date, and also on the day of the Tea, and radio announcements on local radio women's programs. Printed invitations should be mailed at least ten days in advance of the Tea date to membership lists of interested clubs and organizations. Posters made by local artists, school children, or commercial printers should be placed in shop windows all over the community about one week before the Tea date.

All such invitations and announcements should state the date, day, hour, place, purpose of Tea, and admission price. If tickets are printed they should go on sale about two weeks before the Tea. It is a good idea to sell them in quantity through volunteer committee workers to clubs and organizations, so that some estimate of the attendance can be made well ahead of time. Other volunteers can be responsible for single ticket sales in person or by telephone, all far ahead of the party date. This advance selling not only boosts attendance but gives helpful guidance to the committee responsible for planning menu and buying foods.

In addition to the table hostesses and kitchen helpers for any large tea, at a Silver Tea there must be assistants at the door who take money and tickets. Usually tables just inside the entrance, one on each side of door with two women or girls seated at each table, make an adequate and effective way of handling entrance fees. Each guest pays on arrival, either with money or ticket. The fee charged may vary from $1.00 or $1.50 per guest, the advertised regular fee for the Tea, to donations and gifts such as $5.00 to $10.00 or more given at the door by interested local friends of the organization giving the Tea.

Treasure Chest Party Almost any fund-raising event can be a Treasure Chest Party, if the profits from the affair are turned over to a Community or some other Treasure Chest. Father-Son, Mother-Daughter parties, Art Show, Carnival, Good-Fellow Parties, and Silver Teas are typical fund-raisers for this. See also Outdoor Parties.

Here's another kind of Treasure Chest Party. At a community center, church social room, or other convenient place, neighbors, various charity groups, teen-agers gather to wrap mounds of useful gifts donated from their own homes and solicited by notice in local newspapers and by announcements in church and school. The packaged Treasure Chest gifts are to be sold at a church fair, carnival, school bazaar, or elsewhere for some community fund.

Fun at this party is in selecting paper and ribbons, under a leader's guidance, from big supplies of colorful wrappings, gay cord and string salvaged from families' leftover Christmas stock, and also solicited as donations from stationers and other sources. A skilled woman or girl from a local shop can show the workers how to wrap effectively, and tie bows and rosettes. Other workers pile packages in cartons or baskets, write labels on cards, or do whatever is needed.

Menu Refreshments should reward the workers at the end of the wrapping session. Serve something such as hot tea or coffee for grown-ups, cold root beer or other soft drinks or milk for teen-age helpers, and platters of brownies or cookies with the beverages.

The refreshments are provided by committee members of the organization for whose benefit this wrapping session has worked.

Garden Week Entertaining

Annual Garden Week can be established in the community by calling together garden owners and forming a working committee to develop interest in such a Week. Public attention and support for a sustained, annual program is stirred up with a week's program of varied garden activities. The size of the community and the number of outstanding gardens are factors in preparing for the first Week.

Flower Show This working committee may consider as an attraction of first importance a Flower Show, with prizes for arrangements and table settings, to stimulate interest and bring in crowds. The Flower Show may be a one-day opener for Garden Week or be planned as the final attraction for the last day of the Week. It may be free to the public, or so impressive that an entrance fee can be charged. An armory or drill hall, market house, or a shady terrace of a club or other semi-public or public building, or any spacious, fairly cool and shaded area is adaptable to such a Show.

To cover the costs of containers and rent of the display area, local nurserymen, seedsmen, and garden supply stores may be solicited to contribute funds, or to rent space for their own displays, or to give other help. Local home furnishing stores may be solicited to set tables and rent space in which to show flower arrangement bowls, vases, and other accessories.

Flower Arrangement Demonstration can be a feature of another day in Garden Week. The exhibition can be held at a home, on a terrace, in a playroom or porch, with some local woman famous for her garden and flowers doing the demonstrating. Or, a visiting National Garden Club officer, or a nationally-known flower arranger, or the author of books on the subject can be the guest attraction. A fee can be charged for this feature, or it can be a free offering of Garden Week to stimulate interest in gardens and the Week itself.

Flower Arrangement Class may be recruited from those most interested in the demonstration. Local bookstores can recommend books on the subject for preliminary lessons. Women's magazines, home furnishing and garden magazines can supply reprints of articles showing the fundamentals of arranging flowers, including color photographs, diagrams, and the work of well-known experts in the field. There are TV programs in some communities giving demonstration lessons on the elements of flower arranging, instruction in its basic art, practical designing showing tools, holders, and the tricks that professionals use.

Such a class inspired by Garden Week not only aids the immediate show week but subsequently meets regularly through the year. In itself it is an interesting way of entertaining friends and neighbors and it serves as a stimulus to next year's Garden Week and to establishing such activities firmly in community life.

Junior Garden Club Day Another day of this special Week might be designated as Junior Garden Club Day. There are thousands of Junior Garden Clubs all over the country. In one Long Island community one club has members from eight to fifteen years of age. The only requirement for membership is that boys and girls have real interest in gardening. They hold study classes on plant identification outdoors on somebody's lawn, or elsewhere, once a month under the direction of a senior Garden Club member. They also contribute packages of vegetable seeds to Seeds for Democracy, which are distributed to countries in Asia. They make birdhouses and feeders, set them up in local parks, and keep them supplied with food.

Their course in flower arranging often includes special projects, such as using only two kinds of flowers, or each child using only the flowers he has raised. The children give their flower arrangements to children's wards and the lobby decoration of the local hospital, delivering them on certain days and visiting also the wards and rooms of sick children.

One year this club donated its treasury fund to Garden of Fragrance, a special program for the blind at the Brooklyn Botanical Garden. They plant exhibitions of flowers for the annual Spring Garden Show held in their community. Holding their own show one year they won a state award. Under the guidance of a member of the senior Garden Club of the community, they do the tedious tasks and hard work of gardening as well as the lighter and more showy gardening. Among prizes to offer junior gardeners, include *Flower Arranging for Juniors*, by V. S. Marshall (Little, Brown, publishers).

Garden Tea On another day of Garden Week, a Garden Tea might be given by the planners of this community event and committee members for the visiting national Garden Club members, authors of horticultural and flower books, and local officials who may have helped financially or otherwise to make the Week a success. See the section on How to Give a Tea in Chapter 15 for planning, preparing, and serving a big tea.

Weather permitting, this party is outdoors, the tea table on a porch or terrace, or under a gay awning or garden umbrellas. Guests view gardens, tables of flower arrangements or other displays. If there is a guest speaker, the Tea chairman should plan for comfortable places for guests to sit, and a place for the speaker to stand to give his or her talk either before or after refreshments are served.

If the Garden Tea is given to raise money for Garden Week expenses, see Silver Tea instructions in the preceding section. The Tea in a big garden event is important enough to deserve careful planning and sufficient help to assure smoothness and success.

Garden Tour A Garden Tour on two or three days as an attraction of Garden Week is usually a money-maker. Also it is a fine stimulus to more and better gardening, helping the committee to increase general interest in an annual Garden Week. The Tour committee gets permission of home owners to show their gardens. The route from garden to garden is planned to save steps and avoid retracing, and with consideration of the types of gardens in the Tour. In a large community, where various kinds of beautiful gardens are numerous, the Tour might be plotted to show two or more English-type mixed flower gardens in succession, with one-color, or two-color gardens next, then formal gardens, country gardens, and other kinds in sequence.

To make the Tours pay, an announcement should be published in local papers one week in advance and on the morning of the Tour days. Such announcements as well as circulars or cards mailed to prospective Tour subscribers should list names and addresses of garden owners, the time and meeting place for beginning the Tour, and the price. The committee in charge of promotion should also use posters in local shop windows, at the public library, and elsewhere describing the Tour, and ask local women's radio programs to include mention of the Tours daily during Garden Week.

The Tour committee appoints helpers whose one job is to collect the fee from each person before the Tour starts. Others act as escorts and guides, not only to direct the group of visitors from garden to garden, but to ride herd on them to some extent, if there are careless or thoughtless grass stompers and flower snippers among them.

Speakers' Afternoon One afternoon of Garden Week might be Speakers' Afternoon with talks by famous seedsmen, nurserymen, growers, and other specialists, most of whom do not have to be paid for their time and talk. A comfortable auditorium should be used for this, one large enough to make the occasion financially worth while. If speakers can bring color movies or slides showing their speciality or gardens, so much the better for the program. Or, such movies and slides available from growers and seedsmen might be shown by authors of garden books who not only talk about their own specialty but will autograph books at the end of their talk. An admission charge for this program is made to the public and to garden enthusiasts as a source of income toward the Garden Week total.

The Speakers' Afternoon might be preceded by a Garden Buffet Luncheon served cafeteria style in a large, handsome backyard or on a terrace. Light foods are suitable for speakers and audience, something such as a fine, flavorful tossed vegetable salad, chive-cottage cheese, small ham sandwiches, hot or iced coffee or tea, finger desserts such as cupcakes, black-cherry turnovers, small open-face apricot tarts. Or, serve a handsome fruit-and-melon salad, small assorted sandwiches, hot or iced tea and coffee.

Contributions of fruits from local markets, orchards, and gardens can make this luncheon a source of considerable revenue, even if only a $1.00 is charged per guest. But the luncheon is also a convenience and an attraction for those who may have driven some distance to attend the afternoon talks, as well as for guests, speakers, and committee workers who see it as an opportunity to get acquainted and exchange ideas on the Week as a whole and the one they will plan for next year.

Neighbor Parties

There are three kinds of home-community entertaining that especially deserve to be called Neighbor Parties. They are: a farewell party for a neighbor who is moving away, a party for a new family just arrived in the neighborhood, and a housewarming by a family who has built a new home or renovated an old house or added a wing to their small cottage.

Farewell Party A simple party planned as a farewell to a family going away should not be a surprise, since the household is in the midst of packing and other arduous tasks. With permission of the departing neighbors, a friend plans the Farewell at her own home, inviting other friends of the neighborhood to join her in making it a good celebration.

If there are teen-age and younger children in the departing family, children of the hosts and guests have a share in the Farewell with their own hospitality, such as cooking their favorite foods in the playroom and holding a game or dance session while their elders entertain in the dining room and living room. The program depends on the ages of children who will be present and whether there are facilities for separate adult and children's entertaining. Lacking a playroom or other special space for youngsters, all combine in one big party.

This can be supper the night before the moving vans roll away. If there is no playroom then small tables and chairs should be provided for children near the grownups' tables. If there are very young children, they should have party hats, favors, and balloons, which add to their good time.

If the crowd is large, plan a buffet supper because it is easier to serve than a dinner. Emphasis at this party is not on decoration and entertainment but on good food and time for everyone to have his own good-by conversation with the various members of the departing family. For details of preparation, see How to Give a Buffet Supper, in Chapter 15, "Guests for Meals."

One solution of what to serve at this kind of neighborly affair is to make it a Covered Dish Party, to which each neighbor brings a hot casserole or some other item of the menu. All consult with the hostess ahead of time on what to bring, so that there is enough supper for everybody and an interesting variety of delicious dishes. The hosts provide beverages and dessert.

Covered Dish Suggestions: baked macaroni and cheese, scalloped potatoes with anchovies and crumb topping, meat balls and noodles, baked corn and pimiento pudding, baked hash-stuffed green peppers, baked meat-and-cheese stuffed onions, hot ham loaf, scalloped chicken and noodles with crumb topping, shrimp creole. One guest brings rolls ready to brown and serve; another brings a loaf of French bread cut and spread with herb butter ready to go into a hot oven for a few minutes. If salad is a must in local menus, one neighbor brings washed, chilled salad greens and dressing, ready to toss and serve. Dessert might be one of the favorites of the guests of honor, such as chocolate chiffon pie, raspberry tarts, open-face peach or apple pie.

If the grownup crowd likes dancing at neighborhood parties, there should be a supply of good dance records on hand. Everybody sings Auld Lang Syne at the end of the evening.

Other Farewell Parties A good-by luncheon for a girl going away to college, or for a long trip. A dinner for a young couple leaving for a year's assignment in another country. An afternoon open-house for an elderly couple going to the South to make their home. A big Sunday brunch for a favorite college teacher and his family who have been transferred to another university town. A dinner and dance for a young couple moving to another part of the country.

Bon Voyage Party for a couple or for a whole family leaving for a few months in Europe is a popular neighbor party. It is more fun if it is given on the eve of departure. But it is a kindness to let the guests of honor decide when they would like the party, and what kind of enter-tainment would fit into their limited time. Perhaps a luncheon with neighbors would please the female members of the family, or a buffet supper, or a going-away gift shower. An after-dinner coffee gathering that can include the men of the family, too, might be preferred.

Hosts for the party consult with the travelers, and invite other neighbors by telephone or in writing on colorful printed Bon Voyage folder cards decorated with a ship, flags, or other symbols of travel. A group of neighbors may combine their gift money and buy a piece of useful and needed luggage, or a handbag, or sweaters for the couple, or gifts for the children. All such gifts should be easily packable.

Welcome Party A new family in the neighborhood may be welcomed with the same kind of supper and evening party that the neighbors give for a departing family. The host for the Welcome Party selects a date with the new couple and finds out whether they like to play bridge or canasta, or prefer an evening of dancing, or just talking with their new acquaintances, and whether they keep early hours because of young children. The hosts then invite the families who will be near neighbors of the new arrivals. In summer, weather permitting, instead of a Covered Dish Supper neighbors can provide a porch or patio cold supper, or a barbecue meal, a clam bake, beach supper, or other local favorite outdoor party as a good getting acquainted welcome.

Miniature Strawberry Social As a friendly and flattering offering to the new neighbors, the hosts and old neighbors might devise a Japanese Lantern Strawberry Fiesta on the lawn. Everybody invited comes after supper at home and brings a strawberry dessert. Shortcake, baked custard to be served with sliced, sweetened berries, strawberries to serve on ice cream, strawberries left whole with stems on to be eaten after dipping into powdered sugar, and any other favorite local strawberry desserts are featured. The hosts provide coffee, small tables, chairs, china, silver, and hang the trees with Japanese lanterns. Paper napkins in this oriental spirit add to the party atmosphere.

Welcome Dinner or Supper at Home This has been a fixture in American hospitality since the first settlements and towns began to grow. When a new family moves into the neighborhood, their first night's dinner or supper is taken to them by the neighbors. The new arrivals may have to spread their meal on a packing box, but the food is hot, delicious, and tastes of friendship.

Menu is decided by neighbors consulting together and combining their gifts so that the family has a well-rounded meal. Someone makes a big stew of lamb or beef with vegetables, another brings a covered dish of au gratin potatoes or sweet potatoes, one brings a platter of bread-and-butter sandwiches, buttered rolls, or perhaps buttered nut bread; someone comes to the new family's kitchen door with a still-warm cherry pie; another neighbor brings a big vacuum jug of hot coffee, a container of cream, a small box of lump sugar; and another brings containers of cold milk if there are youngsters in the family.

The dishes are left at the door by neighbors with a few words of greeting. And a grateful family on its tired first night in its new home feasts in thankfulness.

Housewarming A housewarming is a party given by the owners of a new home for their neighbors. Or, it is a party planned and given by neighbors for the home owners, either as a surprise or with the co-operation of the family in the new home.

The Homeowner Housewarming Party can be something as simple as "come in for coffee with us and see the new place." Hosts telephone or invite in person all the nearby friends and neighbors to come at 8 o'clock on a convenient evening. The new dining room or family room or a playroom is arranged for serving coffee and dessert. Stools surround a serving counter, or folding tables and chairs are opened up. The tables are covered with seasonal paper tablecloths decorated with spring flowers, snow men, autumn leaves, or midsummer fruits. A pile of matching paper napkins is on a serving table with coffee cups and saucers, necessary silver and big gleaming coffeemakers full of the fragrant, freshly-made brew.

A finger dessert is popular for such parties—date bars, small fruit turnovers, brownies, frosted single-layer cake cut in strips, doughnuts, old-fashioned crullers. Music should be part of the celebration to give the new home a happy air. Perhaps someone brings a guitar and sings. A group of musical neighbors may bring fiddles and cello and the new house is richly serenaded, or someone brings new dance records or other favorites for background music.

Gifts are not essential for a housewarming but tradition and community custom in some areas encourage the taking of a gift for the house. In the early days of American home-building, the gifts were foods—a bag of potatoes, a basket of apples, a dressed chicken or two,

a crock of butter from a cold springhouse, all to stock the larder of the new home. Modern homemakers would appreciate such gifts, too, but their neighbors are more likely to bring half a dozen glasses to add to the kitchen supply, a tray for the barbecue terrace, an insulated ice container, or a big, picnic coffeepot for future parties, and similar housewares.

Some owner housewarmings are much more elaborate. Owners of a handsome new town or city residence, now finished, decorated, and beautifully furnished, may give a housewarming dance, or a tea reception, a Sunday afternoon or evening open house with elaborate high tea or supper, with either extra help or a catering staff. Or they give a formal dinner to their best friends both as celebration and so their friends can see the new place.

A big outdoors Hawaiian feast, the luau, may be just the right sort of gaiety and good food for a housewarming in Southern California,

Texas, and Florida, and for that matter, anywhere else, weather permitting. See Chapter 12, Outdoor Entertaining.

Or a new ranch home owner may hold open house to other ranchers who fly in, or come by car or horseback, and spend several days. The same sort of lively, hospitable week end may be the housewarming of a country home in New England or on an Ohio farm. The idea in all such entertaining is that the new home opens wide its doors to old friends and new, in whatever style its owners can afford or want to observe. For suggestions and details for such entertaining see various sections of this book: How to Give a Tea and How to Give a Buffet Supper in Chapter 15, Anniversaries in Chapter 1, Outdoor Entertaining Chapter 12.

When the party is a neighborhood surprise housewarming, one neighbor can arrange to keep the new-house family at home for the evening by planning a visit ahead of time. A few minutes after she and her husband arrive, the rest of the party appears, bringing refreshments for the evening and gifts for the new home. The refreshments may include large vacuum jugs of hot coffee, containers of cream and sugar, a delicious caramel chiffon pie or walnut layer cake, cinnamon buns, cheesecake, a bowl of apples, peaches, and pears or other fruit.

Sandwich makings are also popular for this kind of party, such as a tray of sliced cheese and cold cuts, a bowl of cheese dip, loaves of bread sliced and buttered. If the party is large, paper cups, paper napkins, and any other essentials for quantity service should be brought along by the surprise guests.

Understanding Our Neighbors The United States Committee for U.N.I.C.E.F. (United Nations Children's Emergency Fund, United Nations, New York 17) issues a series of inspiring, efficiently worked-out programs to aid in better understanding of other nationals, or people of other religions and races who may be living in a community. These Hi-Neighbor Kits, which are large folders complete with songs, games, folk dance instruction, arts and crafts, folk tales, also offer detailed guidance for a season's series of work-together programs. There are also suggestions for a festival week, a one-day-a-week program, special events, such as a pageant, party, or fiesta, parents' day festivity, and other occasions.

These projects may be held indoors, outdoors, in school, church, at home, on a playground or at indoor recreation centers. Material is also provided in the Kit for local radio and TV programs. Drawings of flags are included, and recipes of the five countries featured in each Kit. A new Kit, of five additional countries, is issued each year. The Kits sell for $1.00 each but when bought in quantity, such as for school and other groups, generous discounts are made. The address given above is for all inquiries.

Rooftree Party Long before a housewarming can be held in a new home, another significant and traditional party can be enjoyed by owners and the workmen who are building the house and, in some communities, by neighbors as well. This is the Rooftree Party. The beam in the angle of the roof, called the ridgepole or rooftree, is figuratively the roof itself and the word rooftree also stands for both home and dwelling place. The party is given when the beam is in place, and workmen lay a tree, branch, or bush on it.

In Europe and parts of Asia a tree symbolizes shelter, and when placed on the roof of a new house it means that the house can now provide shelter. The tradition of a rooftree party has significance in many countries.

Present-day rooftree parties in many sections of America are similar to those given in settler days by journeymen English, Dutch, and Swedish carpenters in New England and later in the Middle West. One New York State bush or tree party is a hearty example of this pleasant custom.

As soon as the roof of a new house at Armonk, New York was on, a large green branch was set up on the rooftree. Fashionably arrayed in muddy boots, raincoats, flannel shirts and dungarees, the various plumbers, carpenters, electricians, landscapers, heating contractors, builder, architect, owner, and neighbors toasted the tree as one workman shouted, "Here's mud in your eye!"—the classic salute of modern-day labor to the builder and owner at a rooftree party.

A large table set up by the new residents outdoors near the new structure was crowded with platters heaped high with beef, salami, ham-and-cheese, and pastrami sandwiches. Hot coffee and cold drinks were on hand, enough for second and third rounds.

The architect of this house reports that when owners can't be present for the rooftree raising, it is customary for them to provide food and drink anyway for the tree party. One builder in Westchester County, New York, has attended a tree party for every house he has erected in the last thirty years. He says that the workmen set the time for the party: when they raise the tree it means that they are ready for hospitality to flow. Even in housing developments, according to a builder on Long Island, New York, there's often a party. The carpenters get together, raise the tree, and toast it over their lunch.

Most of the owner and workmen celebrations at noontime last at least one hour. Others held at the end of a working day may include a square dance, large hot buffet supper, and in some communities a blessing of the house, room by room, by a local priest or clergyman.

9

FAMILY-AND-SCHOOL PARTIES

After the Game An after-the-game party can be planned for any age group.

For Young Children Let your children invite their sportsmen friends to come to your home after a junior baseball, football, hockey, tennis, or any other school game. A cooling glass of lemonade with cookies, or glass of milk and sandwiches are sufficient refreshments for these youngsters. They round out the afternoon with games in a playroom or backyard and go home a little later for their supper.

If you are giving the children supper the occasion can look like a party, which to them it is, with balloons, party hats, and a party menu. For this kind of postgame supper your children invite their guests about a week before the date, and they also ask them to get their mothers' permission to stay for supper.

Decorations which your children make, or you buy, ought to be in the spirit of the afternoon's game, with perhaps a (borrowed) football helmet or baseball catcher's mask, or a pair of crossed tennis rackets as a table centerpiece or any other amusing sports figure or design made by the children or found in the toy stores. Favors, such as miniature baseballs, footballs, tennis rackets and other small sports toys, or decks of the *Baseball Card Game,* or the boxed games called *Peg Baseball* and *Pigskin,* can be on the table to be given to the children when they leave for home after supper.

Menus Serve a seasonal supper, such as small chopped beef balls with baked macaroni, buttered soft rolls, ice cream in football or baseball molds, and small cakes shaped like a football or baseball frosted with pink icing and decorated with chocolate icing to look like the leather balls. Milk or hot cocoa or lemonade is the beverage. See Chapter 4, "Children's Parties," for a choice of supper menus.

Teen-agers who invite friends home after a sports event, may enjoy a refrigerator full of sandwiches, milk, soft drinks and ice cream, which will keep them happy for an hour or so. Or, consult with them in advance; they may prefer to cook frankfurters or hamburgers in the playroom or on an outdoor grill. For this have a supply of buns, relishes, soft drinks on ice, and ice cream with brownies or cookies available.

If there is room for dancing, your teen-age children will want some new records as well as their old favorites for the after-supper fun. They will decide whether decorations should be put up, and invitations mailed, but usually their parties after school games are not dress-up and they like them to seem casual and unplanned.

College Boys and Girls may want to bring friends home after a game to a buffet supper and dancing. Consult with them about the menu. Usually they ask for "things nice but not fussy," which means that, in a playroom or dining room, you give them a simple buffet table with the essentials for easy service and delicious but familiar foods.

The menu might be a casserole of browned veal birds stuffed with chopped mushrooms and crumbs, and served with hot rice, small tomato salads, hot buttered rolls, cold drinks and hot coffee. Boys want desserts, such as an open-face fruit pie or layer cake. Or, surprise them with a big ice cream mold decorated with small school pennants cut out of colored paper. (See How to Give a Buffet Supper in Chapter 15.)

Older Guests Neighbors and friends invited to drop in after a game for supper can be happy around a kitchen counter with waffles and bacon or sausages, open-face peach or plum pie, cold drinks and hot coffee. Or, let them make their own sandwiches with split, buttered buns, cheese spread, chicken salad filling, and sliced meat loaf or luncheon meats. Serve an ice cream pie from the freezer, or delicious cinnamon buns, as dessert.

If you lack a hospitable kitchen, you can set up a buffet table in the dining room or living room, and give your guests a chafing dish

Welsh rabbit. Serve it on split, toasted English muffins. With this, fresh fruit for dessert will please some, others will appreciate a big fruit tart, such as black cherry or blueberry cut and served like pie. These are especially good following a cheese dish.

After School Concert or Theatrical If it is your turn to entertain the concert or theatrical stars of your children's school, the hospitality must be planned to please a mixture of ages: teachers, parents, teen-age stage managers and designers, and children from the teens downward to first graders.

The easiest way to feed this kind of crowd is with sandwiches of several kinds, hot coffee for grownups, a fruit punch for teen-agers, chocolate milk drinks for the youngest, followed by ice cream and cake for everybody.

A buffet table in a playroom or cleared living room should be ready with all necessary plates, silver, napkins, and glasses when you come in from the play or concert. For a large crowd, of course, use paper cups, plates and napkins. One or more of the parents and teachers will help you serve.

Let the musical or theatrical stars of the evening cut and serve the cake, which can be decorated with ribbon streamers or bows in the school colors, or with a paper streamer on which the name of the play or musical is written in bright colors. This streamer can be cut from colored paper, lettered with water color paints or crayons, and fastened with gummed tape to thin sticks (such as swab sticks from the drug store); poke sticks into cake so that the streamer stands above the top of the cake. A big, white layer cake with lemon custard filling is a good choice for this, or serve your children's favorite cake. Let them choose their favorite ice cream, too. For the smallest youngsters, have a supply of cookies or frosted small cakes, which most of them will prefer to layer cake.

This same menu can be served to older high school and college students who come to your home after a school performance. But if your budget will permit, this crowd, and the teachers or coaches invited with them, would appreciate a buffet supper and a chance to sit down and talk about the concert or play. For such a supper one hot dish is sufficient, such as a big casserole or chafing dish of cheese-topped gnocchi or lasagne, or spaghetti with a superb meat-and-tomato sauce, or shrimp Newburg, or ham jambalaya.

These delicious dishes can be prepared ahead of time, kept in the refrigerator, and reheated in the oven or a big chafing dish at party time. Coffee and finger desserts, such as narrow strips of fruit cake or tiny fried pies complete this menu. For more details, see How to Give a Buffet Supper in Chapter 15.

Alumnae Parties The easiest way to entertain a large number of old college friends, perhaps an alumnae club, is with a tea, high tea, open house, or buffet luncheon or supper. If it is June and commencement time, a picnic, garden tea, luncheon on the lawn or porch, or other outdoor parties are possibilities. The size of the group, your budget, and your space and facilities for entertaining determine, as always, which kind of party is best. All of them are described in detail with menu, in various sections of this book.

But whichever party is given, the purpose of the get-together is to let old friends and hosts meet in a relaxed atmosphere to talk and catch up on news of each other. Planned entertainment and formal dinners, except for the large home with a cooking and serving staff, are ruled out.

In college towns in Ohio, New England, and around New York state, the first choice by both men and women alumni is a buffet luncheon on a big porch or terrace or in a large, cool house, on one of the days of commencement week. Second choice is a picnic lunch on someone's large lawn or on the campus on Commencement Day after the ceremonies.

These same suggestions for suitable entertainment apply to sorority, fraternity and other school club parties that you give in your home.

Back-to-School Parties For children who go away to school, the best send-off is a big party to which all their friends are invited. Let your child or children decide on the menu for luncheon or supper; and let them make the decorations, invite the guests, and in other ways be responsible for their party. Guests are invited about a week before the party date, either in person or by written invitations. (See "Children's Parties," Chapter 4, for invitations, menus, and decorations.)

Add a school theme to decorations, such as tall dunce caps for every child instead of party hats, invitations which look like old-time school

slates, table decorations which include a little cardboard school house or tin or plastic school bus as centerpiece. Favors can include boxes of pencils and little notebooks.

For College Age A going-away *home supper or dinner with dancing* afterwards is a top favorite with the late teens. So is a *picnic,* and in some communities *a moonlight horseback ride,* or a *swim followed by beach supper.* Depending on what part of the country you are in, a *luau, big Sunday brunch on the porch,* a *barn dance,* or *box supper and square dance* are good ways for your college children to say good-by to their friends. See "Outdoor Entertaining," Chapter 12, and "Teen-Age Parties," Chapter 5; also, How to Give a Brunch, in Chapter 12.

One girl in a Missouri town invited her best beau and several other friends to her home for a good-by supper the night before she left for an eastern college. Several of the boys in the crowd played banjo and guitar, and with the other boys and girls invited for the evening they drove to their hostess's home about sundown and serenaded her with her favorite songs. Singers and musicians then went in to supper, which was a backyard patio and porch supper of Missouri favorites: fried chicken, little hot hominy croquettes (with apple jelly centers), cold baked ham, cold roast turkey, plum jam, relishes, potato salad, stuffed celery, sliced tomato and cucumber salad, hot biscuits, a mile-high chocolate cake, homemade ice cream, and coffee. After supper they danced and made music until the small hours.

Class Reunion The best class reunion parties, according to some old grads, are box lunch picnics on the campus during commencement week or a dinner followed by dancing at a college club house or someone's home, or an open house where there is room for a crowd to gather, move about, and talk. Hospitality for the open house can be a tea and coffee buffet. (See How to Give a Tea in Chapter 15.) *Coffee and canapés* or, when the crowd is not too large, a luncheon, dinner, or supper, are all good ways to welcome old friends and give them a chance to catch up with your life and to talk about their own.

Decorations for any of these should include old class banners and pennants, college colors in the flowers and candles and other accessories, such as small favors on the table. If old films of campus days, past graduations, football games and other school events are available, they make good entertainment after supper. A beloved teacher as guest of honor can add a special quality to the open house or other occasions. A famous old graduate musician, politician, author, can give glamour to the party.

A Woman's College Class Reunion is more often a tea, or luncheon with not so much emphasis on the old days; they prefer talk of today, their jobs, or children. For either occasion, your most beautifully planned tea party, or your most charming luncheon table are recommended. (See How to Give a Tea and How to Give a Luncheon in Chapter 15.) Here's a luncheon menu "les girls" will like: section of cold honeydew melon garnished with crushed, fresh red raspberries, cheese soufflé with crisp bacon curls and large almonds sautéed in the same pan with the bacon, asparagus vinaigrette, small hot rolls spread with herbed butter, parfait of mixed sherbets, chocolate leaf cookies, demitasse.

Here's another menu for such a luncheon: jellied Madrilène with a thin slice of fresh lime in the chilled cup, small piroshki (tiny flaky-pastry turnovers filled with chopped, cooked, well-seasoned meat or chicken), breast of chicken browned in butter with a little mixed dried herbs, fresh lima beans, crusty French bread, fruit salad, coffee or tea.

These luncheons also adapt to home entertaining of sorority and college club friends. See also previous section on Alumnae Parties and the following on Commencement Parties.

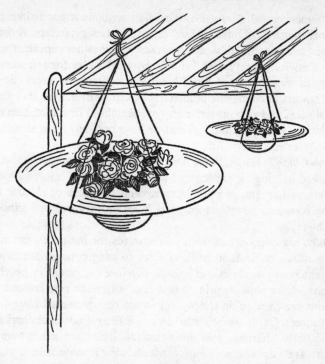

Commencement Parties Parties for the new graduates vary in different communities. Some colleges with beautiful, tree-shaded campuses are usually the scene of lawn picnics after commencement ceremonies, when the weather permits. Other graduating classes lunch together at a school club or dormitory. Others have no such tradition, and graduates join their families after the ceremonies and go to a restaurant. Or, they drive home, perhaps taking a few friends with them and enjoy an especially festive home luncheon or brunch. Or a picnic in the backyard, patio, or on the lawn.

Menus for these vary with different sections of the country, but they should be light and summery, such as this: hot herbed-tomato bouillon with cheese straws, a large gelatin fruit salad with fruit-flavored mayonnaise, hot buttered rolls, floating island and angel cake, hot or iced beverages.

Commencement Summer Dance This night is a good time for a summer dance for a mixed crowd of old and new graduates. If there is a large porch or smoothly-paved terrace, and weather permits, this can be a memorable party with brightly covered tables for refreshments, strings of mixed colored lights hung everywhere, and decorations of fresh flowers in containers hidden in huge straw hats, the hats trimmed with flowers and ribbon streamers (see sketch). For music, hire a college band (wearing white jackets) or have on hand a big selection of good dance records.

One-Color-Scheme Dance This is different and not too difficult to plan. For lighting the garden and porch, use all rose-colored Japanese or Chinese lanterns or white lanterns with rose-colored electric bulbs inside, rose-colored tablecloths, and small rose-colored half-slipcovers for chairs.

Make big bouquets of fresh garden roses for the tables and buffet, and garlands of fresh or artificial roses to hang between lanterns and over any house windows and doors which face the garden or porch (see sketch). Paper napkins printed in a rose pattern or rose-colored linen napkins are plentiful in shops, and so are rose-patterned plates, cups, and saucers. Or all can be rented from a caterer. For written invitations to this party, charming rose-decorated fold-over cards are in many stationery and card shops. So are cards showing a scene from a summer night's dance and other dance ideas.

Menu For any June night dance, this should be light and cool: an icy fruit punch can be part of the refreshments served from a large glass bowl placed in a bigger bowl of ice on a serving cart, with the whole cart as well as punch bowl garlanded with fresh roses or artificial garlands like those made for the windows. Float a few rose petals on the top of the punch when it is first brought out.

A large pale pink gelatin salad (juice from cooked or canned cherries, or from crushed strawberries, is used to make the color) filled with fresh fruits, finger sandwiches of chicken salad, water cress with mayonnaise, and open-face ham canapés on pumpernickel are enough for the main course of supper. Then serve strawberry ice cream and pink-frosted white layer cake, the cake top decorated with fresh pink roses or with a few whole strawberries. Or, in place of a cake, serve tiny fresh meringues and hot coffee.

Another color scheme especially appropriate for a summer night's dance of this kind is blue, using moonlight, big blue moon lanterns, and stars (star-shaped electric lights) as decoration and theme. See also the previous sections on Alumnae Parties and Class Reunions.

High School Commencement Parties may be on this same scale of a big home dance, or a smaller, more simple dance preceded by supper. But today in many parts of the country, the high school commencement dance is held in the school gym, with parents combining their money and efforts to make a gay and delicious supper right in the gym, either before the dance or late at night when the dance ends. This is a concerted community effort to keep their children from late-hour driving after their school party and from going to out-of-bounds road houses, restaurants and night clubs.

Many teen-agers accept the idea of chaperones for their dances, and these community, parent-student affairs provide chaperones who stay out of sight, for the most part since they are elsewhere in the gym making supper preparations. The result is that these parties have been gratefully received by some youngsters because they provide good times of which their parents approve, they cost the boys less, and give everybody a "terrific" dance and supper, better than the class funds could produce, with no family problems afterwards.

Other parties for high school graduates might be any of their favorite outdoor get-togethers, especially *picnics, swim parties, beach parties, clam bakes, square dance* or whatever their crowd is momentarily interested in. See "Outdoor Entertaining," Chapter 15, and "Teen-Age Parties," Chapter 5.

Parents' Night P.T.A. meetings are not always sufficiently relaxed or casual for parents to meet and know each other, and to get acquainted with their children's teachers and with school administrators and other officers. After such meetings, which may be stormy or badly organized or ineffectual, or in some other way disappointing, or when there is no adequate gym or entertainment space for a social hour, a home party may help solve problems and be a means of a better relationship with all concerned.

This kind of At Home or Open House should be simple, and anything but a contrived or dress-up party. Ideally, it is drop-in-for-coffee after the meeting, the emphasis on comfortable chairs, a little refreshment, a quiet and leisurely time for talk. Good things to serve, besides coffee, are cheese, apples, and nuts, or soft cheese spreads with a selection of crisp crackers and toast. Or a pan of freshly-baked gingerbread or cookies. Seasonal changes can appear in this menu, such as cider and doughnuts on an autumn night, hot mulled cider with sandwiches on a wintry night, or tall cold lemonade or fruit punch on a spring evening. See also After-Town-Meeting Parties in "Family and Community Parties," Chapter 8.

Another version of Parents' Night is an open house at school, when teachers invite parents to come to an early evening performance of a play, or perhaps to see a new marionette theatre, or to hear school musicians sing and play. In some schools the refreshments for such an evening are provided by the parents. They should be simple and light, such as a fruit punch or hot coffee for grownups, hot cocoa for children, and an assortment of cookies and small cakes for everybody.

10

KITCHEN PARTIES

Early New England and Middle Western farm and village kitchens, with a coal range, rocking chair, striped cat on the mat and geraniums in the window, were the scene of many kitchen parties. The same kinds of hospitality are still popular although today's kitchens have a different look. A cup of coffee for a drop-in neighbor, hot coffee and a piece of pie for a postman who has come through snowdrifts with a letter he knew was important, coffee and a sandwich in a tiny apartment kitchen for an old elevator man who had to work around the clock because the relief man didn't show up—these are only a few of the many ways the kitchen opens its door with a hospitable gesture.

A comfortably large kitchen is a good place to have an after-theatre or after-movies snack, a visit after Town Meeting or lodge or P.T.A. meeting, an after-the-game buffet. These and many similar, casual meals for teen-agers and grownups are described, with menus, in various sections of this book.

Here's another to add to them. Use the kitchen as a food service center for a teen-age and college dance. When the entire cleared space of living room and dining room is needed for dancing, set up in the kitchen a long folding table or smaller tables pushed together, or a huge round table made by putting a round top (rented from a caterer) on a small table as a base. Cover the table with a blue-and-white or red-and-white checkered cotton cloth. Decorate it with a bouquet of mixed bright flowers, such as anemones, geraniums, and tulips in a pottery or copper jug, or make a centerpiece of an old-fashioned basket filled with fresh fruits, a pair of country lanterns, or big sturdy candles in pottery sticks. Arrange stacks of plates, silver, napkins, a tray of coffee cups, and glasses for cold drinks.

Menu With the kitchen door closed on the music and dancers, the supper can be made ready to put on the buffet table about 10 o'clock. For cold weather this menu can be—whatever your children asked you to serve. Maybe a platter of small meat loaves garnished with sautéed green peppers and a very little gravy, platters of buttered soft rolls or cheese muffins or biscuits, olives, celery, radishes, a big salad bowl of tossed green salad with choice of Roquefort and French dressing.

Or, in place of meat loaf, serve pizzas made with huge round crackers or split and toasted English muffins spread with savory pizza mixture and heated in a hot oven about 10 minutes. Desserts and beverages can be served from a kitchen counter or temporary counter set up for the purpose. These may be ice cream pie, ice cream sandwich of chocolate cake and coffee ice cream, or ice cream with sundae topping or with cake and petits fours, and hot and cold beverages.

At suppertime, open the kitchen door and ring an old-fashioned dinner bell or strike a Chinese brass dinner gong. Your children's guests serve themselves. Trays are essential, unless you have planned to set up small supper tables quickly around the dining room and living room when the music stops. This is practical or possible only in a large house and with extra help.

Guests carry their filled trays from the kitchen buffet to any convenient place to sit and talk. Rented folding chairs may be needed if the crowd is large, or there may be enough seating on living-room sofas, the stairs, assorted stools and benches, and the floor.

Kitchen Work Parties The kitchen party at which everybody cooks or makes something is just as much fun as the suppers and other entertaining that go on in this important room. Among the best of the work parties is a Christmas Cookie Party. For this, keep the guest list small to avoid confusion, perhaps five or six early-teen youngsters with a grownup to guide them. Or, this can be a party of grownups. Either group makes cookies for a community Christmas tree or to be sold at a church, school, or community bazaar. Or the bake may be a family affair in which the children of the household make cookies to give the friends on their Christmas lists.

Plan Ahead Careful planning is necessary to make a kitchen work party a success. Recipes must be studied ahead of time and large, hand-printed copies of recipes made and hung over worktables. All necessary utensils must be assembled ready for use, all ingredients bought. Decide how many times each recipe will be repeated to make the total number of cookies desired. Do not double and triple recipes, because large batches of dough are not easily handled by amateurs.

Follow a Schedule A schedule of work must be made to determine who does what, and when, and where, to prevent useless milling around the kitchen, confusion, and spoiled batches of cookies.

Working Areas Arrange separate work centers such as mixing tables and a table for cutting paper and wrapping. Have a cleared space ready, possibly dining-room table on which to spread baked cookies to cool. As guests arrive, they should choose their jobs, such as cracking nuts, measuring and mixing, rolling and cutting out cookies, greasing bake sheets and other jobs.

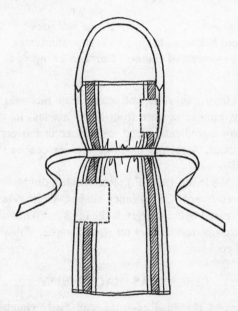

An adult, preferably the hostess should be in charge of the oven to regulate temperature, place baking sheets where they should go and be responsible for all encounters with the oven door. If guests have not been asked to bring their own aprons, give them big, bright aprons made of kitchen towels, and let them keep the aprons as a gift from the kitchen party (see sketch).

Three or four kinds of cookies make a satisfying assortment. For two of these buy your favorite brownie and cookie mixes which are easy to prepare; many teen-agers are expert at making these. Follow directions on the packages. Here are two recipes, also easy to make, and the cookies are delicious.

CHRISTMAS GINGER STARS

Use star-shaped cutters, or cut rolled dough with bird, Christmas tree, and ginger-man cutters. For bird and man cookies, use small dried currants for eyes.

2½ cups sifted all-purpose flour	1½ teaspoons powdered ginger
1 teaspoon salt	1 cup molasses
2 teaspoons baking soda	½ cup shortening
1 teaspoon powdered cinnamon	Currants as needed

Mix and sift flour, salt, soda, and spices. Heat molasses to bubbling, add shortening, remove at once from heat, mix and let cool slightly. Stir in sifted dry ingredients, blend well. Place in refrigerator to chill about half an hour. A second batch of cookies can be started while first dough chills.

Set oven at Moderate (350°F.). Roll chilled dough ⅛ inch thick on lightly-floured board. Cut in fancy shapes. With wide spatula, lift cookies to ungreased baking sheets. Bake for 8 to 10 minutes. Remove cookies with spatula and let cool on waxed paper. This recipe makes about 6 dozen cookies.

CHRISTMAS MACAROONS

2 cups moist shredded coconut	½ cup finely chopped red and green candied cherries
½ cup condensed milk	
1 teaspoon vanilla	

Set oven at Moderate (350°F.). Grease 1 large or 2 small baking sheets. Combine coconut and condensed milk in a mixing bowl. Add vanilla and chopped candied cherries, and mix well. Drop from teaspoon 1 inch apart onto greased baking sheet. Bake for 10 minutes or until delicately browned. Use spatula to remove from baking sheet at once. Let cool on layers of waxed paper. This recipe makes 2 dozen macaroons.

Tray Menu When all baking is finished and cookies are cooling, it is time to reward the cooks with refreshments. When you are planning the details of the cookie bake, plan also for a small tray luncheon that can be put together quickly out of the refrigerator or with a minimum of cooking.

The tray menu, chopped olive-and-cheese or meatloaf sandwich, glass of milk, baked apple with cream, coffee for grownups. Or, creamed chicken-and-pimiento reheated quickly and served on toast, beverage, individual baked caramel custards from refrigerator. Or, individual gelatin salads of vegetables and tuna fish with lemon mayonnaise, buttered soft roll, beverages, small cupcake, doughnut, or fruit tart. Guests carry their trays to living room or glassed-in porch or any comfortable place and rest and talk.

By the time luncheon is finished, the cookies are cool enough to be packaged. For this a supply of small boxes ordered through a stationer or local bake shop and plenty of waxed paper must be ready, the waxed paper to line each box and to be placed between layers of cookies. The filled boxes look their best wrapped in Christmas paper, bright foil, or solid-color tissue paper and tied with colored yarn, cord, or ribbon. Wrapped boxes should be stacked in cartons and kept in a cool place for delivery to bazaar or wherever they are to go.

Christmas Fudge and Candy Party See also 6th Wedding Anniversary party, Chapter 1. Follow general plan for Christmas cookie party. For best results add candy thermometer to list of necessary equipment. Buy your favorite fudge mixes, or this recipe:

CHRISTMAS FUDGE

2 (1-oz.) squares chocolate
2 cups light brown sugar, packed
⅔ cup milk
2 tablespoons light corn syrup
3 tablespoons butter
1 teaspoon vanilla

Break chocolate into small pieces; put in 1-quart enamel saucepan with sugar, milk, and corn syrup. Cook slowly, stirring until sugar is dissolved. Continue cooking slowly, stirring often, until temperature on candy thermometer is 236°F., or a little dropped from the tip of a spoon into a cup of cold water forms a soft ball.

Remove pan from heat, add butter, set aside to cool without stirring. When candy has cooled to 100°F. (lukewarm), add vanilla and beat with wooden spoon. Beat slowly but steadily until the fudge loses its shiny look and sticky consistency and a small amount dropped from a spoon onto a plate will hold its shape. Pour into lightly buttered 6-inch-square pan. Let cool, then cut in inch squares. This recipe makes 1¼ pounds, about 36 pieces.

CHRISTMAS DIVINITY

2½ cups sugar	½ teaspoon vanilla
⅔ cup light corn syrup	1 cup chopped red and
½ cup water	green candied cherries
¼ teaspoon salt	
2 egg whites, stiffly beaten in large bowl	

Combine sugar, syrup, water and salt in 1½-quart enamel saucepan; cook, stirring slowly until sugar is dissolved. Continue cooking without stirring until temperature on candy thermometer is 265°F., or when a few drops of the mixture dropped into a cup cold water forms a hard but pliable ball.

Remove pan from heat at once. Beat syrup slowly into stiffly beaten egg whites. Continue beating until a little dropped from a spoon will hold its shape; add vanilla and cherries. Drop by teaspoonfuls on waxed paper. Let cool. This recipe makes about 1⅓ pounds, about 26 pieces.

HULA HUTS

4½ cups shredded coconut	1 cup dark corn syrup
1 cup granulated sugar	2 tablespoons butter
1 cup brown sugar (packed)	½ teaspoon salt
¾ cup water	

Spread coconut in shallow pan; place in Moderate oven (375°F.) about 20 minutes, or until lightly browned. Let cool.

Combine sugars, water, syrup, butter, and salt in 2½-quart enamel saucepan. Cook slowly, stirring until sugar is dissolved. Continue cooking, stirring only enough to prevent burning until temperature on candy thermometer is 245°F. (a little makes a firm ball in a cup of cold water). Remove pan from heat at once, and add coconut. Mix thoroughly. Drop by spoonfuls on greased waxed paper or pan. With your fingers lightly buttered, shape each piece into small cones or huts; this must be done quickly, before mixture hardens. Let huts cool. This recipe makes about 1¼ pounds, 26 to 28 hula huts.

HOLIDAY CARAMELS

¼ to ½ cup chopped pistachio nuts
2 cups sugar
1 cup light corn syrup
1 cup condensed milk
½ cup light cream
1 cup milk
6 (1-oz.) squares chocolate, broken
2 teaspoons vanilla

Spread chopped nuts in 8-by-9-inch shallow, buttered pan. Combine sugar, syrup, condensed milk, cream, milk and chocolate in 2-quart enamel saucepan. Cook over low heat, stirring slowly until temperature on candy thermometer is 246°F., or when a few drops of the mixture dropped into a cup of water form a firm ball. Remove pan from heat; add vanilla, and pour at once over the nuts in the prepared pan. Let cool a little, then cut in small squares. Let cool completely before wrapping each caramel in fancy waxed paper or colored foil. The recipe makes about 2½ pounds, about 72 pieces.

Popcorn Party for Grownups and Children Follow the general plan of the Christmas Cookie Party. Buy packaged, unpopped corn, but before the party day test it to see if it pops readily. One cup of corn makes about 5 cups of popped corn. Use an electric popper, or a frying pan or hand popper on top of a hot range. Do not put too much corn in hand popper at one time, or popper will fill up before all grains are popped. Shake the hand popper constantly over low heat for speedy, even popping.

For popcorn to eat salty and hot, use a frying pan. Melt 1 tablespoon vegetable shortening and the same amount of butter in large, deep, heavy skillet that has a tightly-fitting lid. Add about ½ cup of unpopped corn, cover, and shake skillet over heat until corn is popped. When popped, sprinkle quickly with salt and stir to season evenly. Serve at once. Or let cool, then package in waxed paper bags to sell at bazaar or add to Christmas gifts.

POPCORN BALLS

3 quarts lightly-salted popped corn (about 2½ to 3 cups unpopped corn)
1 cup light molasses
1 cup dark corn syrup
1 tablespoon cider vinegar
3 tablespoons butter

½ teaspoon salt
½ teaspoon lemon flavoring
Softened butter or margarine for hands

Combine molasses, syrup, and vinegar in 1-quart enamel saucepan and cook, stirring occasionally until temperature on candy thermometer is 240°F., or when a few drops of the mixture dropped into a cup of cold water form a soft ball. Then stir constantly until temperature is 270°F., or use the soft crack, water test, when a few drops of the mixture dropped into a cup of cold water form a semi-hard thread. Remove pan from heat, add butter, salt, and flavoring. Stir only enough to mix, pour over popped corn, and mix well. Form into balls at once with palms and fingers lightly greased with butter or margarine. Use only enough pressure to make ball hold shape. Let cool. Wrap in waxed paper or in twists of red or green cellophane. This recipe makes about 20 2½-inch balls.

If popcorn balls are for Christmas stir about 2 cups finely chopped green and red candied cherries into popped corn before hot syrup is poured over it.

SUGARED POPCORN

2½ quarts lightly-salted popped corn (about 2 cups unpopped corn)
1 cup sugar
¾ cup water

1 teaspoon vanilla
3 tablespoons confectioner's sugar

Combine sugar and water in small saucepan until temperature on candy thermometer is 238°F., or when a few drops of the mixture dropped into a cup of cold water form a soft ball. Stir only until sugar is dissolved. Remove pan from heat. Add vanilla, and stir only enough to mix in flavoring. Pour slowly over popped corn, mixing thoroughly. When kernels are all coated, sprinkle with confectioner's sugar and keep on stirring until syrup on corn "sugars." Turn out onto a large sheet of waxed paper and separate each piece. Serve at once, or let cool and then package in waxed paper bags. Makes about 2½ quarts.

CHEESE POPCORN

2½ quarts freshly popped, lightly-salted corn, (about 2 cups unpopped corn)
1½ cups melted butter

½ cup grated Parmesan cheese
½ cup finely grated Cheddar cheese

Mix hot melted butter with cheese. Pour over warm popped corn, and mix thoroughly. Let cool before serving or packaging in waxed paper bags.

Taffy Pull for Grownups and Children Follow general plan of Christmas Cookie Party. Here are two good taffies for Christmas packages or bazaar sales. Follow the recipe instructions exactly.

For children, pour hot taffy into small greased pans or small greased platters; it is easier to pull a small amount than a large batch. Taffy is ready to pull when the edges begin to stiffen and the mass can be handled. If it cools too long it is hard to handle, but it can be softened by placing in a moderate oven for a few minutes.

Do not grease hands—dip fingers in bowl of cornstarch. Use thumb and forefingers rather than the whole hand. Pull until taffy is cold. Use scissors for cutting pieces; twist and continue cutting until all is cut. Keep pieces separated, wrap separately in twists of colored waxed paper.

OLD-FASHIONED MINT TAFFY

2 cups molasses	½ teaspoon soda
2 teaspoons cider vinegar	1 teaspoon peppermint
2 tablespoons butter	flavoring
⅛ teaspoon salt	

Combine molasses and vinegar in 1½-quart enamel saucepan. Let cook slowly until temperature on candy thermometer is 270°F. (Soft crack, water test.) As the temperature increases, stir to prevent burning. Remove pan from heat, add butter, salt, and soda and stir until candy stops foaming. Pour into a shallow, greased pan or platter. Let cool enough to pull. Pour the peppermint flavoring into the center of the mass, and gather corners toward the center so that flavoring will not be lost. Remove from pan and pull.

When taffy becomes light in color and firm, stretch it out in a long rope, twist, and cut in small pieces. Let cool. Wrap pieces in twists of colored waxed paper. For softer taffy, cook only to 266°F. on the thermometer or when a few drops of the mixture dropped into a cup of cold water form a hard ball. This recipe makes about 1 pound, or, about 50 pieces.

BLACK WALNUT TAFFY

⅔ cup coarsely chopped black walnuts	1 tablespoon cider vinegar
	1 teaspoon vanilla
2 cups sugar	
1 cup water	

Spread walnuts in two greased, 8-inch pans or platters.

Combine sugar, water, and vinegar in 1-quart enamel saucepan and cook over low heat, stirring until sugar is dissolved. Then let cook without stirring until temperature on candy thermometer is 268°F., or when a few drops of the mixture dropped into a cup of cold water form a hard ball. Remove pan from heat; add vanilla, pour into the prepared pans or platters. Let cool until edges crinkle and candy can be handled. Remove from pan or platter and pull until candy is white and firm. Cut with scissors. Wrap pieces in twists of waxed paper. This recipe makes about 1 pound, 40 to 50 pieces.

Other Kitchen Work Parties All ages, or children with one or two adults to supervise, meet in somebody's kitchen a few days before Christmas to fill stockings for other children in hospitals, also for neighborhood pets. Children bring small dime-store toys to wrap, boxes of dog biscuits, toy bones, other small toys for cats and dogs. Stockings can be made from bright felt by the adults. Children add spangles, bright ribbon bows, and Christmas decoration, then fill them and deliver to church, school, community house, or hospital.

Another kitchen party can be held to make wreaths, small table trees, and other decorations for hospital rooms. Guests bring their own greens and trimmings. The host provides wire coat hangers, rolls of wire cord, and assorted Christmas decorations. Gold and silver paint, pictures of professional decorations from magazines, oddments such as small Santa figures, reindeer, sleighs, and candles may be demanded by the artists.

A fruitcake party should take place at least a month before the holidays. This should be planned much like the cookie party. All ingredients should be on hand—also one-pound and two-pound pans, and, for after the baking, refreshments for the bakers. Then, at the wrapping session, loaves are stoutly sealed in waxed paper or foil, to mellow and ripen until time to be sold at a church bazaar or school sale, or some other occasion for raising funds.

11

FOLK DANCE PARTIES

Folk dancing has thousands of devotees, many of whom consider this pleasant recreation a therapeutic art. Its music, activity, and dramatic participation offer a healthy change from business office and other daily tasks which tend to mold the personality in directions it may not want to go. Thousands more, teen-agers and entire families, seemingly like folk dancing simply because it is fun. It is not all romp and stomp; its intricate patterns, movement, and beauty or humor are as rewarding to the dancers as the social good time that is part of such an evening.

And child specialists are among the most enthusiastic supporters of folk play, music, and dancing, believing that the songs and rhythms provide experience which "children can take to their hearts and make part of their lives, and the singing brings gaiety and warmth to the day, stimulates their imagination and creativeness."

If you and your friends are experienced folk dancers, your parties are devoted to learning new dances and enjoying the familiar old ones. But if you and your friends are beginners, you need help from the experts before you can build up a folk dance group. Perhaps a local dance enthusiast can guide you to start, with American square dancing first and later dances of other countries.

Instruction and music for square dancing and the folk dances of the rest of the world are available in exact, detailed dance lessons and diagrams, and in LP and other records, from established folk art centers.

Also see Neighbor Parties in Chapter 8, "Family and Community Parties," and Box Social and Square Dance in Chapter 5, "Teen-Age Parties"

Sources of Information

The Archive of American Folk Song, Library of Congress, Washington, D.C. has preserved on records and tapes thousands of songs and tales from American folklore. Some of this recorded material is sold to the public and it is inspiring and valuable for folk parties and plays, for entertainment at home as well as in school and other groups. Write to the Library's Recording Laboratory for a free list of available records and other material.

Consult your local classified telephone directory for hobby sources, folk music, dance and festival organizations in your city. In New York City where folk dancing is widely popular, there are several established sources of printed material, records, and other information on folk dancing. A letter to them will bring prices, and other facts.

Among these sources is Folk Dance House, 108 West Sixteenth St., New York 11, headquarters for back copies of *The Folk Dancer,* and a book service on the subject. Another is the *Folk Dance Bulletin,* 552 Riverside Drive, New York 27, New York, which consists of dance instruction for beginners, old-timers, and teachers. Bound volumes, each containing directions for 60 or more dances previously published in the *Bulletin* are available, indexed by country, classified as to type of dance (such as educational for schools, camps, and recreational groups) and as to kind (such as waltz, polka, kolo) and as to formation (for example, one couple, two couples, circle). The directions include necessary information about music, names of available records for specific dances, and where they are obtainable.

Folkways Records & Service Corporation, 117 West Forty-sixth St., New York 36, New York, is a long established producer of prize-winning folk records, and is recommended by many educational and entertainment organizations. Folkways publishes comprehensive catalogues of authentic folk music for dancing, singing, festivals, and parties.

And see the section on Neighbor Parties, in Chapter 8, for address and information on folk material available through the U. S. Committee for U.N.I.C.E.F., United Nations, New York 17, New York.

Children's Folk Dance Parties Included in the U.N.I.C.E.F. Hi-Neighbor Kits are directions for children's folk dance parties with music, games, costume sketches, and recipes for foods of different ethnic groups.

Also write Folkways Records (address above) for special catalogue of children's folk music with songs and dance notes.

And see Chapter 4, "Children's Parties," for costumes, songs, and dances for a Gypsy Party.

While evenings of grownup folk dancing are devoted primarily to dancing, in some groups costume parties are frequent, and so are special nights such as Hungarian, Italian, or Scandinavian, at which decorations, costumes, and refreshments are inspired by the foreign country. To make costumes, see dressmaker pattern yearbooks of the nationally-known pattern companies in department stores. You can also buy or rent costumes from foreign shops and rental agencies. Visit foreign shops in your city for photographs of costumes that you can copy, also for decorations and for native accessories to add to costumes you make or rent, and to use in decorating your home for your party. Consult such shops for decoration ideas and seek further help on costumes, decorations, and foods in your local library.

For menus, you might want to consult foreign cookbooks in the library and foreign shops. A local foreign restaurant can supply ideas for a one-dish supper to serve after dancing and give advice on preparing and serving various typical dishes. Some restaurants will send food out, with a man or woman to finish the food's preparation in your own kitchen and to serve the dishes according to their national custom.

Menus Here are several for various folk-dance suppers you may like to try. See recipes at end of chapter.

Austria: Casserole of noodles and ham (called schinkenfleckerln, one of the most popular dishes in Austria), coffee *mit* (meaning with heavy cream or whipped cream), and cherry torte (open-face cherry pie in sweet pastry crust).

Hungary: Poppy-seed pastry, cheese, fruit, coffee.

Israel: Dried-fruit tzimmes, crescent rolls, honey cake, black coffee.

Italy: Baked lasagne, tossed green salad with anchovy dressing, spumone, little cakes, coffee espresso.

Russia: Cheese blintzes with cherry jam, hot tea in glasses. For a larger menu, serve hot or cold borsch with piroshki, then blintzes and jam, and hot tea.

Scandinavia: Open-face Danish sandwiches, chafing dish or electric skillet Swedish meat balls, rolls, apple cake, coffee.

South America: Brazilian empanadas (little meat, chicken, or seafood pastries), small rice custards, coffee or a mixture of hot chocolate and coffee poured from two pots at the same time into cups and mixed with the intricately carved whirl-sticks obtainable at Mexican and Pan-American shops. Whirl-sticks are also sold mail order from such shops through ads in shopping columns in home furnishing magazines.

Spain: Fried eggs Spanish style in chafing dish or electric skillet, buttered crusty rolls, cream or Neufchâtel cheese with guava or quince jelly, coffee, or mixture of coffee and hot chocolate (see above).

Square dance and other American folk parties: serve coffee and doughnuts, or, an oyster stew with crackers; gingerbread, fruit and coffee; or, baked beans, brown bread, coleslaw, apple dumpling, and coffee, or let the dancers bring box suppers.

Recipes for Folk Dance Menus

AUSTRIAN SCHINKENFLECKERLN
(NOODLES AND HAM)

Casseroles of this dish can be put together ahead of time, kept covered in the refrigerator, and put in the oven to bake at suppertime.

1 pound broad noodles	Grind of black pepper
⅔ cup butter	2 cups ham cut in small
1 cup commercial sour	pieces
cream	3 tablespoons dry bread-
6 eggs, beaten	crumbs

Cook noodles as directed on the package, then drain, rinse with cold water, and drain again. Spread out on breadboard and cut in squares. Sauté noodle squares in a little hot butter for 5 minutes, then add the rest of the butter to pan. Combine sour cream and eggs and slowly stir into noodles. Season with grind of pepper; stir in ham.

Set oven at Moderate (350°F.). Butter 2½-quart baking dish, sprinkle with crumbs, and pour noodle-ham mixture into dish. Bake for 45 minutes. This recipe makes 6 or more servings. For larger crowd, prepare it twice, in two casseroles.

HUNGARIAN MÁKORTA
(POPPY-SEED PASTRY)

¼ cup butter
½ cup sugar
6 eggs
½ cup bread crumbs
¼ pound semi-sweet choc-
    olate, melted

⅓ cup ground poppy seeds
(from herb shop or pastry
shop)

Set oven at Moderately Low (325°F.). Grease two 8-inch cake pans, line them with waxed paper, and grease paper with butter.

Cream butter and sugar smoothly together. Beat egg whites until they stand in peaks when beater is removed. Beat egg yolks until thick and lemon-colored. Add butter-sugar mixture and crumbs to yolks, fold in melted chocolate, then fold in poppy seeds and egg whites. Spread in prepared pans. Bake for 30 minutes, or until cake tester comes out clean. Turn cake out on a cooling rack, remove paper, and let cool. Put layers together with peach jam or serve plain. This makes 6 to 8 servings. For a larger crowd, repeat the recipe to make a second torte.

ISRAEL DRIED-FRUIT TZIMMES

These can be made early in the day and reheated in a casserole at party time.

½ pound each dried apri-
    cots, prunes, pears
3 pounds beef brisket
2 teaspoons salt
Grind of fresh pepper
3 carrots, scraped and
    quartered

1 lemon, thinly sliced
2 cups orange juice
4 cups water
4 tablespoons honey

Wash dried fruits, drain, cover with fresh water, and let soak half an hour. Drain again.

Set oven at Moderate (350°F.). Brown beef in a 3-quart, flame-proof casserole over moderate heat. Season with salt and a little pepper. Arrange dried fruit, carrots, and lemon slices around meat.

Combine orange juice, water, and honey and pour over all. Cover casserole and bake about 3 hours. Remove cover, increase heat to Moderately Hot (400°F.) and bake another hour. Add a little mixed orange juice, hot water, and honey if necessary, as there should be a small amount of sauce around the meat. This recipe makes 6 to 8 servings. If the crowd is large, prepare the recipe twice, using matching casseroles.

ITALIAN BAKED LASAGNE

Noodles can be cooked and drained, the sausages cooked and sliced, and all ingredients made ready in advance, to combine at suppertime and to finish in the oven, as directed.

1½ pounds broad noodles
¾ pound small Italian sausages
2 cups tomato sauce
1½ cups grated Parmesan cheese
1½ cups cubed Mozzarella cheese
1½ cups ricotta (Italian cottage cheese)

Cook noodles as directed on package, then drain. Cook sausages in heavy skillet about 15 minutes, or until cooked through and lightly browned on all sides, then slice them.

Set oven at Moderate (350°F.). Pour ½ cup tomato sauce into bottom of 3-quart baking dish. Place a layer of noodles in sauce, top with Parmesan cheese, a layer of tomato sauce, then a layer of Mozzarella. Add a few slices of sausage and several spoonfuls of ricotta. Repeat layers of sauce, noodles, Parmesan, sauce, Mozzarella, sausage, and ricotta. Make the top layer of sauce and Parmesan cheese. Bake for 20 minutes or until top is browned and the mixture somewhat firm. Cut and serve on warmed plates, with or without additions of extra sauce and grated cheese. This recipe makes 8 to 10 servings. For a larger crowd, repeat the recipe, using two large casseroles.

RUSSIAN BLINTZES

If hostess can excuse herself in the midst of the party to make these, or has someone in the kitchen to make them at suppertime, they are wonderful party food. If they seem too much trouble to make, try the quick-frozen blintzes available in many markets. Also buy the excellent borsch which comes in glass jars. Serve it cold or hot, with sour cream and piroshki (small pastry turnovers filled with chopped, cooked, well-seasoned meat or chicken) made in advance and reheated at suppertime.

BLINTZ BATTER

1 egg	⅛ teaspoon salt
¼ cup milk	1 cup sifted all-purpose
¾ cup commercial sour	flour
cream	3 or 4 tablespoons butter

Butter a 2-quart, shallow baking dish. Set oven at Hot (450°F.). Beat egg, combine with milk, sour cream, and salt in mixing bowl. Stir in flour, mixing until smooth. Heat about 1 tablespoon butter in a 7-inch skillet. Pour about 2 tablespoons of batter into the pan, and tilt it to spread batter evenly. Cook until browned, turn pancake to brown other side. Place a heaping tablespoon of cheese filling on each pancake, fold sides in, and roll up. Place in buttered baking dish. Continue making pancakes, filling and rolling them until all are in baking dish. Bake for 10 minutes in hot oven. Serve hot with cherry jam. This recipe makes 16 blintzes.

BLINTZ CHEESE FILLING

2 cups drained cottage	1 tablespoon melted butter
cheese	1 teaspoon lemon juice
1 egg yolk	1 tablespoon sugar
¾ teaspoon salt	
¼ teaspoon grated nutmeg	

Combine cheese, egg yolk, salt, nutmeg, and butter. Beat until well mixed. Add lemon juice and sugar. Use as described in pancakes. This recipe makes filling for 16 or more blintzes.

SWEDISH MEAT BALLS

Meat balls can be mixed in advance, kept in the refrigerator, and cooked in chafing dish at suppertime.

⅔ pound ground beef	4 tablespoons butter
¼ pound ground veal	2 egg yolks
¼ pound ground pork	2 teaspoons salt
⅜ cup rolled dry crumbs	Grind of black pepper
1 cup cream or sour cream	¼ teaspoon ground allspice
½ onion, peeled and chopped fine	

Put meats through grinder, using the finest knife, five or six times. Soften crumbs in cream, then add crumbs and cream to meat, stirring with wooden spoon or kneading with fingers. Cook onion in 1 tablespoon butter for 2 or 3 minutes, without browning. Add to meat mixture with egg yolks and seasonings. Shape into small balls. Cook slowly in butter, turn them to brown on all sides, using two spoons to keep the balls in shape. Add a little hot water to the pan as soon as balls are done. Heat to boiling, spoon over the balls. Serve hot. This recipe makes 8 to 10 servings.

For open-face Danish sandwiches spread small, thin slices of pumpernickel, sweet seedless rye bread, white bread, and cracked-wheat or other breads with softened sweet butter. Cover some with paper-thin slices of seasoned cucumber, others with small cooked, cleaned mayonnaise-coated shrimp, others with thin slices boiled ham, others with very thin slices smoked salmon or pâté. One or two of these is served on each plate with hot meat balls.

BRAZILIAN EMPANADAS

In Brazil these are eaten with the fingers, as snacks.

1½ cups sifted all-purpose flour	1 egg white
½ teaspoon salt	2 egg yolks
¼ pound butter	Hot water

Start oven at Hot (450°F.). Sift flour and salt together, cut in butter with pastry blender until mixture is like fine crumbs. Beat egg white and yolks together lightly and add gradually to the flour-butter mixture. Add a few drops of hot water, just enough to make dough stiff. Break off portions of dough, roll out, cut in 3-inch rounds. Place a generous spoonful of filling on half of round, add 1 olive, and a piece of hard-cooked egg. Fold pastry over, crimp together with tines of fork. Bake 10 to 15 minutes until crust is golden. Serve hot. This recipe makes about 16 empanadas.

FILLING FOR EMPANADAS

1 cup ground cooked shrimp

1 cup ground canned or cooked tunafish

¼ cup ground peeled mushrooms

½ onion, peeled and finely minced

1 teaspoon finely minced parsley

1 or 2 tablespoons small white seedless raisins

2 slices cooked or canned artichoke bottoms, finely minced

1 cup bouillon

16 to 20 pitted ripe olives

2 or 3 hard-cooked eggs

Combine shrimp, fish, mushrooms, onion, parsley, raisins, and artichoke in saucepan. Add bouillon and simmer about 8 minutes or until mushrooms are tender. Let cool. The mixture should be quite moist. Use as described above. This recipe makes filling for 16 to 20 empanadas.

SPANISH FRIED EGGS

2 tablespoons bacon fat with small bits of cooked bacon in it

1 tablespoon honey

6 eggs

Salt and pepper

Sliced green and red pickled peppers from Spanish or Italian delicatessen

Heat fat in chafing dish or electric skillet, mix honey into hot fat. Break eggs into saucer, one at a time, and slip them into hot fat to cook slowly. Season lightly with salt and pepper. When eggs are done, remove pan from heat, cover eggs thickly with the pickled peppers. Serve at once onto warmed supper plates. This recipe makes 6 servings.

12

OUTDOOR ENTERTAINING

A successful outdoor meal is planned with the same imagination, care, and exactness that is given a menu served in the dining room.

Barbecue Luncheon or Supper For either of these, start your planning with a good barbecue cookbook and articles from women's and home furnishings magazines, which show the latest improved and most convenient barbecue equipment and utensils. Such books and articles include menus and recipes for superb meals cooked on handsomely built brick or stone garden barbecues as well as on small mobile grills. Adapt the menus to your locality, your markets, to the size and kind of barbecue you use, to your budget, and to the number of your guests.

Several days before the guest party, cook and serve your planned party meal to the family. This trial meal gives you helpful guidance in timing, seasoning, and serving. For the guest meal invite the right number of friends, which means only the number that, added to the family, can be served by your barbecue cookery with ease.

Invitations For these you may want to use amusing little printed folders especially designed for barbecue entertaining, now available in stationery and card shops. You may also give the invitations in person or by telephone.

Then plan the shopping for the guest meal. Make a time schedule

Also see preceding chapters on Teen-Age Parties, Family and Church Entertaining, Family and Community Parties, and Index for all you must do (see preliminary instructions in the section on How to Give a Dinner, in Chapter 15). Allow time to prepare and put food on to cook, and to make cold dishes to keep in the refrigerator until mealtime.

Decoration Work out a scheme for your garden table, and decide on the silver, china, glassware or their equivalents in outdoor accessories, such as bamboo-handled cutlery, plastic or paper plates and mugs, and similar wares.

If the meal is supper, you may need candles, which should be in sturdy holders with hurricane or other glass shades, or use some other decorative but practical lighting. It may be easier to use two or three small tables instead of one large one. Or give the guests outsize tray-tables, which they can place around the terrace or lawn or wherever they please.

Tableware Bold colors and simple wares are best suited to barbecue meals. A bright blue tablecloth with tomato-red napkins and white or boldly patterned china look especially gay for any outdoor summer meal (and perfect for Fourth of July parties). Another effective barbecue color scheme is a striped linen tablecloth in bright, modern colors, napkins of solid color matching a stripe in the cloth, plates and other china in another solid color matching another stripe. Country baskets or a wooden bowl of flowers, fruit, or colorful vegetables, or an antique pottery container full of geraniums are favorite center-pieces.

Scrubbed bare tables are also popular for barbecue meals, especially those cooked by men. Bright paper or cloth napkins, solid-color paper plates or Spanish, Italian or Mexican pottery plates and other wares, such as a big white enamel coffeepot, are in keeping with the uncovered tables. The wooden bowl for salad can be giant size with long-handled mixing spoon and fork, skewers for kabobs can be extra long, mugs for coffee the brightest of pottery in this man's setting.

A cart to bring the cold dishes from the kitchen saves time and steps, and it adds fun to the party when decorated with amusing banners and colored paper rosettes, or greens and flowers from the garden. Plan the seating of your guests with comfortable chairs, benches, cushions, stools, or whatever your outdoor dining space accommodates.

For any outdoor party, just before guests arrive, use an antimosquito spray *at the grass level* around chair and table legs and in adjacent grassy terrace areas. But be sure that no spray lands on tables, chairs, or buffet counters, or on any of the cookery equipment, service carts, or trays. Some sprays are poisonous, all are smelly, and they fly through the air in all directions.

A barbecue meal should be cooking on the grill or rotisserie, and be almost ready to serve when the guests arrive. The fragrance of the broiling food should be supplemented with thirst-quenching beverages ready on a buffet service counter or cart, and summer appetizers, such as radishes, a bowl of cherries and other small fruits. When the cook is ready to serve his steaks, chops, or other foods, the guests sit down and a hot, wonderfully cooked luncheon or supper is theirs right from the grill.

Barbecue Menus for Luncheons or Suppers:

No. 1. Broiled breasts or halves of chicken; potatoes baked in foil and served with a mixture of sour cream, crisp bacon bits, and chives in place of butter; small hot cheese rolls in foil; iced watermelon, and iced or hot coffee.

No. 2. Broiled ham; sweet potatoes baked in foil; mixed, cooked vegetables chilled and combined with cold mayonnaise in crisp lettuce leaves; thin, warm cornbread. For dessert, parfaits of strawberry and vanilla ice cream alternated with crushed fresh berries, iced coffee or tea.

No. 3. Herbed chicken pan-broiled on the grill; stuffed acorn squash seasoned with onion, butter, salt and pepper and baked in foil; stuffed tomato salads with curry dressing; clover-leaf rolls. For dessert, sliced peaches with vanilla ice cream or whipped cream, iced tea or coffee.

No. 4. Lamb steaks marinated in a mixture of Worcestershire sauce, lemon and tomato juices, then broiled; corn on the cob or cut off and sautéed; cucumber and onion-ring salad in seasoned vinegar; hot garlic bread in foil. For dessert, cold raspberry soufflé, iced tea or coffee.

No. 5. Broiled steaks; quick-frozen fried onions made hot and crisp in foil; broiled, herb-seasoned tomatoes; hot blueberry muffins heated in foil. For dessert, green apple pie and hot coffee.

No. 6. Skewered lamb en brochette: with the lamb cubed, squares of green pepper, bacon, chicken livers, and quartered onions all marinated in equal parts of olive oil and lemon juice seasoned with soy sauce and half garlic bud, then broiled and served with hot saffron rice or wheat pilaf; stuffed celery and endive. For dessert, warm cherry pie or jam tarts, iced and hot coffee.

No. 7. Huge pizzas baked in barbecue oven or in the kitchen, and topped with hot tomato, cheese, and anchovy mixture at grill-side or from a portable broiler; herb-flavored tossed green salad, spumone, coffee espresso.

No. 8. Broiled salmon steaks basted with a mixture of lemon juice, butter, and paprika; casserole of lima beans, hot crisped, quick-frozen shoestring potatoes; date-and-nut muffins; a bowl fresh fruit salad (apple, strawberries, orange, seedless grapes, apricots or peaches, lettuce) with orange-juice salad dressing, and hot coffee.

Patio, Porch, and Terrace Meals without a Barbecue An outdoor luncheon or supper may be cooked in the kitchen and served outdoors. Electric outlets in the patio or on a porch or terrace can be used to cook a superb dish in an electric skillet or other appliances, to make coffee, and keep a hot-tray at the desired temperature for the dishes on it. An electric cart plugged into a patio outlet keeps the dishes on it hot throughout the meal. Plan as carefully as for your best indoor meals. See How to Give a Dinner, in Chapter 15, for help with preliminary details.

Decoration trend for these meals is to set tables with brilliant, modern colors and accessories, and to use decorative garden and terrace furniture, making use of foliage and flowers as background, with tall torchères and lanterns for evening parties. If there is a view or a

lovely garden, or birdbath or feeding stations where birds come and go, the table is placed where guests can enjoy them.

Invitations If the *al fresco* meal is planned as a gala or special occasion for distinguished guests, or for an engagement or anniversary party or other important event, the invitations can be your fold-over informals on which you write, Luncheon (or Supper), the date, hour, place, and To Meet (or, In Honor of) your guest's name. Add R.S.V.P.

If you have a generous budget for the party, you hire the necessary extra help for the day and you may want to indulge in special decorations, which a caterer, florist, or decorator can devise for your garden. A party tent on the lawn might be just right in color and capacity and is a boon when sudden showers descend. Or a flowery pavilion, which is newer, gives a festive air to the occasion. This is sometimes a brightly colored canvas top supported on flower-garlanded posts and decorated with bouquets and greenery. Or it can be amusing and different, the work of some local designer. Small colorful tables and chairs are arranged in this pleasant spot.

Lacking space and budget for this kind of setting, your small city or country terrace or suburban porch can be made pretty with a maypole

theme of ribbons, bouquets, baskets of flowers. Tablecloths and napkins, and slipcovers for chairs, can be in any favorite color scheme in formal damask, country chintz, or striped cottons. Many caterers have all of these for hire. Some hostesses make their own, keeping two or three sets in different colors ready for outdoor parties. Or a foreign theme, for example, bright Mexican colors, or Italian, or Scandinavian wares, might be your choice for such a summer party.

Menus for these luncheons or suppers, unlike those for barbecue meals, may be more elaborate. The first course may be a superb chilled soup, such as crab-meat bisque or cold consommé appetizingly flavored with minced fresh parsley, a bit of fresh basil, or a thin slice of lime in the bottom of the chilled cup and another slice of lime floated on top of the consommé. Or serve a cup of delicious, icy-cold borsch. Such soups deserve to be served in a handsome, chilled, low-stem goblet or colorful bowl placed on a small leaf-covered plate. With them pass tiny, hot cheese tarts.

After the soup, for one menu, serve thin roast turkey or ham slices in aspic garnished with mounds of Waldorf salad in small lettuce cups, a hot vegetable such as new lima beans or asparagus, and oven-browned rolls or lightly-buttered, thin pumpernickel. The dessert may be mint sherbet in tall parfait glasses, thin chocolate-nut cookies, iced tea or coffee.

Other suggested menus are:

Shrimp marinara in chafing dish or casserole, hot rice, tiny hot cheese rolls; for dessert, thin wedges honeydew melon with crushed fresh mint leaves, iced tea or coffee.

Melon ball fruit cup; tomato aspic ring filled with vegetable salad garnished with water cress and deviled egg halves and served with French dressing; finger sandwiches of chicken or lobster salad; for dessert, frozen lime-chiffon pie, demitasse.

Fried soft-shell crabs with tartare sauce; salad of green pepper, carrot, cabbage, and pineapple; small hot rolls; apricot refrigerator cake on tall glass cakestand decorated with small blossoms from the garden, iced or hot coffee.

Lemon gelatin ring of green gage plums and black cherries with sour cream salad dressing; buttered nutbread; for dessert, angel food cake with pineapple sherbet, demitasse.

Jellied tomato bouillon with garnish of a thin slice avocado; fillets of sole amandine; parsleyed new potatoes, thin slices of French or Italian bread; for dessert, fresh peach ice cream with macaroons and hot or iced coffee or tea.

Hot casserole of meat balls with Béarnaise sauce; French-fried zucchini strips; green pepper stuffed with cream-chive cheese and sliced in thin rings on lettuce; for dessert, small gooseberry and currant tarts, coffee.

Chilled ham mousse with mustard sauce; au gratin potatoes; pepper relish; small hot corn sticks; for dessert, spice cake and chocolate-almond ice cream, demitasse.

Smoked sturgeon and scrambled eggs made in a chafing dish or electric skillet at the table; toasted brioche or warm croissants with assorted jams and relishes; for dessert, honeydew melon with fresh lime or lemon, hot and iced tea and coffee.

Warm cheese-and-onion pie (quiche Lorraine); a salad of romaine lettuce and orange segments; herbed toast; for dessert, small meringues filled with red raspberries, iced tea and coffee.

Sliced turkey in hot gravy on toast; a salad of artichoke hearts with sliced tomatoes and celery in mayonnaise on lettuce; for dessert, orange cake and coffee, parfait, demitasse.

Block Parties

A Block Party is a dance, festival, or other entertainment given in a city, town or suburban street. The idea was taken over from foreign-population centers in our large cities, especially Italian districts. Summer block parties of dancing and buy-your-own refreshments are so frequent in many Italian-American neighborhoods that they seem almost continuous. When one party ends, the decorations remain up on lamp posts and grocery store fronts ready for the next party. Bright banners hang high above the street, strings of colored lights add to the festival atmosphere, paper and bunting streamers flutter in the breeze.

At the parties a small but tireless band of musicians makes the occasion irresistible to all ages in the neighborhood. Everybody dances, buys fruit drinks and ices from local vendors and street stands, sees friends, and has a wonderful time. The small fee per dance pays for the music.

The secrets of the popularity of this kind of block party are: no money needed to rent a dance hall, complete informality and easy mixing of dancers so that the neighborhood boys and girls get better acquainted, low cost for couples to dance all evening, and the pleasant coolness of the outdoor dance floor.

Block parties in other communities are more likely to be fund-raising events for school, church, or some local charity. (See Chapters 7 and 8, on Family and Church Entertaining and Family and Community Parties.) Or they may be, like the Italian-American parties, a neighborhood evening of fun, or a private party. For any kind of block party, permission must be obtained from city authorities or police to rope off a dead-end or little-used street. Also permission must be gained from the local health department to set up refreshment stands, whether food is free as in the case of a private invitation affair or is to be sold to paying guests.

Committees are needed to run a block party held to raise money. They must plan all arrangements—secure space, and clean, decorate and rope it off or otherwise enclose it to keep crowds out. Some committee members should make or buy posters to advertise the event, send notice to newspapers, arrange to sell tickets in advance and to take money at the entrance. Another committee is responsible for refreshments.

For either kind of party—invitation or pay—music, color, and lively decorations help set the pace.

Music may be any of these: a pair of hired accordian players to alternate each other in making music for the dancers; a trio of base fiddle, violin, and small portable piano; a large hurdy-gurdy with a good repertoire of dance tunes inside its colorful box and with its own hand operator; a record player with loudspeaker and a large supply of dance records, and someone to keep them playing. Both hurdy-gurdy and record player might be used, the hurdy-gurdy for atmosphere and occasional music, maybe with a costumed, singing operator, and the records for the rest of the dancing.

Decorations Stretch a large "Welcome" and fun banners above the street. Or "Greetings," or someone's name (an honored guest) spelled out in colored lights may be strung across the dance area. Streamers of colored bunting, or long, painted paper pennants can be attached to lamp posts, trees, fences, buildings. Great bunches of green or autumn foliage and out-size gigantic artificial flowers may be used. Decorative lights, lanterns, colored lights to play on dancers add to the scene.

Refreshments for invited guests, or offered for sale at a paying party, might be served from lunch carts, or by a local ice cream parlor using a decorated cart that can stand in one place or be wheeled among guests. Soft-drink bottles in a gaily decorated tub of ice, the makings of ice cream cones, or various flavors of ice cream sandwiches and ice cream-on-sticks make up the load. The attendant might wear a chef's white hat, white coat and trousers, with large artificial flower in his lapel.

Or if this is a suburban neighborhood, co-operative party, refreshments of homemade punch and cookies or sandwiches might be served from somebody's front porch. For any block party neighborhood policemen should be notified and their interest and co-operation secured for the evening. For a private block party they may be needed to keep uninvited guests outside the roped-off area.

Luau

A luau (pronounced loo-*ah*-oo) is an Hawaiian feast, gay, friendly, beautiful—with special music, dancing, and luxurious flowers. It is relaxed and relaxing, and unique as to menu. Like much else from the Hawaiian Islands—the songs, flower necklaces called leis, and the interesting cookery—this spectacular outdoor party has been adopted by other party-givers especially in California and Florida, where climate, foliage, and native foods approximate those across the Pacific.

To give a proper luau you should have a deep barbecue pit, a terrace or patio, professional help, and foods and decorations sent from Hawaii. The helper may be a relative or friend who has lived for years in Honolulu and eaten his way through dozens of luaus. Or the guidance may come from one of the many hired specialists now available for this kind of entertaining. Not so long ago these luau caterers were established only in California, where some of them were in great demand because of a reputation for the authenticity and quality of the luaus they put on for Los Angeles and other local hosts.

But with the increasing interest in Pacific Islands cookery and customs stimulated by colorful, exotic Hawaiian restaurants in many parts of the country, South Pacific shops and mail-order products, and organizations which bring in Hawaiian flowers and foods by air, the catering services have expanded to national coverage. They can make a luau in almost any backyard if it is large enough and planned far enough in advance of the party date.

One such service, Orchids of Hawaii, Inc. (305 Seventh Avenue, New York 1, New York) can bring all the makings of a luau to your door, help create the Island atmosphere with special decorations, music, foods, and flowers, and prepare the special dishes. This organization starts prospective luau hosts off with a small book ($1.00) which tells how to give a luau, includes 33 pages of authentic Hawaiian recipes and lists costs of various services which (with two weeks' notice) may include flying a native orchestra, singers, flowers, tropical foliage, and food from Honolulu to your city on the date specified, complete with a director who puts the luau together for you!

Their services may be shaped to a lower budget, and include only such native accessories as the invitations, tapa paper, fishnet draperies for table, canned food not otherwise available, Hawaiian LP records, grass skirts to wear and to use as table decoration, flowers, leis for everyone, the necessary large ti leaves to cover the table, and similar necessities. The average cost to the host for this budget menu is about $12.50 per person. The cost rises as you increase the order for flowers, leis, other decorations, and include a personal director.

Delicacies, food, cookbook, and decorations from Hawaii do not make a luau. You need several days of advance planning and work. The barbecue pit must be made ready to roast a whole suckling pig. You need good weather, an evening mild and clear, and a terrace or lawn large enough for one long, low table to seat all guests. Luau guests are supposed to sit on mats or the ground, but stateside guests, especially those past thirty, may prefer chairs.

Luau tables are either left bare but decorated here and there with blossoms. They may be covered with broad, shiny ti leaves as in Hawaii, or with a straw or split-bamboo mat, or fish nets. Wooden bowls and platters, green leaves, and hollowed, halved coconut shells hold the foods. Flowers from the garden or those ordered from Hawaii decorate many dishes and drinks as well as the table and are worn by all guests in their hair and as leis.

There may be as many as ten main dishes, a great many relishes, and a continuously arriving variety of lime, orange, pineapple, passion fruit and guava drinks, some frappéed. All of these are decorated with blossoms or fruit or both, and served in frosty mugs, bowls, large footed goblets, and hollowed-out pineapples and coconuts.

In addition to recipes and instructions and much else of authentic know-how available through special catering services and Hawaiian friends, helpful articles on how to give a luau-type supper have been published in women's magazines, with the recipes scaled to family size and using ingredients available in supermarkets all over the country. A request to the magazine editor may bring a copy of the article. Recommended are "South Pacific Foods," by Albert Stockli, in *McCall's,* April 1958, and "How to Give a Luau," in *House Beautiful,* September 1958.

And most helpful of all, *Trader Vic's Book of Food and Drink* (Doubleday & Company) in which the chapter called "A Luau on the Mainland" gives complete detailed instructions for a home luau, with sketches of utensils you can make from coconuts, plus menus and recipes. The book is a valuable source of inspiration and information for a do-it-yourself luau.

Guests are supposed to wear summer sports clothes, the men flowery shirts and shorts, the girls sundresses or shorts and flowery bra-tops. Part of the hospitality is to provide both men and girls with leis, and the girls with grass skirts and flower anklets.

Snow and Ice Parties

Some of the best parties of the year are those inspired by snow and ice sports. They vary, from state to state, both as to the kind of rugged, red-cheeked fun of the sportsmen guests and the warm indoors hospitality that follows. Many winter parties are spontaneous, or at least spur-of-the-moment, depending on the weather. A cold, clear dry day dawns, and you telephone a group of friends who skate or toboggan and invite them for hot food after their cold afternoon. These are not occasions calling for special decorations and entertainment; good food and relaxation are of first importance.

Curling In sections of the country where wintry lakes and streams provide a long, broad expanse of thick ice, the old Scottish game of Curling is played. It is an eight-man game, consisting of two teams of four hearty souls who don't mind the cold, and who can lift the heavy curling stones and send them down the long stretch of ice toward the goal, while teammates sweep briskly with a broom to smooth the way for the rushing stones. It is strenuous fun for players and onlookers.

Ice Boating, sailing, or yachting is a favorite sport in the same crisp weather and the same part of the country, wherever broad, smooth, thick ice invites the swift-flying, beautifully handled boats mounted on runners.

Both of these famous sports are seen on the frozen Minnesota and Wisconsin lakes and elsewhere in the northwest. Families and friends sometimes gather at the lake's edge to watch the fun, with hot tea and coffee and huge sandwiches for these sportsmen. And they are all likely to assemble after the curling match or ice regatta or skating party at someone's home and have a hot supper.

Menus feature a Dutch oven supper of wild duck and rice, or one of the Swedish, Polish, Finnish, or Dutch meat dishes that have become fixtures in the local cookery. Hot rolls, a berry pudding, a tray of cheese and fruit complete the menu. In Wisconsin homes, supper for those ice enthusiasts may be potato dumplings and roast goose, or sauerbraten or baked ham garnished with cinnamon apples. Dessert is usually cheesecake, or apple pie and cheese.

Hot tea is usually waiting for all curlers and yachtsmen when they first come in from the cold. Supper follows quickly, then a leisurely evening around a warm hearth with hot tea and coffee served again, as one for the road. (While we are in Minnesota, see Chapter 4, "Children's Parties," for a children's Skating Party, and a Snow Man Party.)

Ice Hockey does not require such a large expanse of ice as an ice-boat regatta. A smaller lake, a frozen stream or pond, an iced-over skating rink in town or city makes the playing area for hockey on skates. Teen-age skaters and older enthusiasts who follow professional hockey games are devotees of this graceful, intense, swift sport. All over the Middle West, New England, and the Northwest, after-school skaters and Saturday and Sunday skaters play ice hockey. Their best girls usually serve supper at someone's house for the teams when it is too dark to skate any more. And after supper, they dance or pop corn and listen to records.

Menus for these hockey supper parties vary with the community. In Ohio it might be a waffles and creamed chicken supper, or pizzas, or a meatloaf with tomato sauce and a casserole of macaroni-and-cheese, with quince or apple tarts for dessert, and coffee.

In North Dakota, a Mallard duck with wild rice and hot potato salad, is a favorite winter party menu. So are spareribs cooked in the oven and basted with barbecue sauce, followed by apple pudding or a berry pie or a chocolate layer cake.

In Nebraska, the Polish-influenced menus in some areas include a hot pastry turnover filled with well-seasoned ground meat, chicken or game blended with seasonings and sour cream, a hearty vegetable salad, cakes and coffee.

In Oklahoma, the Spanish and Mexican influences often appear in party food with chili con carne, chicken-and-rice, and tortillas as the favorites. Since it is winter and the barbecue pit cannot be used, the hostess may roast a small piglet or lamb in the kitchen oven, basting it with barbecue sauce, and serve it with saffron rice, a salad, and fruit preserves. There is likely to be pecan or fruit pie for dessert, and coffee served Mexican or South American style with bittersweet chocolate stirred into it.

In Idaho, apple pancakes are favorites for any party supper, either served alone with coffee or following a good supper of bratwurst and sauerkraut.

Skating Parties As they do for summer swim parties, teen-agers or boys and girls home from school for winter vacations invite their friends to Skating Parties. They may skate on a sunny, cold morning and come back to someone's house for a luncheon of oyster stew, toasted rolls, pie and hot coffee.

Or, a moonlight night is the setting for a couple of hours of partner skating. Mugs of hot tea and coffee from large vacuum jugs are served right beside the ice. Wieners roasted on a fire of driftwood and a bagful of wood brought along for the purpose, or hamburgers broiled in a long-handled, greased folding broiler or corn popper when the flames subside a little, taste scrumptious in the cold air. A bag of buttered rolls is all that is needed to complete this Arctic picnic.

If it is exceptionally cold, everybody may want to go to the host's home to cook a playroom or kitchen supper of waffles, bacon or sausage, and coffee or soft drinks. There should be a layer cake handy, too, or a tray of cupcakes.

Ski Parties, according to ski enthusiasts, should be relaxing at least for the first part of the evening. After a day on the snowy slopes, a quiet supper eaten from trays or plates on laps around a bright fireplace, listening to records, a little dancing is the pattern many prefer. Foods are "whatever is around," meaning nothing fussed over. Small steaks or chops are easy to broil in a comfortable kitchen, or a big hot beef-and-onion pie made in advance and ready to pull out of the oven, with a flavorsome tossed salad, fresh fruit, tea or coffee, makes a satisfying supper.

In Vermont a country supper may be served to a ski crowd. Such local foods as roast turkey with sweet corn and baked potatoes are favorites, or ham steak with sweet potatoes and maple syrup cooked together in a big Dutch oven or casserole. Dessert may be a butternut cake, or maple gingerbread, maple custard pie, or apples cooked in maple syrup, especially if the occasion is near February 12, when there is a state-wide Maple Festival in Vermont. A festival date in any locality always provides a good excuse for a party, any time of year.

Sledding and Toboggan Parties The essentials of a good sledding party is a hill not too steep but thickly covered with packed snow, and two or three families of youngsters and grownups who like the ancient art of coasting. At this kind of neighborhood party some use sleds, some toboggans, and the mavericks use tin or wooden barrel tops or half of a keg cut from top to bottom, or any other substitute for the smooth but expensive, store-bought gliders.

There is more peace on that particular bit of earth, and more goodwill among the sledders, if one or two adults man the hilltop and more or less regulate traffic. Another grownup at the bottom of the hill can pick up casualties and untangle any crash victims.

The perfect ending to such an afternoon is a big kitchen or playroom co-operative supper, to which parents of the sledding youngsters bring a hot covered dish or some other contribution to the feast. All of the food can be put on a large table with necessary plates, knives, forks, paper napkins and enough chairs and stools assembled for everybody. Meatloaf or meat balls, casserole or macaroni-and-chicken, hot foil-baked potatoes or sweet potatoes are good main dishes for this hungry crowd. Add rolls, jelly, hot coffee, and cocoa or milk for children.

Finger desserts such as fruit, brownies, cookies, or doughnuts are popular at this winter party.

The more professional toboggan and bobsled racers who speed down and around frozen racecourses would enjoy the same kind of informal hospitality, not necessarily a co-operative supper, but a buffet of hearty food, hot and plentiful, with coffee. For these sportsmen a big baked ham or turkey would make a satisfying main dish, with stuffed baked mushrooms, hot rolls, raisin pie, Cheddar cheese, and coffee.

Sleigh Ride Party In some parts of the country this old-time winter lark is still enjoyed, usually as a preliminary to an evening of dancing and late supper. It is only possible where there are long little-used snowy roads and horse-drawn sleighs available (usually at the same stables which rent riding horses and plan hayrides for summer picnics).

One host in northern New York state plans a sleigh ride party for a moonlit Saturday night in midwinter when backroads and former highways of the area are covered with packed snow. The sleighs, driven by stable owners of a nearby town, pick up guests at their homes and drive about an hour, everybody singing as they go. Then guests and host and hostess are delivered to the host's home, (and the sleighs and horses depart for their warm stable).

Menu A fireside supper is welcome after the frosty ride. Menu for this begins with hot coffee served as soon as possible after guests arrive, then a hot dish which had been semi-prepared earlier and is now warming in the oven while the coffee is being made. A favorite in the New York Stater's home is sliced turkey-and-stuffed-mushrooms in a rich cream sauce topped with crumbs, or a savory beef-eggplant-tomato-onion casserole. Rolls are heated at the same time. For dessert, he likes to serve squares of his wife's famous devil's food cake and a compote of sliced peaches and black cherries or other fruits.

Picnics

A picnic is the best of all ways to entertain a few friends or a large crowd in summer. It may be given on the spur of the moment, or planned days ahead. It can be a picnic by the sea, or under shady trees by a little stream, or in a green backyard. You can have a picnic in a nearby park, or miles away on a mountain slope, or in any pleasant spot that encourages relaxation, provides a view to rest and relax the eyes, and is far enough from the noise and smell of traffic so that "Nature can be heard thinking."

When you cook over a picnic fire, let the flames die down to hot coals. Don't cook over flames unless you are using a reflector oven. The easiest and best ways to cook meat, potatoes, and other vegetables are to wrap them in foil for cooking in a folding wire broiler or to lay them on a stationary grill over coals.

Add butter or other fat and seasonings to food before wrapping; the sheet of foil should be large enough to allow a three-fold turnover at the open edge of package. The package must be enclosed in a second wrap of foil if it is to be laid directly on the coals in a folding broiler. A single wrap is sufficient if you are using a stationary grill above coals.

Cooking times vary according to the size of the packages and the depth and heat of the coals, as well as the direction and amount of wind and the weather. Turn package once or twice with a long-handled pancake turner; don't use a fork as the tines may pierce the foil.

Usually a package of chopped beef or a small steak with a slice of onion, butter, and salt and pepper is done in 15 to 20 minutes over hot coals. Half a chicken, with butter, sticks of raw potato, and quartered carrots all sprinkled with seasoning and 2 or 3 tablespoons of water and then wrapped, is ready in 30 minutes. Turn each package several times. A lamb or pork chop, with a few green beans, sliced raw potato, seasoning, and little water sprinkled over all, is cooked in 20 minutes. Turn each package twice. Quick-frozen or bake-and-serve biscuits wrapped in foil bake in 10 minutes; brown-and-serve rolls are ready in about the same time.

Back-Roads Picnics can be fun if you live where old, little-used roads still exist. Often such roads run along beside a small stream, or wind deep into mountain and valley areas, where picnic spots are plentiful. There is a special pamphlet, "Discover the Back Roads," to help you find such byways to picnic spots. It lists maps and guidebooks, too.

For it, send 25 cents in stamps to Pamphlet Publishing Co., 391 East 149th Street, New York 55, New York.

Lunch or Supper on such a jaunt should be what you can pack easily into either fitted car hampers and vacuum jugs or other insulated carriers. Since safe drinking water may not be available at the picnic spot, a vacuum jug of chilled drinking water, another of fruit juices, and an insulated container filled with ice and bottled soft drinks are musts on this picnic. Take the foods you enjoy most, old picnic favorites or newer ones. Everything should be wrapped in waxed paper or foil and carried in a chilled, insulated carrier. Avoid the easily spoiled sandwich fillings, such as fish and other chopped-salad combinations with mayonnaise.

Here's one popular lunch: cold fried chicken, deviled eggs, stuffed celery, strips of raw green pepper and carrots, bread-and-butter sandwiches, hot coffee, cookies, and small fruits or a watermelon.

If a grill or two is taken along on this picnic and the makings of a fire for cooking, omit the fried chicken and include small, foil-wrapped, seasoned steaks or hamburgers to cook, or a casserole of beef-and-vegetables to reheat on the grill. At the same time heat rolls in foil on the edge of the grill and make fresh hot coffee using some of the drinking water from a vacuum jug. If you carry ice cream from the home freezer, it should be as solid as a rock when you start on the drive. Wrap it in foil and place in an insulated bag preferably with dry ice.

Beach Picnics One favorite beach picnic of teen-agers, inspired by good weather and planned by a few telephone calls, is to cook something, such as a big kettle of spaghetti, on a driftwood fire. The hostess brings the utensils and foods, including a saucepan of favorite tomato-and-meat sauce as well as a jar of grated Parmesan cheese. Somebody brings paper plates and forks.

As soon as the spaghetti is tender, the boys lift the big kettle and drain it. Sauce heats in a few minutes over the fire, then is poured over the hot spaghetti, stirred, and everybody helps himself to a plateful, topped with the grated cheese. The hostess or a guest brings a box of small, icy-cold tomatoes stuffed with chopped vegetable salad to be eaten with the fingers. Buttered small rolls go with them, and hot coffee made on the fire. A guitar or other music is part of the fun.

Clam Bake The traditional beach picnic of the Eastern seaboard is a Clam Bake, which may be a private affair, a party for one or two families or a group of teen-agers. It may also be a community event, or a fund-raising affair.

Wherever soft, or long-neck, clams are available, mostly along the New England shore line—according to some old-timers the best ones are north of Cape Cod—this summer feast is popular.

Before the clam diggers get busy finding their victims in the sandy shore, work begins on the pit in which the foods will be steamed. It is dug about 18 inches to 2 feet deep and 3 feet or more square, and lined with clean rounded stones. A hot fire is made in the pit and kept going an hour or two until the rocks are hot through and white-hot on the surface. Then a layer of rockweed a few inches deep is added, and is covered with a large-mesh, wire screen. The washed and rinsed clams are quickly placed on the screen, sometimes with fresh-caught lobsters, washed potatoes, cleaned small fish wrapped in foil, and sweet corn cleaned and rewrapped in the husks. The amount of each is determined, of course, by the number of guests.

One Connecticut clam-bake specialist insists that the contents in the pit be covered with a clean white cloth and sprinkled with hot water. The pit is then tightly covered with a tarpaulin. The steaming continues: 30 minutes for small amounts of food to 2 hours or longer for a larger load.

While the food steams, preparations are made for serving it. The only sauce required is seasoned, melted butter. (To 1 pound of butter add the juice of 1 lemon, ½ teaspoon Tabasco, 1 tablespoon ketchup, 1 tablespoon Worcestershire, and stir. This will make 8 or more servings.) Coffee is made, and rolls are baked on a nearby barbecue, or they are brought from home, already split and buttered.

Paper plates, napkins and forks, and devices to crack lobster claws are essentials. At big bakes, the cooked lobsters are split, cleaned, and the claws cracked by a lobster chef who does nothing else. Some bakes are served to everybody around bare wooden tables set up nearby. At other bakes the hungry boys and girls and grownups who crowd the sandy shore perch on rocks, beach cushions, and the sand, eating from plates held on their laps.

When there is a full moon, a clam bake served at sunset on a summer night is a wonderful picnic by any standard. Guests bring warm sweaters and blankets and stay late after the feast, singing around a driftwood fire.

Home Clam Bake for Inlanders You can have a clam bake even if you live miles inland. Live clams and lobsters can be ordered by mail from various New England areas. Some of the fishermen who make this possible advertise their products in women's, cookery, and home furnishings magazines. One such source is Saltwater Farm, Clam Cove, Damariscotta, Maine. Delivery of your order is guaranteed on the day you select, any place within 1,800 railroad miles of Clam Cove.

The load contains live lobsters and steamer clams with chilled rockweed packed in ice in a ready-to-cook container. This company's catalogue lists prices and other foods, as well as sea decorations which can be ordered by mail.

With such decorative accessories the inland host can create shore atmosphere. He might set up trestle or sawhorse tables and leave them bare except for fish nets thrown across them, and use large clean shells as decoration. If local shops cannot supply such accessories, fishermen's nets (4-by-9 feet) and other nautical items for such a feast are included in a luau kit from The Barrier Reef, 11453 Knightsbridge Avenue, Culver City, California.

It's a good idea to provide guests with homemade or bought bibs for these picnics. Amusing ones can be made of unbleached muslin bound with bright red cotton binding, and the same binding used for ties to hold the bib in place. Cut out a paper pattern of a large lobster claw, then cut claws out of red chintz and appliqué to each bib.

To complete a home clam bake or lobster supper, serve coleslaw, hot coffee, and watermelon. Some hosts include buttered rolls and hot corn on the cob.

Bicycle Picnics A crowd of bicycle riders is a nuisance on a busy highway and they are in danger from motorists and heavy trucking. But if you and your cycling friends live near quiet roads or back roads that lead to beaches or a woodsy camp site or some place with a view that you all enjoy, you can have your own, very good bike picnics.

A small rucksack on the back of each rider, or the handle-bar basket, carries his own lunch or supper or his contribution to a co-operative meal. One rider may tote a folding broiler on which to cook frankfurters or foil packages of chops, steaks, or hamburger. Somebody's bike bears a vacuum jug of iced fruit juice or chocolate milk or hot coffee. The other riders carry wrapped (in foil or waxed paper) sandwiches or other foods to cook, a foil package of raw vegetable relishes and stuffed celery, packaged cookies, chocolate bars, chocolate-covered raisins and nuts.

If the picnic is on a beach everybody swims, suns, then eats lunch. A harmonica player can be a popular addition to this crowd. So is the boy who straps a ukelele or small guitar over his rucksack on his back. A little music makes beach dancing fun. (See Back-Roads Picnics.)

Bird Watchers' Picnic Many city folk as well as suburban and country residents are ardent followers of the sport of bird watching. City watchers know they have to be in their parks at dawn or soon after to catch a glimpse of a thrush or a black-and-white warbler in a sycamore tree and other birds that visit their parks in certain seasons. Burdened with binoculars, these sportsmen walk several miles and after an hour or so over hill and down dale, they are ready—children, teen-agers and adults—for a picnic brunch or food by any other name.

Hosts for these ardent fans can invite them by telephone, a day or so in advance of a bird walk, to stop for a picnic on the lawn after the walk. Or better still, the hosts can transport their picnic lunch to an arranged meeting place in the park or woodland, and have it ready at a specified hour when watchers can gather to rest, eat, and talk about their morning's experiences.

Menu for this should be hearty but simple. Hot coffee, or a refreshing cold drink if the day is warm, should be served as soon as the watchers arrive at the picnic rendezvous. Hot chili con carne from a big vacuum container, and buttered rolls to go with it, tastes good if the day is cool. So do wedges of cheese and an assortment of chilled fruits, such as cherries and strawberries with the stems left on. Another menu is:

cheese or chicken sandwiches, ham-and-potato salad, fancy doughnuts, and brownies or other cookies for the children.

A youngster who has been especially quick, and has identified more birds than anyone else on that morning's walk, deserves a prize. Here's a suggestion—a game called "Bird Watching," for two, three, or four players. It is lively fun to play and also teaches the characteristics of dozens of birds.

Boating Picnics Picnic lunches to be carried by boat—canoe, power-boat, rowboat, sailboat—to an island or across a lake or down a shady river to a shady beach should be light, especially for guests who may not be experienced sailors. On this picnic it is essential that you take the right gear to keep foods fresh, since the exposure to hot sunshine may be prolonged. An insulated ice chest may be part of the boat's furnishing, and in addition, insulated carryalls, vacuum jugs, and bottles are needed for these picnics. If there is no deck to protect the food containers from the sun, they must be covered with a tarpaulin or heavy canvas.

Picnic baskets and hampers equipped with plates, knives and forks, and a picnic cloth add to the pleasure of going ashore and relaxing an hour or so. Canned heat and utensils, or the makings of a picnic fire ashore, can be carried along to provide a hot sandwich, such as broiled strips of ham steak served on buttered rolls or bread. Bring fresh fruit juice for children, and hot coffee for the grownups. Sealed cans of snacks, such as crackers and various filled cookies, provide the necessary sweet finish.

Individual box lunches, packed for all aboard and stored in the boat's ice chest, are popular for boat picnics. If one frozen food, wrapped in a plastic bag to prevent dripping, is included in each box, it helps to keep other foods cold. The box lunch might be: 1 cheese sandwich and 1 sliced baked ham or turkey sandwich, wrapped separately in foil or waxed paper; a small covered paper container of jellied fruits, or a package of quick-frozen, whole strawberries with the stems left on. The hot and cold beverages can be carried in family-size vacuum bottles.

The rule, keep lunch simple, applies as well to the boat with a galley, where guests cook and eat aboard. Cooking aboard is fun for good sailors, especially if an ice chest or refrigerator provides fresh milk and eggs, keeps cold cuts and fruit fresh, and stores a ready supply of quick-frozen, cooked dishes that can be quickly heated for meals. Reheated slices of roast chicken or turkey in a good sauce, soft rolls, fresh fruit, and a hot beverage make a good picnic meal from such a galley. Pancakes or waffles made in the galley are especially welcome on a cool day.

Part of the picnic fun, afloat or ashore, is group singing with a guitar or other instruments. Quartet singing of Gay Nineties tunes and other favorites has been spurred on in recent years by the Society for the Preservation and Encouragement of Barbershop Quartet Singing in America. Address SPEBQSA Headquarters, 6315 Third Avenue, Kenosha, Wisconsin, for information on where to find arrangements and songs for untrained, amateur singers.

The European custom of taking an accordian along on a picnic, whether by boat or any other transportation, is catching on in this country. This sort of singable, nostalgic music sounds especially good beside a lake or cooling stream, and gives a boaters' picnic party a plus mark from teen-agers as well as their elders.

Co-operative Picnic—Bring Your Own Picnic Lunch Several families, carrying a picnic luncheon or supper, drive in their own cars to a picnic ground or other spot they know to be restful and a pleasant change from their backyards and playrooms. Each family may pack its own lunch, or mothers get together a few days ahead of the picnic date and plan a community feed. One makes sandwiches for the crowd, another a large potato or chicken salad, another a cake or freezer of ice cream, one or two bring a hot dish. Foods should be well wrapped, the cold ones in iced, insulated vacuum carriers and the hot ones in vacuum carriers or thickly wrapped in newspapers. These can be reheated on a grill set over a picnic fire. The caravan starts out early on a Saturday morning if the picnic is to be luncheon, or early in the afternoon for an al fresco supper.

Menu depends on whether some dishes will be cooked at the picnic site or whether all are ready to be eaten. Steaks, chops, hamburgers, or chicken halves and foil-wrapped potatoes cooked on a portable grill over hot coals make a satisfying outdoor meal. Add to these favorite family desserts, such as watermelon, or ice cream and cake, and all members are replete and ready to rest a while before the fun begins.

Picnic games, such as toss the ring, horseshoes, croquet, three-legged race, and an egg race (racing your best friends with a hard-cooked egg held in a teaspoon) are old favorites. Grass tennis is fun too if there is room to stretch a net. Miniature golf over bumpy terrain can be hilarious.

Teen-agers like this summer version of the bring-your-own lunch party, and plan this kind of picnic for the beach and other spots, usually with a dance, square dance, or folk dance session to follow supper.

It is also a favorite of city families and their suburban friends. They can plan by telephone to meet at a picnic ground for a long-postponed visit. The city cars may hold picnic baskets, the latest in portable ice chests, portable grills, and insulated containers, with elegant foods carefully packed to keep cold or hot as needed. Or the city-dwellers may take the makings of a country barbecue—chicken halves, chops, steaks or spareribs—to be cooked over a fire using a portable grill.

Amusing, bright flowery-paper or fabric cloths to spread on the grass, an espresso coffee maker, long loaves of French bread or a big round Italian loaf, or long bread sticks, a handsome imported cheese, a case of imported delicacies including caviar and pâté, even canned crêpe Suzettes to be heated in a pan over the grill and served in their own hot apricot sauce—may fill the city family's bring-your-own lunch basket. By careful scheduling the city drivers can plan to leave home before traffic is heavy and to return before city-bound travel is at its peak. (See the Index for Back-Roads Picnics, 9th Wedding Anniversary (Willow or Reed), and other basket picnics.)

Chuck Wagon Picnic In the ranching country, where the chuck wagon was invented because it was a necessity, a modern picnic with the flavorsome dishes that can be prepared on this kitchen-on-wheels is an easy way to entertain a crowd. The wagon and the menu can be imitated in the East, South, Middle West, or any other area, if a host will go to the trouble of making, or having made, a chuck wagon. Or perhaps he has a modern chuck wagon—a big station wagon with electric refrigerator and cooking equipment, storage space, and portable cookery grills and utensils.

To add to the fun, the Eastern host might ask his guests to wear cowgirl and cowboy clothes, and he can wind up his picnic with a dance on a country dance floor, such as many picnic grounds provide, or in a big barn, or on a large home terrace, with cowboy and hillbilly music from records or by local musicians.

Everybody "on the range," that is, at this picnic, may stand up to eat around the wagon, or there may be bare sawhorse or sawbuck tables and benches. Instead of the cowboy's tin plate and knife and fork, you may want to use Mexican pottery, or bright paper plates, napkins, and mugs, and bamboo-handled cutlery.

The picnic may be a breakfast party given before an all-day horseback ride, or it may be luncheon or supper. If there is a real chow cook he will use the two-burner stove on the wagon for cowboy cookery, such as sourdough (yeast dough) pancakes, bacon or ham, eggs, biscuits, and coffee. Add syrup for the pancakes, jam for the biscuits, and cream and sugar for his boiled coffee, and you've got a good, ranch-picnic breakfast.

If the crowd gathers for a moonlight picnic supper and cowboy dance music around the chuck wagon, the cook can produce on that same stove a ranch roast steak, which is thick steak rubbed with olive oil, garlic, mustard and salt and cooked in a pan on the wagon grill until well browned on both sides.

Or, if he cooks old style, he will marinate the steak for two hours or longer in oil and mustard, then coat it thickly with salt and bury it in the hot coals of a campfire for about 25 minutes, turning it once. (Use tongs, not fork, to turn.) It is crusty, charred outside, rare inside. Sliced hot, it is served with potatoes baked in foil in the coals or sliced into a frying pan with bacon fat and onions and cooked until tender and done. Boiled beans or canned baked beans may be heated or served cold with the meat and potatoes. Biscuits or a pan of cornbread are usually a part of the menu. When coffee is ready, the cook will put out a large wedge of Cheddar cheese and an apple pie. Everybody cuts his own cheese and pie.

Round-up time meals, from which you might choose a picnic menu, also include many stewed meat mixtures, such as chili con carne served on hot noodles, and a great variety of wagon-barbecued meats, when there is time to prepare them. Chili loaves made with a mixture of hamburger, sausage, tomatoes, canned corn, sliced olives, and onions are favorites, and so is beef-and-biscuit pie.

A beef stew is always in demand by hungry cowboys. Tacos, a sort of hot sandwich made with tortillas, is sure to be in a chuck wagon menu when there is a Mexican cook in charge. Here is one tacos recipe which you can make and serve wherever you give a chuck wagon picnic, whether in Westchester County, New York, or Florida, or a Cleveland backyard.

RECIPE FOR TACOS

1½ pounds ground beef	1 dozen (canned) tortillas
3 tablespoons bacon fat	½ head lettuce, shredded
1 large tomato	½ pound Cheddar or smoky
1 clove garlic, peeled	cheese, shredded
1 large onion, peeled	Tabasco or Worcestershire
1½ teaspoons salt	sauce (optional)

Brown meat in large skillet using small amount of fat. Add sliced tomato, sliced garlic and onion, and season with salt. Simmer for 10 minutes. Place a large spoonful of the meat mixture on each tortilla, fold over, and brown in hot fat. Drain, and serve topped with shredded lettuce and cheese. Add a dash of hot sauce if it is liked.

Other tacos filled with mixtures of Monterey cream cheese and tomato purée seasoned with strips of green chiles, salt, and pepper are placed in a shallow baking dish, covered lightly with sour cream, and baked for 30 minutes. Wonderful flavor! These are usually served with canned kidney beans drained and sautéed in a little bacon fat or butter.

Dunes Picnic Generous, high-heaped sand dunes and sunny, not too windy days are settings for some of the most popular picnics of the summer according to teen-agers on Long Island's south shore, and in such scattered areas as Michigan, Indiana along the Lake Michigan shore, and countless lake and seashore stretches all over America. Some like to make a day of it on the dunes, especially as summer draws to its end and school vacations are terminating. Families with young children may prefer a shorter dunes picnic, a playtime in sand and water, then lunch, then home.

With packed lunches, iced carriers, insulated food bags, and the makings of a beach fire, the teen-age picnic crowd starts off early in cars or a station wagon or on foot if the dunes are near. Play clothes with bathing suits underneath are the preferred costume for boys and girls. Heavy sweaters go along, too, for by late afternoon the air is cold. They swim, roughhouse in the sand, play cards, checkers, or whatever games were brought along, eat snacks when they want to, and as dusk gathers they make a fire for warmth and cooking. And sing afterwards with ukelele, accordian, or guitar, or all three.

Food requirements vary for this picnic. Usually there are well-wrapped sandwiches of meat and cheese, fresh fruit, and bottled soft drinks in an iced carrier for midday lunch. And for supper, to cook on a portable grill set up over hot coals, wieners and chops, or a quick-frozen dish of meatballs from the iced carrier. Buttered buns go with these, and as many condiments as the lunch kits accommodate— mustard, ketchup, pickles, raw relishes, carrots.

If the crowd likes coffee, the beach pot is a big, white enamel one. A waxed-paper package of ground coffee, the right amount for the pot, is packed in it for the trip to the beach and a similar package of cube sugar. Fresh water for coffee and drinking is seldom available on the dunes, so two or more vacuum jugs of cold, fresh drinking water go along with the lunch carriers.

Hayride Picnic The ancestor of this picnic is the old-time country holiday hayride. The wagon is heaped with clean hay, the host drives his family and neighbors who pile onto blankets laid across the hay, and all sing as they go along a country road to a favorite picnic ground. A dance floor was usually part of the early picnic-grove setting, and some of the guests brought fiddles. After supper they all danced as the moon came up, and until the youngest children were fast asleep in the hay. Then they rode home, singing, under the moon.

Today's hayride picnics are much the same, except that the horse-drawn wagon has been replaced in most areas by an open truck or tractor-drawn vehicle comfortably filled with hay, and holding fifteen to twenty or more persons. In many towns and cities riding stables and entertainment organizations advertise transportation for a hayride. The services of a driver are included in the price, which may be by the trip or by the hour, plus the cost of the load of hay. In suburban or country communities, the local feed and hardware stores can usually recommend a farmer who owns a fine team of horses and a suitable wagon and who is willing to drive hayride parties.

Organized by a school, club, church group, or the host and hostess with youngsters to entertain, the hayride can be an afternoon or evening picnic. Usually the ride is directed toward a picnic spot in some nearby parkland or picnic grounds, where supper is cooked on grills or served hot from vacuum containers. Singing to someone's guitar or ukelele, banjo or accordian, is part of the fun. If there is a dance floor, or smooth dance space on the picnic grounds, dancing or square dancing is part of the program until it is time for the music-filled ride back to town.

Menu for the hayride picnic depends on age and preference of the crowd. If it is a teen-agers' party, consult them as to what they want to cook at the supper spot, and provide them with utensils and foods, which the truck can easily accommodate. To avoid carrying utensils back home again, a box lunch is preferred by most hayriders. An iced carrier of bottled soft drinks or vacuum containers of hot coffee can be included.

Some hosts have supper ready and waiting at a picnic spot for the hayload. A picnic table is laid with bright cotton cloth, napkins are red or blue cotton bandanas, which guests keep as favors. Bowls of iced chicken salad, platters of sliced turkey and ham, buttered rolls or Italian bread to slice and make hero sandwiches, fresh fruit, cake and ice cream, iced and hot drinks—all are miraculously transported there by station wagon ahead of the hayriders.

Whether the guests are young or old, sophisticated guests or the family's assorted friends of all ages, singing belongs to this party, so invite a few who can lead in familiar songs, and one or two who can play guitar, banjo, accordian, or ukelele.

Hikers' Picnic. If the hike is to a picnic site where there are facilities for cooking and foods can be bought nearby to prepare a hot lunch, this is the most satisfactory kind of meal for walkers. During a long hike in the sun foods in shoulder rucksacks are sure to warm up somewhat. It is better to carry only the essentials to ward off hunger, such as a waxed-paper wrapped cheese sandwich (which does not spoil as easily as salad fillings), chocolate bar, packaged cookies and perhaps a small vacuum container of either hot coffee or cold fruit juice or milk.

One host's plan of a picnic for a group of friends who want to walk is to transport the food by car or station wagon to an arranged destination. He has the spareribs broiling, and coffee, buttered rolls, fruit and a good dessert of fruit tart or cake ready when the walkers arrive. After they have eaten and enjoyed a rest by the sea, or wherever the picnic spot, they are all carried home in station wagon and cars, or at least all but the most insistent walkers. See previous section on Back-Roads Picnic, Bicycle and Bird Watchers' Picnics for ideas on menus.

Kite Flying Picnic Take kites along on any picnic and after lunch stage a flying contest. Fun is added to the occasion if there is variety in kite sizes, styles, and colors. Include children's homemade kites, bought models, Japanese and Chinese kites ordered by mail from shops advertised in home magazines or bought in local oriental shops. These are inexpensive and spectacular in color, and are made in fish, bug, animal, flower shapes. If your local toy stores and foreign shops have none, write to Jasmine Gift Shops, Inc., 63 East Fifty-sixth Street, New York 22, New York.

Lobster Picnics at the Shore Lobster may be steamed in a pit with clams, as described in the Clam Bake, or boiled in a large kettle or wash boiler on a hot driftwood fire. For an inland picnic, with a shipment of lobsters from the coast, they can be boiled in a large kettle or steamer, then split, cleaned, and served with seasoned butter to hungry guests.

Some lobster parties include lobster salad and lobster Newburg, made ahead of time by the hostess and offered as part of the feast, with hot corn on the cob, buttered rolls, and fresh fruit and coffee. (See suggestions for a lobster bib and for menus at the end of the Clam Bake section.) There is a government leaflet on how to cook lobsters by thirty different recipes, with a description of types of lobsters, as well as directions on how to eat one. For it send 20 cents (in coins only) to Superintendent of Documents, Government Printing Office, Washington 25, D.C.

Another version of a lobster picnic or cookout has developed, at which skindiving sportsmen in coastal waters bring up succulent loads to be cooked right on the beach, either in primitive clam-bake fashion or in electric boilers and skillets plugged into outlets of the beach houses.

On California's famous Malibu Beach, huge Pacific Coast lobster, crab, abalone, scallops, and fish of various kinds are brought in by skindiver party groups who take turn playing host and fishermen for big shore picnics. (They deep-freeze the extras for out-of-season parties.)

One of these California beach suppers may begin with a superb fish stew with everything in it—shrimp, mussels, lobster, abalone or scallops, onions, garlic, celery, parsley, tomatoes, seasonings of herbs and salt and pepper, and delicate fish fillets added for the last twenty minutes of cooking. Boiled or broiled lobster with butter sauce is also on the menu. Sometimes the sauce is seasoned with fresh dill, or it consists of sour cream with dill, or it is butter and lemon juice seasoned with soy sauce. Grilled fish fillets, stuffed baked fish, sweet crab meat as an appetizer or salad or creamed or scalloped may be there too. This is a gala, luxury feast for divers and guests, the fun being the diving and bringing in the catch as much as the grand-scale cookery and feasting on the beach. (See also Clam Bake.)

Luxury Picnics A luxury picnic is the super al fresco meal, either a handsome luncheon or a candlelighted dinner, transferred by car and station wagon to a picnic setting, the dishes completed there on canned heat and charcoal broilers, and served by servants on handsome china, silver, glassware and linen, on a folding table with comfortable chairs. This is a picnic for guests who have been invited to watch a yacht regatta or an archery tournament, or to go to a racetrack or tennis matches after lunch. This picnic can follow a visit to fabulous show-place gardens on a nearby estate in the afternoon.

Menu for these guests might be an iced cream of asparagus soup garnished with chopped cooked asparagus tips, or a cold creamed curry soup; casserole of chicken breasts with wild rice and garnished with clusters of seedless white grapes; a lemon gelatin salad ring of crab meat and lobster with fresh cucumber mayonnaise made with sour cream and garnished with small endive blades and capers. Dessert is a mold of three sherbets and petits fours, and coffee.

With careful planning of all details of transportation, preparation, cookery, and serving, a gourmet host and hostess can prepare and serve this kind of picnic without a servant. They might serve thin slices of honeydew melon delicately seasoned with cinnamon or nutmeg as the first course. They may substitute a warm cheese-and-onion pie (quiche Lorraine) for the chicken, a superb veal pâté for the salad, they may add a salad of artichoke hearts and black olives vinaigrette, they may bring a frozen mocha mousse in ice to the picnic and serve it with a tender lemon cake.

Besides giving careful attention to planning and cookery, the hosts must arrange to have their guests driven to the picnic spot because they, as hosts, will need to go on ahead, to set up the table and cookery and plan the service for the comfort and pleasure of their company.

Station Wagon Picnic Sometimes a station wagon picnic is a luxury picnic. Or it is a car full of water toys, collapsible boats, life preservers, small sail boats, hampers, sandwiches, cookies, fresh fruit, and vacuum bottles of cold chocolate milk—and a first aid kit—for all the small fry of the neighborhood. This elongated car is ideal for toting kids with all they think they need at the beach, and all you know they will want to eat.

Cookout for House Guests Somewhere between these two extremes of luxury picnic and chauffeuring the young set is a station wagon picnic in which the wagon carries supplies and equipment for a big, neighborly cookout in honor of a house guest. Neighbors are invited to come later, bringing your guest and their own contributions to the picnic. They find you and your husband in command at the picnic grounds. Everything is under control—chicken or small turkey halves broiling on charcoal grills, the smell of coffee in the air, a promising ice cream freezer nearby, picnic table flower-decorated and with a cluster of children's bright balloons attached to a clean stone in the center of the table. Flower-printed paper plates and napkins and paper mugs for hot and cold beverages, picnic knives and forks are all in place.

Menu for an honored guest and friends may start with a cold fruit
soup, which you serve from an iced vacuum carrier, or with very thin
slices of watermelon and honeydew melon. The hot chicken or turkey
is served with a casserole of fresh, summer vegetables cooked lightly
in butter with seasoned crumbs topping, and foil-wrapped rolls made
hot on the broiler. Coffee, ice cream, a one-layer black walnut cake
with mocha frosting complete this supper. See also Luxury Picnics.

13

OVERNIGHT AND WEEK-END GUESTS

If there is room in your apartment or house for an overnight or week-end guest or two, and sufficient kitchen and dining space, and you can include this kind of hospitality in your scheme of living, it can be one of the most satisfying kinds of entertaining for you and your family and much appreciated by your guests.

As in all other forms of hospitality, when you entertain house guests careful advance planning is necessary for success. In the same way that you plan all details of a guest luncheon, dinner, or tea—using pencil and paper and your best thinking—you adapt your experience to the arrangement of a series of guest meals, and all other aspects of a day's or several days' hospitality for the man or woman or a couple who will be guests in your home.

Invitation Start your planning with the invitation, which may be telephoned or written. The telephone call is easier than writing a note, but the written invitation is more considerate for this occasion. It may not be possible to accept an invitation readily at the time of the telephone call, or to express reasons for not accepting. A written invitation gives the prospective guest time to consider whether he or she can accept.

The invitation should be given about two weeks before the date of the proposed visit. It should be specific about arrival and departure times by plane, train, bus, or other means of travel, and about the duration of the visit. Use note paper, preferably with your name, address, and telephone number on it. Many suburban and country hostesses use stationery that has a small map and driving directions included in the address space at the top. They may enclose a card on which such map and directions are given.

Here is a typical invitation that a woman might send an old friend. It can be modified and rephrased to suit the occasion, for various guests, both overnight and week-end visitors.

Tuesday

Dear Hazel,

It's been months since you were here for a visit. John and I would like so much to have you come out Friday, June 4th, and spend the night. The garden is in one of its best moods, and if you take the 3 o'clock train from Grand Central (see enclosed timetable) you'll be here early enough to see the roses and some new plantings.

Either John or I will meet your train at the Greens Farms station. You probably remember that there is a good Saturday night train after dinner, which will get you home before 11 o'clock. Do phone or write me and say you can come.

Affectionately,
(signed) Joycelyn

The invitation may be for a week end, from Friday dinner through Sunday night supper or Monday breakfast. Be specific about the day of the week, the date, transportation, and times of arrival and departure.

If a guest is driving and has not been to your home previously or for some time, include directions, highway numbers, turnoffs, any recent detours or other instructions, and indicate the approximate driving time, for example: "If you leave your place about 2 o'clock or a little later, you should be turning into our driveway about 4 o'clock."

Preparation of the House The invitation accepted, part of your plan of work for the period includes housekeeping time to put the guest room and bathroom in readiness. Wherever the guest sleeps, whether in a guest room, or on a converted sofa bed in the library or elsewhere, or in a guest apartment over the garage, or in a detached guest cottage, you add to his or her comfort if you place a small table beside the bed to hold a lamp, current magazines, a small bowl of fruit, cigarettes, matches, and an ash tray.

Also provide closet space and hangers, as well as drawer space for small things. If the guest shares the family bathroom, show him where you have arranged his towels, bathmat, wash cloth and soap; or point out the door to the guest bathroom where these necessities are in readiness.

Have a Flexible Schedule Before planning meals when there is a week-end guest, decide on some of the other important details of your hospitality. But give your guest freedom to do what he will enjoy most. Do not restrict him to a schedule. Tell him, when he or she arrives, what you have planned, and ask what he would like to do, changing your schedule to fit his wishes.

If you invite him because he needs a day or so of rest, he will appreciate your thoughtfulness if you let him sleep and be lazy. If you invite a guest for golf and swimming, or to go to a local art show, concert, summer theatre, or for the skating, or anything else, say so in the invitation. If you will have other guests at the same time, mention them in the invitation, so that he or she has some idea of the kind of clothes to bring along for possible parties or other activities.

Keep your own schedule flexible enough so that you have time for yourself, and to rest in addition to the necessary housework. If possible, keep the guest out of the kitchen or from helping with the cookery and dishwashing. You have your own easy plan of work and can carry it out better alone. Besides, he is a guest. It is a pleasure to have him in your home or you would not have invited him. Your carefully made plans do not call for putting him to work. If he or she is "family," an old friend so familiar with your home that he would be uncomfortable not helping, that is a different situation.

Menu Planning Well ahead of the week end, plan all menus for the duration of the visit. Do all shopping, except any necessary last-minute pickups from farmer's market, or from a neighbor who bakes rolls and pies for you, or for any similar additions to your supplies. (See advance planning suggestions in the section on How to Give a Dinner in Chapter 15.)

Your plans should include a cup of hot tea or a cold drink, or milk and crackers, or some fruit, offered the guest as soon as he or she arrives. Some people are hungry by 4 o'clock in the afternoon, or after a journey, even a small one, and their spirits rise with a little refreshment.

The meals should not feature fancy or unusual dishes, only those you have cooked and served many times to the family. Simple and familiar dishes relieve you of unnecessary worries and strain. They free you to enjoy your guest until a few minutes before you excuse yourself to set the table and put a meal on to cook.

Friday Night's Menu which is in the refrigerator before the week-end guest arrives, might be a curried cream of pea-and-tomato soup, using canned soups; a wonderful casserole of beef, onion, carrots and potatoes or salmon steaks ready to go into a baking dish; crisp salad greens and a bottle of your favorite salad dressing; a package of brown-and-serve rolls; and a cheesecake.

Skim the soup, and put it on to reheat. Place the casserole in a moderate oven to reheat; or lay salmon steaks in a baking dish with butter, lemon juice, and minced fresh parsley on top, and bake. Brown the rolls during the last fifteen minutes before dinnertime. Place salad bowl and dressing on the table and let some member of the family or the guest toss the salad. If cheesecake is too rich for your family, make an orange meringue pie early in the day. Serve the coffee at the table or in the living room, whichever is easier. On a warm June night, dinner is especially inviting served on a screened porch or at sunset on a terrace.

Plan the cleaning up of dinner dishes and the kitchen with help from your family, or whatever scheme you have worked out to keep you and the occasion from seeming hurried, noisy, disorganized.

Perhaps talk is more important to all of you than watching TV or listening to records, or playing canasta or bridge or some other game. You know what your guest prefers and this should set the pace of the evening.

And if you are old friends, you know what kind of hours he or she likes to keep. Otherwise, soon after he arrives, ask the guest when showing him to his room what hour he likes to retire, and what time he likes breakfast. Also ask what kind of breakfast he likes.

A breakfast tray might be sent in at his specified hour. If he likes a bigger breakfast he will get up and join the family at their regular breakfast time. Or, "come down and fix your own" is best for the late sleeper who strays in to the kitchen long after the family has breakfasted. For him, have coffee measured and ready to perk, bread ready for the toaster, fruit juice or melon waiting in the refrigerator, and a tray on which he can assemble what he wants and carry it out to a porch or elsewhere and enjoy himself.

Saturday Luncheon might be served on a table on the porch, or on trays carried out to a shady side of the house, or as a picnic beside a nearby stream or lake. If you have rainy or cold weather, use tray tables in the living room by a fireplace. For this menu make a ham, chicken, or tuna fish mousse early Saturday morning and place it in the refrigerator. Serve the mousse on crisp lettuce with mayonnaise combined with chopped ripe olives and grated cucumber; with it (bought) croissants or crusty rolls and black currant jam; for dessert, thin slices of honeydew or watermelon and hot or iced tea or coffee.

What you do after lunch depends on the wishes of your guest. He or she may enjoy a walk or just a relaxed afternoon in porch or lawn chairs or by the fireplace. You may have other plans previously discussed and agreed upon with your guest.

Midafternoon Snacks of fruit, or milk and crackers, should be available to your guest each day of his visit, since many people need some light refreshment about 4 o'clock in the afternoon, no matter how delicious or filling the luncheon. Some need a glass of milk or fruit at bedtime. It is a thoughtful courtesy to offer these to your guests.

Saturday Dinner This menu may be influenced by the part of the country in which you live. A Florida hostess might serve wonderful fried shrimp with saffron rice and Indian chutney, grapefruit and endive salad, hot rolls, frozen Key Lime pie, and tall glasses of fruit punch or iced coffee. A New England hostess might serve the traditional Saturday night dinner of baked onion soup, baked beans with crisp bacon curls, pickle relish and coleslaw, Boston brown bread, maple sugar pecan pie, and coffee. For a warm night, you might serve a platter of cold fried chicken, a hot vegetable such as lima beans or new sweet corn sauté, tossed salad, cheese, melon, iced coffee or tea.

Sunday Brunch If family and guests are late risers, brunch is both breakfast and luncheon. The menu should include fruit juice or berries, grapefruit, cantaloupe, or other melon, scrambled eggs, broiled thin ham steaks, toast, or, pancakes or waffles, sticky cinnamon buns or crullers, or baked apple, and coffee. If there are early risers in the house, serve coffee, juice, and toast in the kitchen to any who come downstairs at sunrise, and brunch later as scheduled at 11:30 or 12 o'clock noon.

A *Serve-Yourself-Sunday-Supper* is always a good ending to a guest week end because its informality is relaxing and convivial. The menu might feature cold baked ham or superb meatloaf with reheated gravy, and scalloped potatoes or hot pilaf. Other suggestions: deviled crabs or cold boiled lobster with asparagus vinaigrette, and buttered rolls; crab-meat salad garnished with individual molds of lemon gelatin and chopped olives; chicken à la king on split, toasted English muffins; Italian macaroni and cheese. With any one of these, serve a tossed green salad, coffee, and your favorite dessert, which may be a cold custard with sliced strawberries, or sliced peaches and tender, small meringues. Hot coffee or iced coffee or tea are the beverages.

Arrange to serve supper early enough that guests and family can enjoy their meal and not be concerned with approaching train time or the need to get the car out and start the homeward drive. It is one of the most appreciated courtesies of the visit when host and hostess together drive their departing guest to the station, or come out to the guest's car together to say good-by.

14

TOURNAMENT INFORMATION

So numerous are the sports and games around which families and community groups may want to organize tournaments that a whole book is necessary to do justice to the subject. Such a book, one of the best and most complete on all active sports and games, how to play them, and how to stage contests, is *Active Games and Contests,* by R. J. Donnelly, W. G. Helms, and Elmer D. Mitchell, published by The Ronald Press Co., 15 E. Twenty-sixth St., New York 10, New York.

Armed with such a book, skilled players can organize tournaments or contests for many of the games, such as checkers, croquet, dominoes, backgammon, that are not represented by national associations. These can be worked up simply for the fun of such an event, or to encourage such play in recreation groups, or to raise funds for a new playground, club house or something else by charging admission to the tournament.

For other tournaments, local players may seek out the state or national associations concerned with a particular game or sport and ask for their advice, help, copies of rules, instruction books or printed directions essential to acceptable tournament organization and production. Your local classified telephone directory may be helpful in locating such organizations. The local library may have books on the game or sport, written by an association authority or sponsored by some such organization. The sports goods stores in the community may have books, leaflets, and other information. A local newspaper's information department and its sports editor or writers also may be of help in locating associations to which you can write.

Archery Annual National Target Archery Tournaments have been held in this country for more than seventy years. Today these tournaments are sponsored, with the co-operation of state archery associations, by the National Target Archery Association, said to be the oldest sporting organization in the United States in existence continuously since its founding.

The target archery championships at these tournaments are held in eight divisions: men, women, intermediate boys and girls (ages 15 to 17), junior boys and girls (ages 12 to 14), and beginning boys and girls (under 12 years).

In addition to regular target archery, which is shot on open, level ground, with targets located at fixed distances, there are also flight, clout, and wand shooting. *Flight shooting* is a contest to see who can shoot an arrow farthest. *Clout* is also long-distance shooting, but contestants arc their arrows on a circular target laid out on the ground. In the *wand shoot,* a traditional old English contest, a wand standing in the ground is the target. Contests for crossbows as well as regular bows are included in these tournaments.

The tournaments are open to all archers, and usually admission is free to the public.

There is also the National Field Archery Association which has been sponsoring annual tournaments since 1945, to select champions in eight divisions, men, women, intermediate boys and girls, junior boys and girls, and beginning boys and girls under 12 years. Some of these Field Archery meets have attracted as many as two or three thousand archers on each occasion, all registered bow-and-arrow shooters. No specific qualifications are necessary; anyone who can shoot a bow and arrow is eligible for registering and competing.

Unlike target archery, in which the targets are traditional, the field archery tournament targets are of varying sizes and located in wooded areas to simulate hunting conditions. In general, medals and ribbons are awarded for both types of archery winners. Since 1879, cash prizes had not been given in field archery contests until 1958, when the top eight men and eight women in the N.F.A.A. met to shoot for money prizes, an experiment on the part of the Association to determine whether these field meets are ready for the same kind of tournament competitive effort which golf enjoys.

For all information, dates of tournaments, address of your nearest local Associations of Archery and Field Archery, and how to enter tournaments, or put on one in your community, write National Archery Association, Waverly, Iowa.

Backgammon, Checkers, Dominoes According to manufacturers and importers of these popular games, there are no national clubs or organizations that have set up tournament rules or that sponsor meets and tournaments. In some large-city chess clubs, checker players enjoy membership, and there are countless local checker clubs and backgammon clubs, not only in large cities but in smaller communities as well. Chess club tournament authorities suggest that the backgammon and checkers enthusiasts make their own contest or tournament rules, and with practice arrive at rules on timing and other guidance for judging tournament play and players.

Bowling If your local bowling association or club cannot give you information, guidance, rules, and other help for planning and producing a tournament, write to The American Bowling Congress, 1572 East Capitol Drive, Milwaukee 11, Wisconsin. For teen-agers there is the Junior Bowling Congress, 1913 West 103rd Street, Chicago 43, Illinois.

Bridge For you and your bridge-playing friends, when you want information on duplicate and tournament play, the American Contract Bridge League, 33 West Sixtieth Street, New York 23, New York, recommends *The Beynon Book on Tournament Bridge and Bridge Direction,* by George Beynon. Your library or book store can order the book for you from the League.

Chess For setting up a local chess tournament, consult *The Official Blue Book and Encyclopedia of Chess,* by Kenneth Harkness, published by the U. S. Chess Federation, 80 East Eleventh Street, New York 3, New York. This book is the source of all information on chess and chess tournaments. The author points out that local clubs conducting tournaments may have their own ground rules, outside the scope of the world-wide regulations laid down by F.I.D.E. (the laws of chess adopted by the General Assembly of the world chess federation, the Fédération Internationale des Echecs). In Harkness's book, all F.I.D.E. tournament regulations and all the ground rules of the U. S. Chess Federation have been combined, under the heading, *U. S. Chess Federation Tournament Rules.*

Golf If you want to make your local golf tournament official, consult and follow *The Rules of Golf,* with tournament information included, published by the U. S. Golf Association, 40 East Thirty-eighth Street, New York 16, New York. It is 25 cents a copy.

Ice Skating If you want suggestions on improving your ice skating, *Dick Button on Skates,* published by Prentice Hall, New York, is a book full of good advice. But you will have to be inventive and full of imagination if you want to put on a local ice show or skating tournament. None of the famous skaters has written about producing a skating festival or show.

The big commercial ice shows of the theatre, TV, and the movies are examples that may inspire your best skaters with ideas for a local skating show or tournament. Students and teachers at an art school and in the drama department of a high school or college might combine talents to design a beautiful local skating show, which could include competitive or tournament skating. An amateur theatrical group or little theatre in your community might be pressed into service to write the show, that is, plan the episodes and numbers. The art and drama departments can costume the skaters, and the school band provides skaters' music for the occasion.

This could be sponsored by school, chamber of commerce, individuals, or community, with skaters of all ages from kindergarten to old-timers. It could be worked up into an annual local skating festival to raise funds for any worthy purpose.

Roller Skating The U. S. Amateur Roller Skating Association, 120 West Forty-second Street, New York 36, New York, is the source of all kinds of information on roller skating. The Association's book, *The Amateur Roller Skater's Handbook* contains directions, rules, and information on all aspects of skating, dancing on skates, skaters' games, and tournaments.

Sailing, Yachting Regattas and various kinds of boat races are more popular today than ever. If your local yacht or boat club cannot give you the necessary guidance and instructions for putting on such events, you might write The North American Yacht Racing Union, 37 West Forty-fourth Street, New York 36, New York, which lists many helpful books for young and old sailing enthusiasts. Among these is *The Official Rule Book* of the Union, obtainable from the address above. Other suggestions: *The New Yacht Racing Rules,* by Robert N. Bavier, Jr., and *Sailing to Win,* by the same writer; *Learning to Race,* by Harold Calahan; *Yacht Racing Rules and Tactics,* by Gordon Aymar; and *Race Your Boat Right,* by Arthur Knapp, Jr. These books and others on the subject are available through Sailing Book Service, 31 East Tenth Street, New York 3, New York.

Informal, Home Tournaments are always fun. Chinese checkers, dominoes, checkers, miniature golf, darts, table tennis, ping pong, regattas of handmade sail boats on lake or stream, and favorite card games can be the inspiration of contests to see who wins the most games, or whose boat sails the fastest and farthest. Similar contests are suggested in various parties throughout this book. The contests add excitement to children's parties and diversion for older party-goers.

15

GUESTS FOR MEALS

How to Give a Dinner Young homemakers who have had no experience in giving dinners but who want to know how to give dinners, for their families, friends, important business acquaintances and other guests, can do so warmly, graciously, and *successfully* by following the well-tried planning ideas outlined in this chapter.

If you are a young homemaker and your kitchen space is inadequate, or there is no helper to take care of young children when you entertain, or your kitchen and dining-room or dinner table furnishings are still incomplete as is the case in many young households, or if you don't like order and entertaining—don't attempt a sit-down dinner. Instead, be happy in a much more spontaneous kind of hospitality. Let your husband put a casserole in the oven; or provide make-your-own sandwiches and toasted cheese muffins with cold drinks; or have a waffle or pancake supper, or a picnic, or a pick-up, spur-of-the-moment supper in the kitchen. When the children are older or when you can afford someone to take care of them while you are cook and hostess, then and only then is the time for dinners.

A dinner, to be successful, calls for organization of time, good cookery, and appointments that conform to some degree at least with tradition. These must be combined in an atmosphere of geniality and friendly hospitality. There are rules by which these objectives are achieved. These rules, based on experience, advise you on what to do long before the date of the dinner as well as when the cookery preparation begins and later when the fruits of the planning and hard work are on the table.

Such rules written down seem tiresomely didactic and long drawn out. But once tried and mastered, they no longer seem tiresome. On the contrary there is a thrill, something more than quiet satisfaction, in planning a dinner and bringing it to happy perfection for your husband and your guests.

Two aids are invaluable if you are the hostess in a servantless house. One is a modern serving cart, which wheels easily from kitchen to dining room. And the other is the greatest help and guide at all times, in fact, it is essential to the beginner hostess—a large, complete, general cookbook in which menus are given as well as many recipes and general technique of cooking. Also, you must learn to adapt: general rules made for the many cannot apply to all homes and all cooks. Take what you need from the experience of others and adapt it for your method of work and your home.

Success Tips from Six Young Hostesses like yourself are given below. These women have been giving dinners for three or four happy years, and were asked what they considered most helpful in achieving a successful dinner.

Plan Do-Ahead Dishes the first one said: I plan a menu with do-aheads in mind, dishes I can prepare a day in advance. Then I make sure to stay within the budget I have allowed myself. Next, I work out carefully the time schedule needed for each step of dinner preparation. And finally, I think about my energy and ability, so that I don't take on more than I can do, or include dishes that I haven't cooked several times before.

Use Calamity-Proof Recipes the second hostess said: The only way I can face a really important dinner is to use my calamity-proof recipes. I collect and try recipes continually on the family, and when I find one that we like, which is not too difficult to prepare and is easy to serve, I add it to my permanent menu file. These are the only dishes I will consider putting into a guest dinner menu.

Importance of Marketing the third young hostess said: The market order always seems the most important part of the planning of a dinner. I sit down a week ahead of time, work out my menu, and list everything

I need from wooden skewers to whipping cream. I check all the staples in the kitchen, list any special ingredients, and then I make a day-to-day calendar of shopping. Staples can be bought at once. Vegetables and fruits, for freshness, must not be bought until the day before the dinner or early on the morning of the party day. Meat, poultry, or fish must be ordered several days ahead, so that the shop has exactly what I want when I want it. I buy a dessert for most of our dinners, such as an ice cream pie or cake from my favorite bake shop (where I get wonderful caramel cream cakes), and I order the dessert a week ahead, to be picked up the morning of the party.

That Indispensable List the fourth hostess is like the third one, who always writes down what must be bought and when. But this one writes down every step of what she will have to do on the day of the party, starting with the early morning and going right through the serving of the dinner. She has a poor memory, she says, and can only attend to things if she imposes order on herself, and has a written guide list in the kitchen fastened up on the wall above her work counter. She checks off each job as soon as it is done. Her parties are perfection. She is relaxed, gay, happy, from the time she begins dinner as well as after the last guest at the end of the evening has thanked her for a wonderful time.

Order in the Kitchen! the fifth of the homemaker hostesses said that the order in her kitchen was important to her ease of mind and efficiency. She washes pans as soon as they are used so they are out of the way. She also uses a step-by-step, written schedule to tell her what to do and when to do it. That schedule always allows her at least twenty minutes of rest and time to change quickly from work dress to dinner dress before the final cooking and guests are arriving. She and her husband prepare and serve the dinner at least once for themselves a few days before they serve it as a guest dinner, so they are sure of every step in timing and other details.

The Complete Schedule the sixth hostess said she made a master plan for her first dinner, which was a happy success, and she has followed the plan ever since. It includes every step from exact grocery order to when to set the table, even when to start the coffee as dinner draws to a close.

If all this sounds like bothersome detail and too, too much to undertake, it is important to realize that *giving a dinner is a job full of details, all of which are important*. But planning and serving a guest meal need not be regimented or too much of a change from the usual family meals. If you give your family well-cooked, nicely served, attractive meals, your problems in giving guest dinners are more than half solved.

Relax and Enjoy It That a guest dinner is an especially good, family dinner, with some friends added to the table, is one way to look at it. And since they are guests whom you and your husband want to entertain, you both make extra effort to give them a good dinner, attractively served on time, and one that is a strain neither on your standard of living nor on your energies and ability. It should not wear you out nervously, or demand too much of your time and effort and money. Hospitality should be a pleasure or else be omitted from your way of life.

As host and hostess, your husband and you combine efforts so that each guest receives a warm, friendly greeting to make him feel welcome and to make the occasion stand out for him. You both set the pace for an unhurried atmosphere, gaiety, pleasant conversation, and a good evening all around. Added to these responsibilities, your husband makes introductions, takes care of any tardy guest, assists with the wraps, and attends to any interruptions, such as telephone calls.

At mealtime seat guests according to your previously agreed seating plan, with the woman guest of honor or oldest woman guest at the host's right. Your husband carves and serves and keeps a watchful eye on the table to serve second helpings, and assists in other ways that develop during the meal.

Taking the best points from the above success tips of other young hostesses, here is a detailed working plan for one easy dinner. Maybe you do not need the whole plan, but parts of it may smooth the way for all the entertaining you undertake.

Detailed Working Plan *Step One—Start with Guest List* Invite only a number easy to serve at your table. Invite guests by note on a fold-over card, or by telephone, or in person for an evening about ten days away. Name the hour—that is, invite them for seven o'clock or seven-thirty, whatever is the most convenient hour in your home, and likely

PLACE SETTING

SOUP COURSE

MAIN COURSE

SALAD COURSE

DESSERT COURSE

to be best for your guests. When possible, the intimate, friendly telephone call is preferable to a written invitation for this kind of party. If you do write an invitation, follow some such form as these samples.

To a married couple who are old friends:

Monday

Dear Janice and Bill,

Hal and I are giving a little dinner Saturday night, September 9th, for Hal's Aunt Belle, from Denver. She is a dear and we want you to meet her. Do come and help make our dinner a success. We have asked Dr. Slingo, too. Dinner will be at seven.

Please telephone me and say you are both free to come.

(signed) Helen

To an unattached man:

Monday

Dear Bob,

Hal and I hope you can come to a small informal dinner we are giving Friday night, September 8th. That pretty girl in his office you wanted to meet will be here. Her name is Sue Devon. I threw that in for bait! But in any case, we do want you to come. Seven o'clock. Do ring us up and say you can come.

(signed) Helen

To an older couple:

Monday

Dear Mrs. Pierce,

Hal and I have wanted ever so long to ask you and your husband to dinner at our apartment. We have been so slow in getting settled, awaiting furniture and other things, and the months have rushed by.

But now, on Saturday, September 9th, we are having a small dinner and we hope, very much, that you will come and give us the pleasure of having you both in our home, at our table.

Dinner is at seven.

Sincerely,

(signed) Helen Brooks
(Mrs. Harold Brooks)

Telephone   Dinner, Friday, September 9th.
Saybrook 9-2180   Seven o'clock.

Step Two—the Menu The guest list completed, go to work on your menu. If you invite guests for seven o'clock, they should arrive about five minutes before seven, or no more than five minutes after. Include in your menu plan a predinner, iced juice cocktail with crackers and stuffed celery to be served in the living room. This allows the late stragglers to arrive before guests go to the table. This also gives you time for your last-minute kitchen duties, while your husband is host in the living room.

Have dinner ready to serve at seven-thirty, and serve it, even if one or two of your guests have not arrived. It is inexcusably bad manners to keep hungry guests waiting for late-comers or because of delayed preparations in the kitchen. Careful planning helps you avoid the latter.

Avoid exotic and elaborate dishes. Also avoid too many courses and too many dishes, which cause confusion in the kitchen and in serving. Put the menu together with dishes you have cooked many times, which are easily served by your husband.

Make the fullest use of such equipment as blender, graters, grinders, knives for cutting salad vegetables. Study food advertisements in local newspapers for good buys. Foods in season have a double attraction, since they are at their peak of perfection of flavor and appearance and are selling at budget prices.

Chefs use skillful contrasts to pique appetites. You can do the same with hot and cold dishes in the menu, soft and crisp textures, bland and strong seasonings, tart and sweet flavors, and contrast of color, too, for eye appeal. Study your cookbooks for suggestions on garnishes that add flavor, color, and interest to dishes. A large, hearty meal should end with a light dessert. A light dinner calls for an important, filling dessert.

This menu in the detailed working plan is an easy one to prepare and serve. Besides the juice appetizer served in the living room, the menu includes: fresh fruit cup, glazed ham steak with pineapple rings, apple and sweet potato casserole, asparagus with lemon butter, beet salad, brown-and-serve hot rolls, lemon chiffon pie, coffee. If you are not a pie baker, or don't want to add a pie to your preparations, buy a delicious cake or frozen dessert.

Step Three—Your Master Plan With the list of dishes in front of you, and your best cookbook at hand, write down all ingredients in the recipes. Check this list against your pantry, refrigerator, and other supplies. Then make a shopping list for all needs—fruits, ham, vegetables, as well as any staples, such as flour, salt, sugar, you may need. Add good dinner mints or other candy and cigarettes to the list. Note down the days on which to buy. Fresh things and perishables should be bought on the morning of the dinner; note the day on which to order the ham, and the days for all other supplies.

Check Kitchen Utensils Pans the right sizes? Anything needed at the kitchenwares store? If so, get it and use it several times before party date.

Check Table Settings Decide which linen you will use, and launder it if necessary. Is the glassware ready? Right size, not too small glasses for juice appetizer? Glass dessert cups and matching plates for fruit cup, water goblets? Silver polished? Decide whether to have a low arrangement of flowers with candles at two sides, or a bowl of fruit, or some other centerpiece. Add the number, right size, and color of the candles to your shopping list. Ask the florist for exactly the flowers you want and specify delivery for early on the party morning. They should be arranged for the centerpiece in the morning so that they open up to their best before dinnertime.

Make a Note to Refresh Bathroom guest towel supply, and to renew facial tissue and guest powder supply, soaps, etc. On the day of the party, the bathroom must be cleaned to perfection after the family morning baths, and given a quick look again in the early evening before time for guests to arrive. Plan a cleaning schedule of the whole house. Give the dining room and living room a major cleaning the day before the party, and on the party day late in the afternoon a quick dusting in the living room, including pick-up and putting everything to rights. Put cigarettes in boxes, and place enough ash trays and matches where they are most needed.

Morning of Dinner   Rearrange the refrigerator contents, making room for fruit cups, and salads to come. After you come in from your final shopping for perishables, begin kitchen preparation. Bake the pie and set it aside or in the refrigerator, according to the recipe.

It saves time and wear on the nerves to have all cans opened and out of the way before the cookery begins. So open pineapple and pour it into a dish with the juice. Juice will be used in basting ham, so cover and place the dish in refrigerator.

Open cans or jars of pickled beets, pour into a dish, cover it and place in refrigerator. Open the bottle of capers and any salad dressings; adjust the bottle tops loosely.

Open cans of mixed vegetable juice, to be used as the appetizer. Pour contents into a serving pitcher, cover pitcher and place in refrigerator.

Wash and scrub the asparagus under running cold water—see your cookbook directions for the preparation of asparagus. Wrap it in damp towel and place in the refrigerator vegetable drawer.

Wash lettuce and discard all but the inner, curled leaves. Drain and wrap it in a damp towel and place it in the refrigerator vegetable drawer.

Wash celery; follow your cookbook recipe for stuffing, and stuff the celery now. Place the stuffed stalks on a serving dish and wrap the dish well with waxed paper. Put it in the refrigerator to chill until serving time.

Wash fruits now, but for an unusually good fresh fruit cocktail, leave them whole, and chill until later.

Read the recipe again for the apple and sweet potato casserole. Wash and pare potatoes, boil until tender, let cool, and place them in the refrigerator until it is time to prepare the casserole for dinner.

A ROAST ON SERVING CART AT HUSBAND'S LEFT.

Set the table in dining room. Have it complete and ready for dinner—centerpiece in place, serving spoons and forks beside your husband's plate or on serving cart in kitchen.

Get out all of the serving dishes you will need and place them in a convenient spot in the kitchen or on your serving cart.

Arrange a tray with the right number of glasses for the appetizer and small cocktail napkins. Take the tray to the living-room coffee table or wherever you plan to serve the appetizer.

Eat a kitchen lunch so that you won't get too tired and hungry.

Afternoon   Do the final clean-up of living room; check the cigarette boxes and ash trays.

Get out the dress and accessories you will wear for dinner.

Rest until almost time to start cookery schedule. Then change your dress, put on a large, comfortable cookery apron (not one of those decorative, but useless, small hostess aprons) to cover your dress.

Start Cookery Schedule, which you have worked out according to the recipes you are using from your cookbook. For example, put the ham on to cook in the oven or on top of the stove forty-five minutes or more before serving time, or according to the recipe, so it is almost ready at 7:30 when the first course fruit is served. At that time, turn heat under ham as low as possible, or better still leave it in heavy skillet, which retains heat, while you and guests eat fruit cup. Do the same kind of exact scheduling with the potato casserole.

Put asparagus on to steam, following your recipe as to timing, so that it is done at 7:30. At that time turn the heat off. Cover the steamer tightly and let the asparagus stand in the retained steam until you come out to serve it.

Mix lemon butter in upper part of small double boiler over water. Cover it and let it stand.

Combine sliced or quartered, chilled fruits into dessert glasses. Top each with a sprig of fresh mint and set the glasses, but not their plates, on a cleared refrigerator shelf to chill.

Fix small salad plates, each with crisp lettuce cup. Slice drained pickled beets into each, and top with a few capers and a whirl or rosette of thick sour-cream mayonnaise. (Use a small pastry or decorating tube for this.) Place the salads on a cleared refrigerator shelf.

Put crackers into the oven to crisp for the appetizer tray. Remove after 5 to 8 minutes, and place on a serving dish. Keep them on the back of the stove.

When Your Guests Arrive About this time guests begin to arrive. Take off your apron and with a genuine smile of welcome, join your husband in greeting them at the front door. Your husband brings in the pitcher of chilled vegetable juice, the crackers, and the stuffed celery to the ready and waiting tray in the living room.

When you can excuse yourself, you complete last-minute tasks. You put ice in the water goblets on the table and pour the water. Add butter balls or cubes to the bread-and-butter plates, and attend to whatever is waiting in the kitchen, such as turning the heat on under the lemon butter in the double boiler. As the guests are finishing their appetizer in the living room, you bring the ready fruit cups on their matching glass plates into the dining table, placing them on the cover or service plate at each setting. When they are in place, you invite your guests to the table and with your husband seat them as planned and eat your first course in peace, knowing that all is well in the kitchen.

After all have finished their fruit, you remove the fruit-cup glasses, plates, and spoons, but leave the cover plate in place at each setting.

In the kitchen, when you have brought the last fruit glass from the dining room, you pop the brown-and-serve rolls into the oven where the potato casserole has been waiting on lowered heat, and you now turn the heat up to Hot.

Quickly heat dinner plates and serving dishes under the running hot water, or in electric warming cases. Drain the asparagus, place it in a serving dish, dress with lemon butter, and set on cart. Remove the ham from the oven or skillet to a warmed serving dish and place it on serving cart. Remove casserole from oven and place on cart.

Place the warmed dinner plates on the cart, and wheel it into the dinner table to a position as close as possible to your husband. He lifts his own cover plate from the table to the cart, picks up the dinner plates, and sets them before himself on the table. He lifts the hot foods to the table, placing them where he can easily serve them.

You return to the kitchen and bring in salad plates, two at a time, placing one at the upper left of each place setting. Then you return for the rolls which are ready by this time.

You sit down now to enjoy dinner with your guests. As your husband serves each warm plate and passes it to a guest, the guest hands his cover plate to your husband, who places it on the cart. He begins serving to the guest of honor or the woman at his right.

After everyone has finished, at leisure, after seconds have been offered and enjoyed, you quietly and not hastily clear the table. Remove all plates and their silver, salad plates, all serving dishes and their silver, without scraping the plates. Simply lift the silver from each, so that a quiet stacking is possible on the cart. Salt and peppers are removed at this time and any remaining silver, except a dessert fork left at each setting. Your husband helps by placing dishes on the cart. While you wheel the cart to the kitchen, your husband refills water glasses, puts ash trays about for those who like to smoke at this point in the dinner, and keeps the conversation going until you appear again.

In the kitchen, leave the cart alone. Put the water on for coffee. You now take dessert plates into the dining room and place them in front of your husband. If the table needs crumbing here and there, return to the kitchen for a crumbing tray, and lightly, with some gay word about crumbs needed for the sparrows out the kitchen window, clean off the table.

Coffee Service Return to the kitchen for the coffee tray, which you bring in without the coffee. The tray should be complete with demitasse cups and saucers and small spoons, small sugar bowl and cream pitcher. The tray goes on the table near your place. It is courteous to be prepared also to serve de-caffeined coffee or tea since not everyone drinks coffee in the evening.

Then you bring in the pie or other dessert and place it in front of your husband, with whatever serving silver he needs. You sit down and eat dessert with your guests. Later, at a break in the conversation you return to the kitchen, complete the coffee and bring the pot in, place it on the coffee tray, and serve it.

Or, you may prefer to serve the coffee after dessert is finished. Then you place the tray on the living-room coffee table, and you all can leave the dining room to enjoy coffee in the living room.

Let the dining-room and kitchen duties wait while you have a leisurely cup of coffee and talk. But after a while, you excuse yourself, to clear the table, put foods in the refrigerator, scrape plates and rinse silver. Do it all as quietly and quickly as possible. Turn out the kitchen light and return to your guests.

Tips for the Hostess Guest helpers sometimes present a problem. If you want a man or woman guest to help you with any of your duties during the evening, explain ahead of time exactly what the guest is to do. Don't let helter-skelter running in and out from the kitchen spoil the atmosphere of relaxation and leisurely dining. And no matter how many offers are made to do the dishes, refuse them. The dish washing can wait, and you and your husband can do it after all guests have gone. The success of the dinner demands your presence as hostess after dinner as well as at the table.

If there is a slip-up, an accident, or something forgotten, remedy it as quietly and lightly as possible. Remember that everyone present has had similar experiences and the world has not come to an end.

As experience and practice make the giving of a dinner go more smoothly, you will find yourself thinking of delightful innovations in decoration and menu making. You will develop your own style, something that famous hostesses all have, a style which starts with superb cooking of dishes that your guests praise and ask for again and again when you say, Will you come to dinner.

The accomplished or experienced hostess started just as you are starting, learning from a sound cookbook all the necessary techniques and then trying new methods and new recipes. As she gained confidence, somewhere in those first years, she began trying foreign cookery recipes, and she also began to vary seasonings, to create her own dishes, her own interpretation and variation of some old-time favorites. She hunted out unusual food markets in her own city, sent away for otherwise unobtainable foods she saw advertised in good magazines, visited foreign grocery stores, strange markets, unusual restaurants. She began collecting specialty cookbooks and foreign cookbooks, reading them for what they could teach her.

This new knowledge and her growing ease in cookery, timing, and serving did not mean that she could be casual or slapdash. No true gourmet cook ever is. She abides by an exacting schedule of preparation, timing, and cooking. But her experience makes it all seem easy, almost spur-of-the-moment.

Another habit to cultivate, which can give you as much pleasure as learning more about cookery, unusual dishes, flavors, and seasoning, is to relate the menu to the style of your table. Unusual wares add to the interest of a dinner party. American shops are full of imported earthenware and fine porcelains no more costly than traditional table wares. Many American designers are creating new concepts of beautiful china, glass, silver, and pottery accessories, which are intended for young homemakers' tables. The antique shop, or someone's attic, or auction sales provide much else, such as, Japanese, Chinese, Indian, Early American bowls, tureens, old teapots to hold flower arrangements and leaves and grasses, old baskets which you can spray with white or colored paint and use for fruit and flower arrangements, pieces of old Chinese carving, old lanterns. You can find, as well, fine china and glass, pottery and sculpture, countless shapes and forms and textures in these sales and shops. Some pieces cost less than a dollar; valuable ones may cost many dollars. One or two added to your supply of things for table decoration and used with imagination can add special interest and beauty to your table.

Solid-color linen tablecloths are available in department stores and linen shops in such colors as avocado, orange, light blue, brown, gray, hunter green, maize, mint green, pink, red, sand, turquoise, ginger and blueberry—colors that suggest unusual, beautiful, or dramatic table color schemes. And of course, traditional linen damask in white and pastel colors, hand-screen-printed linen cloths and others in rayon-cotton mixtures are among the most popular tablecloths today. Young homemakers who have inherited old damask cloths and find them too large or too formal may have them dyed—the damask takes dye wonderfully—and cut to more useful sizes. Every scrap in the new soft coloring can be used, small ends being cut into napkins or tray cloths.

See the Index for dinners in various chapters throughout this book. Also see Charts on food colors for further menu and decoration help.

How to Give a Luncheon In general, planning and all procedure for giving a luncheon are the same as for any other guest meal, and especially like the planning of a guest dinner. First, read the preceding section, How to Give a Dinner. Then make a lighter, simpler menu than a dinner menu. The usual luncheon formula is two or three courses instead of four or more, as in dinners. Plan all details as described in

How to Give a Dinner. Study the general instructions; adapt them to your kitchen, your budget, your menu, and your problems of serving a guest meal without help or with a helper in the kitchen. For your table, see the sketch of a luncheon place setting.

Today almost any kind of meal served at noontime is called a luncheon. It can be light, simple, as informal as tossed salad in a wooden bowl with a sandwich and an iced drink. It can also be a menu of superb dishes in the tradition of elegant entertaining, handsomely served in handsome surroundings. Between these extremes there are many other kinds of luncheons. The degree of formality you hope to achieve depends on your menu and your plan of serving as well as the setting and decoration of your table. So in the preliminary planning for a luncheon, the menu should be related to the style of the table, your home and your way of life.

Why give a luncheon? Because it is a pleasant way to bring friends together, to entertain a house guest, or renew acquaintance with old college friends; to discuss business with an employer, partner, or employee, or club president; or to honor a new bride, or introduce a a new neighbor.

Here are various luncheon menus for such occasions, and ideas for color schemes and table decoration. From them you can combine

menus suited to your needs and work out table decoration adapted to your home, your supply of tablewares, and your color preference. For a small gathering of close friends, invite your guests in person or by telephone. For more important luncheons, send a note ten days or one week before the date, on fold-over or informal cards.

Summer Porch Luncheon for a Friend This is a small easy-to-do-luncheon. Iced fruit juice, tossed fresh-herb garden salad in a wooden bowl, toasted cheese muffins, iced coffee, and fresh currant tarts is a simple but good menu. This luncheon was given in Manchester, Vermont, to a visiting woman's page editor from New York. The salad was fragrant with freshly cut herbs from the garden of the hostess. The editor and other guests were especially appreciative of the care with which each dish had been prepared and the simple but effective decoration. The setting included a scrubbed pine trencher table on a screened porch, hunter-green straw mats, large yellow, hem-stitched linen napkins, yellow pottery plates, very large Swedish peasant water and juice glasses, green pottery cups and saucers for hot coffee, and tall amber glasses for those who wanted their coffee iced. The centerpiece was a brown pottery jug full of zinnias.

Winter Day Luncheon for Club or Sorority Friends Menu: honeydew melon-ball cocktail, curried chicken with curry condiments, rice, small mixed green salad, French apple cake, tea or coffee. For the table: your prettiest pale green, modern china, or solid white china, or white with small green leaf motif, sparkling modern, undecorated crystal water goblets and fruit cocktail glasses, green majolica leaf-shape salad plates, apple cake served at table onto crystal dessert plates. Serve the demitasse in small green cups.

Summer Garden-Club Guests Menu: chilled cucumber soup garnished with chopped fresh parsley and capers in a glass cup or small bowl set in bowl of ice, thin hot cheese strips, chicken-and-sweetbreads shortcake, fresh raspberry mousse, tea or coffee. The setting: an air-cooled dining room and your prettiest flower-embroidered linen mat set and napkins. The centerpiece is made of fresh flowers in a carefully worked out arrangement, such as a Japanese pewter fish with tall but delicate branch of a flowering shrub, and a low cluster of blooms of whatever is at its best in the garden that day.

Another centerpiece idea is to use miniature garden tools, rake, spade, and hoe, the handles crossed in the center of the table, with fresh trailing philodendron or other vine wound in and out over them and among small pots of bloom (see sketch). For the table: china in

solid-color pale grey or white; salad plates of antique glass in red or bristol blue; dessert glasses to match salad plates, or of another antique pattern.

Luncheon for College President or any distinguished person in the community. The menu: hot or jelled Madrilène with sesame-sprinkled melba toast, creamed crab meat in avocado half, small celery hearts,

black olives, radishes, hot rolls, lemon sherbet, large soft fresh macaroons, coffee, or tea. For the table: your nicest silver trays, candy
dishes, other pieces; a luncheon cloth of fern-printed, white Belgian
linen, white linen napkins, your prettiest china, such as Spode or
Wedgwood or a handsome antique Chinese or English pattern, or any
favorite good china; etched crystal glasses, and a tall epergne of fresh
fruits as centerpiece.

Luncheon for New Bride Menu: hot deviled crab meat appetizer in
crab shells or ceramic ovenware scallop shells; salad of endive, sliced
olives, and grapefruit with orange dressing; hot raisin muffins; coffee
jelly with mocha-flavored, whipped cream topping, and demitasse.

Put small tables for four around the room, cover each with a pale
blue tablecloth, and use assorted colored napkins on each table, such
as one rose, one pale yellow, one orchid, one of a deeper blue than the
cloth. Make simple slipcovers of blue cotton or linen for the party
chairs at these tables. On each table place a small silver or glass tumbler
or mug holding a bunch of violets or little bouquet of mixed small
flowers. China should be solid-color, pale pink Wedgwood or other
good ware. Serve the coffee jelly on glass dessert plates. Use blue
demitasse cups, or assorted antique cups and saucers of various colors
and patterns.

This same menu and scheme of small tables was used for an
Engagement Luncheon by a Chicago hostess.

**Luncheon for Local Teacher, Librarian, Music Director, P.T.A. Offi-
cers, etc.** Menu: baked onion soup in individual casseroles, herbed
toast, white meat of chicken and almonds in a salad, hot crusty crescent
rolls, baked apple, coffee or tea. Use handsome trays such as red
lacquer, or wicker which has been painted pale grey. Use your best
embroidered linen napkins and plates to harmonize with the trays, for
instance, grey pottery on the lacquer trays, flowered china on the grey
trays. Serve dessert in apple-shaped, glass dessert dishes and beverage
in cups to match luncheon plates. Carry trays to a fireside table, or out
to the porch, or to a table by a window with a view.

If the luncheon is large, for family and several guests, use the dining
room and either seat all around one large table or use two tables. Mat

sets are always easy to use, but if you have cloths that you like, such as screen-printed, flowered linen cloths or hemstitched linen crash, by all means use them.

Other Luncheon Menus A very simple and delicious luncheon is made with one hot dish, such as a chowder, stew, casserole, or a meat or fish pie, and tossed green salad, hot brioche, fruit, and coffee.

Other interesting luncheons are inspired by the season. A New York favorite in June is broiled young chicken, new asparagus, and the first strawberries up from the South. Another New York spring luncheon is broiled Hudson River shad with the roe, crisp bacon, escarole salad, rolls, half of grapefruit.

Broiled salmon steak is a popular luncheon dish in many West Coast homes. With the salmon serve new asparagus, parsleyed small potatoes or potato puff, crusty French croissants or any local baker's favorite bread, mixed fruit sherbets served in tall glasses, and coffee. These salmon luncheons sometimes begin with a cup of hot minced-clam bouillon, or a cream soup of minced clams garnished with freshly-ground black pepper and celery salt.

Patio Luncheon in many parts of California and in New Mexico is popular because guests make their own salads from a big, iced buffet selection, or they eat a fine Caesar salad with cold smoked salmon or sturgeon or iced boiled salmon, a moist dark bread such as fresh pumpernickel, and iced fruit juice or hot coffee to drink. Or the luncheon is a fruit platter salad with hot coffee and pound cake with inch-high mocha frosting.

Salad Luncheons any time of the year are popular. They are easy to prepare and serve. The main dish, the salad, can be a platter of fruits California style, such as halves of fresh apricots, peaches, nectarines, fingers of ripe pineapple, cantaloupe and watermelon, blueberries or red raspberries, and sprigs of water cress or very tiny curls of the inner heart of Boston or butterhead lettuce.

Cooked and raw vegetables combine in a good salad. On crisp lettuce, make mounds of cooked peas, asparagus tips, lima beans, sliced boiled potato which has marinated in tart French dressing; add

sliced raw cucumbers and miniature tomatoes hollowed and filled with horse-radish mayonnaise. Serve buttered hot rolls with either salad and a beverage.

See Index for luncheons in various chapters throughout this book. Also see Chart on food colors and food go-togethers.

How to Give a Bridge Luncheon A bridge luncheon is a small menu of delicious, light luncheon dishes served to friends before an afternoon of bridge.

Invitations The invitation is usually given in person or by telephone, or if the party is a very large one with several tables of bridge, a written invitation is sent. For this you might use printed or engraved and decorated small invitation fold-over cards which are plentiful in stationery shops and wherever playing cards and correspondence note papers are sold. The phrasing printed on such cards is usually Luncheon and Bridge, or, Come for Luncheon and Bridge, on the cover. Inside is printed something like this, to be filled in:

Date————————————
Time————————————
Name———————————— Telephone number
Address———————————— R.S.V.P.

Or, you may use your personal engraved invitation fold-over cards which have your name on the cover. Inside you write:

Please come for luncheon
and bridge
Wednesday, October Fifth
One O'Clock
42 Lancaster Place   R.S.V.P.
Gladwin 2-2121

Menu Diet-conscious friends will bless you if you limit the food to something as simple as a chicken sandwich, superb fruit or vegetable salad in crisp lettuce cup, and a hot or iced beverage. Other menu suggestions:

A gelatin ring salad of vegetables or fruit, small finger sandwiches, caramel custard, and beverage.

A cheese soufflé, ripe olive open-face sandwiches, sherbet, and beverage.

Ham, salmon, or smoked tongue mousse, endive salad, toasted whole-wheat roll, blueberry meringue tart, and beverage.

Most hostesses who are serious bridge players prefer to serve luncheon, when the group is small, in the dining room or on a screened porch on one or two tables or on trays, keeping the bridge tables which have been set up with their chairs free for the game.

Others like to use matching small tablecloths and cover the bridge tables, setting them simply with silver, glass and china, and then serve one of two ways: buffet, letting guests help themselves at a buffet table and take their plates to the small tables; or the hostess serves the plates in the kitchen and brings them to the guests at the tables. Whatever is easiest for your space and for the number of guests should be followed. Luncheon should be ready to be served when your guests arrive.

Decoration Linen, glass, china, and silver for this party should be attractive, perhaps different from the wares you use for other luncheons and for suppers and dinners. Some gift shops and table ware departments feature special bridge luncheon plate-and-cup sets. Whatever plates and other pieces you decide to use should be appropriate to the menu and easy to manage at a small table or on a tray. These might be a medium-small decorative plate perhaps unusual in shape, a water tumbler with sturdy base or a low-footed goblet, a cup which does not

slide on its saucer, a luncheon-size napkin to match the cloth or china pattern.

As usual for the best effect, co-ordinate the colors of the wares with the tablecloths and with your room in which the players are entertained. Table centerpieces are omitted when lunch is served on bridge tables. Instead the score cards with partners' names written on for the opening game, two unopened packs of cards, and a sharpened pencil with an eraser are placed in the center of each table, to be picked up when luncheon is finished and the tables are cleared, cloth removed, and tables left bare for playing.

The young homemaker hostess needs to exert as much care in planning all details of a light menu as of a larger menu for luncheon or dinner. These smaller menus require the same careful attention, imaginative yet practical scheduling for the shopping, preparation, timing and serving. For general guidance in all such details, read How to Give a Dinner and adapt that information to the detailed organization of your bridge luncheon.

Also, an older married friend, an in-law, or some other experienced hostess will be glad to help you plan and give your first bridge luncheon. It is usually easier to learn the short-cuts and the little niceties of service when helped by an experienced friend. For a Bridge Tea see section on How to Give a Tea later in this chapter.

Dessert and Canasta Many neighborhoods enjoy simple afternoon parties of canasta and bolivia, or any other currently popular game. Groups of women meet to play for an hour or so, with inexpensive prizes as the trophies to carry home afterwards.

One of the most popular plans for these afternoons begins with dessert. Guests are supposed to omit dessert and coffee or tea from their luncheons at home. Then their canasta hostess serves them with a dessert and beverage when they arrive for the afternoon. Popular desserts for this are mixed sherbets and cake, meringue with ice cream and fruit, such as sliced peaches or stewed blueberries, or brick ice cream with frosted cupcakes, or a special fruit compote of black cherries, cooked dried apricots, section of canned pear, with a spoonful of grenadine poured over fruit, served with cookies.

How to Give a Brunch Brunch is a late morning meal, both breakfast and luncheon. Because of its informality and ease of preparation and service, and because it fits into the way of life of many Americans, it has become the favorite guest meal of young homemakers. This is also true for city career girls and all sorts of busy men and women in teaching and professional jobs in small towns, cities, country locations, too. At its best, brunch is leisurely, the foods simple but delicious, the table interesting.

Brunch probably owes its menu and unhurried manner to the British country house breakfast, which consists of a buffet of hot dishes, a big table, comfortable chairs and time to enjoy both the dishes and the company around the table. And the British breakfast is flexible. If it is announced for 9 o'clock this means only that the first array of foods will be ready at that time. If you come down at 10, you find that breakfast is still going on, hot dishes have been replenished and the arguments about what is in the *Times* that morning are only warming up.

The way of life of few Americans permits this kind of breakfast except on holidays, Saturday and Sunday. But the obvious pleasures of such an informal and sustaining meal encourage all of us to offer this kind of hospitality to our guests, calling it by its American name, brunch.

If you have overnight guests on Friday night, brunch at 11 o'clock or a little later on Saturday morning is a perfect way to feed them and any additional guests, neighbors, and drop-in friends. What you serve depends somewhat on the season and on your table cooking equipment, such as electric warmer for keeping food hot on the buffet, a toaster, perhaps an electric skillet or chafing dish. Such devices are the secret of easy brunch service.

Your guests serve themselves at the buffet and sit around one large table or two or more smaller ones, which have been set with linen, china, glassware and silver for breakfast. Or, they pick up a decorative tray ready with silver and napkin, serve themselves, and find a comfortable place to eat and talk, at a large group table or smaller tables.

Menu In winter, a brunch might include a hot cereal, such as quick-cooking oatmeal in a double boiler on a buffet grill and the essential top milk or light cream and brown sugar to go with it. In warm weather, an assortment of crisp cereals in their unopened, one-serving size packages can be heaped in a big punch bowl or decorative basket, from which guests choose the kind they prefer. In any season, have ready a pitcher of iced fruit juice on a tray with glasses, or, a platter of iced cantaloupe or honeydew melon pared and cut in serving pieces, and freshly cut lemon or lime quarters to go with them.

One guest is asked to make toast at the brunch table. Another may attend to the coffee and pour it for all comers. You bring in hot brown-and-serve rolls or freshly made popovers. The tray of jams makes a bouquet of color in the morning light: black cherry, greengage plum, gooseberry, currant, apple jelly. In a hot chafing dish on the buffet, make freshly scrambled eggs seasoned with a quick grind of black pepper. In an electric skillet kept at low heat, there is crisp bacon which was cooked and the fat drained off before guests arrived. There may be creamed chipped beef in a chafing dish to be served on lightly-buttered toast. Waffles may be made at the table or on the buffet and served with delicious syrup and crisp bacon.

In place of hot rolls, brunch may feature a fine coffee cake or sticky cinnamon buns, since the guests will not expect to eat again before the evening meal and many enjoy a sweet pastry with their coffee. You might serve an assortment of miniature Danish pastries from a good bake shop, or a fine poppy-seed or prune Hungarian coffee ring, or some other coffee pastry.

Other menus for brunch:

Fresh berries and cream; corned beef hash or any other hash, such as roast beef, lamb, chicken, or turkey; poached eggs, toasted muffins, jam, coffee, applesauce-cinnamon cake.

Half grapefruit, small broiled chopped cooked meat cakes, mashed potato patties, warm corn bread or sticks, jam, sticky cinnamon buns, coffee.

Warm baked apple, cream; browned rice patties, broiled ham slice; heated brioche or croissants from a French bakery, jam, pan of warm gingerbread, coffee.

Ham hash patties browned and served with cream gravy on toast; warm compote of plums, peaches, pears; pecan coffee cake, coffee.

Chilled orange or pineapple juice; pancakes, butter, syrup; small link sausages in electric skillet; stewed cherries, Sally Lunn, coffee.

Broiled half grapefruit, scrapple, poached eggs on toast, jam, crumb cake, coffee.

Mush sliced and sautéed in butter, grilled Canadian bacon, biscuits, applesauce, Danish prune pastry, coffee.

Cooked dried apricots with grated orange peel; creamed, hard-cooked eggs on split, toasted English muffins; crisp bacon, thin apple cake, coffee.

Grapefruit shell full of grapefruit and orange sections and one or two cooked prunes; sautéed chicken livers and mushrooms on toast, broiled tomato halves, extra toast and jam, coffee.

Strawberries in orange juice, broiled kippers, hash-browned potatoes, scrambled eggs on toast, extra toast and jam, crullers or doughnuts, coffee.

Decoration and Tableware In general, breakfast tablewares are used on the brunch table. These are often bold, solid-color plates, cups, and saucers, or a fruit-and-flower patterned china. Or, a delicate imported, thin porcelain of pale color, the favorite breakfast china of Europe. Whatever the pattern, coffee cups should be of a good size. The best silver cutlery adds a gracious touch, but raffia-wrapped cutlery or bamboo handled knives, forks, and spoons also are at home on this table. You may use a tablecloth or mat set, the cloth solid-color linen, or striped or checkered if the pattern does not clash with the china.

A centerpiece is not essential on the brunch table, but if the table is large, a flowering plant or bowl of fruit adds pleasant color. Or, be amusing with some unusual piece, such as a fat Italian wicker boot filled to overflowing with fruits. Or, a big shell from the beach, scrubbed and lined with fresh green leaves and filled with small bunches of red, blue, and pale green seedless grapes, washed and ready to eat.

For basic instructions on the details of planning, shopping, cooking, and serving, as well as on how to co-ordinate menu, color scheme and table settings for best effects, read the previous sections on How to Give a Dinner and How to Give a Luncheon. See the Index for brunch parties described in other chapters of this book.

How to Give a Buffet Supper The average dining-room table, even an extendable one, has its limitations, which make it difficult to serve a large group of people comfortably at a seated luncheon, dinner, or supper. By serving buffet style from this same table, your number of guests may be much larger, the work of preparation easier, and the foods off the beaten path, even for beginning cooks, and therefore with unusual eye appeal and appetite satisfaction. The result can be an atmosphere of informal hospitality and a good time for all concerned, host and hostess as well as guests.

Let's begin with the good time for the hostess. Long before the day of the party, you, the hostess, will have to do the same kind of detailed planning and scheduling of tasks and preparatory work that you must do for a dinner or any other kind of party. Much of the kitchen preparation for buffet meals can be done a day in advance, which eases the schedule on the party day. The problem of serving is also simplified because guests serve themselves.

Guidance for you in all steps of planning and preparation is in the first section, How to Give a Dinner which should be read and studied whether your buffet supper is to be large or small. And if it is to be a buffet luncheon, also read How to Give a Luncheon and make use of the menus and decoration ideas given there. If it is to be a buffet tea, or reception, see the following section, How to Give a Tea.

Invitations You and your husband having decided on a date for the buffet supper, you give the invitations about ten days to one week before the party. For a small party invite your friends in person or by telephone. If you are entertaining more than eight, mail a written invitation which may be on party note paper, small fold-over cards which are printed for this purpose (and sometimes have a colored party sketch on the cover) and are in all stationery displays. Or mail your personal engraved or printed fold-over cards which have your name and your husband's name on the cover and are blank inside.

Only the simplest, brief phrasing is used for this invitation. Inside write something such as:

Buffet Supper
Sunday Night, at Seven

Mary Ann and Will
(Please do come!)

2308 Lake Place   R.S.V.P.
Orchard 5-6976

Menus Invitations mailed, go to work on the menu (for advice, see the section on How to Give a Dinner) and make those detailed plans for shopping, preparation, arranging the house and table, and for the last minute jobs and the serving schedule on the night of the party.

This buffet menu should make use of those dishes that can be made ahead of time, such as aspics, a mousse, and casseroles which can be made the day before the party, and of table cookery equipment—table warmers, chafing dish, grills.

For a small party the menu can be as simple as: chilled juice appetizer, one delicious hot casserole, such as chicken and mushrooms, rolls, jelly, a tossed green salad, and dessert, such as pie or cake, and coffee.

For a larger party you may want the menu luxurious enough to include two or three hot dishes, a cold mousse, an aspic, and those famous standbys of buffet meals—a whole baked ham and a cold roast turkey—two or three relishes, such as chutney and beet relish, one or more desserts, and coffee.

Between these extremes are many tried and successful buffet supper menus. Here is a favorite menu of a couple in New York who work in television. They usually show a new movie after their suppers, which are given on Saturday nights. For these they do all the cooking and serving, but hire a part-time maid to come next day to help with the cleaning up.

Their living room is very large, being two rooms thrown together, their kitchen small but well laid out and complete with the latest in all kinds of useful equipment and utensils. Their favorite supper menu is chilled mixed vegetable juice with tiny round sliced onion sandwiches, lobster and shrimp Newburg made in a chafing dish and served on thin slices of toasted bread, stuffed Belgian endive and celery, and their special ham rolls, which are small, thin slices of boiled ham spread with chopped water cress mixed with thick mayonnaise and rolled and fastened with cocktail picks. For dessert, they like to serve a Linzer torte, which they buy at a neighborhood Viennese bakery. Sometimes they serve, by request, individual cherry jam tarts made by the hostess, with coffee, of course.

Here's another buffet supper menu from a New York couple—the husband is English and his wife is from the South. Their parties, for which they hire a part-time helper in the kitchen, begin with two or three hot canapés served from a large electric table grill. Their favorites are cheese puffs, bacon-and-olive rolls, small fried oysters, which earlier have been dipped in batter and crumbs and are fried until browned and then kept hot on the table grill.

For a big, gala supper to entertain friends and business partners, the menu always features a large chafing dish of hot pasta, such as spaghetti with meat balls, cappelletti (Italian for "little hats") with tomato sauce, sea-shell macaroni, or some other form of pasta bought at an Italian grocery store and served with tomato and Parmesan cheese sauce. As an alternative, they serve a casserole of baked noodles with

cheese, onion, tomato, and anchovies in the sauce. In addition, cold boiled salmon on an iced platter, and gelatin ring salad of mixed vegetables with a well-seasoned mayonnaise, buttered toasted rolls, frozen eggnog, black walnut cookies, coffee.

Other Buffet Menus:

1. Deviled eggs, small celery hearts, and olives as appetizers, hot casserole of scalloped oysters, coleslaw with horse-radish mayonnaise dressing, a tray of buttered, sliced assorted breads cut in strips, orange cake, coffee.

2. Hot appetizer of small patty shells filled with chicken curry, open-face tiny ham sandwiches, sliced meat loaf, pickle relish, sliced cucumbers, hot casserole of corn and green pepper pudding, small blueberry muffins, caramel icebox cake, coffee.

3. Hot casserole of creamed, hard-cooked eggs with browned crumb

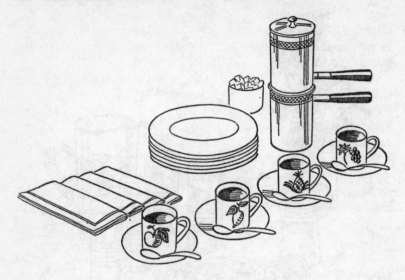

topping, buttered toast, baked ham, raisin relish, mixed vegetable salad in cupped lettuce leaf, ice cream pie, date and nut strips, coffee.

4. Cold roast turkey or capon to be sliced at the table, cold smoked sturgeon or salmon, cold sliced boiled or baked smoked tongue, cranberry jelly, mustard sauce, buttered toasted rolls, small molds of jellied tomato aspic garnished with escarole and Roquefort dressing, hot chocolate sauce in small chafing dish to serve on ice cream sandwich of devil's food cake and vanilla ice cream, coffee.

5. Thinly-sliced cucumbers in sour cream, small lettuce hearts to eat with them; jellied lemon salad ring of cherries and almonds, the center filled with thick fruit-juice mayonnaise; sliced boiled ham decorated with thin strips of dill pickle and all covered with aspic; hot casserole of chicken, mushrooms, and noodles with browned crumb topping; toasted slices of Italian or French bread; very small meringue tarts with any seasonal filling, such as fresh strawberries or cherries in summer, or cooked apples or a chocolate pudding in winter.

Note that any menu prepared for a large number means that many dishes must be doubled or made twice or more often. For instance, if the above menu is served for twelve, you will make two jellied salad rings, two platters or one very large platter of ham in aspic, two casseroles of chicken and noodles, and so on. Follow cookbook directions in each recipe. Use sets of matching casseroles and matching salad platters for best effect.

Arranging the Table When you put your menu together and have written down the shopping, cooking, and timing details and other plans for seeing it serenely on to the table the night of the party, it is time to plan the table itself. See diagram to guide you in placing plates, silver, napkins, and various other essentials for buffet service.

The table may be left bare with only protective pads used under hot dishes. Or, you may use a handsome linen cloth in color or white or an embroidered and lace-trimmed family tablecloth too large to use on any but a buffet table. You may want to use your best china for this party, or you may have collected other wares useful for buffet service, such as solid-color pottery plates or imported earthenware plates with brilliant flower designs or animal figures. This is a party at which you can mix your wares and be original in color scheme and decoration. At a buffet supper on a screened porch, you may want to use country-store wares, modern reproductions of old stoneware, early English blue-and-white china, milk glass, checkered cotton or paper tablecloth, and big dinner-size paper napkins—depending on the crowd.

To clear a dining room or living room for ease of service, the table should be pushed back along one wall where it is easily reached from the kitchen and is also accessible to guests. Put on it, instead of a centerpiece, some unusual decoration, such as a row of inexpensive, small Japanese baskets full of fruit and flower arrangements, or a row of tall candlesticks holding lighted candles and centered before them a cornucopia wicker basket holding fruits or flowers, leaves and grasses. Use a piece of Mexican tin sculpture, or an African or Indian carved figure and garland it with fresh flowers. For this table a handsome tureen or a fine porcelain epergne might be filled with small packages of good candies wrapped in bright foil papers.

As in giving a dinner, the buffet table is decorated, and all of its china, glass, silver, large serving spoons and forks, the napkins, salts and peppers, candle warmers or electric warmer are in place and ready, early on the day of the party. Follow the diagram of the table top as a

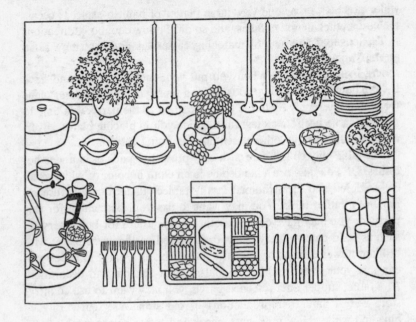

guide for placing dishes, but modify the arrangement to fit the service of your particular menu. A tray for coffee and another with a pitcher of ice water and glasses might be placed on an adjoining side board unless your buffet table is large enough to include them.

Buffet Service One plan of service: each guest is given a decorative tray and when he has served himself at the table, he will take one of the small, folded tray tables available in the room and open it up where-ever he will be most comfortable—at a chair, sofa, window seat, piano bench near guests with whom he wants to eat supper.

Another plan: if you have the space, provide square or round tables that seat four guests each. These add to the comfort and the success of your party, and with them trays are not needed. Such tables may be borrowed or rented from a caterer, club, or perhaps neighbors. They should be covered with tablecloths and left unset except for a small container of cigarettes and ash trays. Given elsewhere in this book are suggestions on how to make cloths for these tables. Solid-color and white damask cloths and others of cotton, and linen may be bought or rented from a caterer.

The covered tables may be left undecorated or garlanded with greenery placed low around the cloth. Napkins for these gay tables should be of dinner size, in any pretty color that goes with the cloths. If cloths are rented, matching napkins, of course, can be ordered with them.

As guests begin to arrive at the party hour, appetizers and glasses of chilled juice are brought in on a tray to the living-room coffee table or passed around to first arrivals. When more guests come in and are enjoying their appetizers, you excuse yourself and bring hot dishes from the kitchen, placing them on the electric or candle warmers on the buffet table. Then bring in cold dishes, such as aspic or salad, placed in larger serving dishes of cracked ice.

When everything is in readiness on the table, you announce that supper is ready and you invite your guests to serve themselves. They go to the table and serve their plates with whatever they want and then sit down, as described, at small tray tables or the larger tables to enjoy their supper.

While guests are coming to the buffet table, you stand near one end to help serve and your husband does the same at the other end of the table. You also keep an eye on the various dishes on the table, replenishing or replacing them as needed. With a large guest list this means that you bake two casseroles but bring only one in at the beginning of supper. When it is nearly empty, replace it with the untouched, second casserole, which has been kept hot in the kitchen. The same is done with other dishes, the molded aspics, salads, and whatever dishes your hungry guests are depleting at the table.

When all guests are served, your husband or one of the men guests serves a plate for you and you join one of the tables or sit down with a group of guests for supper. Your husband serves a plate for himself and finds a place to sit with another group of guests. You both keep a watchful eye on guests, to suggest seconds, relishes, rolls and other refills.

When the main dishes have been served and seconds to all who want a second helping—most people do!—your guests carry their used plates and silver to a serving table, or one end of the buffet table.

From there all are taken to the kitchen by you and your husband without haste or clatter. The remaining casseroles, platters, and serving dishes, their warmers and all equipment and silver used in serving the supper, are also cleared away to the kitchen. Only the table decoration remains and the waiting coffee tray.

Dessert plates are brought in at this time, with serving silver for the dessert, freshly-made coffee for the coffee tray, and then dessert itself. You serve the dessert while your husband serves the coffee to everyone.

See the Index for various buffet and buffet tea parties in chapters throughout this book.

How to Give a Tea A tea is an afternoon party which can take on various degrees of formality. In its simplest form, it is a gathering of friends to drink tea, partake of light refreshments, and talk. In its more formal aspect, it is a reception for a visiting notable, the new club president, or some other important person. Also, a large tea is the kind of open-house hospitality well suited to various family occasions, such as a Sunday afternoon reception in honor of a son who has just been ordained in the priesthood or the ministry, or for a son or daughter who has completed study at a missionary school and is about to leave for foreign duty. Also a tea, because of its light menu and the daylight hours, is ideal for entertaining elderly members of the family. (See section on Birthdays in Chapter 1.)

For a young hostess a tea is one of the least complicated forms of entertaining, as well as the least expensive, for a large number of guests. The size of your living room and dining room and your supply of wares for the tea table determine the degree of formality and the atmosphere of the occasion. All details must be planned well in advance of the date, as for any other form of entertaining.

Invitations should go out about ten days before the party. A simple card is usually sent for a tea, such as your calling card, or a fold-over card or any card which has your name or monogram on it, or a card which has printed on it something such as, "An Invitation to Tea" or a little drawing of a steaming teapot.

If you use your calling card, simply write below your name:

Tea
Thursday, March 5th
3 to 5 o'clock

And if your address and telephone number are not on the card, add them. If you use fold-overs or other informals write the same kind of invitation, adding your name if it is not printed or engraved on the card.

Menu The customary menu for a tea includes plain bread and butter, the bread cut very thin and crusts left on; assorted small sandwiches; small hot canapés and cheese tartlets; pound cake cut in thick slices and then into narrow, long pieces easily picked up and eaten with the fingers; tiny cream puffs, miniature cupcakes, jam-filled cookies, petits fours. Fine-quality mints or other candies, and fresh salted almonds, pecans, or filberts, belong on the tea table with the two beverages, tea and coffee, and their accompaniments.

As for other parties, the tea menu must be planned, food shopped for, and the preparation done with exactness. Read your cookbook on how to make and serve tea, and on how to make tea sandwiches. One of the serious chores preceding a big tea is making the sandwiches. They should be made early on the day of the tea, which means that you or someone else must schedule morning time for the job.

They should be varied and delicious, with one or more sweet fillings, such as currant jelly with cream cheese, marmalade, or apple butter. Others of thin ham or chicken, cucumber, and water cress mixed with mayonnaise are favorites. Nut bread and other unusual breads should be used as well as paper-thin white bread. The fillings should be thin, and the round, square, triangular, and other small, shaped sandwiches should be just the right size to be picked up and eaten from the fingers. (They must be kept fresh until tea time. Place them on platters, cover securely with waxed paper, then with a wet towel, and place in refrigerator.) The number of sandwiches needed? Some hostesses count on a minimum of three for each guest invited, others four sandwiches each.

The sandwiches are such an important part of the tea repast, because of their variety, necessary freshness, different shapes, and unusual fillings, and to make them is so time-consuming that many experienced hostesses order them made outside the home by experts. In all cities as well as many smaller communities, there are catering services, food shops, restaurants, or other sources of good tea sandwiches. Even in small towns, there may be retired cooks or a butler who can be relied upon to help out at local parties, and who will make sandwiches and other foods in their own kitchen and deliver them on the day of the party.

Some such service may be available to you if you will make inquiry and should be considered, unless you have friends or relatives, or a skilled maid who can make the sandwiches for you in their own kitchen. This frees you to work on the remaining morning preparations for the party.

For correct and effective service of a large tea, you need at least one helper who stays in the kitchen, and two friends who will pour tea and coffee at the table at all times during the afternoon. If it is a very large tea, an experienced maid is needed to help remove used plates and cups. She should wear a fresh, trim, black uniform with small white apron.

As for any other party, you should schedule the morning of the party day to include a final light cleaning of the dining room, living room, and the bathroom for guests. You must clear a clothes closet or provide other space for guests' wraps. Caterers also rent suitable racks for this purpose, at little cost.

Arranging the Tea Table The size, style, and location of the tea table are of the greatest importance to the success of the party. If you have a dining room and the table is small, convert it into a side table for used dishes. Then create a larger table for tea: put two sturdy bridge tables together and cover them with a pad (bought from a housewares store) cut to fit them. The tablecloth for the doubled table must hang almost to the floor because the bridge table legs must be hidden.

You may prefer to rent a suitable table, with pad and damask cloth to go on it, from a caterer, or borrow a table from a club or church that gives teas. If you do not have a dining room, place the tea table in some strategic spot in the living room, such as at one end or in an alcove, where it will be of easy access from the kitchen and to the guests yet out of the stream of arriving and departing people. Ideally, there should be close at hand a sideboard or some kind of serving table, perhaps your small dining table, on which used cups will be placed. Otherwise guests must put their used cups down on the tea table, or hold them uncomfortably long before you or a maid can remove them to the kitchen. A small folding table, or tall butler's bar opened up and covered with a handsome tray, can also be used for this.

The tea table should be arranged during the morning of the party day—all silver, plates, napkins in place according to the diagram. If flowers and candles go on the table, place them where they look well and do not interfere with service.

The table must be large enough to accommodate a big tray at each end, one for tea and the other for coffee. Coffee cups in their saucers, with spoons, are placed on the table around the coffee tray, and tea cups around the tea tray. Small plates, folded tea napkins, and the foods are between, placed so that guests can easily help themselves. Exactness of placing, such as cup handles all in one direction and teaspoons all on the right side of cups in the saucers, add to the effective appearance of the table.

The table may be covered with white damask or a fine lace or embroidered linen cloth, although present-day hostesses use whatever attractive cloths they may own that go with their china and other wares on the table. A fine antique table may be left bare except for protective mats under the trays and any hot dishes. There are no chairs at the table except a chair at each end where the tea and coffee pourers sit.

The tea and coffee trays are not covered with tray cloths. The tea tray may hold a silver teakettle on small alcohol lamp or two teapots, one for tea and the other for boiling-hot water, a silver strainer, sugar bowl and tongs or spoon, small pitcher for milk, a small dish of thinly-sliced lemon and its tiny serving fork, and a china bowl matching the tea set, into which the dregs of cups are poured when guests come to the table for second helpings of tea.

The coffee tray holds a silver samovar or a coffeepot, a cream pitcher, sugar bowl and tongs or spoon. If you have handsome silver tea and coffee services, they add beauty and importance to the occasion. But charming English and American china and porcelain tea and coffee sets, antique porcelain services, or a fine Russian brass samovar for hot water on the tea tray as well as contemporary-design wares are used by many.

The tea and coffee sets should be in harmony with each other or, preferably, they should match. That is, if a modern coffee set on a modern brass tray is placed at one end of the table, the tea service at the other end should be in the same style. Thin china cups and saucers, delicate, attractive tea plates, and handsome embroidered or hem-stitched tea napkins, like fine silver, add elegance to this party, although interesting, highly successful teas are given in studios, modern houses, and many homes, with wares as varied as Kentucky mountain pottery, German and Scandinavian ceramics, and Japanese and Chinese tea services either in fine antique patterns or the austere new imports. What to use must be your decision, based on what is in your supplies. But you must be guided in where you place the wares on the table by the traditional layout for easy service.

The "correct" darkened, candle-lighted room for a big tea is not popular with younger hostesses, especially when the tea is given in some such setting as a room in a high penthouse apartment with a magnificent view, or in a mountain or country house, a suburban home facing a colorful garden, or a college campus residence with a glimpse of lake and wooded areas. These hostesses consider that tea is the thing, in a pleasant room with a chance to sit and talk with people you haven't seen for a long time.

Tea Service It is customary to ask two friends to serve at the tea and coffee trays for the first hour, and two others to replace them for the last hour. The guest hostess at the tea tray may make the tea, using boiling water from the tray kettle or from a pot of boiling-hot water just brought in to the tray from the kitchen. For this she uses your favorite blend of tea but never one of the flower-scented varieties. A supply should be in a covered caddy on the tray, because she will make fresh pots of tea several times during the afternoon. If this is too complicated for her, the teapot can be freshly filled in the kitchen and replaced on her tray as needed.

As guests arrive they are greeted by you and shown where to leave wraps. First comers chat with you and then go to either tray and are served according to the way they like their beverage—tea with lemon, tea with milk, coffee black or with cream. They place their cup and saucer on a tea plate, pick up a napkin, help themselves to sandwiches and other foods, and stand about talking or find a place to sit.

As more guests arrive you make introductions and see that all go to the table and are served. You suggest second cups to any guests with empty cups. You also see that the table is kept replenished. For this the kitchen helper is essential. She keeps kettles of freshly drawn water boiling ready for the tea tray, she is constantly ready with freshly made coffee for the coffee tray. She can refill milk, cream, and sugar containers. She removes wrapped sandwiches from the refrigerator and refills table platters.

Your guest hostess at the coffee tray gives the empty coffeepot to the maid or helper, and she brings it in refilled. You and a guest helper also may carry off used tea cups, plates, or spoons which guests have put down on the serving table or sideboard. But if the kitchen helper is wearing a maid's uniform, it is preferable that she come into the dining room or living room from time to time to clear away used dishes and make refills at the beverage trays. If you have a dining-room maid for the occasion, she, of course, does all such clearing away.

As early comers finish their tea and their visit with you and friends, they leave after you have had a final brief chat with them, thanked them for coming, and if possible seen them to the door. Late arrivals must not find a depleted tea table, but fresh platters of sandwiches and cake, and steaming coffee and teapots.

Much of the smoothness, gaiety, and pleasure of the afternoon not only depend on your early, careful planning and the good quality of the foods and beverages, but on the co-operation between you and your guest hostesses. They may be a sister and an in-law, an old friend and a new one, but they can be of the greatest help to you, especially if they are familiar with tea parties. As a young hostess you need such help at your first big tea, and you should not be shy in asking more experienced friends to help you launch your first party.

Tea Reception or Open House If you plan a large tea, reception, or open house to help introduce a new teacher, or garden-club speaker, or some other notable, then the invitation should say so. Use fold-over cards which have your name on the cover, or an informal card with your name and address at the top of the card. And write:

Tea
Thursday, March 5th
To Meet
Mrs. George Brown, Garden Club President
3 to 5 o'clock

21 Pine Tree Drive   R.S.V.P.

It is customary at this sort of presentation tea to have a small receiving line just inside the living-room entrance. It consists of the guest of honor and perhaps a club officer or some other important guest next to her to make introductions. If there is a maid or someone else to open the door and show guests where to leave wraps, the hostess also stands in the receiving line and makes the introductions.

As soon as a guest is introduced to the guest of honor and speaks a few words to her or him, and to others in the receiving line, the guest passes along out of the way and goes to the tea table and is served. Then with cup and saucer, napkin, and tea plate in hand, she joins a group of friends who have preceded her.

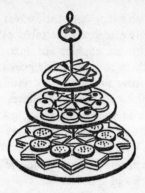

The menu for this reception is the same as for a large tea, except that for men guests there are such additions as hot appetizers, tiny hot biscuits, heartier sandwiches, and often a bigger dessert, such as ice cream molds or fruit with cake. If you plan to add a hot dish, such as a chafing dish of creamed seafood or chicken, and a salad, this tea becomes a Buffet or High Tea, and as such should be served from 4:30 to 6 o'clock instead of 3 to 5 o'clock, which is noted on the invitation with the words High Tea.

Use same cards as for other teas:

High Tea
Sunday Afternoon, March 5th
4:30 to 6 o'clock
For Our Son, Father James Walsh
Mr. and Mrs. J. R. Walsh
21 Pine Tree Drive   R.S.V.P.

See the Index for other tea and buffet receptions in various chapters of this book.

Tea for a Few Friends If you have telephoned three or four friends to come in for a cup of tea, you do not need the formalities of a large tea table. You may want to serve them seated around the dining-room table, which for the occasion is covered with a pretty tea cloth. Your tea tray, which you made ready in the kitchen, is placed at the head of the table. You sit down and pour tea at the tray, pass the filled cups and saucers to guests and they help themselves to sandwiches, cake, cookies and whatever is placed on the table within easy reach.

Tea plates and folded tea napkins are near one guest, who helps you serve by passing these along to other guests. A small centerpiece of fresh flowers, or a rose floating in a crystal bowl of water, adds that pleasant touch which only flowers can give.

If you serve this tea in your living room, set up a bridge table or use any table large enough to hold the tea tray and necessary accessories. Cover the table with a pretty tea cloth. Place the prepared tray at one side, from which you serve. Provide folded tea napkins, tea plates, cups and saucers and spoons.

When your guests have arrived, bring in a pot of freshly made tea and another of boiling-hot water. Return to the kitchen for a plate of sandwiches, and another of hot canapés, such as tiny puffs filled with hot creamed crab meat, or a plate of hot cinnamon toast. If you have a tea cart, use it to bring everything in at one time. Place it near the tea table and serve from it and the table.

Your guests sit around the table, you pour tea for everyone giving each guest what she wants as to sugar, milk, lemon. Then place the cup and saucer with its spoon on a tea plate and hand it with napkin to the guest. They help themselves to the sandwiches and canapés. Later, when you go to the kitchen to refill the pot, you bring in a plate of frosted cookies, petits fours, or pound cake to cut and serve at the table.

As with a large tea, it is important to have a ready supply of boiling water in the kitchen, and some reserves of sandwiches waiting in the refrigerator for any extra guests, or drop-in husbands who come by to pick up their wives. Good candy, salted nuts, or candied peel are welcome additions to this table.

A Bridge Tea A bridge tea means that friends are invited to play bridge early in the afternoon, and refreshments are served afterwards. For a small group, simple tea foods, such as sandwiches, tea or coffee, and a dessert, such as sherbet or fruit compote or a meringue with a good sauce, are served onto individual, small decorative trays in the kitchen, and then carried in to each guest at the bridge tables.

The hostess may prepare her dining room ahead of time, setting the table for tea to be served either buffet or with her guests seated around the table. If she has arranged the table for buffet service, her guests help themselves as at any tea and go back to the bridge tables to enjoy their repast and talk.

Since it is awkward to cover the bridge tables with tea cloths while guests are moving about the room, the tables are usually left bare. Hence the popularity of the individual tray service for the buffet tea as well as for refreshments served from the kitchen. Such trays can be made ready ahead of time, with napkin and silver on each, and placed near the buffet tea table on a serving table or sideboard. Each guest picks up a tray, is given tea or coffee, and serves herself to whatever is on the tea table.

What to serve after an afternoon of bridge varies according to custom in the community. Some guests enjoy an elaborate tea, such as pastry shell filled with creamed mushrooms and turkey or chicken, or waffles hot from the kitchen, which means there must be a kitchen helper or maid, served with a sweet sauce, such as brown sugar or caramel. Some hostesses offer a superb buffet menu or high tea after a large bridge party. This includes salads, an aspic of sliced turkey or ham, a hot cheese pudding or soufflé (if there is sufficient kitchen help), sandwiches, and sherbet or fruit compote, with cake, petits fours, and the coffee or tea.

This lavishness is not popular with young hostesses, because they can't afford such menus and because they and their friends are usually on slimming diets. The trend among them is to serve hot or iced tea and coffee, really good small sandwiches, and a choice of desserts, including sherbet with cookies, small fruit tarts or apple turnovers, or something as simple as macaroons or other bake shop cookies. (See also "How to Give a Luncheon," Chapter 15.)

16

HOW TO GIVE A FOREIGN DINNER

There are two ways to give a foreign dinner. The easiest is to prepare a menu and several dishes of the country in which you are interested and serve it to your guests as you serve any other dinner, on your best china, linen, and silver.

The other way is to use wares and decorations of the country that inspired the dinner, and prepare the foods and serve them as nearly possible as they are cooked and served in their native country. This calls for more imagination in the planning, more budget, and perhaps a good bit of research and shopping for ideas, accessories, and decorations. But the results are worth this trouble. Your dinner can be unique, taste good, and provide an evening's fun and conversation for friends and family.

Your local foreign food shops, gift shops, and other stores may have what you need for such a dinner. Also visit foreign restaurants for ideas and recipes. You may want to have a restaurant prepare dishes for your party and perhaps send a waiter to serve them in native style. At a foreign dinner your guests should sit down not only to good food interestingly different from their usual home meals, but the setting and atmosphere, by its color and authenticity, should give them an evening's visit to another land.

In cities where there are many shops and restaurants of other countries, the planning, shopping, and decoration for foreign dinners is

Also see Costume Parties, Folk Dancing, in the Index

easy. But wherever you live, foreign foods and accessories can be ordered by mail from advertisements in magazines. Book stores carry, or can order, books on foreign cookery. A cookbook of the country you are interested in should be studied and the dishes for your proposed dinner prepared once or twice before the party.

The traditional foods and cookery of most countries vary from province to province within the country. With changed living conditions brought on by war and other influences, long established food habits are being modified, old customs are disappearing, and new ones begin to alter the way of life of people of all classes. The dinners described here as samples for your foreign parties are typical for comfortably well-to-do families living in "good times." The extremes—meals of poorest laborers, banquets given by rich landowner families—are something else again. Both may show up in the research you do in cookbooks of the countries which interest you.

Chinese Dinner Chinese food has been popular in America for so many years that many hostesses are familiar with enough Chinese dishes to make a delectable home dinner without further research. Using any one of the many American books on Chinese cookery, you can try out one or two less familiar recipes, add it to your established favorites, and produce a delicious Chinese feast in your home.

Menu Your first Chinese dinner might be very simple, one easily put together with the excellent quick-frozen, cooked dishes prepared by Chinese food companies in America and distributed widely to markets and grocery stores. These include Cantonese-style, quick-frozen dinners in one package, and also egg foo yung, fruit rolls, chicken or shrimp chow mein, beef chop suey, sweet-and-sour pork, egg rolls, fried rice, and various other favorites. This menu might begin with hot egg rolls served as appetizer, followed by chicken chow mein as the main dish, with hot rice. Add preserved fruits and fortune cookies to the menu and serve hot tea throughout the dinner.

Another easy Chinese menu that makes use of quick-frozen foods might begin with hot fruit rolls served as appetizers, followed by egg foo yung, sweet-and-sour pork, with hot (mustard) and sweet (plum) sauces. These are sold under Chinese labels in many stores. Of course, hot rice and tea are served throughout the meal. Add a few chopped scallion tops or chives to the egg foo yung gravy. Serve ice cream with chopped candied ginger on it for dessert. If quick-frozen Chinese dishes are not available for this type of simple but delicious dinner, see the recipes at the end of this section.

For That Chinese Atmosphere If you want to give a more atmospheric and authentic Chinese dinner, adapt the following suggestions. Chinese hosts prefer a round table. Each place setting consists of a medium-size plate with small covered soup bowl on it, a small bowl for rice nearby, a porcelain spoon, a pair of chopsticks, and a small round cup without handles for tea. Host and hostess sit together in the seats nearest the kitchen door. The guest of honor and his wife sit directly opposite, and other guests are seated according to their importance around the table from the guests of honor toward the host and hostess.

Chinese etiquette calls for the host to disparage or belittle his food and his cookery. He must apologize for the dishes served, their inferior quality, their too-few numbers as unfit for such notable guests. It is up to the guests to disprove these libelous statements by praising all the virtues of the food and eating extensively through dish after dish until they have partaken of all on the table.

Informal and Formal Dinners At an informal dinner, when guests come to the table, hot soup is at each place in the covered bowl on the small plates. Each guest removes the cover of his soup bowl, drinks his soup with his porcelain spoon, and replaces the cover on the soup bowl. Bowl, cover, and spoon as well as the small plate under them are taken to the kitchen. Immediately from four to eight heaping platters of hot food are placed in the center of the table, with a large pot of hot tea and a large, covered dish of hot rice. When the host opens the rice bowl by lifting its lid, it is an indication that he is ready to serve the meal.

Dishes are not passed at a Chinese dinner. The first helping is served to the guests by host or hostess. Afterwards all help themselves, or gentlemen (presumably with the longest reach) serve the plates of the ladies sitting next to them. Hot tea is poured into small cups throughout the meal. No sugar, cream, or anything else is added to the tea.

A formal dinner may include, besides rice and tea, as many as thirty-two dishes. These include four varieties of fruits, such as canned or fresh plums, grapes, pineapple, four dishes of nuts, melon seeds, and lichi nuts, and four of various sweet-sour pickles, also small dishes of thin strips of cooked chicken, giblets, ham, hard-cooked eggs. The eight "large" dishes in such a dinner include those strange luxuries former travelers to the Far East used to describe such as shark's fin, bird's nest soup, and steaming duck.

The others are such favorites as the intricate, difficult-to-make transparent dumplings filled with finely minced chicken or other stuffings, many kinds of filled rolls of paper-thin pastry made of rice and potato flour, scrambled eggs with vegetables, omelets of many varieties, stuffed fish baked or fried, Chinese mushrooms cooked with peas, braised abalone, fried shrimp, lobster in various dishes, and chicken in several of the fifty to sixty traditional recipes the Chinese prepare with this fowl.

At both formal and informal Chinese dinners, as a guest finds himself unable to eat any more he puts his chopsticks together, and gesturing with them to the other guests that he is through eating, urges them to continue feasting and to take their time, enjoy their meal, and "don't stop because I've stopped."

If you plan to attempt a dinner with true Chinese atmosphere, decide on your menu, try out the recipes once or twice on the family before the guest dinner, and begin to collect Chinese wares for your table.

Invitations Having decided on date, menu, and guests, the invitations should go out. In card and stationery shops there are many party fold-overs decorated with small Chinese designs. Or, buy sheets of richly decorated Chinese paper, cut into strips, and write the invitations on the undecorated side. Fold, and mail in envelopes decorated with Chinese lettering or other design. You can, of course, invite your guests by telephone.

Decoration and Accessories These are available in many shops and by mail and include Cantonese porcelain tablewares and colorful lacquer bowls, boxes, and other dishes; they are relatively inexpensive. Plates, bowls with covers, serving dishes for various foods, rice bowls with covers, handleless cups, teapots in traditional Chinese designs or in the newest solid white porcelains as well as many small dishes are in such displays.

Low-cost split wood chopsticks in cellophane or paper wrappers add to the fun at your dinner and should be included in your purchases for the table—see chopstick instruction in the section following, on a Japanese Dinner. For guests who can't use chopsticks, provide bamboo-handled forks. Knives are seldom needed at a Chinese dinner.

The table is more dramatically oriental if left bare. If you want to cover it use split bamboo, reed, or straw mats and simple white or solid-color linen napkins. (In a Chinese home, servants pass steaming hot towels, folded into small squares, to guests after the finger foods of the first course.)

When buying covered bowls for soup, also buy matching porcelain spoons to go with them. To light the room ask at the same shops for Chinese lanterns. See the source list for Japanese dinner, to order lanterns, or write Quong Mee Yuen, 16 Pell St., New York 13, New York. You can also use Chinese candlesticks of pewter, ceramics, carved wood, or whatever you find in Chinese shops.

A large pewter or ceramic fish or duck makes a handsome centerpiece for the table either with cover left off, the lower half filled with water and one or two flowers floated in it, or left empty except for fortune cookies and kept covered until the end of the meal. If these cookies are not available in local shops, write Lotus Co., 436 Pacific Avenue, Department G 1, San Francisco 11, California, for prices on fortune, almond, and sesame cookies, and leaflet on tablewares.

After Dinner Chinese checkers is a good game for this crowd. Or, entertaining Chinese films are available: The Asia Society, 18 East Fiftieth Street, New York 22, New York, publishes a comprehensive list of films of various aspects of Asian life, for low-cost rental. Write to this Society for the list which includes several on China, such as *Understanding the Chinese* (rental $4.00 a day for 2 days) color, 10 minutes, obtainable from Audio-Visual Department, World Affairs Center for U.S., at U. N. Plaza, Forty-seventh Street and First Avenue, New York 17, New York. Also *Peiping Family* ($4.00 a day) black and white, 21 minutes, from American Museum of Natural History Film Library, Central Park West at Seventy-ninth Street, New York

24, New York. Also *Sampan Family* ($4.00 a day) black and white, 16 minutes, from the same source, and also from the Audio-Visual Center, Indiana University, Bloomington, Indiana.

Recipes for Simple Chinese Dinner

If you do not use quick-frozen Chinese dishes and make up your own menu, here is one easily prepared: barbecued spareribs and butterfly shrimp as appetizers, chicken chow mein, rice, preserved fruits, fortune cookies, hot tea served throughout the meal.

BARBECUED SPARERIBS

3 pounds pork spareribs	1½ teaspoons salt
1½ cups soy sauce	2 tablespoons honey
1 clove garlic, peeled and crushed	1 tablespoon cooking sherry (optional)

Wash ribs, remove gristle, dry on towel, cut in pieces of 2 or 3 ribs each. Combine remaining ingredients in a large bowl and mix well. Place ribs in bowl; let marinate in sauce 15 minutes or a little longer. Drain; broil under moderate heat until well cooked through and browned on both sides. Serve 2 or 3 small pieces hot, as appetizer on plate with 1 or 2 butterfly shrimp. This recipe makes 8 servings.

BUTTERFLY SHRIMP AS APPETIZER

1½ pounds jumbo shrimp	½ teaspoon pepper
2 eggs	Deep hot vegetable oil for
3 tablespoons flour	frying, with drop of
½ teaspoon salt	sesame oil added

Shell shrimp but leave tail on. De-vein and wash shrimp, then split along back, but do not cut all the way through. Dry on towel. Beat eggs, flour, salt, and pepper together in mixing bowl until they make a smooth batter. Dip shrimp in one at a time and coat completely. Remove with chopsticks or fork and drop into hot oil, at 300° to 350°F. Fry until golden brown. Serve 1 or 2 very hot, with appetizer spareribs. This recipe makes 8 or more servings.

CHICKEN CHOW MEIN

4 tablespoons soy sauce
2½ tablespoons cornstarch
¼ cup water
¼ cup vegetable oil
Salt and pepper
2 cups sliced Chinese celery
  cabbage
2 cups (drained) canned
  bean sprouts or shredded
  raw string beans
3 cups shredded celery

2 cups shredded onion
1 teaspoon sugar
2 cups chicken stock or
  bouillon
2 cups finely shredded
  cooked chicken
4 cups (canned) fried
  Chinese noodles, reheated
  in oven
2 hard-cooked eggs, cut in
  strips

Mix soy sauce, cornstarch and water, and set aside. Heat oil, about ½ teaspoon salt, and a dash of pepper in 3-quart deep (metal-base) casserole or in a large, deep skillet. Add all vegetables, sugar, and bouillon, and mix well. Cover and cook for 10 minutes. Add starch mixture and chicken. Stir and cook until sauce thickens and boils 2 or 3 minutes—it should look clear. Place crisped, hot noodles on large deep Chinese platter, or individual plates. Serve chow mein on top of noodles. Add garnish of egg. This recipe makes 4 to 6 servings.

Japanese Dinner Japanese cookery is no longer a novelty in many parts of America, because importers of Japanese foods, furnishings, decorations, and accessories are doing a brisk business in many communities. Japanese-inspired architecture in homes and public buildings, and Japanese theatre, art shows, and movies have become familiar in the larger cities. There is a Japanese department store on New York's Fifth Avenue and there are handsome new Japanese restaurants in New York and elsewhere. These as well as excellent small, less well-known restaurants in many communities have helped to popularize Japanese foods in America. The few favorite dishes are easily prepared and Japanese atmosphere is not too difficult to achieve at your table. Its informality and the delicious food provide fun and good eating for you and your guests.

Preparation In Japan, dinner guests kneel-sit on cushions on the floor and eat from individual small, square tables on low legs placed in front of them. For your Japanese party the table around which you place your guests also should be low. One or two large square or round coffee tables are just right for this. The table is left bare and the authentic Nippon atmosphere is heightened if it is of red or black lacquer. Your guests will be more comfortable if they sit on plump cushions or on low wicker stools or pads around the table.

In Japanese homes each diner has a tray of red or black lacquer placed before him on his individual low table. On the tray in traditional position are various dishes as the meal progresses. When you give your Japanese dinner, formal order in arranging all dishes is necessary if you want your table to look oriental. Only essential dishes and utensils are present. There are no table decorations. Hot, steamed napkins are passed on a lacquer tray before eating.

All necessary wares are easily found today in dime stores and many Japanese import shops—unadorned white, black, or brown teapots and handleless cups, others in bold orange, yellow, or red, and many decorated with traditional flower and fruit designs. You need, besides teapot and cups, plates, covered soup bowls or cups, covered rice bowls, a large covered lacquer rice box and paddle (this is a flat wooden spoon for rice), and small dishes for pickled vegetables.

Japanese lacquer baskets and trays, lanterns, and other decorations are available from the same shops which sell tableware, such as the Jasmine Shops listed in the Index, and the grocery store, Katagiri and Co., Inc., 224 East Fifty-ninth Street, New York 22, New York. If your budget permits, the same shops can supply short, light, cotton kimono-style jackets in blue or black, with bold red, black, and white designs on the back, for guests to wear at dinner and keep as favors.

Invitations When your dinner is planned, the date set, and the shopping for wares almost completed, send out your invitations. Look for miniature Japanese fans in dime stores, toy stores, and oriental shops. Write invitations to dinner across these little fans, then slip them into suitable envelopes for mailing. Invitation note papers decorated with Japanese doll, landscape, or other detail are in stationery shops. Or you can telephone the invitation.

Set your table with individual trays, each holding the first course, or use straw or split bamboo mats before each guest. On each tray or mat are five items with which a Japanese dinner begins: a small decorative dish holding two or three pieces of pickled radish, cauliflower, or other vegetables, a small covered bowl of hot rice, small covered bowl of clear hot soup, porcelain spoon (out of deference to Western diners), and cedar-wood or bamboo chopsticks. (This type of chopstick is thrown away after each dinner. In Japanese and Chinese families each member has bone, ivory, or lacquered bamboo chopsticks, which are washed after every meal and used again.)

Menus for dinner in Japanese homes are simple. The soup course (described) is followed by a fried fish or meat dish or both, with rice and grated radish and more pickled vegetables. Hot tea is served throughout the meal. Sometimes sweet cookies are served at the end. The total amount served, by American standards, is a light meal even when the Japanese chef adds specialities such as skewer-cooked, small, whole fish, chicken cooked with vegetables, shrimp, and a special holiday or regional festival dish to the menu. A great deal of trouble is taken by Japanese cooks to make the dishes look attractive, using time-honored methods to cut vegetables and other foods in fanciful flower shapes and combining them in eye-catching arrangements.

At a Japanese dinner the lid of a bowl containing hot food may be difficult to remove because of the steam, and a Japanese guest holds the bowl firmly by one hand and removes the lid, placing lid upside down on the table. If he eats rice with chopsticks, he holds the rice bowl in the palm of his left hand, and eats with chopsticks held in right hand. Lids are replaced on the little bowls when these first foods have been eaten, and the dishes are removed to the kitchen.

To follow the first course, you may serve tempura (delicious hot shrimp and vegetables) and you probably will want to serve the Japanese meat dish that is such a favorite with Westerners. This is sukiyaki, now so popular in this country that a number of imported and American-made special cookery devices for it have been put on the market, so the dish may be cooked as the Japanese do it, at the table or on a tray nearby. You can also use an electric skillet, or a chafing dish pan on an electric grill on the table.

The host or hostess begins to cook the sukiyaki while guests are drinking their soup. When the soup-course dishes are removed, plates are brought in for guests and a covered lacquer box of hot rice and its paddle. The sukiyaki continues to cook, and if tempura is included in the menu these tidbits are brought in, very hot, to be eaten while guests keep an eye on the sukiyaki cook and his skillet. Of course hot tea continually refills the small cups around the table.

Condiments, such as soy sauce and plum sauce, in small Japanese ceramic bottles or pots are placed on the table. The host opens the covered rice box, serves each plate with a mound of hot rice, then serves the sukiyaki onto the plates. He uses chopsticks, selecting hot meat and vegetables with care and placing them quickly and effectively on the rice. Guests help themselves to soy sauce and plum sauce if they like these on meat and vegetables.

When this main course is finished, sweet cookies and ice cream may be served, as a concession to American appetites. The Japanese serve flower-and-fruit-flavored jellies in hollowed out orange or tangerine shells, when there are young girls at the table. Fresh strawberries are a wonderful and frequent Japanese dessert.

Using Chopsticks Before going on to the recipes, here is chopstick information from the Japan Tourist Association. To use chopsticks, place a stick in crotch of thumb. Hold stick in place with bent tip of third finger. Place second stick between tip of thumb and side of index finger, with index finger resting a bit on the top side of the stick. Move second stick by moving index finger up and down. Don't move first stick. Adjust sticks and practice until you can make lower tips come together easily. Pick up cluster of rice or small morsels of sukiyaki between lower tips of sticks and convey to mouth.

After-Dinner Entertainment If you plan ahead of time, you can show Japanese movies. Some are free loan, such as one called *Japan,* color, 26 minutes, Ideal Pictures, Inc., 233 West Forty-second Street, New York 36, New York. Or, the charming, *So Small My Island,* color, 29 minutes, also free loan (but $2.50 shipping fee) from Ideal Pictures, Inc., 58 East South Water Street, Chicago 1, Illinois. Or, others on the Japanese family and arts, and dramatic moving pictures made by Japanese film companies. Write to Ideal Pictures, Inc., for all information.

Recipes for Japanese Dinner

CLEAR SOUP

Season any good chicken bouillon, strained clear, or vegetable broth with a little powdered ginger. To the vegetable broth add a little dashi (dried concentrated fish broth), or celery salt and a little soy or shoyu sauce. Place thin slices of raw leek or lightly-cooked mushroom in each bowl. Or cook thin strips of cucumber a few minutes in the hot bouillon, then remove the cucumber and place in soup bowls. Pour seasoned hot bouillon over the vegetable. Each serving should be from ¾ to 1 cup.

SUKIYAKI

For an outdoor dinner or supper, sukiyaki makes a dramatic show-off dish for a host who likes to cook on the terrace. The oriental saucepan or skillet placed on a hibachi or any small grill is the center of interest. On a nearby table in a handsome lacquered tray lined with fresh grape leaves are the ingredients of the dish, ready to be added to the cooking pan as needed. Reed and wicker tables, chairs, trays, pads and stools, red and black lacquer dishes, boxes, trays and covered bowls add to the oriental atmosphere.

For any sukiyaki dinner, indoors or out, here are Japanese instructions for four persons: Prepare a table big enough for a skillet or pan on electric or other heat in center of table or beside it. Use a wide, heavy skillet or pan; place the platter or tray of prepared foods near host, with sauce at hand and five pairs of chopsticks on table. Cook uses one pair for lifting foods from platter to skillet and for turning foods as they cook, or to add new ingredients to the cooking pan for second helpings. Guests use chopsticks to reach into skillet, helping themselves to meat and vegetables as soon as they are cooked.

Ready on the table is the covered lacquer box or basket full of hot rice. Pickled vegetables also should accompany this dish. These are usually lengths of broccoli, long, broad slices of carrot and radish, and pieces of cauliflower cooked to the par-boiled stage in seasoned vinegar; they should be crisp.

FOR THE SKILLET

1 large piece beef suet

1 pound beef tenderloin, sliced paper-thin across grain

2 tablespoons sugar

½ cup soy sauce

½ cup beef stock or bouillon

½ cup cooking sherry (optional)

4 scallions, cut slanting in 2-inch lengths

1 cup celery cut slanting in thin slices

½ cup thinly sliced fresh mushrooms

5-oz. can (⅔ cup) water chestnuts, drained and thinly sliced

5-oz. can bamboo shoots, drained and cut in slivers or diced

5 cups small raw spinach leaves, stems removed

1-lb. can (2 cups) bean sprouts drained

Let meat stand at room temperature about 20 minutes before cooking. Combine sugar, soy sauce, and beef stock; mix well and pour into Japanese ceramic bottle or bowl with handle. Have all vegetables chilled; arrange in symmetrical rows in lacquer tray or basket lined with fresh grape leaves, leaving room for beef. Cover tray closely with foil or waxed paper and keep in refrigerator until party time. Then arrange sliced beef in the tray and place beside the table, with the bottle of soy and bouillon mixture.

Heat large electric skillet at 360°F., or follow directions for heating whatever cookery device you are using. Rub skillet or pan with suet and let suet stay in pan until about 2 tablespoons of melted fat have accumulated; remove suet and discard it. Add beef and cook briskly about 2 minutes, turning it over and over with chopsticks to cook evenly. When just browned, pour soy mixture over beef, push meat to one side, let soy mixture come to boiling. Turn skillet heat to Low (220°F.). Add vegetables in separate groups—scallions, celery, mushrooms. Continue cooking about 3 or 4 minutes, and stir each group of vegetables without mixing all together; push contents to one side, add remaining vegetables in separate mounds. Cook 3 or 4 minutes and stir each vegetable until hot and lightly cooked.

Vegetables should be crisply tender, not mushy. Host serves guests

plates with hot rice, then with sukiyaki over rice. Or guests help themselves to sukiyaki from the skillet onto rice on their plates and usually
add a dash of soy sauce to their hot food. This recipe makes 4 servings.

For a party of eight, prepare 2 tables for 4 guests each, 2 trays of
raw foods, 2 skillets or cooking pans and let your husband or a guest
take charge of one pan. Adds fun to the dinner if guests take turns
adding ingredients to the sukiyaki skillet and then serve other guests
as well as their own plate.

TEMPURA

At some Japanese dinners, after the soup, shrimp and vegetables
dipped in batter and deep-fried are served snapping hot, while the
sukiyaki finishes cooking. Called tempura, these delicacies have become as popular with Americans as the sukiyaki main dish.

BATTER

1 egg	1 cup sifted all-purpose
1 cup ice water	flour

Beat egg, mix with water smoothly. Sift flour into egg mixture
stirring gently. Do not beat briskly or whip. Cover bowl, chill 20
minutes in refrigerator.

Oil: Some Japanese cooks use a mixture of vegetable oil, such as
peanut and olive, with a drop or two of sesame oil added. Pour about
2 inches of oil into a deep-fat fryer or heavy kettle. Heat to 300°–
350°F. and keep temperature at this level during cooking; use a frying thermometer, with its tip in the oil.

Have foods ready, such as shelled, de-veined whole shrimp with the
tails left on, scallops, small chunks of boneless white fish, pieces of
cooked breast of chicken, slices of uncooked broccoli stem and leaves,
strips of green pepper, very thin slices of large radish or carrot.

Dip pieces lightly in batter, place 2 or 3 at a time in boiling oil. When
light golden brown, remove with chopsticks or fork, drain on thick
paper toweling a few seconds, and serve at once to guests. Continue
frying a few pieces at a time until all guests have been served with a
selection of 2 or 3 pieces each.

If your husband is cooking sukiyaki at the table, and you attend to the tempura in the kitchen, a guest is pressed into service who hurries the hot pieces in to the festive table. Japanese hosts serve fresh-grated horse-radish or soy sauce with these hot delicacies.

Mexican Dinner For a Mexican dinner, the favorite foreign dinner of hundreds of Americans, there are many canned food specialities from this below-the-border country in local food shops and grocery stores. These include tortillas, packaged enchilada dinners, sauces, and a tacos dinner as well as other ready-to-heat-and-serve native dishes. If these are not in your local grocery stores, write to Foods of Mexico, Ashleys, Inc., Station A, El Paso, Texas, for price lists and order blanks.

Invitations can be written on Mexican postcards (but mailed in envelopes) or on folders or children's stationery decorated with Mexican donkeys, flowers, angels, and Mexican children. In some shops cards with reproductions of modern Mexican paintings are available. They make refreshingly different invitation cards, and like other postcards should be mailed in suitable envelopes.

Decorations To serve this type of easily prepared Mexican dinner, or a party with more atmosphere, you will find native decorative and tablewares in great variety in many American shops. Pottery plates, the colorful heavy glassware, giant pottery bowls to hold glowing displays of the fruits so popular in Mexico, boldly woven and dyed tablecloths and napkins, even Mexican furniture and rugs to transform terrace, playroom, or dining room are in many stores. Bright, intricately designed tin candlesticks, animals, birds and other decorations; ceramic angels, birds and fruits; gaudy paper flowers, cutouts, and ornaments; boldly colored baskets, trays, and mats are included in these displays.

Mexican cotton skirts, shirts, slippers, big straw hats, Indian blouses, and other costume essentials are also available, if your party budget permits you to include such items on your shopping list. They make much appreciated guest favors, and everybody dresses Mexican as soon as he arrives. If your local shops cannot supply you write to Fred Leighton, Mexican Imports, 15 East Eighth Street, New York 3, New York, for price lists.

Arranging the Table A Mexican dinner, because of its informality, gaiety and the brilliantly colored accessories, lends itself to patio and terrace serving. Indoors or out, if you want it to look Mexican, use a bare table with a bright pink, orange, or green hand-woven runner thrown across it, and place settings for your guests composed of Mexican pottery plates, glassware, cutlery with raffia-wrapped handles and solid-color linen or cotton napkins. The table may also be arranged for buffet service with plates, cups and saucers, and all else needed.

For either service, make a flamboyant background of flowers, foliage, and fruit, a large display perhaps along a stone wall or against a trellis of the terrace or against the dining-room wall, of pottery bowls or baskets, wooden trays, lacquered basket trays, all filled with carefully arranged showy fruits, as many tropical varieties as your shops can supply, and clusters of ripe red and yellow bananas, peaches, plums, oranges, tangerines, persimmons, lemons, limes, a cantaloupe or two, a watermelon or casaba cut in half, and the fruit scooped out with a ball cutter, the shell refilled with melon balls and ripe berries or other small fruits. Guests serve themselves fruit cup from the melon, as an appetizer before the first hot course is ready.

Menu Many Mexican dinners begin with a soup, followed by a "dry soup," which is rice or vernicelli cooked in bouillon until all the liquid is absorbed. This is like the pilaf of Near Eastern meals. Some form of tortilla is served next, or with the "dry soup," and then a bean dish. Sometimes there is a green salad. And this is followed by a sweet dessert, perhaps one made of bananas, or a custard with caramel or other sweet sauce. Coffee, very black and hot, made in a drip pot is served into cups containing a little hot milk.

Here is such a menu: sopa de papa (potato soup), sopa seca de arroz con jamón (dry rice soup with ham), quesadilla (tortillas stuffed with cheese), garbanzos con tomate (chick-peas with tomatoes), ensalada de ejotes (string bean salad), fresh fruits from the buffet, and Mexican coffee. Nougat or other candies and small besos (meringues) should be placed on the table in colorful arrangements in tall pottery epergnes or other decorative holders.

Recipes for Mexican Dinner

For most American appetites, the above menu seems too large and too heavy. But with kitchen help, or some of the dishes prepared ahead to be reheated at dinnertime, the whole menu is not difficult to prepare and serve and is not elaborate by Mexican standards. Omit the salad and some of the desserts if necessary, or omit the dry soup although it makes a pleasant, starchy balance to some of the richer dishes.

SOPA DE PAPA
(Potato Soup)

3 large potatoes	¼ cup tomato sauce or
¼ cup vegetable oil	sieved, canned tomatoes
½ cup thinly sliced celery	2 quarts beef bouillon
1 small onion, peeled and	(canned)
finely chopped	Salt if necessary

Pare and slice potatoes thinly. Heat oil in soup kettle, add potatoes with celery and onion and cook for 5 minutes or until hot and oil-coated. Add tomato sauce and bouillon. Cover and cook over moderate heat until boiling. Reduce heat to simmer and cook until potatoes are tender. Taste, and add salt if needed. This recipe makes 6 or more servings.

If the soup is made early in the day, skim and reheat it at dinnertime in a large soup casserole. Serve in the casserole on buffet, into individual Mexican pottery bowls.

SOPA SECA DE ARROZ
(Dry Rice "soup")

½ clove garlic, peeled	1 pound baked or boiled ham
½ cup vegetable oil	cut in thin slivers
1 cup rice	2¼ cups boiling water
1 small onion, peeled and	½ teaspoon salt
minced	½ teaspoon pepper
3 tablespoons tomato sauce	
or sieved, canned toma-	
toes	

Brown garlic in hot oil in 2½-quart, flame-proof (metal-base) casserole; remove garlic and discard it. Stir rice into hot oil and cook until lightly browned. Add onion, tomato sauce, and ham; stir and mix. Stir boiling water into mixture, season, and cover tightly. Cook over moderate to low heat for 30 minutes. Do not stir. Let liquid cook away. This recipe makes 6 servings.

Serve from casserole onto plates with tortillas. This with tortilla represents bread in the menu. But you may want to serve crusty French or Italian bread with the salad or garbanzos.

QUESADILLA
(Tortillas stuffed with Cheese)

This is a recipe to be cooked on the buffet table or near it in an electric skillet or chafing dish and served hot from the pan to the guests.

12 tortillas (canned, or bought in Mexican store)	12 tablespoons Monterey cream cheese or grated Cheddar

Place a spoonful of cheese in the center of each tortilla, fold over, and fasten with a wooden pick. Place in hot, lightly-greased skillet or chafing dish. Brown lightly on both sides, until melted cheese begins to run out. Serve at once. This recipe makes 6 generous servings. If the tortillas are large, prepare 6 instead of 12.

GARBANZOS CON TOMATE
(Chick-peas with Tomatoes)

1½ cups chick-peas	⅓ cup vegetable oil
4 cups water	1 teaspoon salt
1 clove garlic, peeled and minced	½ teaspoon pepper
1 large onion, peeled and minced	1½ cups tomato sauce

Soak peas overnight in salted water to cover, 1 teaspoon salt to 1 quart water. Drain. Pour peas into 2½-quart, flame-proof (metal-base) deep casserole. Add 4 cups water, garlic, onion, oil, salt, and pepper. Cover and cook over moderate heat about 1 hour. When peas are almost tender, drain liquid off, add tomato sauce to peas, and continue cooking slowly until peas are tender. Serve hot from casserole. This recipe makes 6 servings. It can be made early in the day and reheated at dinnertime.

ENSALADA DE EJOTES
(String Bean Salad)

2 **pounds string beans**	**Grind of fresh black pepper**
4 **tablespoons olive oil**	**Crisp lettuce leaves, thin**
3 **tablespoons cider vinegar**	**strips pimiento, avocado**
3 **tablespoons minced onion**	**slices, and chilled cooked**
1 **teaspoon salt**	**cauliflower**

Clean beans, cook in a little boiling salted water until they are tender. Let cool; chill in refrigerator, then drain. Mix a dressing of oil, vinegar, onion, salt, and pepper. Vary the amount of oil to suit taste. Pour over beans, lift and turn with two wooden spoons to coat beans. Serve heaped in lettuce, top with criss-crossed pimiento strips. Add a few slices of avocado and cauliflower as garnish to plate. This recipe makes 6 servings of salad.

Near Eastern Dinner To many Americans, one of the most enjoyable foreign cuisines is the food of the Balkan and Middle Eastern countries. This delicious cookery is well known here because of the Armenian, Greek, Turkish, and Syrian restaurants long established in many cities, and the flaky, light-as-air concoctions of their bakeshops—56-layer pastry, for instance.

These restaurants introduced yoghurt to America. Health foods stores took the hint and made it big business. The same restaurants introduced meat cooked on skewers, now known to every American with a backyard barbecue and featured in a few phenomenal dining places in sensational, frightening fiery displays—kabobs on flaming swords—carried by red-coated waiters.

You can ignore kabobs, with or without flames, and still serve an authentic and delectable Near Eastern or Middle Eastern dinner, but you must include yoghurt in the menu; under various names including the Armenian madzoon, and kumiss originally from the Mongols, it is an important part of such a dinner.

Decoration Near Eastern and Middle Eastern wares are not plentiful in American shops, because most Arabic, Iranian, and other importers from their part of the world concentrate their efforts on rugs. But in gift departments of large stores, antique shops, and in better gift shops, you may find a few decorative objects from the Near East, such as brass, copper, and ceramic bowls, copper coffeepots and platters, brass trays, and large silvered-copper trays that fit on the top of carved folding tables. These tables and smaller brass and silvered-copper trays and footed bowls are used for fruit, sweetmeats, and the small cups of sweetened coffee always served after such dinners.

Divans are placed around large tables for dining in some Near Eastern homes. Others have become Westernized and use chairs; this is a long step from the ancient days when, in some homes, hosts and guests sat cross-legged on the floor around a magnificent feast arranged on a richly-colored, hand-woven cotton cloth, the cloth printed in color and design to look like a rug. These floor cloths for dining protected the precious family heirloom rugs and at the same time were decorative, adding their own special quality to the scene. They were much like the Indian cotton prints, plentiful today in our shops, which Americans use for window draperies and bedspreads. (The Persian Bazaar, 40 East Eighth Street, New York 3, New York, has plentiful supplies of the light-weight Indian cotton prints, heavier Persian cotton prints and small tables and other Near Eastern accessories.)

On the floor cloth, platters of hot meat and game, rice or wheat pilaf, eggplant in various cold and hot dishes, luscious fruits chilled in snow brought from the mountains, and several pickled vegetables and salads were arranged within easy reach of all. Goblets of sherbets, trays of sweetmeats, and tiny cups of coffee, or mint- or rose-flavored tea were served after these dinners. Servants brought silver bowls of hot water perfumed with orange blossoms and other flowers with towels for hand washing to guests around the feast. (Knives and forks were unknown.) Such dinners sometimes lasted several hours or all night, with music and entertainment by storytellers and dancers.

Service You can serve a Near Eastern dinner effectively and beautifully on the floor, using an Indian cotton print as the floor cloth over the rug, and cushions around its edge on which your guests sit cross-legged and help themselves to your good dishes. They should be young guests! Americans, unlike Orientals, are not trained from babyhood to sit cross-legged on the floor. Older guests will find the floor tiring and may resent the awkward position and the clumsiness of their Western clothing.

You may prefer to use a large Indian cotton print on the dining-room table with your best silver, solid-color linen or embroidered napkins, and your best china. If it is flower-decorated French or Bavarian porcelain or a Chinese pattern, so much the better. Some Chinese wares of the nineteenth century were made for the Near East trade, and are still being made in some parts of China, and imported by America. They are just right for this dinner. If you have found other Asiatic plates, platters, and bowls in your shopping, use them for either a floor dinner or one served at the table.

It will add oriental atmosphere to the occasion if you also provide small tables in the living room afterwards for the coffee and sweets. Some of the charm and color of oriental homes is achieved if these tables are wreathed with flowers. The brass or silvered-copper bowls on them should be lined with fresh leaves and filled with fresh or dried dates, figs, and raisins, pine and pistachio nuts, nougat, small sweet cakes and cookies made with honey and nuts, and various flavors and colors of the candy known as Turkish paste. Fresh flowers, especially roses, mimosa, and freesia, should be used to decorate the dining room and living room.

Invitation When your plan for such a dinner is ready, the invitation should go out by telephone, or in notes on flower-decorated fold-overs. Then make your final choices of dishes for the menu.

Menu should include appetizers of pickled fresh vegetables, such as artichokes, small green tomatoes, celery, peppers, or the famous vegetable cocktail that Armenian gourmets prefer to all others. (Recipes for these and dishes following are at the end of this section.)

In addition to the appetizers mentioned, include one or two cold salads of which eggplant salad is a favorite. Sesame-seed bread or any thin unleavened bread should be served. (An excellent one found in most grocery stores is packaged as Euphrates bread wafers.) If you omit breads, prepare one of the Armenian bread entrées, such as sou beurek, a meal in itself to some U.S. appetites. In either case, pilaf (pilaff, pilau) should be in the menu. It is served with the meat and vegetables. If you can shop in a Syrian or Greek store buy the cooked and dried wheat called bulgur and make pilaf by the recipe at the end of this section, or buy in speciality grocery stores an American-made, semi-prepared, packaged pilaf. You can also use rice for the pilaf.

If you do not serve cold pickled, stuffed grape leaves as an appetizer, you might serve this delicacy hot as one of the main dishes; it is one of the best and most typical. Other main dishes (serve one) are stuffed eggplant, and roast leg of lamb with potato plaki. All dishes are put on the table at the beginning of dinner, with a cup of yoghurt at each place setting. They are not passed. Guests help themselves and are helped by other guests to everything.

By the time all the guests have sampled all of the good foods you have prepared, they will be ready for a little relaxation in the living room, with coffee. This sweet black coffee, served in miniature cups, is only made after dinner is ended and guests have left the table.

The dessert, such as tissue-paper-thin pastry filled with honey and nuts can be ordered from Near Eastern bakeshops and restaurants in your community. Or serve sherbet, or stewed dried apricots sweetened with honey and topped with a spoonful of *kaymak* or yoghurt. The *kaymak* can be bought in a restaurant, but if you will take the trouble to make it, the results are worth the effort.

There are many collections of Near Eastern records, which can give your guests the best from these lands once full of singing and dancing. Your local record shops can order them for you, or write for catalogue and price list to Folkways Records. (See Index.)

"Folk and Traditional Music of Turkey" is one of these; recorded in the Balkans, around the Black Sea, and in various parts of Turkey in Asia Minor, it contains epic, love, wedding, mountaineers' songs, and others. A similar record of Greece includes music from Crete, Epirus, Macedonia, Cyprus, and various neighboring areas, with notes on historical background by authorities of the folklore archives in the Academy of Athens. Instruments heard on this record are lyre, lute, bag-pipes, drums, horns; many types of folk songs and dances are included. The catalogues list many others, such as songs and dances of Armenia, shepherd and folk songs, Arabic songs of Lebanon and Egypt, love songs and dances.

Recipes for Near Eastern Dinner

COLD PICKLE APPETIZERS

Prepare these pickles about a week before your party. Select celery, small green tomatoes, slender young eggplant, green peppers and cauliflower. Wash, drain, and cut all into convenient pieces for serving. For 1 quart of cut vegetables use:

¼ cup mixed whole spices	2 cups cider vinegar
1 clove garlic, peeled, and sliced	1 tablespoon allspice
	2 tablespoons sugar
Salt	

Make layer of mixed vegetables in glass or crockery jar, sprinkle with a few mixed whole spices. Put garlic in cheesecloth bag and hang down into jar to be removed after day or so as desired. Sprinkle layer of vegetables lightly with salt. Repeat layers of vegetables, whole spices, and salt until jar is full.

Heat vinegar, allspice, and sugar to boiling in an enamel saucepan. Pour over vegetables slowly, to let them absorb as much as possible. Fill the jar with water and cover. Let it stand in a cool place for a week. Taste after 2 days, and remove garlic if flavor is becoming too powerful. If vegetables seem too mild, prepare another 2 cups of hot vinegar mixture, drain off some liquid from pickles and add the fresh hot vinegar mixture to jar. This makes generous servings for 8. Pickles should be cold, and served at beginning of meal.

VEGETABLE COCKTAIL

2 green peppers, chopped	1/16 teaspoon pepper
2 onions, peeled and chopped	1½ teaspoons salt
2 ripe firm tomatoes, peeled and chopped	1 teaspoon finely cut, fresh mint leaves
2 cups ketchup	½ cup juice of pickled grape leaves (bought) or mild vinegar
¼ cup pickle relish	
¾ teaspoon Tabasco sauce	
1 teaspoon Worcestershire sauce	

Combine chopped vegetables. Mix remaining ingredients together and stir into vegetables. Chill in glass jar in refrigerator. Makes 8 servings. Guests help themselves from the chilled bowl onto their appetizer plate. Serve with unbuttered slices of thin sesame-seed bread or any unleavened bread.

PICKLED ARTICHOKES

8 large artichokes	1 cup olive or peanut oil
3 medium onions, peeled and sliced	1 teaspoon salt
	½ teaspoon pepper
Juice 3 lemons	1½ cups water
1½ tablespoons sugar	

Wash and drain artichokes. Use scissors to cut tops off each petal; use short sharp paring knife and dig choke out of center of each. Place trimmed artichokes in enamel saucepan, add onions, lemon juice, sugar, oil, seasonings, and water. Cover tightly, bring to boiling, then cook on low heat for 1 hour. Do not uncover while cooking. Serve cold, with any juice from the kettle poured over artichokes. This recipe makes 8 servings.

EGGPLANT SALAD

Like the vegetable cocktail, this salad is served with thin slices of unleavened bread. If you serve this at your dinner, omit other eggplant dishes.

1 large eggplant	3 tablespoons cider vinegar
3 tomatoes	1 teaspoon salt
1 onion, peeled and chopped	½ teaspoon pepper
	Crisp lettuce
2 tablespoons chopped fresh parsley	Sliced ripe tomatoes
	Black olives
3 tablespoons olive oil	

Bake eggplant whole in Moderate oven (350°F.) for 30 minutes or until soft. Let cool. Peel off browned skin, and chop coarsely. Scald tomatoes, remove skins, and chop these coarsely. Combine onion, parsley, oil, vinegar, salt, and pepper with eggplant. Serve on crisp lettuce leaves. Garnish with slice of tomato and ripe olive. This will make 6 to 8 appetizer servings.

SOU BEUREK

This is hearty enough for a main dish after the pickled appetizers. It is called a bread entrée in Armenian cookery. Omit it from your menu if you are serving pilaf and potatoes.

Pastry

6 cups sifted all-purpose flour	1 teaspoon salt
	Water
3 eggs	Cornstarch
1 tablespoon melted butter	
1 cup milk	

Sift flour again into mixing bowl, and make a "well" in the center. Beat eggs and pour into the well center. Stir to mix with flour, adding butter and milk gradually, then salt. If additional liquid is needed for good dough texture, add a very little water. Dough should be firm. Divide into 8 balls. Sprinkle each lightly with cornstarch, wrap in wet cheesecloth. Let stand at room temperature about 1 hour. Once during the hour, sprinkle cloth lightly with cold water so that the dough does not dry out.

Start oven at Moderate (375°F.). Roll each ball out into a thin sheet just the right size for a round baking pan. Grease pan. Place a pastry layer in the pan, cover it thinly with meat filling (see p. 421), repeat pastry layers and filling, making the top layer pastry. Press contents of pan down lightly and evenly. Cut with thin, sharp knife in 6 to 8 servings. Pour melted butter over the top. Bake for 30 to 40 minutes, or until lightly browned on top. Serve hot. This recipe makes 6 to 8 servings.

Meat filling

6 cups ground lean lamb	3 eggs
4 large onions, peeled and chopped	¼ cup chopped ripe olives
	1½ teaspoons salt
3 tablespoons oil	¼ teaspoon pepper
1 cup hot water or bouillon	½ pound butter, melted

Sauté lamb and onions in hot oil until the meat is lightly cooked. Add water, mix, and let cook uncovered until liquid is absorbed and meat is lightly browned. When ready to add to pastry layers, beat eggs, combine with lamb, olives and seasonings. Complete recipe as given above.

PILAF

3 cups bulgur	6 cups chicken, beef, or lamb bouillon
¼ pound butter	
1 small onion, peeled and chopped	1 teaspoon salt
	¼ teaspoon pepper

Set oven at Moderate (375°F.). Stir bulgur into melted butter in 3-quart heavy (flame-proof) casserole. Add onion and sauté 2 or 3 minutes or until onion is lightly browned; add bouillon and seasonings. Mix well. Cover and bake for 30 minutes. Remove from oven. With 2 forks, lift and stir wheat, return to oven and bake uncovered 10 minutes more. All liquid should be absorbed; pilaf should be fluffy and light. This recipe makes 6 servings.

When using rice in the above recipe, use only ½ small onion, or omit. If you like saffron rice, add ½ teaspoon saffron to the bouillon when mixing into the sautéed rice.

STUFFED GRAPE OR CABBAGE LEAVES

12 green grape or tender cabbage leaves	¼ cup uncooked rice
	1 teaspoon salt
1 pound ground lean lamb	½ teaspoon pepper
2 onions, peeled and chopped	Juice 1 lemon
	⅓ cup tomato sauce
2 tablespoons chopped fresh parsley	½ cup yoghurt

Set oven at Moderate (350°F.). Wash leaves and cut away heavy stems. Cover with water and boil a few minutes, until half cooked. Drain but save liquid. Combine remaining ingredients, except yoghurt, in mixing bowl and mix well. Put spoonful of meat mixture on each grape leaf, roll up, fold ends under to make secure packages about 3 inches long and not more than ¾ inch thick. Place in rows in shallow baking dish. Mix yoghurt with liquid in which leaves cooked and pour over rolls. If necessary, add sufficient hot water so that rolls are completely covered. Cover the baking dish. Bake for 1 hour.

Test rolls for doneness and bake longer if necessary. Serve hot, 2 rolls to each guest. This recipe will serve 6 guests. Stuffed grape leaves can also be served cold as an appetizer.

STUFFED EGGPLANT

This is a favorite main dish for many Near Eastern dinners.

2 eggplants	¼ cup chopped fresh parsley
Salt	
3 tablespoons butter	2 tomatoes, peeled and sliced
1 pound ground lean lamb	
1 onion, peeled and chopped	½ cup water
	½ cup tomato sauce

Wash eggplants, cut lengthwise into quarters, salt generously, and let stand ½ hour. Then slit fleshy side of each piece down the middle but do not cut through the rind. Sauté eggplant in butter about 5 minutes. Sauté lamb with onion and parsley 5 minutes, or until lightly cooked.

Start oven at Moderate (350°F.). Grease shallow 2- or 3-quart baking dish, place sautéed eggplant in dish, skin side down. Spread sautéed lamb mixture over eggplant. Cover with tomato slices. Pour mixture of water and tomato sauce over all. Cover the dish and bake for 30 minutes, uncover it and continue baking for 10 minutes more. This recipe makes 6 servings.

This is easy recipe to double; use two identical baking dishes, or one very large baking pan.

POTATO PLAKI

1 cup sliced onions	2 pounds potatoes, pared
1 clove garlic, peeled and mashed	and cut in half-inch cubes
	Salt and pepper
½ cup oil	3 cups water
1 cup chopped tomatoes	
½ cup chopped fresh parsley	

Brown onions and garlic in oil in a large skillet or saucepan 3 minutes; discard garlic, add remaining ingredients. Cover, bring to boiling, lower heat and simmer for 45 minutes, or until potatoes are done. This recipe makes 6 servings.

KAYMAK

Armenian cooks in America say that no hostess in her right mind would spend the time to make kaymak if she can buy it at a Near Eastern restaurant. If she can't buy it, they suggest she substitute yoghurt as topping for any dessert of stewed fruit or light honey pastry.

But if you want to add to your culinary laurels, here is the recipe. From a farmer secure 1 quart *unpasteurized* heavy cream. Heat it in a shallow pan on very, very low heat. With ladle, lift cream up and pour back into the pan until bubbles begin to form. Keep this up for ½ to 1 hour. You'd better sit on a high stool near the stove for the job.

When top surface is thickly covered with cream bubbles, turn heat off. Let cream stand in the pan in warm, not hot place for 2 hours. Then place it in refrigerator overnight. With sharp knife cut thick top layer of cooked cream off, roll up, and remove from liquid. Discard liquid. Slice kaymak, and serve on stewed dried apricots, other fruits, and pastries—wonderful flavor. This recipe makes topping for 8 to 12 or more desserts.

TURKISH COFFEE

The small, tin-lined copper Turkish coffeepots hold only four or five small cups of the brew. So be prepared to make coffee twice or more often for a large dinner party. If you do not have one of the imported coffeepots, use a small, heavy saucepan. It is important that each guest receive his share of the foam, in Arabic the "face of the coffee."

1½ cups water	4 tablespoons finely pulver-
4 teaspoons sugar	ized coffee

Measure water into heavy saucepan or pot. Add sugar; bring to boiling. Stir coffee in. Bring again to boiling. Allow brew to froth up 3 times; then remove from heat, and add a few drops of cold water. Spoon some of the foam into each demitasse cup and pour coffee in. This recipe makes 4 demitasse servings, or 8 very small Turkish cups.

17
CHARTS

Foods for Color-Scheme Luncheons, Dinners, and Suppers

Black

blackberries and black raspberries in fruit cups, salads, gelatins,
  sauces, ice cream
broiled mushrooms
caviar
coffee, demitasse
dried currants and raisins in compotes, open-face tarts, pies
prunes, stuffed, also cut in fruit cups, salads, compote, open-face pies
  and tarts, also in gelatin molds
truffles

Blue

blueberries and huckleberries in fruit cups, salad, sauces, ice cream,
  muffins
plums, in fruit bowl, fruit cup, salads, gelatin molds

Orange

apricots (dried), cooked for desserts, pies, tarts, fruit cups, salads
candies, mints, bonbons
carrots, raw and cooked

gelatin desserts and salads
kumquats, fruit bowl, salads, garnishes
melons (some)
oranges, orange filling in cake,
    frosting on cookies and cupcakes; sherbet, soufflés,
    ice cream, orangeade, salads, fruit cups
    whole, unpeeled in decorative arrangements
        with leaves and other fruits
peaches, some canned varieties in fruit cups, salads, open-face tarts,
    pies
pumpkin, whole, also gourds and squash for decoration
squash, steamed
sweet potatoes
tangerines. See oranges

Brown

baked beans
Boston brown bread
browned crumbs, browned rolls, meats, fowl
browned top of bread pudding, custards, etc.
burnt almond ice cream
butterscotch sauce, pudding, ice cream
cake, chocolate, mocha, spice, caramel; also frostings and fillings
caramel candies, ice cream, cookies, sauces
chocolate candies, ice cream, pudding, various desserts, sauces, cookies,
    soufflés
chutney, with ginger in it
coconut combined with molasses, chocolate or butterscotch in cake
    topping, other desserts, candies
coffee-flavored ice cream, custards, puddings, soufflés, frostings, other
    desserts
croquettes, various kinds, with fried-crumb crust
croutons
curried dishes
dates, figs
doughnuts

gingerbread, cakes, cookies, sauces, candied ginger as topping
lentils, lentil soup
maple syrup, candies, sugar, sauces, frostings, fillings, pies
molasses, candies, sauces, fillings, pies
mushrooms
nuts, especially sautéed in fat
pumpkin, pies, soup
spice cake, cookies, cupcakes, frostings
waffles

Green

artichokes, asparagus, avocado, broccoli, Brussels sprouts, cabbage
candies, mints, bonbons, Turkish paste, gum drops
capers, celery, chives
cream of pea, asparagus, spinach, water cress soups
cucumber, peel left on
gelatin desserts and salads (lime, mint)
grapes, seedless
gooseberries, tarts, open-face pies
green beans, limas, peas
greengage plums
green peppers
herbs (fresh)
honeydew melon
ice cream and sherbet with mint, lime, or pistachio flavorings and
    coloring
limes and lime-flavored desserts
mint, fresh, also in candies, gelatin, jelly, desserts
olives, pickles
parsley
pistachio nuts, frostings, ice cream, puddings
salad greens, water cress
zucchini

Pink

apple, crabapple, quince jellies
applesauce, flavored with cinnamon candies
cake, cookies, cupcakes frosted with pink
candies, mints, bonbons, others
gelatin desserts and salads
grapefruit, pink variety, or use spoonful grenadine on each half
ham, also many cold cuts
lobster
nectarines (some)
raspberry sherbet, sauce, gelatin
rhubarb, stewed as dessert, in open-face tarts, as pie filling
Russian dressing
salmon, also salmon bisque
shrimp, also with Russian dressing as cocktail sauce
strawberries, in ice cream, other desserts
tomato bisque (more pink than red, if cream is used)
watermelon, can be red or pink

Red

apples, red if peel is left on, in fruit cups, salads
 whole in decoration with leaves and other fruits
beans, canned kidney beans, for chili con carne
beef, rare roast, also corned beef
beets, cooked as vegetable, also in borsch
bologna, other luncheon meats
cherries, cherry desserts, in fruit cups, salads, garnish, ice cream
chiles, also sweet red peppers
 chili sauce
chipped beef (dried beef)
cocktail sauce
cranberries, cranberry jelly, desserts, sauces, sherbet
currants, fresh, in desserts, garnish, open-face tarts
frankfurters, other speciality meats
gelatin desserts and salads
guavas

jellied madrilène
ketchup
paprika sprinkled on various dishes, and sauces
pimiento in appetizers, salads, other dishes
    also as garnish
plums
radishes
raspberries, in fruit cups, salads, desserts, sauces, as garnish
red cabbage, cooked, also in salads
strawberries, and in fruit cups, desserts, salads, sauces
tomatoes, salads, cooked, sauce, aspic
watermelon

White

apple, pared, in fruit cup, salads
banana in fruit cup, salads
blanc mange
bread, rolls, biscuits
cakes, cookies, cupcakes, white frosting
cauliflower
celery
chicken breast, in various dishes
coconut
coleslaw
cornmeal, white, in mush, pudding
cottage cheese, pot cheese
crab meat
cream, whipped, creamed soups especially potato, sauces, also sour
    cream as garnish
endive (Belgian), braised, also in salads
fish, especially in white sauces
hominy
ice cream
leeks
macaroni, spaghetti, other pastas in butter sauces
marshmallows, as topping, in desserts

meringue, small meringues, meringue topping, meringue ring filled with
   various desserts
onions, scallions
parsnips, turnips
pears, pared, in fruit cups, salads
potatoes, mashed, boiled
rice
vichyssoise
yoghurt

Yellow

apricots, fresh
bananas as decoration in fruit bowl
bisque ice cream
cakes, cookies, cupcakes with yellow frosting
candies
cheese, also in sauce, various dishes
cream of corn soup
curried dishes
custards, custard ice cream, pies, sauces, desserts, zabaglione, floating
   island
egg yolks, hard-cooked, grated as garnish
gelatin desserts and salads
Hollandaise, mayonnaise, mustard sauce, other yellow sauces
lemons, lemonade, lemon pies, filling and frosting for cake, cupcakes,
   cookies
melons (some)
peaches (some varieties canned) in fruit cup, salads, open-face pies
   and tarts
pineapple, in fruit cups and salads, also as garnish
saffron in rice and other dishes
squash
tomatoes, small yellow variety as appetizers and in salads

Punch to Serve Fifty

1½ cups lemon juice	6 oranges, sliced very thin
1 cup orange juice	2½ quarts sweet cider
1 quart hot tea	2½ quarts iced gingerale
3 cups sugar	

Combine lemon and orange juices, hot tea, sugar and orange slices in a glass jar or pitcher. Chill and ripen in refrigerator until just before serving time. Then combine in large punch bowl with cider and gingerale, stir well. Add block of ice, ladle punch over ice. Serve at once. Makes 6½ quarts, 52 punch glasses.

Quantity Cooking

HOW MUCH TO BUY FOR 50 PERSONS

Beverages	Each serving	Market order
Cocoa	¾ (measuring) cup	½ lb. cocoa 1 gallon plus 1 cup milk
Coffee	¾ " "	1 lb.
Juices	½ " "	6 qt. plus 1 cup
Juice concentrates, frozen	" "	9 6-oz. cans (or see label directions)
Punch	½ to ⅔ cup	2 gal.
Sugar, for coffee and tea	2 lumps	1⅛ lb. lumps
Tea	¾ (measuring) cup	50 tea bags or ¼ to ½ lb. loose tea

Bread

Bread, sliced	1 to 2 slices	6 pullman loaves
Buns, rolls, biscuits	1 to 2 pieces	50 to 100 pieces
Butter for bread and rolls	1 pat (½ in. thick)	1¼ lbs.

Cereals

Cooked cereals	⅔ cup	Consult directions on packages
Dry cereals	¾ "	" "
Macaroni, noodles, other pastas	¾ "	4½ lbs.
Rice	¾ "	6¼ lbs.

Dairy Products

Cheese (Cheddar, Swiss, etc.)	3 oz.	8½ lbs.
Cottage cheese	⅓ cup	8½ lbs.
Cream, light for coffee	2 tablespoons	1¾ qts.
Cream, for whipping	1 heaping tablespoon	1 qt.
Milk	1 cup	3½ gal.

Desserts

Cake		
Fruit Cake	1 slice	5 lbs.
Plain sheet	1 slice	3 or 4 pans (according to size)
3-layer (10-in.)	1 "	7 or 8 cakes
Fruit compote or cup	⅔ cup	9 qts.
Ice cream		
bulk	No. 12 dipper	2 gal.
brick	1 slice	depends on size (buy large-quantity size)
Pies, 9-in.	1 wedge	9 pies
Pudding	depends on size	follow directions on package
Pudding sauces	2 tablespoons	1¾ qts.

Fish

Fish fillets for baked fish or sautéed fish	¼ lb.	14 1-lb. packages (or check number of servings per package)
Crab meat for cocktail	3 oz.	10 1-lb. packages (or check number of servings per package)
Oysters, to scallop	2 or 3 oysters	6 qt. or check number of servings per quick-frozen package
as cocktail	4 or 6	Buy by peck or bushel (200 to 300 oysters)

Other seafood and fish, buy quick-frozen, check number of servings per package.

Fruits

Apples for sauce	½ cup	20 to 25 lbs.
Apples for pie	(9 pies)	about 20 lbs.
Bananas	1 each	50
Berries for shortcake	½ cup	6 to 7 qts.
Canned fruits	1 serving (depends on kind)	3 No. 10 cans or 7 or more No. 2 cans
Cherries for pie	9 pies	9 to 10 lbs.
Cranberries for sauce	¼ cup	4 lbs.
Dried fruits		
apricots, stewed	¼ cup	10 lbs.
dates	5 or 6	6 lbs.
peaches, stewed	¼ cup	10 lbs.
prunes, stewed	¼ cup	10 lbs.

For quick-frozen fruits, berries, and mixtures, check package directions for number of servings.

Meats

Beef, for loaf or burgers	6 oz.	18½ lbs.
Beef, rolled rib roast	8 oz.	25 lbs. before boning
Frankfurters	2 franks	9 lbs.
Ham, baked	6 oz. (approx.)	18 lbs. to 20 lbs. boneless 20 to 22 lbs. with bone
Lamb chops	2 small to medium	50 lbs.
Lamb, roast	6 oz.	4 to 5 leg roasts
Meat for stew	6 oz.	18½ lbs.
Steaks	8 oz.	25 lbs.
Veal cutlets	6 oz.	18½ lbs.

Poultry

Chicken, for à la King		20 to 25 lbs. (ready-to-cook weight)
Chicken, to fry, casserole	¼ chicken	13 chickens
Chicken to roast	½ to ⅔ lb.	35 to 40 lbs. (ready-to-cook weight)
Turkey to roast	½ to ⅔ lb.	35 to 40 lbs. (ready-to-cook weight)
Turkey, for creamed turkey, etc.		15 to 16 lbs. (ready-to-cook weight)

Salads

Potato, meat, fish, poultry	½ to ⅔ cup	7½ to 8 qts.
Head lettuce	⅙ to ¼ head	12 heads
Lettuce for garnishes		4 to 6 heads
French dressing	1½ to 2 tbs.	1½ qts.
Mayonnaise	1 tbs.	1 qt.

Soups

All varieties	1 cup	20 to 25 cans (according to directions)
Crackers	2 each	1 to 2 lbs. (according to variety)

Vegetables

Canned	½ cup	11 No. 2 cans
Asparagus	4 or 5 stalks	20 lbs.
Beans, green	½ cup	24 to 30 lbs.
Dried beans and peas	½ cup	13 lbs.
Beets	½ cup sliced, or 2 or 3 small whole	25 lbs.
Broccoli	½ cup sliced	25 lbs.
Carrots	½ cup sliced, or 2 or 3 small whole	13 lbs.
Cauliflower	2 or 3 pieces	13 large heads
Celery	1 or 2 small stalks	8 bunches
Corn on cob	1 or 2 small ears or pieces	50 to 100 ears
Cucumbers	¼ cup sliced	10 cucumbers
Eggplant	½ cup	13 medium-size eggplants
Onions	¼ to ½ cup	20 lbs.
Peas in shell	⅓ to ½ cup	39 lbs.
Potatoes, baked	1 potato	26 lbs.
to scallop	⅓ to ½ cup	26 lbs.
Sweet potatoes, baked	1 potato	26 lbs.
other methods	⅓ to ½ cup	26 lbs.
Spinach (and other greens)	⅓ to ½ cup	27 lbs.
Tomatoes, sliced (also cooked variously)	3 slices	25 lbs. or 30 medium tomatoes

Quick-frozen vegetables, all varieties: read label for number of servings per package, and buy accordingly.

Candies, small for individual paper cups	1 to 2 tbs.	5 to 6 lbs.
Jam and jellies	2 tbs.	7 or 8 8-oz. glasses; 1½ lbs.
Olives	2	2 qts.
Pickles	depends on kind	2 qts.
Radishes	2 small round	10 bunches
Syrup	¼ cup	3 qts.

For free quantity sandwich recipes, write to American Institute of Baking, Consumer Service Department, 400 East Ontario Street, Chicago 11, Illinois. And from Department L6, same organization, you can also get free, step-by-step diagrams showing the best ways to cut wedding and anniversary cakes, and also layer, square, loaf and sheet cakes for church, club and school affairs. The number of servings from various cakes is also given.

Menu helpers for meals for 50 or more: for club, church, or school, free folder of menus, recipes, and amounts to buy is available from Hotel and Institution Department, Armour and Co., Union Stock Yards, Chicago 9, Illinois.

Consumer Service Division, National Canners Association, 1133 20th Street N.W., Washington 6, D.C. has free, 40-page booklet of recipes for appetizers, soups, sauces, entrées, sandwiches, vegetables, desserts, punch made from canned foods. All recipes are for 50 servings.

Also, "Recipes for Quantity Service," a book prepared by the Agricultural Research Service, may be obtained from the U. S. Department of Agriculture, Washington 25, D.C. These are tested recipes from the Department of Agriculture's Institute of Home Economics and are designed for 25, 50, and 100 portions. Price is $2.50.

Similar leaflets of menus, recipes, and helpful hostess information for serving large numbers are available free from the Home Economics Division, Research Laboratories, Swift and Co., Chicago 9, Illinois;

Home Economics Department, Box 56, Campbell Soup Co., Camden 1, New Jersey, and Pineapple Growers Association, 215 Market Street, San Francisco 5, California.

The Bureau of Commercial Fisheries, U. S. Fish and Wildlife Service, U. S. Department of the Interior, Washington 25, D.C. has a 1959 film release on Outdoor Fish Cookery. This 16 mm film, running time 28 minutes, is both entertaining and instructive on the subject of big outdoor cookery events—Indian salmon barbecue, a clam bake, an oyster roast, political fish fry, and lobster broil. Rental information on this can be obtained by writing to the above bureau.

INDEX